THE
WIND
IN
A
JAR

THE WIND

N A JAR

John Farella

University
of
New
Mexico
Press
Albuquerque

Library of Congress Cataloging-in-Publication Data

Farella, John R.
    The wind in a jar / John Farella. — 1st ed.
        p.   cm.
    ISBN 0-8263-1407–4
    1. Anthropology—Field work. 2. Anthropology—Philosophy.
I. Title
    GN34.3.F53F37   1993
    306´.01—dc20
    92-28684
    CIP

DESIGNED BY

LINDA MAE TRATECHAUD

*For
Glenn,
Helen,
Jim,
Norman,
and
Marjorie*

CONTENTS

PREFACE

I wonder how to think about people's lives and experiences so as not to take from them what matters, what is important. We have this tendency to look for or to impose order and pattern, but the categories of peoples that we create and the types of experience that we assign to these categories seem to remove what matters from people and their lives. It also seems to be a way of avoiding or not listening to what others have to say.

This is difficult to talk about. We are so habituated to classifying experience rather than having it, to saying convincing things about understanding rather than listening.

Renato Rosaldo tells a story near the beginning of his book *Culture and Truth*.[1] He says that an older Ilongot man will tell you that he used to cut off heads because "rage, born of grief, impels him to kill his fellow human beings. He claims that he needs a place to 'carry his anger.' The act of severing and tossing away the victim's head enables him, he says, to vent and, he hopes, throw away the anger of his bereavement."

Rosaldo goes on to talk about his own attempts to understand and explain what is for the older Ilongot man a self-evident truth. And he goes through various attempts at making anthropological sense out of the statement, none of which work very well. Rosaldo says that it took him fourteen years to understand. When he and his wife returned to the Philippines in 1981 she was walking along a trail and fell to her death. And he started to grasp the meaning of what these men had been saying.

---

[1] *Culture and Truth: The Remaking of Social Analysis.* (Boston: Beacon Press, 1989), pp. 1–21.

I don't know quite what to say about this. I use his example rather than my own, because I feel as if a part of what I have to say in this preface is captured by his description. That makes it at least partially his idea, and I don't want to steal it. But I feel uncomfortable assigning my meaning to the description of his wife's death; it is all right for him to do it, but not for me.

When Navajos talk about people who have done fieldwork among them they will sometimes say that these people are stealing, stealing their culture, their ideas, the things they care about. I feel reluctant to steal Rosaldo's experience, but I suppose I will get over it. That is the business I am in.

When Rosaldo uses this example he uses the word *force*, as in "emotional force," to describe his experience and what the Ilongot men are saying. Implicit in this is the self-evidence of truths that matter. If you listen to people telling you about the things they care about, what they are saying will make sense. I like the word *passion*, or *intensity*, better than *force*. In order to have a chance to understand anything that matters, we need this passion. The first part of this is the passion for understanding and for truth generally, and, for Rosaldo, the second part is the passion for understanding the specifics of what the headhunter meant.

You have to care about getting it right, about understanding what the world has to say to you. And as a part of this you end up being dissatisfied with your own, and with others', approximate and partial descriptions. Rosaldo, at some level, knew he was getting it wrong for all those years.

We have a huge repertoire of strategies for diminishing the intensity of life or removing it altogether. The application of Aristotle's idea, genus and species, to people and experience, is the most basic and damaging of these. We really believe in these categories, and professions (as contrasted with jobs) are completely based on the ownership of certain slices. Categorizing an experience necessarily makes it less intense. Like dealing with the category death, or grief, or mourning, or funerary ritual, rather than with our friend or lover's death.

Sometimes the categorization is useful, as in some clinical situations. When my daughter has strep throat, there is something that can be done about it. When we treat people with AIDS as diseased rather than as sinners, there is the possibility of behaving towards them as humans rather than shunning them.

But usefulness is overdone as a rationale. Mostly we think this way out of habit. The habit is based on and reinforced by the control it gives us over experience It takes the force, the passion, out of what others have to say. And we can feel less, more in control and subdued. As if intellect really mattered and really brought understanding.

In anthropology today, there are two extreme strategies for diminishing the intensity of our experience of others. The first of these is method, rigor. Method takes the intensity out of experience at the point of attack. It insists that one focus here and not there, and ignore much of what matters, what cannot be digitalized. Rigor promises the mastery of experience. One will be able to know and therefore to control. And of course in any chronic obsessive act one feels less, sidesteps or deintensifies.

There is another way of not listening that is more sinister. Over the last twenty years this strategy has been discussed under the heading of *interpretation*; more recently the word *text* is used in anthropology (*postmodernism* is more generally used). But this way of looking or, I suppose, of not looking has a long tradition, and it is based on feigning or emphatically insisting on open-mindedness. Before anthropologists interpreted, they talked about relativism, which essentially was an emphatic insistence on being nonjudgmental. The *reductio ad absurdum* for nonjudgmental is to not believe in and therefore not pursue truth.

The problem with this, aside from it being dishonest and wrong, is that when you talk to people they tell you about truth, about their passion, about what matters to them. And if they bother to talk to you at all, they care a great deal about you understanding it. A part of that understanding is that you feel something, that you respond with some sort of intensity. As in "Aha! That is exactly the way it is"; or, "That is bullshit!" Rosaldo's initial response to the old men was simply wrong; they were talking about passion. He was responding politely and reasonably. Anthropologists are supposed to behave like this around natives; around each other they argue.

Categorization, method, and that most absolute of methods, emphatic open-mindedness, are simply ways of editing and controlling experience at the outset. People who are well socialized in Western thought are pretty much able to avoid life.

Opposed to this way of knowing is taking experience and

people personally rather than categorically. It involves listening or paying attention. You more or less accept discomfort and chaos at the outset. That is, rather than trying to avoid uncertainty, you accept it. The most you can do is accept; I don't think anyone really seeks uncertainty. But at the foundation of this acceptance is a faith that somewhere in the process of talking to and watching people and feeling confused, it will all make sense. Instead of editing at the outset you go after what you care about and hope that it shakes out.

Over the last few years I have made efforts to explain this to people. Mostly, people give me their own examples of these sorts of things that they care about. These are all different kinds of people and they care about all different sorts of things, but the thread they offer is always in transforming what is usually categorical into the personal. Sometimes it is about the utter nonsense of categories.

I would like to give a few examples of this that others have given me. The example from Rosaldo's book was suggested to me by Gilbert Quintero.

My oldest daughter gave me an example. She lives in Los Angeles. God intends this as a punishment against me. Obviously I have failed as a parent. She works with some sort of anarchistic political organization that is too well organized. They are trying to monitor government and change laws, that sort of thing; and they approach this in a real grass-roots, populist way. I was talking to her about the ideas in this book and she told me about a Los Angeles skid row mission that has been in existence for a very long time. It turns out that during the Reagan/Bush years the Salvation Army, missions, these sort of organizations are real growth industries, in fact they grow at a phenomenal rate. It never occurred to me that these would prosper during times of indifference but it makes sense. Kind of an American success story.

The mission runs these ads on TV to get people to donate money. And for as long as my daughter can remember they have been the standard ads about "help the homeless," citing statistics, showing anonymous people making the generic plea that we are all so familiar with. The other day when she was cooking dinner and had the TV on, one of the mission ads came on that was different. She stopped what she was doing and she listened.

This is Joe Smith, said the ad, and it showed this man. This is his wife Susan and his children Mark and June. Joe is thirty-eight and has worked as a commercial artist for fifteen years. Eighteen months ago he was laid off. And the ad went on in the same very personal way. My daughter listened, remembered, was bothered.

A third example. There is an instance that Carlos Castañeda recounts in one of the Don Juan books that depicts the utter failure of categorization. These are generally stories about shamanism and magic, and Don Juan is this kind of primitive sorcerer, a wild Indian. One day Castañeda is in Mexico City, and a well-dressed suit-and-tie businessman says, "Hello Carlos." And he does a double take and it is Don Juan. What are you doing here, says Castañeda in complete amazement. Oh I was just talking to my broker about purchasing some equities to add to my portfolio. I have to go to the bank now, but let's do lunch.

There is a recent example of something that is ultra personal that we habitually transform into the categorical. In this case the woman involved insisted on not being treated as a category. The woman was raped. And she came to the conclusion that the way that newspapers reported rapes—keeping the "victim" anonymous and reporting the incident generally instead of graphically contributed both to rapes continuing and to her continued victimization. For her this was not a categorical experience but a very personal one. She wrote about her rape very graphically and personally and the *Des Moines Register* published her account over a series of weeks. Another part to this is that other papers picked the story up, but edited it so it would not be so graphic, so upsetting.

As an extension of the same idea, Michael Ghiglieri is writing a book on male violence. While he was researching and writing this, you kind of avoided him; he wanted to tell you one horrible story after another. He wasn't real cheery to be around. But the part of the book he could barely face and then only very late in the writing was the personal account of a woman he knew who had been badly brutalized.

So this book is about these sorts of things. It is against certain ways of organizing our thoughts and our actions. It is an attack on categorizing experience and people. Therefore it is anti social science, anti Aristotelian, anti any sort of ownership of knowledge, anti organization or bureaucracy. And it is opinionated, not open-minded. These are all ways of taking the punch out of what the world has to say.

I have had a number of people read this and support me in this endeavor. They seemed to understand what I had to say and think that it was worth saying. They include my wife Linda, Sheila Berndt, Eva Bading and more recently Cindy Knox and Barbara Leviton. Very early on a man named Greg McNamee gave me some encouragement.

There are several people who helped as critical readers. This is a really valuable thing to have, people who take the time to care about what you have to say and try to make it better. Two people who were very valuable, and very different, were Miranda Warburton and Scott Thybony. Not every insight, observation and anecdote is a gem, Farella, says Miranda. Scott is much more polite; he kind of hints at what he doesn't like. Thanks.

Charlotte Frisbie encouraged and critiqued (some of these I will address momentarily) as did Roy Wagner. A long time ago, I had Roy as a teacher. I still have some books I stole from him. He was extremely good at teaching. He managed, and still manages, to convey ideas that matter. And he gets enthusiastic when he likes something. Charlotte gets excited in different ways, real honest and direct. Jeff Grathwohl, who was at the University of New Mexico Press, was really encouraging at a time I needed it. After he left Elizabeth Hadas took the project over and edited the book and was real helpful. It's nice to have people like this in the world. They take an interest. Let you know what they think.

Charlotte made two observations that need to be included. First, she correctly notes that there are many Navajos, including many singers, who are very strongly in favor of, and work at, cultural preservation. It is not just an Anglo anthropological trip, but a Navajo one as well.

Charlotte makes a second point that was also made differently by Miranda. I tend to write using the masculine almost exclusively. Their point is about pronouns, but I think the critique more general. In an earlier book I addressed this (specific to pronouns) in a footnote, where I cited something Ursula LeGuin mentioned in *The Left Hand of Darkness*. She in effect said that in English the neuter and the masculine pronouns have the same surface form. And although this is true as far as it goes, it doesn't really address what these women are saying. I think for them the pronouns and the masculinized writing are much more of a personal thing, something they've been uncomfortable with for quite some time. I don't really know what to do about this, other than to acknowledge it. I'm uncomfortable for the most part with the neuter words we have invented in the last several years; and the he-and-she sorts of things get cumbersome. I suppose ultimately the most honest thing to say is that I tend to think and write in kind of a masculine way, so much so that any other way seems rather dishonest or odd. So I guess this is how I have to do it. I am not insisting on my correctness in this, nor am I not taking what others have to say seriously. I just don't know what else to do.

Each one of the chapters in the book is a story. And it is self-contained; that is you can start reading anywhere, or if you don't like something go elsewhere. Because of this, some information is placed at several points, creating some redundancy. But the book is not only independent stories; there are certain threads that connect the whole. so if you were to read the whole thing there would be, hopefully, a kind of cumulative understanding of these themes.

An earlier version of Chapter 6 appeared in *Diné Be'iiná'* (Fall 1990; volume 2, number 1, pages 107–25).

There are a lot of people in this book. On the one hand I want to reveal them, but on the other I want to keep their lives private and not expose these people. This is a funny way to feel, but I feel that way all the time. So I do a variety of things to conceal who these people are while at the same time trying to keep things honest. Miranda Warburton has pointed out to me that this is paternalistic. She is correct; but I tend to be that way. Ultimately trying to both reveal and conceal is pretty difficult.

As I said at the outset and will say again, I care about the meaning in life and in what others have to say. And I wonder how to understand it, see the pattern in it, and write about it without removing much or all of what matters. I don't know the answer to this, but I do know a fair amount about where the answer isn't, about what cannot possibly work. But I don't have a formula for doing it correctly. This book and these stories are an attempt in that direction.

BEGINNINGS

I
INTENT

This book is somewhere between a collection of essays and a beginning- middle-end sort of book with a unified theme. In small part this is intended, but in much greater part it just happened that way. The stories are about some people and some places I have known and some experiences I witnessed or was otherwise part of. My memory of it is more a series of snapshots than it is like a movie. But the snapshots are in the same family photo album; as such they are connected.

The most obvious connection is that these photos are taken by an anthropologist of some people he is studying. Sometimes someone else is holding the camera and I am in the picture, but not usually. But as with many things that initially appear obvious, there is also an inaccuracy in describing things in this way. The particular separation that has me as the observer and them as the object of study works rather poorly, and as time goes on, it works even more poorly. This is not to say that there is only an us (with me becoming a member of their group), or only me (with the others being an extension of my unconscious or something of the sort), or only a they as the scientist would maintain. It is just that the separation shifts, moves about, sometimes appearing strongly, occasionally, at least for a moment, disappearing completely. Ultimately, however, people like me need the separation and we tend more towards an I/you view of things than an I/thou relationship. We never quite join, nor do we completely separate; we tend to hover somewhere on the periphery, not knowing exactly where we do feel comfortable but knowing that when someone else tries to get closer or more distant, we don't like it.

The second connection in this book is thematic. There are certain patterns and ideas that repeat and repeat. This was not part of any grand plan; these are just things that are stuck inside of me somewhere and won't go away. Even with the exorcism ritual of writing about them, they remain. I will have more to say about these themes later and throughout.

There is another linkage that, while ultimately personal, is not solely mine. It has to do with discovering and conveying, writing about, the meaning, the things that matter, in people's lives. It is why I write about these things in this way, or more correctly, in these ways. This personal connecting thread starts as a reaction to the ways in which we remove what matters from people's lives—the ways that we depersonalize and objectify in the name of accuracy and understanding, making the living inanimate, a reverse genesis. As social scientists we are the very worst at this. By the nature of what we do, we put ourselves into contact with people and in the act of writing about them we kick the life out of their stories.

MEANING

Man likes to define himself as the one who seeks meaning, or who creates it and/or imposes it on his world. The one who questions, searches for answers, looks for what matters in it all. What this really tells you is that we are a species that is particularly fond of grand definitions of itself.

Today we are more involved in editing the meaning from experience than in seeking or creating it. As a part of this, we ignore what others have to say. At the same time we loudly complain of the absence of anything that matters in our lives. People say they want their existence to be more meaningful. They want their work to matter, to make a difference. They want their marriage to be more intense, to have better communication with their spouse, to share more, argue less. They don't really know their children, and so on.

And yet we vigorously sidestep those events that matter to humans. We avoid the uncertain, the painful, and the tragic and are surprised that the joy, the passion, and the beauty disappear with them. We promise that birth will be both safe and beautiful, that people will die only of old age after having worked things through and resolved things totally with their families—

the beautiful, peaceful, and correct death, carried out in conformity to a very rigid etiquette for dying. New possessions take on huge importance, product quality is equated with quality of life. We insure ourselves beyond all reason so as to be able to keep these possessions and maintain the ability to purchase new ones. And the desire for security becomes hugely addictive; we gradually increase the dosage of protection that promises us peace and safety. Then we wonder about the excitement that is gone from our lives.

We have stopped listening, and created huge industries that eliminate the painful messages from the world. I recently watched a television news special on the twentieth anniversary of man walking on the moon interspersed with commercials for Aetna insurance and Gallo white zinfandel.

We devote our best efforts to avoiding those messages with the strongest meaning. And people speak louder and louder, I guess out of frustration at not being heard or taken seriously. As the volume increases, we make an even greater effort to screen out and insulate ourselves from these sounds. The people speaking care about what they are saying, but to the bystander it is simply noise.

The urban affluent travel to work in a climate-controlled Mercedes, passing the projects and other desolation that they will not see. The windows are hermetically sealed and a Blaupunkt stereo fills the interior and even further insulates the traveler from the world outside. On leaving the automobile a Walkman is surgically implanted. The rich live in the suburbs or in city fortresses. They want quiet, a world with no visual, auditory, or emotional noise, a very small protected world. Various sorts of security systems protect them from messages they would rather not sense.

For the less affluent a boom box is permanently attached to the side of the head.

There is a bleak poetry in the world living on the edge of our consciousness. The louder it gets the more we increase the magnitude of personal noise to distract from the unpleasantness of the message. When the kids are yelling we turn up the TV. In a city, people fill their space with louder and louder music to offset the clamor created by everyone else for the same purpose. You can buy white noise machines, noise to screen out noise. Or you can buy sounds that should be meaningful and use them as noise. My personal favorites are those recordings of nature from pseudo outdoor outfitters—really clothing stores to make it look like you've been there or are about to go. Places like Eddie Bauer that inhabit suburban shopping malls. There are recordings of the ocean, the woods (however woods sound), whales singing B. B. King songs. There is an optional scent machine to go with it.

Soon there will be a boom box that no one can carry.

There are two things I take as basic to the pursuit of meaning. First, what matters is there for the taking. If we pay attention we will understand what is being communicated. The world is not trying to trick us or otherwise hide from us. But we do make rather extreme efforts to confuse ourselves, to hide from these messages and to rationalize this in terms of the mystery of the world or the difficulty in understanding, that sort of thing.[1] There is meaning and it can be found. We don't need to invent or enhance it.

Second, the pursuit of meaning necessarily produces discomfort. Much of what matters to humans is unpleasant. When we see or hear about certain things, and actually think about them, it makes us sad and angry. These emotions are certainly not the only products of understanding, but they are the ones we try to avoid.

There is in addition an even more fundamental discomfort that we seek to do away with: the discomfort of uncertainty, of not knowing, of hearing messages that are out of our control, and that confuse or frighten. And we have certain basic habits of thought that reduce or eliminate this fear while at the same time eliminating anything of importance from what is being said.

ANTHROPOLOGY

Anthropology is a part of what we are talking about, a part of those habits of thought that bring comfort and familiarity and do away with what is important in people's lives.

At one time anthropology prescribed discomfort as an avenue towards discovering meaning. Ethnographic fieldwork

---

[1] Bishop Berkeley said, "We have first raised a dust and then complain we cannot see." (*Principles of Human Knowledge*, p.3).

was the means to that end. The requirement was that you live in a setting where there was a likelihood of experiencing something different and where you were certain to experience discomfort. Anthropologists like to romanticize this in various ways. They call it culture shock, or they write elaborate accounts of what it is like. All of which makes it appear much more glorious and dramatic than the actual experience.

This is a bit difficult to explain if you haven't been there. With fieldwork, everything doesn't work. Your proposal doesn't work, your methods stink, the machinery works episodically when it wants to, the outhouse blows over, the people who are supposed to work for you don't show up or show up two hours to four days late and they are drunk, your marriage goes to hell, your lovers have affairs with other people. Nothing works.

Your function in the community is giving people rides when they show up at your door unannounced, and since you aren't doing anything, at least anything that anyone in their right mind would think of as work, it is difficult to say no. Or it is in being manipulated into giving loans of money that never get paid back; you are the one in the community with money all the time. Anglos are never broke, never completely broke.

Kind of strange work for a grown-up.

From having been there, you were supposed to write about, capture, that experience. People used to think, or at least say, that the written work was based on the fieldwork. And this produced its own discomfort because you were never completely sure about what you wrote. There were parts that were guesses, parts that were incomplete; you were never sure that you really knew. But to paraphrase Evans-Pritchard, you did the best you could under the circumstances. This knowledge of our limits is not new; everyone knew it and talked about it, but few people wrote about it.

Today people are completely enamored with discovering that the writing of ethnography was not always accurate, honest, or true. That it was often, usually, or always fiction or autobiography. There are two responses to this discovery. The one is ethnographic strategies that emphasize truth. And the other consists of writing strategies that emphasize style. The people who advocate each of these approaches see them as a response to the mystery of the world. I see them as just another generic form of Valium, epistemological tricks to do away with the discomfort, especially the uncertainty, associated with these sorts of situations.

Before proceeding with this I want to introduce a distinction that I heard put forth by Orson Welles; it was during a very late night television interview on an obscure cable station. He said that the highest form of art and the best representation of truth is to create something that is unreal but true. I am very taken by this idea even though I am not completely comfortable with his wording. There is a contrast that needs to be drawn between an idea, something so correct that it forces you to see the world differently, and the detailed description of that world. Not acknowledging this difference or that there is a difference produces the two essential errors, the two chronic but escalating symptoms, of social science.

The first is relativism run amok. Cultural relativism was anthropology's idea. It is the notion that people saw the world, and solved its problems, in different ways. Not better or worse, but simply differently. Exactly how different was subject to debate; but there was enough contrast that you were supposed to respect it, and, as a part of that, question your own ability to know another's world.

At some point people discovered or acknowledged that the thing called cultural relativism applied not just to the world of the native, but had something to do with the ethnographer as well. What ethnographers reported was not exactly correct or real. From the fact that ethnography was, to use Welles's term, chronically unreal, it was concluded that there was no truth (except of course this one), that it was relative, a figment of the ethnographer's imagination. And from the fact that there was no completely real ethnography, it was concluded that there is no truth in ethnography or that (really the same thing) all ethnography is equally good or true. Or, to paraphrase Flaubert, style becomes the only thing. We are still living with the fruits of this unfortunate idea, and they aren't very interesting.

The second error is made by those who think themselves scientists and fancy that they are emulating science, those who reify the pursuit of truth. They start in the same place as the amok relativists; that is, they note the unreality of ethnography and conclude that because it is unreal it is untrue. The remedy they seek is to make it more real. The idea is that if they add more detail, more data, to their description, this will make it truer. And of course it simply makes it worse, less like a portrait of people, more like a paint-by-the-numbers kit.

Good ethnography can be, perhaps tends to be, unreal but true. Ethnographies resemble nativistic movements. At some level they are correct; people, not just the natives, but administrators, missionaries, and anthropologists, are quite taken by them. But the shirts don't stop bullets and the plane piloted by LBJ hasn't come with the stuff.

It is difficult to see the attraction of reductionism, the reification of truth, or of relativism, the narcissistic pursuit of style, when they are viewed only as ideas, because obviously there are a lot better ideas. The basis for their attraction is in something else—their promise of control over experience. The pursuit of science enables you to bound the world rather severely, look here and not there, and fill your time with gathering data. It keeps you busy no matter what, and you can do the business pretty much irrespective of whether or not there are any natives to talk to. It makes research, fieldwork, seem like actual work and nicely medicates ethnographers who go crazy when there is nothing to do.

Open-mindedness, or feigning it, also does away with uncertainty and dissonance. You can only feel uncomfortable if you believe that there is something important in the world to discover. Then you worry about missing something, or about getting it wrong. Again I can't help thinking of Flaubert, who initially wrote wonderful, true things that he thought completely imperfect and who then completely screened out the world in pursuit of the perfect word, sentence, paragraph and produced perfect works that are lifeless.

And this brings us back to the habits of Western thought that essentially achieve the same end, the reduction of dissonance through the removal of uncertainty: the elimination of meaning through the creation of knowledge. The most fundamental of these habits of thought is interpretation, creating an illusion of understanding by dismantling contexts and messages. We assign someone to particular sets associated with categories we are somewhat comfortable with and, as a part of that comfort, take as real. We take the person and his or her statement apart and in the act of reduction claim understanding of the parts that we have created. And through a supposed understanding of pieces we claim knowledge of the whole, of "what he means."

"She is Navajo"; "Navajos believe this"; "this is what she means." Or, "He is schizophrenic"; "we used to believe his words had meaning but now we know that they don't, they are merely a symptom, a manifestation, of what is biochemical and genetic." The categorical replaces the personal even when, or perhaps especially when, it is extremely personal.

The dismantling takes the strength out of the message, but we ignore this, or more likely we seek it. Typically by taking it apart we gain control of what is being said. The first level of control we call understanding or knowledge. Transforming the unusual and powerful into the familiar and tame—the domestication of meaning. Through knowledge we believe that we can go to the second level of control, to be able to change what is being communicated. Thus a physician believes that he can transform human pain and discomfort via a diagnosis. If the diagnosis is correct, he can change the message. The person, now patient, no longer talks about malaise, but how much better he feels.

Our creation or imposition of meaning does away with it, eliminating or transforming what is being said into something we can understand and not be too uncomfortable with.

Each profession claims ownership of particular ways of taking things apart, of particular sorts of categories, so as to differentiate itself from other professions. A part of anthropology is also, it turns out, to look askance at the categories of other professions. This in fact was its basis for coming into existence, to argue that the way we looked at humans was accurate, insofar as it was accurate at all, only within a restricted context.

The particular categorical abstraction that anthropology owns is culture. By means of this, it describes difference between peoples (note: not *people*, that term is owned by psychology, but *peoples*). We create categories of people—the Nuer, Navajo, Trobriand Islanders—and assign categories of experience to them. Thus intimacy becomes kinship, one's relationship with God becomes world view, fear and anger become witchcraft, death becomes ritual, and the ideas that people hold most true become belief.

When you study anthropology you learn a great deal about these categories, especially about which of them particular peoples fit into. The Navajo language is of the Athapaskan family; they are southern Athapaskan along with other Apacheans. Their (more recent) traditional subsistence and settlement pattern is seminomadic (I'm not sure what semi anything is let alone seminomadic. I think it might have something to do with living in a trailer with the wheels off.) pastoralism, their kinship is matrilineal, their marriage matrilocal; and so on.

A part of this profession is to quibble about the categories. Something should be here rather than there; they aren't in this category but in that—that sort of thing. But the belief in categories *per se* and in the fact of categorization as an efficient and relatively accurate means of mapping the world is never questioned. I guess that we are simply unable to think about it differently.

At the point where you know a great deal about such things and have developed the habit of wondering about them, you go and do fieldwork. For me this was with the Navajo. This quickly undermined anything at all that I thought I knew. I'm not sure whether all fieldwork does this or if it is just this particular group of Indians that is especially bloody minded. To me they have always seemed different, special. Not always or even usually pleasant or comfortable to be around, but having a more correct outlook on a great deal that we habitually muddle up.

The initial impression is that the way that Navajos have been described is incorrect. To a budding researcher, this looks like an opportunity; you can show up the previous ethnographers and provide a true description of these people. If you are diligent and obsessive, and not too self-critical, you will discover something that you are able to market as truth.

It turns out that this is what you are supposed to do in anthropology. The task is to discover that our categories don't describe the natives, and this needs to be discovered over and over again. It goes on forever. After you discover that the categories were wrong and put forth new ones, you discover, or someone else does, that the new ones don't quite work either, and then again, and again. For the scientifically minded reader let me point out that new does not mean better; there is no evidence overall that we are getting better maps. They are simply new and different, not new and improved.

As a part of this, anthropology loves anomalies. You first discover one, and then you make sense out of it. It is not difficult to discover anomaly; it is merely an artifact of taking categories as real. If you believe in rigid boundaries that separate classes of things, classes that are real, then you will always be taken by something that is in both classes, or in neither, or that is sort of between them. You can produce or discover anomaly at will.

But the more basic error is in the fences we build in the world. Having built them and repaired them and insisted that they are where they are, we ultimately come to believe in their existence. We forget that we constructed them and think that they are a part of the order of it all, that they are discovered and not built. People who build highways have this same belief about pavement.

When you start asking Navajo people either/or questions over time, you discover very quickly that they don't know their own culture. After they go to college they learn it from reading Kluckhohn and the like. There is one community with a lot of medicine men, one that is always referred to as traditional by those who know about such things, where I had the following conversation over and over again: Are you a medicine man? Yes. Do you believe in the traditional religion? Yes. Are you a Catholic? Yes. Native American Church? Sometimes. Well, which is it, traditional, Catholic, or peyote? Yes.

Or consider one of the old standards, matrilocal residence, the prescription that a couple live with the wife's family after marriage. Where does a man live after marriage? is the query. It's up to him, comes the response. But I thought you were supposed to live with the wife's mother. Yes, that's right. So that is where you are supposed to live? It's up to him. Where did you live? I lived here. Where is your mother in law? She's dead; I'd rather not talk about her. After my own fieldwork I could no longer give or take multiple choice or any sort of objective tests.

I keep thinking about the way that the Navajo and most other people in the world think about the hermaphrodite, the incorporation of difference that is defined as and that generates completeness. And I contrast that with our own insistent attempts at manufacturing difference and individuality. In our world a person is male or she is female. And we have surgery to eliminate the ambiguity if the genetic material can't decide. In our world there is an immense tragedy in ambiguity, in theirs it is the potential for everything, for completeness.

Imagine a people in the world who shared a belief in individualism. If they were truly individualists they would not cite that in a prescriptive way, because that would be a denial of the belief. That is, they wouldn't say you are supposed to be an individual, which in itself would be a denial of individuality. If you asked them about what a person should do in an abstract moral dilemma, they would respond, It's up to him, and they would mean it.

What if this group were studied by another group, whose whole basis for existence was in the notion of group belief. Who defined the very idea of group as people who shared beliefs. And who, to further complicate the picture, had their own group notion of individuality, which was not a true individuality at all, but some sort of caricature of cowboy movies. One error in thinking, categorizing is more than enough, but if we add to that the transformation of what is the essential noncategory, individuality, into one of Aristotle's metathings, it really gets confusing.

The studiers would watch and they would talk to people about, say, marriage. The person would answer, as best he could, about who you could and could not marry, where you lived afterwards, and so on. The person doing the study would take this to be a statement of what Navajos believe and/or do. He would hear similar things from people living nearby and then write authoritatively on the Navajo. When a different person studied it later, or in a different place, or simply asked the questions differently, he would get a different result.

Rather than question the premise of what you are doing, the categorization-of-shared-knowledge idea, you create other categories to explain the difference. And you have, to name a few, regional variation, individual variation, the ever popular social/cultural distinction; that is, a difference between what people say or believe and what they do. And today it is the bad-data category, that non-idea that people before did ethnography poorly and that we can do better by trying harder.

My attempt here is to say something true about some Navajo people, the place where they live, doing anthropology, and myself, in that order of importance. Oswald Werner, when talking about postmodern ethnographies, likes to say that the natives are a lot more interesting than the ethnographer. He is completely correct. Malinowski, in his own way, also conclusively demonstrated this.

My starting point, as is my custom, was more in the direction of knowing what I didn't want to do rather than in having a precise idea about how to convey what it is I cared about communicating. So I experiment with different ways of describing the meaning that I care about so much. Unfortunately, "experimental ethnography" is one of those pseudocategories in rather heavy use today. And it tends to be used by the people who emphasize style.

My own particular set of experiments is oriented differently. My goal is to arrive at better representations of the way things are. I want my description to be truer, a more correct picture of the world out there. I am interested in discovering these people and their world, and then in writing correctly about that. I have rather little interest in writing about me and even less about anthropology and anthropologists. My goal then is the same as that of the truth-seeking ethnographers, the ones who think themselves scientists. And it is very unlike that of the people who emphasize style. But I think that the style of science, the emphasis on methodology, produces its own form of dishonesty and untruth that I would like to try and avoid. It is simply too easy to treat, to do away with, discomfort through technique, through obsessive ritualization.

Ultimately I am neither a stylist nor a scientist since I see the tendency of both to reify as distorting rather than enhancing discovery and representation. What that leaves is some stories with reflections. You see I also cannot simply tell the story; I have to think about it and tell the readers my thoughts, hit them over the head with the meaning. This is why the people in my tribe write poor fiction: they cannot simply let the story speak for itself; they need to make sure the reader gets the point. We think a lot about experience, sometimes to the point that we eliminate it.

2

CONNECTEDNESS—
PLACE, PEOPLE, AND
JOURNEYS BACK

 A generic Christian missionary has just come to the
house of the middle-aged Navajo man to whom I am
talking. The missionary has, to summarize, told my
friend that he must believe in something for which he
has absolutely no evidence. That is, he must have
faith. In addition, the major events of the religion the
missionary is peddling occurred in places he has
never been to or seen. To summarize my friend's response,
"How can you believe in this? Have you ever been to Jerusalem?
Have you ever been to Bethlehem and seen where this Christ
was born, or where he died? How can you believe in something
you've never seen? How can you say you know this when you
don't see it every day so that you are reminded of what happened there, when the memory of those events isn't a part of the
world that surrounds you?"

In trying to approximate how it is there are certain patterns
and themes, certain abstractions, that at least hint at the mood.
There is first the importance and sense of place. You have this
impression initially and it persists. And, the people who live
there, both those that have been around for a while and those of
us who came more recently, will emphasize the place.

As to the people, the impression is much more episodic and
vague. You remember initial bits and pieces, but nothing very
strong and clear. Later the episodes connect up and you can see
them as part of a larger whole, but not initially. So there is a
connectedness, and there is that connectedness with the place as
well, and as part of that a sense of return. People don't start out
here and stay; they return.

And finally, and most important, the place and the people are part of a pattern, an order, one that you must acknowledge and live within. Conscious purpose and will do poorly here; you cannot bully the place or the people.

PLACE

Anglos call this place the Colorado Plateau. It is large, extending over parts of four states. Overall, it is rather dry, in some places very dry. There are mountains with forests and snow, areas of piñon and juniper with less precipitation, and sagey expanses with no trees and even less water. The Plateau is also cut by canyons, the Grand being one of the more spectacular examples.

With variation in elevation goes a diversity of life. In the small, wet canyons there are lush deciduous forests; at the tops of the mountains, tundra; and of course everything in between. And with diversity of life generally you get diversity in human life. There are a variety of niches that have long been exploited. You can see this in the variety of people today. And you can see evidence for it in what remains of the past; in what the people who were here before left behind. There are pieces of stone transformed into tools, fragments of pottery, and what remains of houses of stone; later the tools are metal, the houses are log or lumber, or occasionally, for those who meant to stay, they are again masonry. There are also hints of what people did to make a living—terraced areas that were fields, fractured stone where agave was roasted, barbed wire fences to contain cattle, twisted pieces of rail and ties from a logging operation. When you see these things and hear people's stories, you have a strong sense that people have always been here, and you feel connected to them.

A part of the initial impression is of harshness. The descriptions of early explorers in this part of the world conveyed a mood of frightened wonder. More recent travelers have a similar reaction; they see this as a harsh, difficult place. This is especially true when they look at it through a car window. When they occasionally do stop and get out it feels very hot and they are instantly thirsty, the air is so dry. If it is a "rest stop," they find that there are chemical toilets, water being so scarce and remote. And the people on tour will always ask, in a sort of confused or even hostile awe, How could these people live here? You hear this question especially often at large prehistoric ruins.

Over and over. How could these people live here? What did they eat? And most important, where did they get water?

But this superficial first impression is deceptive. It is not an easy place to make a living, but you can do it. The environment demands that you pay attention, that you know what is going on and live within that. It is not a world that you can control. The place instead emphasizes an inner control, a self-discipline, developing habits of living that coincide with this environment. When you attempt to impose your will, to forcefully shape this world, something inopportune happens. A part of it is aesthetic, a part of it is that control to the exclusion of living in the place ultimately fails here. The town of Page and the dams on the Colorado River demonstrate this. They have not only done away with the beauty, they have created an ecological disaster. But the aesthetic and the environment are really a part of the same whole, two different aspects of the same reality. If you create ugliness you will, by definition, destroy the other aspects of the world of the Plateau.

And finally for the people who live here, meaning is found and expressed in stories that are structured by and anchored in this place. Individually and collectively there are the stories about coming to live here. Everyone, of course, somehow arrived. But they didn't stay. They didn't feel an initial love of the place and a need to be here, although they did remember it and at least implicitly felt a fascination for it. Because the stories tell you about locations in great detail and with a sense of awe. For some reason the individual or the people telling the story left, often in search of, very literally, greener pastures. And then they return. Sometimes they stay for good, sometimes they leave and return again.

In the stories there is a sense of past connected to present, not in a deterministic cause-and-effect way but in a patterned sort of way. This is where I came before, or my ancestors came and this is what it was like, what it means. So the paying attention becomes very detailed and is passed along in the form of these stories.

THE PEOPLE

For Hopi people the stories begin with their birth from the Earth, near the mesas where they currently live. The place is in the Little Colorado River gorge. The place they came out is literally called the Earth's vagina. And I'll tell you something, that is exactly what it looks like. It is interesting that when we politely interpret the religion of others we get the abstract and the concrete all wrong. We politely talk of Native Americans thinking of the Earth as their mother, but we virtually never talk about the literalness of this. Politeness that is false, translating their ideas into our own image.

And they left and traveled to different places, according to the myth, for a large piece of time. And then they returned. Once a friend of mine asked an old Hopi man about this. He said, "Why, after traveling to and being in such lush and wonderful places, did the people return to the bleakness and the difficulty of the mesas?" The man said, "In those easy places, our religion, our way of life would not survive."

This is very important. Their religion, their way of life requires close attention to things. They need to watch closely that world around them, look for the order in it that allows them to live there. They ceremonially make note of that pattern; they mark the moments in it that matter. They have a ritual cycle that follows and creates that tempo. This ceremony happens at this time, then this, and so on. The Kachina dances are the most spectacular part of this, but not the only part.

We have always viewed Hopi religion through the lens of our own most sacred belief, that events in the world are of two classes, causes and effects. We have said that Hopis believe that these ceremonies cause the rain to come, the seasons to happen. But I don't think that is right. I think that they punctuate time and are a celebration of it. People say if you don't do the ceremonies, or if you do them wrong, then things will go wrong. But I think that the wrong is in forgetting the tempo of their world. It comes from not having paid attention to or knowing what matters.[1] The magic, as with all magic, is in watching and paying attention, not in anything else. If you are

---

[1] In talking about this with Oswald Werner, he noted that since there is an exact correlation between the ceremonial cycle and the seasons, there is no way of knowing, and it is irrelevant, which precedes the other.

bored with life you always want something spectacular, but knowing your world is spectacular enough.

The religion also mandates that the people on these mesas need to behave in a certain way towards each other. If they don't, that too will make a difference in the world around them. It is not a life of ease certainly, but neither is it a life of hardship; it can become that if you don't attend to and live in the world of the Plateau, and instead try to control and transform it. If you are arrogant you won't do well here.

The Navajo place of emergence is not so nearby. It is always referred to as over in the North and East somewhere. But they traveled here, left at least once, and returned. If you believe the archaeologists, they have only been here for about six hundred years. And yet everything that matters to these people—their religion, philosophy, world view—is located, encoded in the place. This is where the twins killed that particular monster; you can see the stain in the rock; it is the blood from that. And the indentation is where he fell, the small rise is where Monster Slayer stood; that ridge is a part of the skeleton of the one he killed; and so on. Or this is where my father showed me about hunting while he told me the story of how game was created and how hunting came into being. These stories that we think of as very general are almost always told and thought about very personally.

The Navajo origin story describes their emergence from the Earth, their travel to the northeastern reservation, then to the West, and then back again. As with Hopi religion, we need to be careful in how we look at this. In our lineal arrangement of time we see the things that happened before as causing what happened after; a subset of this is in seeing the return to a place as being chosen, caused by what went before. As if we learned from the past and decided to come back. But this theme of arrival and return has little to do with conscious purpose. It would also be incorrect to say it just happened. There is a pattern in it, but it transcends our notions of will and mind.

ARRIVAL AND RETURN

My introduction to the Southwest in general and the Navajo specifically was during spring break from being a fifth-year junior in college. (In those years, if you graduated you went to Vietnam and got killed.) I had recently been married and the two of us and another couple headed for, among other places, the Grand Canyon. After that, we dropped the other couple off and headed for a place called Navajo National Monument which is in the western part of the Navajo Reservation. I'd never been in this part of the country before, never really saw Indians, never really knew much about the Southwest. I was an undergraduate student in anthropology, which in the late sixties was semipopular, which is as popular as it ever was. I certainly knew nothing at all about Native Americans. I was more interested in every place else—Middle America, China, and especially Africa. I also had no plans to study or be involved with Indians. Anthropologists can be snobs; American Indians were too acculturated, not exotic enough. This trip did nothing to alter my lack of interest.

We got there in the late afternoon and camped out of the back of a Ford station wagon. The campground was what you would call primitive or rustic, just dirt with a few fire rings. It was on a shelf with piñon and juniper trees and it overlooked a small redrock canyon, a tributary to a larger drainage, which is not to say that anyone could remember water being there. It was pretty and a nice place to be, but cold at night in April. The elevation there is about 7,200 feet, and when you come from California, you tend to know very little about the Colorado Plateau and the mountains of Arizona.

I talked to one of the rangers about Keet Seel. This is the largest Anasazi ruin in Arizona. It's under an overhang, and when I finally saw it I was impressed. In order to get there you had to walk or ride a horse about seven miles. You followed a live drainage, not a creek really, kind of a wash with water in it that was inside a canyon. You followed the canyon until you came to Keet Seel, off to your left. Today you can't go out there unless there is a ranger in residence. Then there wasn't that much traffic, and I guess they figured if you were willing to walk you were not interested in doing any major damage. Remoteness always works better than preserve and protect.

If you didn't want to walk, there was an Indian who rented horses. But you had to rent him as a guide along with the horse. It cost ten dollars for the horse and ten for him, which seemed like a lot of money. It turned out that he was going to take two Frenchmen there the following day.

Next morning I started walking when it was warm enough
to move and get out of my sleeping bag. After a while the Indian
and his two clients rode by on some very emaciated horses. I'd
been around horses most of my life, a little in the suburbs, but
mainly on my uncles' cattle ranches. Suburbanites treat horses as
pets, which is not such a great thing to do with an animal whose
essence is a combination of fear, size, and stupidity. Cattle
ranchers mostly treat horses matter-of-factly. They are a tool; they
need to be taken care of, but not coddled. But I never knew that an
animal that gaunt could still live and more or less function.

I walked along for a while. There wasn't really a trail, or
more accurately there were many trails worn by sheep and other
stock. You were in sand a lot, and occasionally in mud. Not
difficult walking really, but not so pleasant either. It was difficult
picking exactly the right way to go. With some experience you
learn there isn't one. This in fact is soon obvious, but it takes
longer to accept than it should.

I started to follow the horses' tracks, figuring that this man
knew where he was going. The horses weren't very far ahead
and occasionally I would almost overtake them, at which point
the Navajo would put them into a trot, a life-threatening activity
for these skin-and-bones animals. And although these animals
weren't the pride of his herd, he didn't want to have to refund
the rental money. Soon after, the horses' tracks started to lead
me through quicksand. At first I thought this was a coincidence,
but it was too consistent. As it occurred to me that the Indian
guide thought that I was taking advantage of him and cheating
him out of his fee, I started to laugh. I was fairly near the riders,
and he looked back seriously and then he smiled. And then the
horses' trail got better. I think the fact that I laughed about it
made a difference.

Ten years later, after going to England to prepare for East
African studies and then on to Northwestern for more African
studies, I was back at Navajo National Monument camping in
the old campground, although maybe not in the same spot. My
first fieldwork was going to be on the Navajo Reservation, and
my professor had gotten some money for me to do it.

It was June. I was in a tent trying to find someplace to live
that wasn't a tent. I thought there must be a proper and correct
way to do this. This is one of the reasons you go to graduate

school; you want to do fieldwork and think that there are secrets that allow you to do it. At some point during graduate education you expect to be told these secrets. Like they're going to take you into a room and tell you the correct way to find a hogan to live in, how to haul water and that sort of thing, tell you about the Navajo rental market for budding anthropologists. You go to the fourth hogan north of the wash, she is the Navajo who handles summer rentals of hogans for anthropologists. A part of the same thinking is that you need some sort of license, some credential to do fieldwork. As if the Navajo in charge of these matters is going to show up and ask you to show your badge or your degree.

It turns out that it doesn't exactly work that way. That June there were thunderstorms every night and some days. It never rains in June. June is the driest month in an otherwise very dry, completely arid part of the country. I took the weather personally.

Every morning, for about a week, I would show up at my professor's trailer located in a small trailer park behind a trading post. It had plumbing, heat, and was dry inside. I was dirty, muddy, and covering the mud was dust. You would think that rain would suppress or eliminate dust. I had not slept. When there is lightning, my very strong assumption is that I have to stay awake and count the time between the flash and the sound. When it gets down to a second or two, I get very religious.

He'd be sitting there drinking his coffee in the morning sun and he would say, each and every morning, "It's real unusual for it to rain at this time of the year." End of conversation, me on my way. The secret, it turned out, was to go into complete strangers' homes and to ask. There was no secret; that's the secret. The same secret of all the great religions of the world, the self-evident truth that you arrive at out of necessity, when you are tired of being rained on, not sleeping and dirty.

There is a mood here. Superficially it involves plans, especially plans for a life—they tend not to work out. You end up in a place and you don't remember how you got there. Usually you invent reasons, describe a trail that leads directly to that present moment. It creates the illusion that this is what you wanted, this is how it happened, but it isn't. You get to the place and just aren't sure how it came about. Later you invent reasons.

Which brings me back to the theme of conscious purpose,

cause and effect, that sort of thing. In this southwest part of the world, especially with the Navajo, plans don't work. But there seems to be an order, a pattern, that you can tap into and have a sense of the future, maybe not knowing exactly where you will end up but having a notion of at least the direction of the destination. This sounds mystical, and in a pure sense it is. But not in the sense of Don Juan and magic tricks, in the more mundane sense of being connected to something larger, being a part of a process that you can sense in the world around you.

As a rule, we look in the wrong place for mysticism. People bored with their lives, dissatisfied people, will try to invent a spectacular other world, one that you can supposedly touch. Sometimes it is inside, sometimes outside. I am intensely suspicious of this whole business—people who invent other-world powers and gods and insist on their unique and different truth. I am also intensely suspicious of those people, scientists, who insist on the unique truth of the natural and relegate things they can't explain but that clearly exist to the category of nonsense.

We need to be careful when we look at this sort of thing. As a part of our desire to build fences and place things in the proper pasture, we tend to convert things that are best viewed as both/ and into either/or. Two examples of this are this natural/supernatural division and the division between experience and explanation. In terms of the first set, people tend to prefer one type of explanation or the other and they tend to insist on the essential difference between the two. They also are absolutely convinced that there is something essentially wrong with people who choose and emphasize the other type of explanation.

As to the second distinction, most people tend to prefer explanation to experience. Other ways of saying this are that we convert novelty into expectation and that we don't like surprises. There is a difficulty in simply being a part of something, living in a moment, without being able to explain it. The result of this is that we limit our experience to the realm of things we have answers for. I think that the world, the order of things, is transparent, not hidden and mysterious, but I think that most of us are too afraid to look and so we impose the idea of mystery to rationalize our fear.

I used to live with an old man who looked into and at the future. Sometimes he chewed datura, sometimes he looked into a crystal, often he just looked without props. He would always describe this spatially, as in seeing a long distance, or a long way off. He tried to teach me about it, especially the datura. For whatever reason, he thought this safe and appropriate for me. In this he was correct. My experience was auditory, not visual. He told me that if I listened closely, I would understand the voices and the other sounds that were present when I went off alone. He also was correct in this.

But when you tell a story like this, it raises questions: How can you explain it? How could such things happen? My answer is that I don't really know, but I think I know something about where to look for an answer and where not to look. The old man knew a lot about things, he'd watched the world very closely. He could spend an hour telling you how a spider wove its web; he could describe the social organization of an anthill. He also knew a great deal about people. In Gregory Bateson's terms he knew a lot about the pattern that connects, about the ways that living things are joined and the world organized.

I would try to talk to him about there being more: ghosts, spirits, the magical. I think that he found enough magic, and enough sorrow, in his world without this being necessary. He really didn't think it a correct question. He just didn't have this contrast in his mind, in the way he saw things. Maybe there were ghosts; there certainly were memories, and if the memories were strong enough they became tangible. Things came into existence somehow—there are stories about that—but no one knows such things for sure.

There was an order. It wasn't hidden, but apparent. But most people avoided looking at it and seeing it. They wanted the world to be different, to take the direction they desired, and so they wouldn't look into the distance. If they did, they would have to face the fact that life was not going to be exactly what they wanted it to be, was not completely subject to their wishes. So they avoided looking or looked selectively. It was that simple. There were things, living beings, that had existed before, you could see their shadows in the rocks; they no longer walked here, just their memories in stone. Just because you can't normally see something or hear it doesn't mean it doesn't exist. You know that from listening with the datura.

So a part of being in this place is this strong sense of the world around you having a form or shape, an order or direction, that you can know and be a part of but that doesn't necessarily concern itself with you. And a part of getting to know this world and the people in it, especially the Navajo, is in the surprises, in the profound sense of anomaly that you experience with some frequency. You see this initially not as an artifact of your own thinking but as a feature of the world you are entering.

When I was still at the beautiful but wet campground, another student and I went to town, or a kind of a town. Towns on the Navajo Reservation are the condensation, more correctly the effluent, of the worst of all worlds. They contain government both from Washington and modeled on it. If that isn't bad enough, they contain bad curio shops and terrible restaurants populated by tourists. To that add bootleggers, missionaries, and trailer parks. But there is something even worse. The towns were built in places that were special, places with water near or on the surface, where populations have existed since there were people. You can see that these were places of beauty, and they aren't anymore. It is difficult to completely transform beauty into ugliness, but in these places they managed it. Southern California without the beaches.

We went to town to see a movie. This was before there were theaters and the movies were shown on certain nights in schools or, in this case, the chapter house. One of the things that you are supposed to know about Navajos is that they don't like corpses. If you are in the anthropology business that is one of the rules. Another one is that they have witchcraft stories which include cross-generational incest, and that too is a touchy subject, discussed not at all or with difficulty.

This is one of the products of anthropology, these factoids, bits and pieces of information about the rules people live by. Anthropologists can say things like "This is what Navajos believe," or "They don't marry this or that kind of cross cousin." That sort of thing. Items, lists of attributes that purport to describe a people. If you know enough, do enough reading before you start fieldwork, you don't have to go or you can stay in a motel nearby.

The movie shown in the chapter house that night was

Harold and Maude. It is a story about the relationship between an old woman in her seventies and a young man, sixteen or seventeen. They meet at funerals, which they both love to attend. Just any funeral; not anyone they know. They are both enamored of death. The movie portrays their love of death and their love affair with each other.

This can't be, you think. You are sitting there watching this; you are in the middle of the high desert, but the town doesn't know this, doesn't know that towns don't belong in this place and you are watching this very cult, very avant garde movie about things that should horrify Navajos. You are off balance, there is a strangeness. It isn't what it is supposed to be, isn't the way the compartments in your head have it organized.

After you are there for a while you pretty much give up on rules and categories; you regard them as a figment of Anglos' collective imagination. But occasionally it comes back very strongly—this sense of the bizarre, of anomaly, of what should be separate being joined.

Later, during a longer stay on the reservation, I participated in an all-Navajo basketball league. The all-Indian team was called, of course, the Cowboys. The Sioux probably call their basketball team the Seventh Cavalry. Initially I thought this was being accepted, being a part of things, belonging, that I was special. Later I learned that any Anglo that wanted to, or anyone else for that matter, could play. They just didn't want to.

You learn a lot playing basketball with people, although that wasn't why I did it. The schools where we played and practiced had showers and you get tired of sponge baths, especially in the winter. Other Anglos would play for a while and then they would quit. This was particularly true of missionaries, especially Mormon missionaries.

Navajos know what basketball is like, and they re-create it here in their own setting and in their own way. The re-creation looks the same but it is not. It has the same appearance—ten people on two teams moving up and back on the court. But there is an important difference: there are no rules. This is an anarchistic basketball game. Not in the sense of fights or bomb-ings, but in the sense that the game gets played, and resembles basketball in other settings, without any obvious authority. There are two referees, but they don't really call fouls unless there is an obvious consensus on the part of both teams that one should be called. But a whole game can go by without a foul being called.

The referees are a part of the re-creation, making it look the same. If you don't watch too closely it seems like the games you see in high school, college, on TV. But it really isn't. People haven't worked on things, run plays and the like; they just go out and do the pattern. Similarly, if they are losing, there are, as I recall, no very serious attempts to alter it. There are time-outs and talk of it, but no real attempt to force anyone to do something contrary to their nature. If a large clumsy person insists on thinking of himself as, and attempting to play as, a small fast guard, then so be it.

As a newcomer, a stranger, you get beat up a lot. Part of this is the testing of someone new and different. It also has to do with size. If you are a foot taller and fifty pounds heavier then most of the people you are playing against, they will play what is euphemistically called a very physical game against you. You need to learn to retaliate rather than expecting the deity in the striped uniform to make the world a better place for you.

When there is a tournament, teams will recruit new players, and that is when a lot of Anglo missionaries show up. It's strange to see what happens. The first thing that these people get upset with is the lack of fouls being called. There is a refusal of authority figures to behave properly, to intervene and impose justice on the world. And these missionaries are not upset because they are personally fouled or hurt (being a missionary necessarily includes the expectation of, and even the desire for, suffering). They get upset because things just aren't fair. People break rules and nothing happens. Again, this desire for justice from on high is probably a part of the genetic makeup of a missionary.

The second thing they get upset with is the lack of reasonableness. Plays are not followed, strategies are not changed, people don't do what they need to in order to win. The Navajo players won't sacrifice their own individuality for the benefit of the team, in order to accomplish the goal of winning or at least of playing better. Probably another gene in the missionary species: means/end thinking, which includes sacrifice for the greater good.

These basketball games look the same, but when you watch

closely or get involved it's different. The only other thing you need to learn to get along in these games is to be able to chew snuff while moving full tilt up the court and not to swallow it when someone hits you with an elbow. Keeping the snuff between your cheek and gum instead of in your stomach is probably the hardest thing to learn.

Navajos appear to anthropologists to have culture, as if they have rules and behave in certain systematic ways. It is a pattern certainly and it looks a lot like a pattern governed by rules, but when you start to describe it something happens. Sometimes it disappears, sometimes it changes. Often it seems as if you need at least one more dimension to portray what you sense is there.

I guess what you learn from *Harold and Maude* in the chapter house and from basketball is that you are not only missing something, you are just looking at things in completely the wrong way. And the error in perspective is very large, very basic. It is not just in details or in getting better or more accurate data. You are just way off on the level of abstraction. You are used to seeing things in terms of rules, as man being governed by and more often determined by context, and here you find individuality. This is not the individuality of American cowboys, which is just about as rule-governed and context-determined a social phenomenon as you can get. This is different. If you take it seriously, it knocks the pins out from under the whole social science business. It is probably not very surprising that the people in the social science business don't take it seriously.

To end this beginning, I want to tell you about the man who led me through quicksand. When I came back to the reservation, I ran into him. Actually I first ran into one of his children. He had between twenty-five and thirty children, and he had four wives.

He was a man of tradition. He wore the hair knot. He knew Blessingway, a brief unspectacular ceremony by our standards, only the one night and there are no masks, no spectacular magic, but it is the core of the philosophy. It celebrates life, the passage of time, transitions. There is a promise in it. It says that if you lead life in a certain way, paying special attention to the sheep, there will be growth and abundance, riches not necessarily in the personal sense, but in the sense of having a large family, being able to care for them, and the like. And being able to help those other kin that call on you for help. Being able to be a generous man, not needing to be stingy or impoverished and having to beg others for things.

At a certain point in time, Blessingway came into existence and made this promise. Before that the world was more dangerous, more uncertain. Before that the things that mattered involved power and danger, hunting and, with that, being involved with the spirits of the wild. Blessingway and Changing Woman said, "You can worry less now; the world is safer. Live a proper life, take care of the sheep, the corn, your family, and the good life will follow." I knew this about tradition and about Blessingway; people had told me and I'd read about it. But I always understand the abstract better if I can see or experience a tangible representation of an idea.

I remember driving up to this man's home, which was about a mile back from the edge of the mesa. From his house there were trails leading out onto the surrounding land and leading down off the mesa and into the drier grasslands below. It was the kind of thing you saw with all animals, not only man, on this plateau. Water and grass are the requirements in this environment; neither is abundant. Living near the edge meant that you could take advantage of the changes brought by the difference in elevation. Elk do the same thing, as do deer, as do the animals, coyotes and men, that prey on them.

When you came onto his house, the single most striking thing was the size of the corrals. They were immense and meticulously maintained. They could easily hold a couple of thousand sheep. Here in the early 1970s was a glimpse of life fifty years before.

After that time Navajos were told that their land was overgrazed and that there were too many sheep. They had to do something about it, regulate the size of these herds. They went through the process of talking about it and agreeing to do something to correct it. Decisions like this take a long time; for Navajos they take forever. They work toward consensus, to get everyone to agree.

The head of the BIA got impatient. He felt this urgency about what was happening to the land, about what was going to happen. He felt that he needed to do something. This, I think, was a particularly courageous man. He felt he had to act, and he knew that everyone would remember and hate him for it. (He was, by the way, correct in this; Navajos universally remember and hate him.) But he felt it was his responsibility to try, while knowing that with action there would be consequences. Courage in the government bureaucracy is so rare, it being a niche exclusively inhabited by invertebrates. At the same time this was a man without wisdom, but then wisdom is not really something that Anglos and especially Americans have. They are too brash, too arrogant. They believe too much in their own strength and their own power to influence and to make a difference.

In some cases rangers came to people's homes and shot the animals in front of them. In others, the "excess" sheep and the goats were gathered up and put in corrals and pens. But of course there wasn't enough feed or enough water for them. Some of the animals died and the remainder were shot. The carcasses rotted or were partially burned while what remained rotted. People who raise livestock look at animals differently from those of us who only experience the remains of these animals in cellophane in the supermarket. And pastoralists, people who herd and watch animals every day of their lives, have a particularly intimate and strong relationship with the flock.

The Navajo call the sheep, "my mother, *shimá*; my grandmother, *shimá sání*." They are sustenance, nurturance. The small boy herding the sheep feels frightened when he is alone and away from home. But he feels safe in the midst of the flock, surrounded and protected by them. The feelings persist into adulthood and they are constant, a part of life. In a sense you are always in the midst of the sheep. Anything of value that you possess derives from them. In your house you can hear them, smell them, and see them. Occasionally you slaughter an animal, but there is an ambivalence about doing this. You and your family want the meat, but you have known the sheep for a long time and you also feel sad in the death. You share the meat and you don't waste it. Everything gets used.

The sheep were rounded up, killed, and burned during the depression—when people were without and some were starving in cities. What was a terrible thing became incomprehensible.

The man who lived near the edge of the mesa, and who had led me through quicksand until I laughed, had been successful. He'd lived properly, he'd taken care of the sheep. And the sheep,

Blessingway, and Changing Woman had kept their promise. The herd and his family grew together; the sheep are the sustenance for the family, and the family is needed to care for the sheep. When the sheep were gone, some of the children had to go, usually to Mormon placement. This is an arrangement where you can place your children with fairly well-to-do Mormon families, not for their lives, but to be educated in schools that are usually better than those found on the reservation.

Forty years after the sheep were murdered, the corrals still waited. They had been maintained through those years of nonuse. For what? Maybe as a sign of what had been, or maybe in hopes of the old times returning. Or maybe he couldn't stand to have it any other way. He couldn't tear them down and he couldn't let them deteriorate. To tear them down would be to give up hope; to let them deteriorate was not his way.

But the basic rules of life were changed here. And there was no getting over that; in fact this man didn't get over it. I'm not sure whether the Navajo as a people did either.[2] Another one of those interactions that say very clearly who is in charge. They say we, the government *Wáashindoon* may have given you these sheep and encouraged you to raise them, to replace raiding and warfare, and you did well with them. But we can take them away any time we feel like it. The fact of us not intervening or imposing our will does not mean that we will not. It also says to a people that we will solve your problems, which is another way of saying that the people need to be taken care of, that they are incapable of making decisions and caring for themselves.

A few years after this the corrals were gone, not his doing. The man's home was on a rather rich, easily accessible coal bed. Even on the first visit, the strip mine that defaced this mesa, that scarred the earth, could be heard from his house. And in just a few years his home was a part of that mine, a huge open pit that feeds a coal-burning generating station seventy miles away. But it is not a total loss because the smoke, the ash, and the sulfur dioxide blow back, return here.

---

[2]Counter example: The parents of a friend of mine saw the reduction coming and sold off most of their livestock in a gradual manner before it came. They put the money into savings bonds and used the proceeds to finance their children's college educations.

When you experience this, you get very angry at the coal company. There is a foolishness in this. What else would you expect from a coal company? The anger is also misplaced or at least needs to be redistributed. The Navajo tribe, which means the Navajo politicos, lease that property to them. Local older Navajos have tried to sue the tribal government for violating their religious freedom; the mesa is a sacred place. It is *dził ba'áád*, the female mountain. But you can't do that. Native Americans are not protected by the Bill of Rights in their dealings with their tribe. The tribe is a sovereign nation that does what it pleases, which translates to mean they act pretty much like the corrupt, indifferent Anglo politicians who serve as the model for this way of government.

SYSTEMATIC LIES

When you write about others you try to do it honestly, but you always impose a systematic lie. Not just occasional fibs and mistakes, but distortions that are an extension of you. Some lies we professionalize. In social science we write objectively and dispassionately about people, leaving the people out, taking an experience and making it into something that is more pure by being more reasonable. In fiction or that subset of fiction, the educationally oriented documentary, the purity is in the creation of superficial caricatures. For Indians this involves making them into something purely good and beautiful, or completely ugly, or making them noble victims of depraved Anglo politicians.

One of my lies is already apparent. I like anarchistic individualists and dislike government and change. My favorite movie is *Butch Cassidy and the Sundance Kid* and, while I would prefer to be like Sundance, I am more like Butch. ("Just keep thinking, Butch, that is what you are good at.") I have difficulty in seeing a world of man beyond very small units—individuals, families, and moments. More and more I can't see tribes, nations, and the like. It angers me, and upsets me in other ways, to see individuals harmed, especially when such harm is inflicted in the name of the greater good. As when a man's sheep, his way of life are killed so as to make the world a better place.

When you try to capture a people in words, you quickly discover there is no purity (pure description is the benchmark of dishonesty), only rough edges and a few redundant themes. In describing the reservation world this is apparent. It is neither purely grim nor is it only beautiful. If you wallow in beauty or in the ugly, you have missed something, left something out. It is pieces of things that combine into wholes but that don't fit together. It is an all-Navajo basketball team called the Cowboys; it is Christians who pray with corn pollen; and it is, today, tract houses in the middle of nowhere. It is waiting, empty sheep corrals; it is a strip mine raping the sacred land; and it is corrupt politicians. It is these anomalies, things that are supposed to be separate living together.

It is also meaning. Things occurring that matter, that you are witness to and a part of. And for people like me, with my particular pathology, it involves thinking about, reflecting on, trying to purify and distill out that meaning. The world is, after all, supposed to make sense, behave in an orderly fashion. As the old man with the datura said, the meaning is there for the taking; you only need to listen. We avoid it because there is a part of it we don't like, can't accept, don't want to face. Like a world I care about that is changing. I want the past to stay. I want it there for me, not because it makes sense or is better for the people involved. When we can't actually physically control the world, we edit and in other ways limit how we look at it. We see this, but overlook that. And of course all we ever end up seeing is our own image in a mirror.

3
THE WIND IN A JAR

 It is very difficult to explain why you go to graduate school. Occasionally, pretty much by accident, it turns out to be practical. But you don't really go for practical reasons. Learning is not the reason, because of course you can do that anywhere, including universities, without enrolling or seeking a degree. Needing a rite of passage has something to do with it. And there is a desire to get money so that you can do fieldwork. At the time it seems as though you need to be a part of some sort of formal institution to have a shot at this.

As soon as you are enrolled in graduate education, you want it to be over, particularly the part where you have to be at the university taking classes and having other people tell you what to do. The culmination of graduate school is in getting funded to do research for your dissertation. This money, if you get it, is kind of a stamp of approval and it is the practical means to being able to live with the Indians.

I was in San Diego when I found out I had been funded. This wasn't my home. That summer I met a linguist in Ann Arbor and fell in love with her, and she lived in San Diego. When I heard that I had money I went downtown and bought a Stetson cowboy hat, embarrassing to admit, but I needed something tangible to celebrate the funding and as a sign to the world that I had made it. I wore it for a few days, and then put it away somewhere. It is like getting a tattoo at the end of boot camp to show the world you are now a man of importance and then wearing long sleeve shirts for the next sixty years.

This was about as close to perfection as life can get. The beginnings of relationships are wonderfully intense and this was a special relationship anyway, not easy but very important. And I had the money. Combined with this, there was no requirement, as yet, of having to prove anything. There was not yet the opportunity to fail in either the relationship or the research or, worse yet, to be mediocre. This time was pure hope, all expectation, passion, excitement. I was expecting to ride this out for at least another few months.

But, of course, I was wrong. My professor had somehow managed to find me. He was on the phone calling about enlisting me in one of his semigrandiose schemes involving going to the reservation and tape recording a ceremony.

Would I be a part of this? Tough choice. Love, passion, and the perfect woman versus living in the dirt somewhere with a bunch of people I couldn't understand and who very likely would be unsure about me. Warmth and comfort versus being cold and alone on the reservation in November. One of the requirements for being an anthropologist is that we habitually make the choice of being cold; not only that, but we think the choice obvious. We make it without thought or reflection. Others, people who are not of this calling, have pointed out to me that this is odd, different. I cannot explain why we are like this.

One of my teacher's other students, Allen, was living with a singer. He was herding sheep and doing other jobs for him and learning to speak Navajo. He was also learning Hebrew as a part of rediscovering his Judaism. He would write Hebrew/Navajo puns, which had a limited but very dedicated following.

The Navajo man was learning the Night Chant and was going to have his teacher perform the ceremony over him as a part of that learning. He had asked Allen to, more or less on the sly, record parts of the chant to help him remember. All the stuff written on chants will talk about the singer's phenomenal memory, and about rules for not putting sacred things into a permanent medium. But people have cheated on this for years; it is pretty common to have a medicine man show you a piece of cloth with a complex sandpainting drawn on it. Or more recently they'll use spiral notebooks.

In a way they are cheating, but in another way they have enough knowledge to follow the idea of the law without obeying its letter. The idea about permanent media is that you don't imprison the forces of the universe. And people with knowledge can, through prayer and ritual, release these powers without destroying the representations. If you ask them about the drawings they won't give such an elaborate answer, they'll say something very matter of fact. Like, I can't remember it otherwise; for these people the pragmatics of the moment matter more than elaborate and abstract rationalizations.

But in this case the man was cheating; he wanted Allen to record things in such a way that the teacher wouldn't know. And this was characteristic of this particular traditional singer; he was an operator. He was clever and seemed to care very little about what others thought of him. He was Coyote. He was the first singer, and one of the first rural Navajos, to have a phone. People would call him for emergency medical treatment, sometimes in the middle of the night. Take a little corn pollen and I will see you in the morning. At the time it was strange and funny to see him singing or praying a little into the phone to cover the person until he got there. I always wondered if there was a Yellow Pages section headed "Singers," which was then broken down as to specialty. The phone was gone fairly quickly, in about three months, because the bill never got paid.

He was also a bootlegger, and very successful at it. Technically this is illegal; in fact, it is quasi-legal. A large number of upwardly mobile Navajos sell wine. To be successful they have to be rather responsible people. If they sell to underage people or violent drunks or customers who make trouble, the police will shut them down. If a bootlegger drinks, he won't do very well. This man was successful. He was always driving a new truck, never did have a driver's license.

Allen had casually told our professor about the tape recording. This man is also an operator. This is unusual in anthropology, where the primary requisite for fraternal admission seems to be ineptitude at anything human and especially at anything social. He had contacted various agencies and managed to come up with relatively large sums of money in a very brief time, something virtually impossible to do. Allen had tried to tell him to slow down, but this isn't such an easy thing for him to do once he gets rolling.

The community where this was all happening was towards the east of the reservation, up against some spectacular mountains. It was and still is an area that people call traditional. It's a nice place. There are some irrigated fields; people's homes are neat. Most people still lived in hogans, had sheep, and several still drove the old Conestoga wagons that the government had given them after returning from Fort Sumner. The only change people had made was to replace the wooden wheels with automobile tires. These wagons did a very lucrative business in the spring and winter pulling stuck pickups and automobiles out of the mud. Allen had a new fuel-injected Volvo. It was funny to watch the wagon with the Volvo in tow. Two dollars was the going rate for getting unstuck; coincidentally this was the price for a pint of sweet wine, tokay or Twister, from the local bootlegger. It's cold in the winter and even in the spring.

On the census rolls all people in this area gave their religion as Catholic. A Franciscan priest who had lived there for about forty years was responsible for this. He had quite an interest in learning Navajo and especially in learning about Navajo religion. He was a very curious, very disciplined man—two qualities that we assume are paired but that almost always exist separately. His superiors must have been ambivalent about him, but the local people were quite fond of him. He has been dead for some years, but even today the locals tell stories about him and poke fun at him. They particularly like to mimic him speaking Navajo. He had a deep, very distinctive voice, very un-Navajo-like. And when an older man or woman speaks as he spoke there is laughter, and then they tell their stories.

He told people that there was no difference between being Catholic and believing in the traditional religion, that they were two parts of, really two representations of, the same whole. He also made no attempt to convert anyone, while at the same time pursuing in his inquisitive and disciplined way that study of Navajo religion. I think he was really studying or looking for truth and he thought that some Navajos had a few good ideas on this. Enough to keep him very busy for forty years. And to keep later scholars busy for another (so far) twenty years stealing the little priest's materials.

Anthropologists don't know how to study rehicion. They always think that they are studying someone else's beliefs and if they are respectful and open-minded, people will talk to them. But people aren't telling you about belief. They are telling you how the world is; they are talking about the truth. And passive, atheistic social scientists are always missing the point. Singers liked talking to the priest, a religious man looking for ideas. They had something in common.

He also, ironically, found exactly the right way to "convert" Navajos—don't push. "Should I become a Catholic, Father?" "It's up to you." "Is it better than the traditional religion?" "It's another way to know the same things, to answer the same questions."

There is this same wonderful irony throughout the history of southwestern Catholicism. Often the Franciscans or Jesuits would have a large initial success with conversions in certain groups of Native Americans. Their journals describe their euphoria in this with references to the grace of God and all that sort of thing. But after a fairly short while, the priests noticed that the Indians weren't doing the Catholicism right. Initially they would attribute the mistakes to the newness and the lack of practice. So they'd try to teach them how to do it correctly. But no matter what the priests did and how hard they tried, the Indians couldn't get it right. At Easter the Yaquis would still have a man in a deer head leading the procession. In their journals, the euphoria quickly becomes anger. Imagine these guys in their black robes covered with dust sweating like pigs in the hundred-degree heat getting more and more pissed off and not being able to do anything about it.

The people in this community liked the little Franciscan and he liked them. He and the other philosophers in the community shared a great deal. His superiors were happy about the conversions, but stayed bothered that the Catholicism wasn't done the right way. Stupid Indians, no matter how well you explain it, they can't get it right

When I arrived on the scene in early November these Catholics were getting ready for a Night Chant. It is difficult to describe Navajo ceremonies briefly to those who are not familiar with them. The whole system is very involved; Anglos have spent a great deal of time studying the system in general and Night Chant specifically and still don't really understand it. In fact the studies often produce more confusion than anything else. In general, the ceremonies are used for healing. A patient and his family hire a singer to perform a ceremony as a treatment for whatever it is that ails the person. The singer is more or less in charge and responsible for the whole business although quite a few other people formally and informally help out. Ceremonies are lengthy, expensive undertakings, not resorted to casually.

The Night Chant is one of the more spectacular of these. It is often referred to as *yé'ii bicheii* or the *yé'ii bicheii* dance. *Yé'ii* is a class of beings. The term is often translated as "masked god," although that doesn't quite capture it. For example, the powers that animate the mountains that support the sky can appear as *yé'ii*, but so can many of the forces that brought disease and other misfortune to the world of man. It is more correct to think of them as one expression, one manifestation, of the powers in the universe.

In this ceremony, as in some others, men put on buckskin masks and appear as *yé'ii*. Anglos always describe this as a re-enactment of a mythical time, and the dancers as masked impersonators. But, here again, that isn't really correct. It isn't so much a re-enactment as it is a re-creation, bringing the essence of that past moment, that prototypical time, into the present. Although that doesn't really capture it either, as what is represented here tends to be atemporal rather than arranged lineally into a past, a present, and a future.

Before people put them on to dance, the singer prays to the masks, giving them pollen and then blowing life into them so that they kind of puff up or stand up. The idea is that these are living breathing things. Putting the mask on is associated with power. For some of the dancers it resembles a possession state or an altered consciousness. Afterwards they will talk about feeling different, not being aware of their actions, needing to be shaken, slapped, or otherwise aroused by others. For some it isn't like that at all, but is a completely matter-of-fact endeavor.

There are rules about wearing the mask. You don't speak with it on, but you make this kind of "ho ho" sound. In the underworlds the beings were different, as if they were half man and half animal, but more like a primal, less speciated or differentiated being. This is what the Night Chant and other ceremonies are about, the times of creation when the potential for all things was put in place. And the sound the dancers make is a part of this. The first world time is when there was one language, a more abstract less differentiated language, and all life spoke it. It was before we started to talk and think differently, before there were different species of animals, different peoples, and different ways of thinking.

For nine nights this is sung about, prayed about; stories are told, sand paintings are made that depict this time. On the last night, the *yé'ii* dance until the light appears in the east. This is what they call the *yé'ii bicheii* dance. So they appear in their masks and their breech cloths; it is night and they make their sounds and the singer sings in this falsetto. It is as if you are back in the beginning somewhere; this is what it feels like.

But, as I said, there isn't only this public part of things. There is a great deal that is quiet and, to varying degrees, private. That happens inside the hogan; conversation, prayers, singing. There are the sandpaintings, the prayersticks, and all of the different medicines.

In the Night Chant there is knowledge and there is power. In the Navajo world, the one derives from the other. The knowledge is acquired; one person teaches it to another; the student memorizes it over a period of years. Once you have learned it, it belongs to you: it is yours to do with as you want. But it is only momentarily yours because everything that is known ultimately returns to the universe and is forgotten.

This certainty about knowledge ultimately being lost is a part of the Navajo story of things. "One day we will wake up and it will be forgotten; it will be as if we never knew it. The words will all be forgotten and with that, the Navajo way will be gone." This is a powerful idea—that we possess, hold, and control things only for a moment, that we keep nothing forever. You find it everywhere. The thread that goes out to the side of the rug exists so as to free the animating force of that creation. The design of a pot is interrupted so as not to hold those powers in check. A sandpainting is created over a period of days. It beckons and then contains the powers it depicts. These are used by the medicine man to aid the patient and then released. The sandpainting is destroyed and the remnant is disposed of so as not to imprison these deities. A prayer ends with a portion that releases the powers it has beckoned, as does a song, as does a ceremony. Someone or something that dies decomposes or disintegrates; it is not correct to attempt to embalm or preserve it. There is sadness in the death but also the joy of knowing that there will be future generations. They are essentially linked, parts of the same whole.

The only stories of permanence, of things lasting forever, are about witchcraft (and today about Christianity), which is always concerned with personal immortality, sacrificing the life-stuff of relatives and using it to live on. Immortality is not a personal thing; continuity and connectedness are in future and past generations.

In this knowledge is a respect for the powers in the world, an acceptance of correct and proper use but a prohibition against the permanent possession of what is ephemeral. In the ceremonies you can see a willingness to nudge things very slightly, but beyond that to accept the course of things. Contained within this concept of knowledge is something very personal, something that happens between people. Knowledge is in interaction. A man teaches other men; the gods have taught man and in the prayer, the song, the ritual, the interaction continues; and there is also thought and reflection, man interacting with himself about knowledge.

The Night Chant and everything else are about this, about process, not about things. And in this simple notion there are some striking ironies. There is one story, the incident of the Whirling Logs, that is often included as a part of the Night Chant.[1] It takes place near where the waters come together, which refers to an area near the junction of the San Juan River and one of its tributaries. The hero arrives at this place where there is a body of water, in the midst of which there are logs spinning as if in a whirlpool. On the shores are sets of *yé'ii* that seem to assure that the movement of the logs will continue, while at the same time containing the logs and their motion within a particular space. This is nicely depicted in several sand paintings.

Quite a few of the stories mention something like this, an area bounded by masked beings who somehow protect that space and assure that the movement will continue. On a larger

---

[1] In his book *The Nightway* (Albuquerque: University of New Mexico Press, 1990), especially pages 37-40, Jim Farris discusses where this incident belongs in the ceremonial scheme of things.

scale this is a description of the Navajo universe, bounded by the four mountains that are the hogans of the *yé'ii* and where various sorts of processes are in motion.

In the Night Chant, there is the whirling and the flow of the river. The actual place of this story is today under some very still water. A dam was built there around twenty years ago and we the people have managed, at least for the moment, to still the movement, to convert that process of the Navajo stories into those still deep waters that Anglos like so much. And we control those waters, ideologically with various Bureaus, physically with dams, so as to make them useful.

Against this backdrop of essential process, we anthropologists arrived to preserve this ceremony, to record it and place it in a vault somewhere so that it would never be "lost." We were there to build another dam, to take a world of movement and make it hold still, to embalm it. Even when the Navajos had forgotten it all, we would have it preserved in jars somewhere, forever.

We weren't the first to attempt this particular act of preservation. In the late 1800s Washington Matthews chronicled the Night Chant. He tried to record what he could, the sandpaintings, drawings of the masks, prayersticks, and so on. He also recorded some of the stories, the songs, and the prayers. In general he wrote them based on a translator's English, but, in the interests of good dam building, he would transcribe key words, names and so on, in Navajo. The problem is that he was rather deaf, so his transcriptions, although they look very nice and even scientific, have only occasional similarities to anything real.

The book in which he wrote about this is quite large, pretty, and impressive. Today it would be a coffee-table book. I recently went to look at it in a university library near where I live. They have two copies and they store them in a vault. Now that's really preserving something; make it so that no one can see it and hurt it, that way we'll always have it.

When you attempt to discover the world of others, you end up with a caricature of yourself. As a people we believe in things and we believe in these things as separate from and often instead of people and relationships. Knowledge is one of those things. It exists in books and even in vaults, or, better yet, in books in vaults in universities. When it is in minds, we still think of it as a thing, an artifact, not as something that is alive, that is moving and changing. When we teach we are supposed to put things called facts into people's heads. And then we give objective tests, to measure how many things the students have in their minds. Or we create an encyclopedia—a compilation of knowledge. It is fixed, an artifact rather than a product of interaction. It exists on its own, apart from people.

And, of course, all of this shows that we weren't listening, that we had missed the point of the epistemology we were treating as an object. We were at this Night Chant in another attempt to transform the Navajo account of process into an entity that would last forever. And in this case we were going to preserve what was still very much alive. We weren't trying to discover something Navajo; we were trying to make their ideas into our own. Their epistemology and ours are opposed and incompatible, and if you care about any sort of truth you have to decide on the correctness of one or the other.

In the tradition of Matthews before us, we were deaf, we didn't understand, and what we don't understand we attempt to keep, building a dam to hold the water, to stop the whirling of the logs.

And like all preservationists, we operated on the premises of technology and attention to detail. We would be able to preserve more completely and more accurately because we had better stuff, better equipment, and we had better methods to rationalize, to ideologically power these machines. We had these Nagra tape recorders with a million reels of tape. These were (maybe are) state-of-the-art recorders. They were used for movie sound tracks, to record outdoor concerts, and so on. And we had these big mothers with batteries galore. We had earphones on and wind shields over the microphones. One constant about the Navajo Reservation is the wind. It either blows hard or is intolerable. So there we were with these tape recorders; there were always two of us doing the recording. One of us was a "backup." An essential part of any technological endeavor is to have a backup. Don't want to miss anything.

When you obsess about technology, you exclude understanding. But you don't see this. In fact, you rationalize the use of technique as a means to, or as part of the effort to, understand. It is one of those highly addictive sorts of endeavors.

Once you start with this process there is no escape, recording without understanding, paying attention to the machines, keeping the arrows on the dials from entering the red zone. Having recorded it accurately and not understanding, we think that a better recording, a more accurate machine, will bring comprehension. So we improve methods and machines, use video instead of just audio, and when that fails add more cameras and recorders. We still don't understand, but once the process is begun, reflection, thought, and questioning vanish. We instead keep trying for the perfect recording, the perfect representation that will last and not change, the picture of Dorian Gray.

What matters in the ceremony that we were trying to put into a mason jar is what it meant; what it said about that moment; what it said about the beginnings, the Navajo, man in general. We were trying to substitute technology for meaning. We did not understand what was being said, sung, talked about. And we tried to make up for this with our earphones and our state-of-the-art recorders. We tried to preserve and control the sound and the wind so as to preserve what we didn't understand. The illusory promise was always that you could go over it later. When you have data, you can go over it anytime. The wind that we eliminated from the recording was an important part of what we should have kept. It was a part of the meaning, a part of the story and of the chant. We thought it was noise rather than information.

We looked totally ridiculous in this setting. I can't remember if we knew this or not. I'm fairly certain that I felt it and that Allen felt it. Navajos take it for granted that Anglo anthropologists look silly; in fact they probably regard it as an essential part of the job description. In addition they ask stupid questions and say even stupider things. We fit that description quite nicely.

But of course we ignored this. We were on a mission. And we were into some very serious equipment with archival-quality audio tape looking like two of the original Mouseketeers monitoring the launch of a space ship. There was nothing about what we were doing that was funny.

What a strange contrast. We were witnessing a part of what had gone on in the beginning when the ancestors of these people were still inside the earth, still trying to create the future. And we were trying to transform the ancient into the modern with our machines while the ancient remained aloof and indifferent to our success or failure.

On the last night I was watching and listening to the masked dancers re-creating the beginnings of the chant and of Navajo history. I felt as if I were traveling to that time, to the underworlds and the dark world without moon and stars lit by the glowing horizon. My hearing became focused and my vision tunneled and my consciousness lapsed. I can remember the intensity and the clarity of this, also the peace and the certainty—no doubts, no questions—but I was certain about my nature, man, the world. I don't remember the content of this certainty, or whether it had a content. I only remember the feeling.

There was a stranger, an intruder on the edge of my hearing. It didn't belong, it was not a part of that moment. I tried to will it out, but as soon as will emerges, the moment is necessarily lost. It was *The Star Spangled Banner*. That travel to the beginning and that focus had been real, while hearing the national anthem just as surely was not. For this moment reality and its opposite had changed places.

The song in the distance ended and I heard a voice speaking over a loudspeaker system. He mixed his Navajo and English and talked about the finals of the All Indian rodeo, how important it was, how glad everyone was to be there, how they appreciated the crowd, and so on. Typical Western rodeo announcer; this one just happened to be an Indian and he was imitating all those Anglos he had heard. The content and inflection were identical, the jokes the same, as were the repeated allusions to patriotism. He just spoke a different language some of the time.

I knew what was happening. I knew what it looked like. There were a lot of Indians dressed like cowboys and cowgirls. And doing their best to act the way they thought these role models acted. It was happening at the rodeo ground nearby.

The gods near me danced and the distant riders tried to stay with the bulls, getting hurt pretending that it didn't hurt. The dancers danced and the chant went on. I wanted this modern noise to stop and the ancient to continue.

Things were out of synch; they didn't fit properly together. Which meant that the rodeo didn't belong. I felt off balance, as the saying goes. It wasn't right, I had come out here to study Indians, man in some sort of natural state. Changing perhaps, but reluctantly, trying to hold onto tradition to keep the old ways. Having the evil and powerful white man in the Uncle Sam clothing forcing modernization on the noble red man. A BIA official dragging people to the rodeo.

I just wanted that part of this place to go away, to cease to exist. I tried not to see or to hear it but, just as the sound had intruded on my reverie, that part is there and continues. This lack of comfort with the present and romance for the past feeds the desire to preserve and hermetically seal the traditional so that it doesn't decompose. We need to imprison the Navajo in our vault so we can continue to have at least the illusion of this romance with difference.

But the more basic difficulty is that we don't acknowledge these two sides as being a part of the same reality, the same whole, this thing we call Navajo. For me this particular juxtaposition is disturbing. For an older Navajo there are parts that disturb but no real discomfort with the fact of difference or with change *per se*. Many people who were at the sing later went and watched the rodeo. The contrast that I experience and that I find disturbing is not one that disturbs them. And the difficulty in describing this whole is that I don't recognize it as such. I only see the two parts as separate, one that I care about and the other that I feel alienated from.

These people didn't know how to be and didn't care about being what I wanted them to be. This was natural man with a lot of garbage around his house, sometimes drinking heavily and violently, and having a rodeo beginning with *The Star Spangled Banner*, while a bunch of old medicine men who thought they were Catholics were trying to have a sing. These Indians didn't even know how to be Indians, in addition to which they didn't seem to mind.

That night I dreamed. There was a *yé'ii*, one of the masked dancers. He was riding a bull at the rodeo. The cinch, the bull rope, that he held on to was a large set of rosary beads strung firmly around the animal. I'm not sure, but I think his hand moved occasionally from bead to bead. The Night Chant singer was the rodeo announcer and was singing one of the songs of that ceremony, while everyone stood out of respect. The rider ended up being thrown into the dirt and as he got up I could hear him say, "Shit."

The next morning we were out in the open, recording what was going on. There was the incredibly ancient medicine man arranging things so as to pray and to sing and do the details he was supposed to do. He was the teacher. The man that Allen lived with was the pupil and the patient. And this particular ceremony was part of the teaching and, in a way, part of the initiation. He was not only learning what details and what knowledge mattered but he was being ritually empowered. Having the right stuff put into him so that he could do the ceremony. Playing around with the powers of the universe is a dangerous business and it is important to act and do things correctly.

Allen and I were sitting there kind of cross-legged in the dirt. Dressed Mouseketeer style, watching our machines and their dials, feeling somewhere to the left of bizarre and looking even more bizarre than we felt. The very old man looked in our direction, as if he saw us for the first time. In fact he was seeing us for the first time. It turned out that his vision wasn't too good, and on this morning was the first light clear enough for him to see us. He looked in our direction, incredulous, looked away, looked back to see if we were a persistent apparition or had disappeared by that time. Classic double take. He and his pupil exchanged conversation, we continued recording, watching our dials and the like. Allen's expression started to change from that of the incredibly bored to that of someone who had just noticed that he was naked in front of an audience of girl scouts.

"What's going on, Allen?" I ask. I didn't know what they were saying. At that time I didn't know much in the way of Navajo language. But then I didn't need to know it, I had a recorder and tape that would last for 500 years. Allen says he's not quite sure, but the old man seems to be upset about us being here. I said that I thought our coyote friend had talked to him and it was OK. "So did I," says Allen. "Maybe he forgot," says one of us, giving our trickster friend the benefit of a doubt he richly deserved, while momentarily holding onto some hope for us.

"What's going on now?" says I. "He wants us out of here." "Just for now or forever?" "I'm not sure," says Allen. So we pick up the recorders and go back to Allen's hogan. For the next few hours we're in limbo. We want a clear situation. Of course the singers have gotten on with their business and could care less

about us. But we operate on the assumption that we are important and that they are in some sort of a confab discussing the
relative merits of recording versus not recording. Whether or
not it is better to compromise the integrity of the sacred so as to
be able to keep it forever.

At some point we screw up the courage to go ask; actually
we get tired of waiting. "Oh, I guess you better not do it,"
comes the reply. "But will you record a few songs with the small
recorder, the one no one can see?"

We called our professor a little later on. We were glad it was
over. We'd not seen the situation for what it was, and tried to
make it what we wanted it to be. This, by the way, is one of the
very strict rules of con men; their whole game is contingent on
the mark insisting on seeing things as they aren't, but instead as
he hopes them to be. The professor suggested something that
others in the preservation game had used. The idea is that you
make a deal that you record something that a person knows
now, and then store it away somewhere in a vault and don't play
it or listen to it until some future date, like the singer's death, or
ten years, or when no one else knows the ceremony. He told
Allen to go back and say that if they let us record it we wouldn't
play it for, I think, fifty years.

Stranger and stranger. The archaeology of knowledge, another artifact to collect and put on the shelf. Somewhere in the
book *A Hundred Years of Solitude* is the story of a village. The
people there started to forget the names for things so they wrote
them on each object. On the top of a table was scrawled the
word *table*, on each wall, the word *wall*. And so on. And as their
dementia gradually worsened they soon forgot what the words
meant. When outsiders came they entered a village of people
who had forgotten virtually everything, with these names
scrawled everywhere. Strange and sad. How can we confuse
knowing with an object? If the Night Chant was forgotten, who
would understand these endless recordings arranged by name
and date, these objects designed to store ideas? There would be
no one to tell us what they meant.

It would be like the word *table* scrawled on a table. We
would look at it very closely, perhaps we would transcribe it,
photograph it, measure it to see how wide and how tall it was,
see what color the letters were, and so on. But what does it

mean? You only have the chance to discover this while the knowledge lives; the tragedy is that in the act of recording and preserving you don't have the time or the inclination to ask, to discover.

Some years later Allen and I talked about this. We had both spent a time studying the ideas of some old people and the more we learned the more we became troubled by the end of knowledge, their prediction that someday it would all be forgotten.

For the old people this was a part of what they had to teach, a part of the truth that they knew and saw. They looked things squarely in the eye and could see them as they were, and this is why we spent this time listening to them and studying what they had to say. But as a part of this, we didn't want these thoughts to come to an end; we wanted somehow to keep them alive, not let them die. And of course the more we insisted on this, the more we were unable to see the world as it was, to appreciate what they had to teach. There are two different and opposed ideas— wisdom and control. And in their wisdom they sadly accepted what was inevitable; and in our desire to possess and hold, we understood nothing.

A few years ago I heard a new trickster story. Coyote appeared as an old but active man. He was fat and he acted as if he wanted to learn things. Coyote acts this way a lot, but he never really learns. Just when you think he has the idea, he'll do whatever it is he is being taught, incorrectly.

Like when the gods in the beginning are trying to decide between living only for a while and then dying, or living forever. They throw a stick into the water and pronounce that if it floats they will not die, but if it sinks they will live only for so long. It floats and everyone is happy. But then Coyote comes and throws a stone ax into the water while making the same proclamation. He looks like a fool and incurs the anger of the others, but of course he is correct. Living only so long and then dying is the only thing that makes sense. The rest of us directly pursue what is immediately desirable. He seems sometimes to do that, sometimes to be a fool, or, more correctly, to fool others. But when wisdom is required or when wisdom dictates a difficult, unpopular decision, he is the one who somehow stumbles onto what is correct.

In this story I heard recently, Coyote is traveling and comes to roost in this one community where he presents himself as someone with knowledge, someone who knows how to heal and how to bring wealth. He walks around with his chest out and says, "I am the one that knows everything. I can solve any problem. I know how to bring riches. I am the one who is the chief when it comes to knowledge." Of course, everyone thinks this is very funny and laughs about it.

But a very big chief in the East hears about this, hears about this man that knows everything. And he sets out to talk to this man. This chief from the East owns knowledge. He has several homes that he travels between daily. In each of these you can see the knowledge that he owns. It is on shelves everywhere in the form of paper, and in other places in plastic form, and in still others in magnetic form, and then again in electric or lightning form. This chief owns so much knowledge that he hardly has any place left to keep new knowledge. So he builds bigger homes with more space. At some point he was afraid that he would lose some of it, so he had duplicates and then triplicates made of what he owned. You can't have enough back ups of knowledge.

But even though he owned all of this, he wanted to have more. And his terror was that something would be forgotten, lost, before he could possess it. It was said by many people that this had happened before. There was a certain old woman who had known about something, and when she died it was forgotten. When the chief in the East heard these stories he was sad and he trembled with fear.

So he went to Coyote, who was in human form, and he said, "I would like to possess what you know. I can capture it and put it into a form so that it won't be forgotten, and I can put these replicas where they will live forever, where it will never be forgotten." Coyote was very pleased by this idea, because although Coyote knew everything, he could remember very little, and the little he remembered he didn't understand, he didn't know what it meant.

The eastern chief showed him how to capture voices in a box and how to capture images of people with another box. And Coyote thought that if he could get someone to sing over him he would be able to capture that sing and later be able to perform it. He had this image of himself as a great singer; he would open his mouth as if to pray or sing and the voice that he had captured would come from the box and the people would think it was his. "What a great man" they would all say. "He knows everything."

So he told the eastern chief that he knew some things that were about to be lost, and that there was a man who wanted to learn these things from him. That this knowledge was very valuable, very special, very sacred and that he could help this eastern chief to possess it, to have that knowledge forever. He said with some importance that he was about to have a ceremony and that he was going to teach some of this knowledge to this very old man. "I know this," he said, "and I am going to teach him about it. You see I am a very great chief; I know everything and people come from everywhere to learn it from me. But I need you, the chief from the East, to give me some valuable things so that this old man that wants to learn can travel here."

The truth was that he was going to have this singer sing over him, as if to teach it to him, Coyote. But he turned it all around. And the valuables he would get from the eastern chief would be used to pay the singer. And while it was taking place the eastern chief would be having people capture the sounds and the images of the ceremony and then Coyote would own it forever. And people would say what a great man he was, and how powerful he was, that he could remember so much after only one ceremony.

The singer he had chosen was very old. He couldn't see in the normal way but had other ways of coming to know things. During the ceremony Coyote ran all around. He would sometimes lie or sit down and appear as the patient and he would sometimes act like he was in charge, telling everyone what to do and bossing them around. He didn't really pay much attention. He knew he didn't have to because when it was all over it would be there for him. The ceremony went on, and on the last day the Blessingway prayers were said. In a way they consecrated what had gone on during the previous days and nights. They were also a necessary precaution: if anything had been done improperly during the chant, they were a protection for those mistakes. The chanter who saw differently, not with his eyes, said this part a little differently.

A few weeks later Coyote got copies of the recordings. But they were tapes of mariachis singing various health awareness commercials for a Spanish radio station in Chicago. There was one about fetal alcohol, another about children and lead, one about diet cholesterol, and so on. So in a way I guess they were healing tapes. It made no difference to Coyote because, being a Navajo coyote, he didn't understand Spanish. He of course thought that the reason he didn't understand was because of the sacredness of the songs and the fact that they were sung in a special way so as to keep them secret. For a while he became very popular lip-synching to the mariachis. People liked the music (especially the songs about safe sex) and they thought he was very funny pretending he was singing like a great medicine man.

The chief in the East was very happy. He had the knowledge. He now possessed it, owned it. And he put those original recordings into a vault, a hidden place, so that they would never be lost. He never listened to them because he didn't need to. When you possess something there is no need to use it; it is yours forever. Besides, if you use them you might wear them out.

And in a few hundred years, after the people have used and disposed of four other worlds, they will open the vault and the chief's heirs will play his possessions and of course they will be blank. A part of the story is that you can own and know things only for so long and then they are forgotten. And when the chant is forgotten, the tapes also will not remember. It will be as if the knowledge never existed.

PEOPLE

4

ANDREW

He made a habit of coming home like that, dirty, hung over, and tired. Sometimes you could see he'd been beaten, probably while he was passed out; that is how it usually happens. If he didn't go off like that for a month, you started waiting for him to leave, and everyone got increasingly uneasy. Not for a tangible reason, not because of fear of him or of wanting him to leave, but because we were all a part of and habituated to this pattern. It was the way things were, and, like all humans, we hated novelty. If he didn't go, his wife would start an argument and that would cause him to leave. Or I might give him money or drive him somewhere.

That last time was different. He came back sick, not just tired-and-hung-over-sick, but really sick. He was jaundiced; on his reddish-brown skin the yellowing looked almost golden. And that afternoon he died. We all just watched; there was nothing to do, nothing at all to do.

The local Christians, including his wife and daughters, said that just before he died Andrew embraced Christ. I think this was supposed to make us feel better. This is the sort of thing that zealous Christians are always doing—quickly assigning meaning to life events that really don't make any sense and, more importantly, are difficult. The Christians had been assigning meaning to Andrew's life for the last twenty-five years. He hadn't wanted them to; in fact he hadn't wanted them to a great deal. But with Christians that seems to encourage rather than deter. The more upset and angry you get, the more they harass and badger.

Missionaries are the absolute worst thing about living on an

Indian reservation. They're worse than tourists, which is saying a lot. It's a little hard for me to understand my vehemence in this regard; it is the sort of anger usually reserved for ex-wives and/ or people running for office and I guess anyone at all who makes a career out of helping others.

I guess there are three reasons, really three ways in which I need to see myself as different from these people. First off, they are trying to alter what I want to keep; I want pagans to stay pagans.

The second thing is that they try to do good. It is basic that people who seek to create goodness necessarily (key word) do harm. Of course, they think that they just need to try harder. The basic premise is never questioned. In the class of the good we have not only missionaries, but loving wives and mothers, caring social workers, psych nurses, military types, and so forth. All very dangerous, very harm-doing people.

But the greater part of my anger is toward the missionaries' lies. I care about true things and I despise falseness. Their basic lie is in the claim that they have knowledge of things that no one can know about, that Andrew will live in some sort of eternal bliss because he made a last-minute switch, for example. And when you question the lies, you become a bad Christian because your faith isn't strong enough or some equivalent nonsense. Dumb idea piled on dumb idea. Along with this they assign these simple meanings to events and problems in human life that have no answer, or many equally incorrect answers.

Andrew and the Christians had been at war. Most of the major battles were fought in his family. The occasional help that came from allies on the outside made it certain that the war would not end, that no resolution could occur.

There is a pattern to their war that I do not like. It includes men and women, alcohol and Christians, and illness and people dying. And most important it goes on and on, repeats generation after generation. When I see or am a part of a tragedy, my tendency is to feel sadness and anger. When I see tragedy repeated, when people should know better, I am enraged, beside myself with fury.

I used to see tragedy in isolation, as occurring occasionally but not regularly. A bad thing happening to someone I knew. But now I never see it that way. The tragedy in people's lives is part of a pattern and it has a theme which, while varying slightly from family to family, is amazingly consistent.

This change in perspective comes from staying with things longer, staying in relationships. When you are only present for brief moments you can't see pattern. You have the illusion that things improve or that troubles are only there for a moment. If you stay connected, you see the play re-enacted generation after generation, on and on.

When you are involved with the Navajo world you have relationships that don't end. You may be away from people for years or for decades, but the relationships continue. And something occasionally happens to remind you of their permanence. It may be a phone call after fifteen years from a person you knew, or a letter. This is after you've moved two or three times so that no one could still know where you are. The letter or the conversation pretty much always starts where it left off; there is almost no small talk. It starts with things that matter, that are personal and involve relationships. You talk about changes and constancies in the network of relatedness, the people you both knew. It is not always that you felt terribly close to these people in the past; often you felt unimportant or intrusive or marginal. So intense intimacy isn't the reason that knowing each other lasts.

When it first happens you are surprised, almost shocked. But after that, it is simply a matter of course. I think the reason it is like this is that this is the way man in general does relationships. We Anglos are the exceptions and it is our way that is strange and odd, knowing people for brief moments, disposing of them, and moving to a new and equally disposable relationship.

Navajo stories, what we call myths, always involve relationships. There are stories about the creation of kinship; they talk about the necessity of man being with others and of behaving in certain ways towards each other. There are many stories with many actors and in many forms. But there is one in particular about relationships between men and women. It is an old story, set very near the beginning of time.

In translation it is usually called "men versus women." But a more correct translation is "where people moved opposite." This conveys several things. It has the man-versus-woman or battle-of-the-sexes part. But there is also the notion that men and women move about on this earth differently, that they think differently, that there are essential differences between them.

The story begins with the creation of sexuality. In the next instant, First Woman[1] commits adultery. First Man suspects that something is going on and he is worried; he can't sleep and he obsesses about his wife. Does this sound at all familiar to anyone? So he follows her and sees her meeting and having sex with her lover. When she returns they fight. His mother-in-law, of course, gets involved. They argue about control, who is the strongest, and so on. And they decide that they don't need each other, that things would be better if they lived apart. They are living on the banks of a river, so the men stay on one side and the women go to live on the other side.

What brings men and women together, sexual desire and our general need for and incompleteness without the other, is also what drives us apart. But when they are apart, they become intensely desirous of each other. In these stories, their constant state of sexual arousal is graphically and repeatedly described. The hermaphrodite, who lives with the men, also talks to them about the necessity for the sexes reuniting and staying together. "Otherwise where will new generations come from? Where will thinking of various kinds come from?" His argument is of course the rational side of things. Everyone is familiar with the various rationalizations covering male-female relationships. We have all used them many times without success. Reason really has nothing to do with it; males and females are together out of a very fundamental necessity.

They get back together. And they again test their reasonableness. They are ritually cleansed after their separation and, as with all ritual, a four-day period of sexual abstinence is prescribed. They of course don't, or can't, follow it. You can trust a religion with stories like this.

Here is the nature of man-woman relationships. They are intense, they are necessary, and they have certain characteristic,

---

[1]This is a man's version of the story. I could never get women to talk to me about it. They would laugh, get embarrassed and make an off-color remark directed at me. The published versions of the story are also all from men and translated by men.

recurrent difficulties. What to do? There is no answer or solution, no prescription that will make it all right. But some sort of resolution is possible if you accept the givens of human existence, if your starting point is what necessarily is and cannot be changed, rather than what ideally should be. In this case that is the acceptance of the necessity of being with one another.

There is no final answer because there is no final answer. The truth is that the gods couldn't solve the difficulty, so they turn it over to man to do with it what he can. It is up to you as individuals, they say, to figure it out, to decide for yourselves. The ultimate Navajo moral imperative is not something as mundane as the golden rule; it is the statement "It's up to you." There are no pretend, try-harder solutions to eternal problems. The best that we can do is to accept the givens of life, and momentarily resolve difficulties in terms of these givens.

HOW ANDREW AND ELAINE MOVED OPPOSITE

Andrew and Elaine had been together for between twenty-five and thirty years. They mostly fought; that is the part of their relationship that initially and most easily comes to mind. But they were together for the duration and everyone knew that. Here their fights were a way of being related, not a means towards ending their relationship.

Andrew was fifty-something and she was about ten years younger. They'd married when she was in her teens. They had nine children, although by the time I knew them there were just eight; within that year there would be seven, and ten years later there are five. It seemed like their primary motivation for being parents was to breed allies or soldiers for their wars with each other. The girls were on their mother's side and they were raised like that from the beginning. The boys initially were raised by their mother, or an older sister, and then they gradually moved toward their father and their brothers and cousins.

In describing herself, Elaine would first and emphatically say that she was a Christian. *Christian* here meant that she belonged to the particular brand of Protestant mission in the community. On the reservation, these missions come in all different flavors. This is very important to the missions but irrelevant to everyone else.

From the community's perspective, the mission offered two services that mattered. The first was a private elementary school. The second was a clinic staffed by a couple of old women who called themselves "nurses," rather nice women who had no concept of the harm that they did. When you walked into the clinic, the first thing you saw was a sign that said, "If you have a black widow bite, go to Fort Defiance." (There was an Indian Health Service hospital there. It took somewhere between an hour and a half and several days to drive there, depending on the weather.) I'd never seen so many black widows. In the winter they got cold and shared your house and your outhouse. You'd wake up to one dangling above your face. The most common bite happened fairly late at night when you couldn't see under the seat of the privy and sat down and got bitten.

Elaine worked for the school as a cook. A benefit of the job was that her kids went to the school free (usually there was tuition). Jobs are not plentiful on the reservation, so being employed like this mattered. It also increased the importance of the mission and its Christianity in her life and gave the Christians at least six years towards indoctrinating the children.

They were taught that their father was a sinner. He was in the wrong first and foremost because he wasn't a Christian. There were other things, but they derived from that. For one, he worshiped Satan. Of course he didn't call it that, he called it the traditional religion. But since the only true belief was in Christ, the native religion had to be Satan's. Essential missionary reasoning.

There were other ways in which this was obvious as well. You just had to look and see what happened at the traditional ceremonies. There was drinking and fighting; sometimes people were raped and even killed. It couldn't be anything but the work of Satan. Or the children could look at their own family. Their mother worked, went to church, and led an upstanding life; their father ran around, drank, and didn't have a job. But, of course, he didn't know any better, hadn't seen the light, and so on. It wasn't that he was a bad man; he just didn't have Christ in his life. If you loved him you would talk to him about Christ. He would get angry, but again that was Satan. What absolute nonsense.

Andrew is difficult to describe. He wasn't always easy to like. When he was drunk he was annoying. At many other times he was working on getting drunk and he would be very manipulative in trying to get money or transportation. You always had to be on your guard somewhat, and it's unpleasant living like that. Our own society places a tremendous importance on privacy, so much so that we assume that importance is a feature of society in general. It is uncomfortable living where the rules are different.

The essence of Andrew was in how consistently unremarkable he was. For everyone else the most important thing was his not being a Christian, but for him that didn't matter so much.

If you asked he would say he was a mechanic. And he was pretty good at keeping the local pickups running. When you drive through the reservation, you see lots of seemingly abandoned cars and trucks around people's houses. This is where people get parts, and the mechanics have a comprehensive knowledge of the locations of various years and models.

He'd worked as a fire fighter, like a lot of Navajos. They travel all over the country fighting fires during the summer months. It pays well. They do it with other Navajos and they only have to be away from home temporarily. Plus it is kind of quasi-heroic, quasi-warrior-like. Andrew stopped doing this, he said, because he couldn't pass the physical because of arthritis. I don't think that was the reason, but I don't know another one.

The thing I remember best about him was that he did not accept authority. He wasn't defiant like an adolescent or a protester of the sixties. He just didn't accept the right or power of anyone or anything to have control over someone else. He was indifferent to coercion and he stayed clear of government. I've always had the strongest trust for people who are reluctant in getting organized.

The traditional religion was important to Andrew, not as important as it was to his wife, but it mattered. As with everything else, in his belief he was unremarkable. In ceremonies he did what he could to be a part of things and to help. But he didn't have any special knowledge, just that desire and willingness to be a part. Maybe he was too young; singers are usually older. Perhaps in his limited participation he was starting to learn.

The stories of Andrew's religion describe gods or beings that are like him. Beings that are a little wild and out of control to begin with. They take odysseys that involve the characteristic trials and difficulties. In the process they learn a great deal about different, seemingly unrelated things, like where to find a special medicine or a particular car part. At some point they are called on to put it all together, to synthesize these unrelated facts and do something with that knowledge. And most importantly, the beings in these stories don't accept authority. Gods that don't even believe in the power of other gods.

Andrew saw me, or at least wanted to see me, as a friend or companion. For me this was a problem. In part this was because I don't like people expecting things of me. I tend to feel trapped and avoid demands or expectations, which of course is simply another way of being trapped. This sort of society is built on reciprocity and expectations; they don't need or expect spontaneity.

I also wanted to stay out of the war between these people, to be neutral. This was incredibly naive. As soon as you show up you are part of the movie.

Why did Andrew have this interest in me? I'm not sure; probably the simplest and truest thing to say is that he liked me. Even now when I say that I get uncomfortable. Another thing was that he and I were both marginal. He was always on the border of his wife's community and his wife's family. And he was somewhat peripheral to his children. A part of this is probably built into being Navajo. He'd moved from his own family to his wife's community, to where her relatives lived. And, of course, in such situations you are never really quite accepted. In any marriage there is the blood-is-thicker-than-water element. There are of course other males in the same situation in the community. You tend to drink with them; you also drink with your in-laws, and later on with your sons, later still, your daughters' husbands. When you are drinking, generations don't exist. Everyone calls each other brother. But afterward, the drunkenness counts against you. The way you connect is what keeps you apart. I think it is also built into the Navajo way of things that fathers are peripheral to the children, just as the mother is very important.

A few times I went with Andrew to visit the family he was born to. His mother was alive and so was an older brother. He wouldn't go there sober, and he wasn't well received; no one was rude exactly, but there was no warmth, no welcome home. Something must have happened somewhere along the line. Someone, a nephew, had drowned under mysterious circumstances in the past. At the time Andrew mentioned this, I remember thinking that he had some responsibility or was held responsible.

Once we went there when he had a sore knee. He wanted them to help with a ceremony to fix it. There was talk, and a great deal of reluctance. This is very unusual. In these matters a family is supposed to help. Implied in the presentation of an illness and the request for help are bad feelings and bad thoughts—in this case the bad thoughts the mother and older brother had for Andrew. One of the things he was asking them for was to participate in something that would heal these feelings. Ritual transforms the very abstract and universal into the concrete and personal. And in the focus on detail, there can be an emotional and familial healing.

I think that this is what Andrew wanted. Finally they agreed on a brief rite. Some sort of healer sucked an object that looked like a small arrowhead out of the knee. You could see that Andrew was pleased. He was asking his mother and brother to care about and for him. For some reason, they wouldn't. Andrew was short on belonging, on having people care about him and take an interest in him.

In any family war, there are swing votes; all people don't stay clearly divided, but a few try to bridge the parental and family schism. They go back and forth or they mediate. There are also outsiders who try to help, benevolent intruders. These are the elements that are necessary if conflict is going to continue without resolution. If boundaries stayed clear, the conflict would be self-limiting. One side would win, the other lose. With a lack of clear boundaries, you can battle on forever. Temporary respites without solution. More of people moving opposite.

In the separation-of-the-sexes story, the swing vote was the hermaphrodite. In this family three of the children tried to keep from completely siding with Andrew or Elaine, the drunks or the Christians. They were Woodrow, the oldest surviving son; Ellen, the second oldest daughter, but in many ways the oldest; and the youngest child, Robert. They each had different ways of going about it.

I knew Ellen the best and I liked her a great deal. She was about my age and she was open and candid. She was a homely woman who had a strikingly beautiful four-year-old son. He was not beautiful in the sense that we talk about children being attractive, which is mostly polite lies, but possessed a true and striking beauty.

Her husband, James, was about ten years younger than she; he was not the boy's biological father, but he tried to behave like a father. He did his best, but he was very young and he had not had a father himself. So his knowledge of parenting was more in the realm of theory; still he did his best.

Ellen was the adult in her marriage. Thinking on it, I can't imagine her as ever having been anything but an adult. You see this older-woman- younger-man marriage fairly often. The plan is to impose maturity on the young man. Or, failing that, to have maturity somewhere in the relationship. Someone has to be in control.

I think that a part of her candor with me was motivated by simply needing someone to talk to, someone of her own generation. Also, I think that the fact that I didn't despise her father counted for something. She had difficult things in her life and she had happy things. And she didn't insist on imposing only one color or shade of emotion onto the world. She took things as they came and was afraid of neither joy nor sorrow. She didn't try to protect herself by insisting on optimism or pessimism.

She was most like her mother, but she cared most about her father. You could see this, you could see her worry when he was gone. You could see her lack of anger when everyone else was enraged about and with him. Her caring and concern weren't the obligatory, prescribed love of the Christian. She simply cared about her father.

When her parents' fighting had gone on too long or gotten too severe, Ellen would get ill. There are many ways of explaining this, but the simplest would be to say worry made her ill, or that her parent's anger was hurting her. This is the way that Navajos talk about it, and for me it is a correct description of how such things occur.

When I had lived there just a short time, she got seriously ill. It ended up being a tubal pregnancy with the tube rupturing and the life-threatening emergency that sometimes creates. When the trouble began, her father had been away from home for almost a week. This was longer than usual for him. He had left on the heels of an especially difficult and violent argument with his wife. When this happened the women in the family would spend a lot of time at the mission; they would pray for Andrew's salvation, talk to especially the younger missionaries, commiserate with each other and the old nurses, that sort of thing. They were mad as hell, but they were supposed to be caring. Ellen would go, but her concern was different, genuine. She was worried about her father and among other things she prayed for him.

Looking back on things, I think that Ellen was worried that her father was going to die, or perhaps if you are a Navajo you would say that she foresaw it. At the time this didn't enter my mind, but later on it often would. I'd really never known death; it was a stranger to me. And the violence and inopportune deaths I would experience over the next decade were not yet part of me nor anything I was able to anticipate. I think Ellen knew what could and ultimately was going to happen. I'm not sure if she was trying to stop it, delay it, or was simply trying to have some contact with her father while he was still alive.

When she got ill, something very odd happened. Her father came home, stopped drinking, and he and Elaine started working together to take care of their child. It was a startling contrast to what was usually there. Together the parents hired an herbalist, who prayed over and gave medicine to the entire family. They took it together over a two-week period and the mother brewed it and made sure of this. So much for the Christians against the heathens. When Ellen needed to be taken to the hospital, they both took her; when her son needed care, he was cared for by Elaine. It was very simple and clear-cut. Their daughter needed care and they gave it to her.

But as with everything else there is a cost. When you are married and go back to being your parents' child, it does something to your husband and to your own marriage. When he is ambivalent about being an adult to begin with, a part of the choice is made for him. At the moment when Andrew was the responsible parent and he and Elaine cared for their daughter, the husband entered adolescence, not permanently, but for the duration of her illness. This is how the cycle continues; one generation is momentarily well, the next becomes ill in different ways. Simple continuing story.

With her illness Ellen could get her father back and get her parents together, or at least less separate than they usually were.

It worked very nicely, but she didn't stay ill. And then the trouble would start again. It always does. Things are not just broken or fixed, but over time seem to go back and forth. In the Anglo world we don't understand this. We attach labels to events and to people which fixes them in time and stills their movement.

Andrew wasn't the first to die. His oldest son was. If I were an objective creature, Woodrow's death would have mattered more to me than Andrew's. He was younger; he had a wife; they had two children. He worked at one of the open-pit copper mines in Utah. He seemed to have gotten out of the cycle of hopelessness that was a part of the lives of many younger Navajo males. He was successful—job, family, somewhat educated. He'd made it. He would come to visit about every other weekend. Ellen was especially close to him.

Woodrow moved between his parents in a different way than did Ellen. His mother was proud of him and so was his father. He described himself as Christian, went to church and seemed to, for the most part, fit into that religion. But on occasion, when he was visiting, he would go away to traditional ceremonies. Sometimes it was with his brothers, often with old friends. Sometimes he would drink there, but it didn't have the serious tone of his father's or brothers' drinking.

His father didn't always like Woodrow's Christianity and his mother sometimes thought critically of his attending the ceremonies. But the criticism and disapproval weren't very serious or intense. Woodrow's life was too good and things went too well. There was nothing to criticize seriously; the way he lived demonstrated the quality of his life. And this was pretty much acknowledged by everyone.

One weekend he came to visit. And late that night there were a lot of people driving in and out of the camp, coming and going. Woodrow had been killed. He'd been run over by a car that evening. And after the car had run over him, it returned and backed over him. That is all anyone ever knew about it. So many questions without any kind of answer. Would the answers help? Almost certainly not; but we always seek them in the hope that the reasonable will do away with the pain of the irrational. When we have the reasons the pain persists. We all know this, but each time it comes up we look for the reasons again. If I just knew who or why.

And the final one who moved in between, who mediated the family relationships, was of course the youngest child. In families with trouble, the youngest one always matters. He was seven and looked exactly like his father. Both of them wore the same Indian Health Service glasses, with the apparently obligatory broken frame held together with the white adhesive tape. I don't think that I've ever seen a pair of these glasses without tape; maybe they're manufactured this way. The glasses were the same shape, the lenses the same thickness. When you saw them together you almost had to laugh. Identical versions of the same person but in different sizes. Everyone called the boy Andrew Junior although that wasn't his name. He really cared about his father, but as the youngest he was primarily cared for by and tied to his mother.

In the summer they would have large, month-long Bible conferences at the mission, all kinds of people coming from all over to do Bible study. This always precipitated a phenomenal drinking binge on the part of the males of the community. It would have been a wonderful time to be in the bootleg wine business. All the girls and Andrew's junior would be taken to the Bible study by their mother. And every so often Andrew would show up and more or less fall asleep, pass out under the ramada just outside the fence that enclosed the mission. And somehow his junior would extricate himself from the grasp of his mother and of Jesus and go and make sure his father was all right. And then he would just sit there with him.

If you read about Navajo kinship, they talk about the primacy of the mother-child relationship. And there is a truth in that. But what statements like this always miss, those social-scientific rules about a culture, is the individuals, the people. It misses this deep affection between Andrew and his junior.

He was also glue for the rest of the family, and again you see this a lot with a youngest. Everyone may be fighting each other, but they agree on caring for and about the last born. There is a Navajo word for the last one, *lók'eeshchąą'í*, the caboose.

PATTERN

In the social science business you can't just tell stories about people, you look for cycles and for wholes in places where others only see independent elements. Explaining these cleverly is the essence of this particular profession. There is also something more personal in trying to analyze and explain things. I'm not completely sure what, but I have some ideas.

It first has to do with distance. To be in and a part of this war is not very pleasant, not anything I could easily accept or even tolerate. So I transform these people into objects and, perhaps, don't get too upset about the futility and sadness in their world. Of course it doesn't work, but that never changed anything. A second part, the big lie of western thought, is that if you understand something you can do something about it. Symbiotic relationships generally, nicely exemplified here in the relationship between Christians and alcoholics, are the definitive disproof of that idea.

One of the most transparent cycles and one of life's universal truths is that Christians, or their equivalent, and alcoholics, or theirs, need each other. If you find a person who pursues goodness in life, you will necessarily find that they have ongoing relationships with bad people. They will try to transform the bad into the good, thus reaffirming and establishing their own goodness.

The Christian gets everything she needs from the alcoholic. It is truly remarkable. There is something to be zealous about. There is suffering. There is the fairly constant reaffirmation of there only being one correct zealous Christian way to live. And when one wavers, the drunkard serves as a very tangible reminder to stick with that one Christian way. And there are some fine opportunities for forgiveness.

The alcoholic in a relationship with a Christian is in a similar fortunate position. He always has a reason to drink. Being preached to is always good. A good wife is even better. Other popular reasons are one's wife paying more attention to the church than to her husband, the wife and church turning his children against him, and so on. But the most important thing of all is that the alcoholic has constant opportunities to be forgiven. The alcoholic needs to be forgiven and the Christian needs to forgive, and at some point this becomes the basis of the relationship.

It is not only Andrew and Elaine who are connected in this way, but the entire community. The men are together in their alcohol and the women in Christ. When Andrew was home for a while, Elaine's preaching would increase. Or the same thing would start with one of the other couples. Andrew would go to friends and they would start to drink as a group, usually near home. There would be fathers and sons, uncles and nephews, and in-laws. They were no longer separated by relational distance and by generation, but were all brothers in sweet wine.

The women would go to the mission, they would talk to the priest, the assistant priest, and so on. The message was always the same about Satan, alcohol, the traditional religion. They needed to pray and to more actively fight the whole business. And for them, too, the generations would disappear; they were all children of God the father.

And then the men would return, beat up, tired, and not looking too well. And after being angry for a short period, their wives would forgive them. After a while it would start all over. Occasionally there would be a respite, as when Ellen or one of the other children got ill. But they usually got better, and if they didn't, the effect even of a death was very brief.

So you do this social science ritual; you explain or invent these cycles and claim knowledge and understanding as the product, but something doesn't happen. No matter how correct or brilliant the explanation, it makes no difference. The understanding doesn't bring peace, in fact in many ways it makes living with tragedy even more difficult. And it also doesn't enable us to control, to bring change to the world. Here it is not the entire world, just these few people we came to know.

Here is something that doesn't matter, that is false, a distraction, superimposed on something that does, that is real. You would think that people would get to the real, get past the bullshit and have a chance at something that matters, but they never do.

Christ and sweet wine simply aren't that important, but we transform them into symbols that lives are based and lost on. We take these two things as having crucial importance. And while we obsess about that nonsense, lives are wasted in avoiding what does matter—the relationships we have and the contact we make with others.

The Navajo story of the separation of the sexes, of people moving opposite, is about relationships being both necessary and difficult. We exist with each other; there is no alternative; and as a part of that, there is difficulty. In the story there is, if not the promise, at least the potential for hope; things can be made better, perhaps, if you can accept the givens of man.

Converting the trivial into the profound hides what we care about and need, and it necessarily means that we will end up pursuing the impossible. It means that we have taken our chance at meaning and blown it. There is something upsetting in this.

There is something else that makes it much worse. And that is that it continues, goes on forever. You find this same battle and the same pursuit of these false symbols generation after generation. Men die and women suffer.

At Andrew's grave, the preacher spoke of the miracle of his conversion. He talked about how he'd accepted Christ and therefore avoided eternal damnation. We should all feel grateful and hopeful for both him and others in the same plight. And it was important not to give up trying to help those others, to keep trying to reveal to them the light no matter how bleak it seemed. Andrew's story was an inspiration to all. He'd strayed but returned to the flock. In heaven he would live in eternal peace.

These guys always have the same answer. You have one of the eternal and profoundly difficult questions, and they tell you that this is what it all means. If you question it, they cite some nonsensical Bible verse. But the bottom line will be that you have to have faith. One of the universal truths is that if you have to convince people that something is true, and you need to demand faith, then the idea must be false. It is like having a girlfriend or real estate agent who says, "Trust me."

The funeral did not satisfy or heal; it couldn't. Lies don't heal. We would all like them to. We would like words like "Everything will be all right" or "It is for the best" to fix things. But they don't. And all that funerals like this do is cause people to lie about their pain and their anger.

What matters the most about that moment was that Andrew died alone. He was surrounded by people who in some way cared about him, but who never really knew him. It wasn't that he was deep or mysterious or hid himself from others. You simply cannot know a person whom you spend your life trying to change. All you ever see is what needs changing, the potential for change, and everything else that fits into that particular framework. The rest is invisible. And in this there is a loss that cannot be mourned, the loss of someone close who was a stranger, with whom you made contact only as a potential convert.

We all felt this, but it was more apparent in Ellen. There was something else that she at some level knew. And that was that the deaths would continue; they had to. That is the problem with solutions like last-minute conversions. They work so well, giving everyone what they need, that people just keep using them.

There are no relapses after death. Andrew and those sons that follow him remain perfect Christians, perfect fathers, husbands, sons, forever. There is no more drinking, no more anger, no more fights, no more imperfection. You are loved forever. For Andrew there was the promise in death of what he had wanted but never obtained in life.

Elaine got what all Christians seek, pain rationalized by some higher good. Andrew had accepted Christ. She had done her job and now she could remember him with love and supposedly in peace. They could both look at the moment of death as lasting eternally and as defining their relationship. No subtleties, nothing unresolved, the perfect solution.

AFTERWARD (PERFECTION CONTINUES)

A short while ago I taught a college anthropology class and mentioned living in this community. A younger Navajo man came up afterward and talked to me. He was Elaine's sister's son. I had known him when he was a small boy. He told me how his father had died; he had been run over at a squaw dance.

A few weeks later Ellen called me and I talked to her for the first time in many years. We talked about our children, my ex-wife, her husband, our parents and relatives. This is always what you talk about. If it's one hour or ten years, this is where you start. She talked about her father, the person more than the others that we are related through.

Another brother had died the year before. He had just gotten out of some sort of alcohol rehabilitation. And, of course, he'd gone on a binge to celebrate. And he came home, just as Andrew had ten years before, jaundiced and sick, and he died. When his three children got a little older they would wonder and question who their father had been.

Of the two remaining brothers, the older will also go the way of Andrew. Or he might die more abruptly, as Woodrow had.

That leaves Andrew's junior, now an adult. When we talked, Ellen was the most concerned for him, I think partly because his fate was not yet decided and because you always worry about the youngest. There was a chance that he would survive and even do well. There was also the fear of something tragic. But not the same as his father, his brothers, or his uncle. I think Ellen is afraid that he might kill himself. As I said, she knows about such things. She has this sense of patterns, the ability and, most important, the courage to see them; and she does not allow her own wishes to impair or color her vision.

The pattern she sees includes a seven-year-old who watched his father die. Who felt that he should have done something. And it happened in a context where an answer to the loss was provided. A false answer, one that did not and could not explain away the issue at hand. The other part of it is the choices he sees life offering. In this family things are either black or they are white. If you are a male the assumption is black. When there is a mistake in a man's life, it is not just a mistake but evidence of corruption and evil. The only perfection is in redemption at death.

It seems a little less clear for the women. The goal is still perfection but they seem more accepting of mistakes.

A part of the people-moving-opposite story is the essential difference between male and female, and usually between man and woman. The female side of things owns nurturance and with it compassion. They are qualities that are not very strong on the male side. In this story, however, the nurturance is elicited and not simply given. It occurs in response to someone not being able to take care of himself. It says that you need the help of the other to live, to survive. In the Anglo world there is a rule that every junkie needs a loving mother. Sin must occur so that compassion and forgiveness follow. And forgiveness is the only love they know.

I worry about Ellen and junior. She will survive, I have no doubt about that, but I hope that she doesn't experience any more sorrow, especially the loss of Andrew's junior. He has had sadness for his life and, with it, questions about tragedy and what it all means, and there is no one who can answer his questions and tell him truthfully about those difficult things that matter.

There are only the lies, and the family insists on these. They value the untruths more than they value people. Or probably they don't know anything else. Or maybe at a certain point of experiencing the tragic, you have to invent a lie to explain it, to make it bearable. Maybe that is why people get strung out on

Christianity, just too much bad stuff happening. Too many losses to mourn, so you embrace a lie which says the losses aren't really losses.

I hope that junior doesn't die. I hope that Ellen knows other things in her life.

As a species we try very hard to make sense out of sorrowful things. I used to talk to old Navajo men and women about death. "What," I would ask, "happens after death?" They all had the same initial response: "How do I know? I never died." They would then go on to talk about future generations and, starting from the very beginning, generations of living beings (all life not just man) living to old age and dying, making room for the new generations and the new ideas that follow. The meaning was in this, a sense of the continuance and repeating pattern of life, not in any sort of personal immortality. It is simply not a question to be taken or answered personally.

Christianity and the Navajo witch stories, of course, take the opposite point of view. Their basis is the notion of personal immortality, of living forever as we are now. Process is denied and an entity is created, and the entity is eternal.

Since I am neither a Christian nor a witch, the idea of personal immortality has never rung true. It just doesn't make sense. There have been too many dramatic changes in my life and in those around me. Staying a particular way, keeping a particular me forever can't be right. What those old people said about the process of life and the continuance in generations seems real to me; it seems to describe what is, not what should or could be, and there is usually a peace in the thought.

But when these generations don't continue, or when they create ugliness rather than beauty in the world, there is no peace. You hear this from the old people all the time, continually mourning the youth, their children and grandchildren. They are saddened by it, but they accept it anyway. What else can they do?

Andrew and Elaine combine the worst of two worlds, the traditional and the Christian. They have made themselves eternal, immortal in these future generations. They have somehow endlessly re-created their present in the future, in their children and in the generations that follow.

I wonder how to deal with tragedy that seems eternal, that goes on and on. Where can we look for an answer to this? We could say that death on this earth doesn't matter because we go to a better place eternally. Heaven is a shopping mall in Cleveland where you can only watch the Indians play every day on a large-screen TV. The idea is false and even for those that try to believe in it, it doesn't work, doesn't satisfy. Focusing on future generations is a way of making sense out of sorrow in the present, but it makes the repeating pattern even more tragic.

The way of dealing with it we have talked about, preferred by us social-science intellectual types, is through explanation that masquerades as elegant. We pretend that we understand the why and the how of something, using such labels as poverty, ethnicity or culture, and alcoholism, codependency, and the like.

But there is no impact, no power, in this knowledge. It neither changes what is nor satisfies as a portrait. Rationalization may help some to tolerate the intolerable, but I never found much comfort in it. What happens to people, especially the bad things, always seems too personal for abstract explanations. It isn't just some poor alcoholic Indian dying; it is Andrew. And it wasn't just the poorly educated Indian children of a screwed-up family, it was Ellen and junior and Woodrow and the rest. It is all very personal, and the abstract explanations seem without relevance and have no impact.

So what are we left with? I guess we are supposed to mourn. That is the current popular thing to do with loss; you cry and get angry and work things through, whatever that means. But how in the world can you mourn or resolve a process that is perpetual, that continues and that you know will occur repeatedly with future generations, with the children and grandchildren of Andrew and Elaine?

Stupid questions really. But I keep asking them even knowing they are stupid and that they cannot be answered. Questions like this, trying to find answers that satisfy, keep us from seeing the world as it is. The wisdom in this particular system is in Ellen. She can see things as they are and she can live in a world of repeating tragedy. Most of us have to see it differently, see hope or view something as changeable. See events and a future that is different from the way it is, creating instead a soothing illusion.

5

WALLACE

It was never completely clear why he had killed her. At the trial he said that he couldn't remember; he had been drunk and had no recall of those moments. Maybe it was someone else who came after he had left. He didn't know.

Fifteen years later he maintained his amnesia. He would occasionally talk about the trial and about the time immediately before her death, but not about the killing. Only once did he tell the story of what happened. And then he insisted that it was not from memory but from what the police said had occurred.

After they finally caught up with him, and into the trial, his anguish was so complete and so accurate that it was unconvincing. It was a despair that he must have learned when he was in Bureau schools; it was not the sort of thing that an Indian would have cared about or believed. You learn despair and guilt, the proper way to act, from the missionary Anglos—the ones who come to the difficult places and live in them for years trying to help, to educate or Christianize, to bring morality to the Indian. You learn that if you feel bad enough you will be forgiven by those who have power over you.

For us as a people, remorse and forgiveness are two of our most sacred beliefs. When someone is convicted of a crime, the judge always begins a maximum sentencing by saying that the defendant showed no remorse. And the TV evangelists who sin offer a caricature of what remorse is supposed to look like.

As we grow older we learn to lie more subtly, more convincingly. We learn that there are no pure emotions, only mixed feelings, and that some are more mixed than others. But Wallace never had; his expression of grief stayed pure and intense. Convincing only to born-agains and school teachers, the ones who watch Jimmy Swaggart, with the tear-sensitive makeup, cry on TV while holding the microphone and never missing a camera cue. The intensely perfect, convenient grief.

Wallace's two boys had been there to see and hear their father kill their mother. The state had thought them too young to testify but they were not too young to remember. They had watched him strangle her and pour bleach down her throat. What must that have been like? We read about these sorts of things all the time, but stop for a minute and imagine what it must be like watching your mother being killed, being unable to do anything, watching, feeling if you make a noise or try to interfere that he will turn his anger on you. And then after he fled, being there with her.

He was always afraid that when his sons were old enough they would seek him out for revenge, to hurt or kill him. One of every man's basic assumptions is that the way that he feels and thinks is shared by the rest of the species. As time went on and he knew they were growing older, his fear increased. They lived in Phoenix, quite near by reservation standards. A white Christian couple had adopted them soon after their mother's death.

When I was still living there, the oldest son did come. Wallace got a letter announcing a visit sometime soon, and his terror grew out of control. He would run off, come back after a few days. He didn't know exactly when his son would appear, and he was too dependent to stay away for very long.

He was there when the son came, and it was nothing. The now-adult child had been raised in forgiveness; I'm sure that is all the Christian couple had taught in those fifteen years. The young man came to tell his father that he no longer hated him, that he had forgiven him. He suggested that his father become a Christian, so that he could heal, so that he too would be forgiven.

Wallace pretended that he believed his son. Of course he wanted to, so he lied to himself. He told me about it and tried to convince me of the lie. But Wallace knew too much about pure things, pure feelings and emotions. He knew about pure anger and hatred with certainty, and he kept trying to create or find pure love. He knew that the boy could not forgive him and put aside anger, hurt, and fear completely. That ultimately the teaching of the Christian couple could only create more convincing lies; some ways of being human simply cannot be real.

After he killed her, he had run away into the wilds and the canyons. The FBI was called in. They are the ones that have jurisdiction over these sorts of things with Native Americans. They tracked him for several days. He said at the time that he wanted to die. But he brought food with him and stayed near water or carried enough with him. When they caught up to him he was in a rock overhang on a canyon wall. He says they rappeled down from above. Over the years he would tell two very correct stories about that moment. The one was that he could see them as they got to the entrance of the overhang and could have shot them and gotten away; the second was that he came at them with a rifle so that they would kill him, or alternately that he screamed at them to kill him, that he didn't want to live, his grief was so intense.

But, of course, he hadn't been killed nor had he killed himself. Above all else he knew how to survive. And as a part of that, he knew how he was supposed to feel, supposed to act, but when he thought no one was looking he would stop. You never knew what was inside of him; of course he didn't know either.

The newspaper account gave a slightly different version. It had been a Navajo policeman who had tracked him to the cliff edge. In the newspaper interview, he said that they just waited for him to come up. There was no hurry. Wallace either had to jump, fall, or come to them. Might as well build a fire, make coffee, and get comfortable. I'm sure that this drove the FBI agents completely berserk.

Once I was with Wallace at a trading post in one of the larger reservation towns. He and the Anglo woman who ran it were talking in Spanish, kind of a pidgin Spanish, dueling with words, each trying to outdo the other. When he was momentarily somewhere else, she urgently and excitedly whispered his story to me. "Did I know about him?" she asked, while nervously looking around for his return. She described in immense detail how he had killed several women, how he had escaped and hid in the canyons for months. They had to track him with dogs, she said, and even then he escaped, living like a wild Indian. What a dangerous man he was. She got more and more excited as she talked, adding more and more detail. The woman was fascinated. This was a story about Jesse James or Geronimo. Later he told me some very detailed stories about her. So it goes.

There was this mutual strangeness between him and women, especially Anglos. They had the same fascination that the trader expressed. I never have understood it. He wasn't especially charming or attractive. I guess that they were drawn to the danger, his potential for violence, or maybe they were simply attracted to someone who cared so intensely.

I first met him when I was on the reservation for the summer. The teenagers I was working with as interpreters were more than reluctant to go to his house; they were afraid of him. And they made the harsh jokes about him that frightened children, ashamed of being afraid, make.

At the time he was living with a woman he'd been with for about a month. She was blind. The story was that a previous husband had poured something caustic into her eyes. You could see scars, so it could have been true.

But in this relationship each of them expressed a truth that was more important and which transcended the details of a correct and accurate story. The theme or the pattern of their lives was played out before you. As you watched them, they seemed to be trying to change that theme through and with each other. But when you watched a little closer or a little longer you saw that it wasn't a change at all, just more of the same, a repeat of the pattern. They needed each other momentarily, to have an excuse to be, and to continue being, the way they were.

In her eyes he continually looked for and found the story of her blindness. Through this she said, "I am the victim. Look at what the world has done to me and has always done." To her and especially to her blindness he responded, "I once created victims, but no longer; I will take care of her and I will make up for what was done to her, and for what I have done to others." Through his devotion to her he would atone, and with atonement people would care about and for him.

He would express tremendous anger at the man who had blinded her—the man who had given Wallace the opportunity to care for her and thereby remedy the harm he had done to others. I have worked at other times with people who have this violence in them, and they always express rage at others who are violent. They have a very strict black-and-white moral code, which they of course fail at fairly often; but the reality of their actions changes the morality not at all.

The two of them were absolutely always together. He was the caricature of one who cared, helping her, talking gently to her, waiting on her. Purity and goodness. It was terribly uncomfortable to watch; you felt embarrassed. But whatever he did for her, it was never enough. She wouldn't scold. She would hint or reluctantly ask. She felt bad about bothering him, but of course what else could she do. Or she would try to walk across a room and bump into something, or try to cook when he was gone for a moment and burn herself. In all of these actions was the gentle cruel message that he didn't quite do enough. "No, of course I'm not angry; I don't blame you. It isn't your fault I am crippled, that I have this cross to bear. I know you do your best." And of course he would then have the additional burden of her shame, brought about by his failure. If he had only been more aware. And so he would foolishly try harder to accomplish what was impossible. If he could only do it correctly it would make the woman care for him, give him the perfect love.

His effort was toward purity, toward perfection. To him a relationship with a woman meant either murderous rage or perfect love. And the more he felt rage, the more he sought to express only caring. The more anger he had for her helplessness and demands, the more he tried to compensate for her blindness. He could make up for what that other man had done to her. He was different, better. He would care better than anyone ever had.

They lived with his mother and father. The old man was between seventy and eighty and his mother was in her fifties. Wallace was her first born; she was fifteen when she had him. The old man had married an older woman with a young daughter. And when the girl was older, he married that daughter. Navajos do this on occasion; and in the past Mormons would do it. It seems incestuous to me, and I think a part of the problem that Wallace had with women came from this. It meant that his grandmother was his mother and his mother was his sister. When you have funny generations, children don't do very well at becoming adults. Wallace did very poorly at it; it also seems to be something of an issue for Mormons. Their "Families are Forever" bumper stickers reflect this. If you are forever a member of the family you are born to, you won't do very well with marriage, with creating a new family and a new generation.

The mother seemed angry, almost as if she felt that he had betrayed her with his new wife. The old man was aloof, distant. He had given up on things in his family being very different. The practicalities of the situation were that they all lived in a one-room hogan, about twenty feet across. Sleeping and making love to a woman in the same room where your parents are would be very difficult, to say the least. I think his wife used this, found it a convenient excuse.

There is this remarkable redundancy about our lives. For Wallace it kept centering on trying to be good enough at caring for his wife and his mother, and hating them both. In seeking perfection, all he ever found was murderous rage. In the contact he sought, all he ever found was abandonment; he had little trouble finding objects to practice perfection on, but none stayed. He had always been rejected by those who claimed to care for him; he must have thought that if he acted correctly they would care. And he must have kept trying to be caring so he wouldn't be like them, that he would be different and better. We live in these traps that are just this simple and this silly, but we take them with intense seriousness. We base our existence on these lies.

When Wallace talked about the beginnings of his life, he would start by saying, "I was born dead." Everything subsequent elaborated on this master theme. He was taken out into the brush by his grandmother, who had delivered him, and left there. As a rule, Navajos are afraid of corpses, and dead babies are no exception. His grandfather came and wanted to know where the baby was; he went and got the baby and brought him back to life. Some people don't care very much about rules.

As a young boy, Wallace remembers being angry at his father and wanting to protect his mother. In those days his father drank and people hid from him. He was a very large, strong man. He remembers his father passing out and several members of the family and some neighbors tying him up while he was unconscious. He wanted to keep his father away from his mother. She was young and she didn't want to be with this old drunken man; he had to protect her, but of course he couldn't. And in some way she made it clear to the boy that it was his fault. Echoes of his mother in the eyes of his wife.

When he was about six, the people from the government came. They wanted to take the children and educate them. There had been schools on the reservation for some time, but they didn't pursue the children in the remote areas, at least not effectively. For some reason when he was six, they got serious. There were other things happening around the same time; the Great Depression was one; the massive stock reduction on the reservation was another.

The depression had some effect on the Navajo—not so much in terms of wages where there wasn't much to begin with—but the stock reduction made the people instantly poorer, not just economically but spiritually. Maybe the schools were a convenient way to have the children taken care of in a difficult time. Or maybe the stock reduction and the schooling were a part of the same whole, the government and the BIA taking governing Indians seriously. A demonstration of who was in charge.

The school that he went to was about sixty miles from home. This was the time of travel by horses, by wagon, and on foot, on trails and roads of dirt, mud, snow, or ice. It meant not only that he went there to live, but that visits would be infrequent. It was unlikely that he would see his family except for summers.

There are many people, mainly men, of his generation that tell this story. A fifty-to-sixty-year-old man describing what it was like when he was six and was taken from his home and his family. In the memory there is always confusion, not understanding what is happening and how his parents, especially his mother, could let it happen. There is the memory of at one moment feeling safe and nurtured, being in the midst of warmth, family, the sheep, the hogan. And in the next moment they are taken to a distant unknown place. They no longer feel the warmth and the safety, but only the cold and the loss and, as a part of that, the anger. This is how a six-year-old would remember, in strong primary colors, not subtle shades or hues.

The people in these schools had a mission. It wasn't that they didn't care, but that the caring was expressed in that mission. And they were themselves willing to experience harshness, as well as being willing to inflict it on others, in order to accomplish their goal. They wanted to civilize the Indians, teach them practical and social skills, as well as educate them. And as a part of that they taught them Christianity. These always go together, are always a part of the same whole, a part of helping those that don't need help until you begin this process. Teaching them to be imperfect Anglos.

You can see all of this expressed in the photographs of the Indian schools in Phoenix or Oklahoma or Tuba City. The location doesn't matter; the pictures are identical. There are before photos of long-haired Indian savages. And the pictures taken after; their hair is shorn and they are in the very uniform uniform, the wool serge suits with the white shirts buttoned to the collar, even in the middle of the desert. The women school teachers are always to one side, standing very erect, their dresses to the floor, buttoned completely to the neck and their hair tightly done. In the photographs they look proud of their charges, proud of what they are accomplishing.

When Wallace was six, he was taken to this setting. The first time they came for him, he knew in advance when they would arrive and he disappeared until they left. The next time there was no notice and they took him. And his story is the same as all the other stories that these men tell you.

There is a tremendous sadness in this, and it is intensified by the fact that it happened to a generation, that their stories are all the same. Standard stories are never about hope or joy, and when you hear them you look urgently for variation or nuance. When you find none, you know you are in trouble.

As a people we chronically do this sort of thing. We begin with the belief that we know what is right. And then we immediately and impulsively start to act on what we fervently believe to be correct. But the enthusiasm quickly wanes. We lack any sort of commitment or follow-through.

Navajos are importantly different in two ways. They think before they act. Both as individuals and as a group. And they tend not to speak for or impose their beliefs on others.

With Indian education we initially thought that we had to take away these peoples' languages and traditions and replace them with our own. But within a few years we wanted them to keep their own languages and ways of life and superimpose Anglo education on top of that. A fervor for what is right, combined with ambivalence and lack of commitment. This should be on a bronze plaque somewhere as you enter this country.

We do poorly at educating Native Americans. (In the last several years we are also failing at educating everyone else, so equal education may well soon be at hand.) But with Wallace's generation it was a complete disaster. They lost their families and their traditions and the effort to make them into Anglos, to educate them, failed completely. We created these in-between people.

I'm not sure how long he stayed at the school. He probably isn't either; time is different when we are adults looking back. It was more than a year, because when he tells stories of that time he mentions each of the seasons. His strongest memory is of a Ute woman who cared for him, probably one of the dorm matrons. Again that perfect love. He says she was like a mother to him. He says he forgot his own mother; this wasn't true, but he needed to express his anger. And he needed to prove to the world (and himself) how independent he was, how he didn't really need his mother.

People who experience this loss never get the closeness thing right. They have learned not to trust another person being there, so they try not to need or they try to love safely, in a way that avoids the possibility of loss. But, of course, they need so desperately that none of the strategies or rationalizations ever work.

Towards the end of his time at the school, Wallace got sick. He didn't eat and lost weight. He probably noticed that everyone got worried, or that they were alarmed by the weight loss. And he continued his fast. He was sick enough that they sent him home. There was no school for him after that.

So in addition to his pattern with women, there is the second theme of manipulating and controlling situations. In this case he did it through illness. The socialization of the sociopath. In order to create one, all you need to do is take away his insides and make his survival dependent on how well he can manipulate different, often harsh, contexts. Finally you need to reward and excuse behavior according to the display of appropriate affect. How easy this is.

Navajo morality is different. People don't excuse misbehavior simply because you feel bad. Navajos acknowledge the existence of bad feelings, but individual and group responsibility is something else, something separate. The one has nothing to do with the other.

When Anglos on site, teachers, missionaries, administrators, first saw this, they took it as immorality. They would see, for example, a young boy hurt a girl and show no obvious remorse. And, of course, a part of their mission was to change this, to bring morality to their charges. The children learned to display sorrow and tears, and whatever else was required. And when the teachers saw a child break a rule and cry, they felt good. They were succeeding.

In the short time he was at the school, Wallace learned that the Anglos wanted him to feel bad. They would care about you if you appeared to feel certain ways, and they would ignore you if you didn't. And this display of proper feeling persisted. But the correctness of a six-year-old was false in this middle-aged man. Again, it was too pure.

On first meeting Wallace, one was struck by how fluent he was in English, something very rare in the men of his generation. He had learned this in a real school, a place where Indians do learn English: Leavenworth Penitentiary. And I learned later how well he could speak Navajo, not just the everyday variety, but the technical poetic talk of the old people. He understood them and their ideas, and he was someone they felt good talking to.

That summer my professor needed someone to translate and I suggested Wallace. He was excited. One reason was that he would be doing something that mattered; he always wanted to be important and this work seemed important to him. Second, he would earn a wage. And third, he and his wife would move to where my professor was staying, where they would have some privacy. Paired with Wallace's excitement was his wife's fear. They would stay in a tent, up on a hillside that you could only get to by a fairly steep, narrow path. It wasn't dangerous, but a little difficult. Practically this meant that Wallace would have to lead his wife to and from the tent. It meant that she would have to completely rely on him. The game they played with each other was over control, and the balance of power was changing.

After they had been there three days, Wallace came down to my professor's trailer and woke him at about three in the morning. He was pounding on the door and very alarmed. He said his wife was real sick; she couldn't move. They managed to get her down the hill and into the car and drove her the eighty miles to the emergency room of the Indian Health Service hospital. She disappeared into this particular medical maze while Wallace and the professor were left sitting in the waiting area. Wallace went to the rest room and when he came out he was different. I was told about it later, but I saw the same thing happen with him at other times.

When he was in the rest room, he drank the alcohol in the vials where you put thermometers. Alcohol in hospitals is mostly not denatured; it is cheaper to just use alcohol without adding the poison.

He came out, not drunk exactly, but different. The distance and reserve he normally maintained were absent. A lot of ribald, obscene remarks. Jokes about sex and women that would have made anyone uncomfortable. He must have thought this was the way to connect, to get close. It was strange and uncomfortable.

He then disappeared. Later we found that he'd gone to the bootleggers in town; we didn't see him for several weeks. The physicians said there was nothing wrong with the wife; she was hysterical, or scared of her husband. Take your pick. By the time Wallace came back, she was gone. He wouldn't talk about it much other than the disparaging remarks about her, her dishonesty, how she had lied, how good he had been.

There are a few people in my experience, fortunately not very many, who become totally different after even a small amount of alcohol. This total difference is never for the better. The people seem evil—a strange thing for me to say. I don't really believe in evil, but that is what it is like. There is a real terror in this, that switch; they seem possessed. Or maybe people who are always on stage simply shouldn't drink. Maybe for the sociopath *in vino veritas* actually means something. I can't explain it; I only know that it was like a toggle switch being turned on or off with even small amounts of alcohol.

When he was sober he would express the perfect love for this woman; then the switch and it was the perfect hate. And it was a hatred for women. Even more than that a hatred for the female, femaleness, *yin, bik'e hózhǫ́*, whatever you call it. He didn't tell me about this; he simply assumed that I shared this rage, that it was the way all men felt. It made me uncomfortable.

There is a peculiarity about this. In the Navajo world there is something very important, very powerful, very special about the female. This idea is pervasive, but you can see it centered in or begin to understand it through certain gods or symbols. The one is Changing Woman, White Shell Woman, the Earth, Earth Woman. She is *shimá*, my mother. For she provides for and nurtures all. Any Navajo can tell you about her, tell you that she is the mother, the provider, the one who cares for the beings that live on the surface of the earth. The essential nurturer.

From my perspective this always seemed like half a story. The world of humans can't be divided into a perfect good and a perfect evil. It seems always more grey than it does black and white. And yet with these Navajo gods, at least on first glance, it is black or white.

We have talked about the other half elsewhere. It is centered in the underworld story of the sexes separating and "moving opposite." Here women are portrayed as lustful, adulterous, and dishonest. The sexes moved apart and lived on opposite sides of a river; women masturbated and resorted to bestiality out of lustfulness, and of these acts monsters were born.[1] This is the Pandora's box of Navajo creation, the explanation for the negatives (and some of the necessary unpleasantness) of human existence.

Contained within these stories, often hidden, is this ambivalence about the female. She is portrayed as the perfect nurturer and mother, possessing the very power of creation, a power that is both feared and respected. A part of this is men's fear of something they cannot understand. Something that is so important, that is also so dangerous.

I wonder if there is a universal ambivalence about nurturers. On the one hand, the gratitude at being cared for, at having one's needs met. But there is always an uncertainty. There is hunger, and you wait and wonder. And then the relief and, I suppose more than relief, pleasure. But I suspect anger in the waiting and, more important, anger in the dependency. There is always this rage at having to depend on another, at them having that kind of power and control over you.

He must have felt this toward the wife he killed, this extreme ambivalence. No, not quite that; ambivalence means feeling two

---

[1] This, of course, is also half a story. The males did the same things, but, apparently, nothing was born of their sexual improprieties.

ways. I think he felt one way at a time, one extreme way and
then its opposite, and then back again. Purity of feeling and
purpose. The rest of us feel ambivalent, always, about relationships. They matter but they are dangerous. We want closeness
but not to be smothered, and we especially want to avoid loss.
That is ambivalence. The pathology was in the purity, the lack of
ambivalence. And with purity are the seeds always for the
opposite—the purity of the other half.

That week when he killed her, he must have felt that pure
love and desire for his wife. He must have known or thought she
was having an affair. He would try to talk himself out of that
reality, try to use reason and persuade himself that it wasn't so.
And the more he lied to himself, the stronger the thoughts
would become. He would imagine her with the other man,
imagine other men with her, dream about it. But he would try
to convince himself it wasn't so, not with the one he loved so
purely, not with that perfect female symbol.

This must have been exactly the way that First Man felt.
First Woman claims illness and needs to be taken to the banks of
the river every day. First Man starts thinking about this, it works
on his mind. One day he follows her there, sees that she meets
someone, is having an affair. He returns home. He goes into his
house by himself; he can't stop thinking about it. He doesn't
sleep. The next morning he can't eat anything. And so it goes.
The love and desire, the betrayal, and then what? No simple
answers in this, just the question over and over.

If the suspicion became certainty, there would be attempts
at forgiveness, trying to rationalize the imperfection. Perhaps he
would blame it on himself. It was his own flaw that caused the
perfect person to violate his trust.

People use forgiveness in an attempt to avoid loss, but of
course the loss has already occurred. Sometimes people just
won't admit it, so they spend their lives believing in things like
forgiveness or that the infidelity was their own fault. They were
drunk, worked too hard, weren't attentive enough. It doesn't
really matter what you try. The reality is that perfect love is
gone. Sometimes so is the other person. Sometimes you lie to
yourself and to each other so that you can stay together and
maintain at least the illusion of what you desired.

At the time he killed her, he was a bootlegger. The illegality of alcohol on the reservation assures that bootlegging flourishes. There is some legal risk, but not too much. The police tend to look the other way, especially if you are related to them. They enforce the law when a bootlegger is associated with trouble—violence, underage sales, and the like. Bootlegging is a means of upward mobility, a way to make a profit and save, to live out the American entrepreneurial dream. It also, almost paradoxically, requires that the bootlegger abstain from alcohol and generally stay out of trouble. A bootlegger who drinks is quickly out of business; he drinks his profits, gives the wine away, or when he is unconscious or otherwise vulnerable has the wine and money stolen.

Wallace was bootlegging and he was successful. That week his wife starting drinking and getting mean, and he was drinking right along with her. Jealousy and anger were the precipitant, and the alcohol would intensify those feelings he was trying to deaden. And at some point they started to argue or disagree, or say mean things to each other. The rest is forgotten, but at some point he killed her. He woke up next to her and she was dead. He couldn't remember what happened. His boys had been there but had run away.

He got into his truck and drove to a remote canyon and then he left the truck and started out on foot. He had a rifle. He kept alive, he says, the way the old Navajos kept alive. He set snares, cooked with a small fire, gathered plants. He kept moving.

He was tried in federal court in Prescott, one of the privileges of Native Americans accused of felonies. The trial took place quickly. The feds don't like these cases; they are more of an annoyance than anything else. After all, they deal with big cases, spectacular decisions about esoteric points of law, not some drunk Indian killing his wife. There is no one else around who cares much about the outcome. Liberals don't like the cases because they don't like to look at Indians who act less than perfect. The involved Navajos stay away. There is no outrage on the part of Anglo society for the victim. After all, it is an Indian; this is what these people do to each other.

He told the same story at the trial that he told years later. He didn't remember, maybe she killed herself while he was unconscious. Or maybe someone else came into the house. He didn't know; it wasn't him. His attorney's name was Whymper, very likely a not-so-good omen. After all was said, they arranged a plea bargain. He would plead guilty to a manslaughter charge rather than murder and would receive five years in federal penitentiary. Why? Probably they simply weren't interested in pushing what they considered a domestic dispute between Indians. Also, getting young sons of an accused to testify is a rather tricky business.

At the sentencing he got the five years for manslaughter and then, unexpectedly, five more for bootlegging. He was transferred to Leavenworth, Kansas. He spent seven years there. After five, he said, Attorney General Robert Kennedy came down and held hearings on some Native Americans. He said they offered him parole and he refused. He was afraid to go back. Afraid of what? He didn't know; he was just afraid.

There is, in our species, this need for structure. This need to be confined and restricted, the terror of freedom. This is difficult to admit but very easy to see. People will always give reasons why they are not free, the things that have to be different before they have freedom. Relationships, economics, and jobs are common reasons for seeing oneself as trapped. They see freedom as being given or allowed, something that needs to be provided, rather than something that simply is. The error, the trap, is in seeing it in the world out there, rather than in an attitude or a way of looking at things. It is in seeing it as material, rather than as a product of the mind.

Wallace needed the structure; sociopaths always do. He was in a minimum-security area outside the prison walls, lived in a single room by himself, and was involved with agricultural tasks. This was his world; he avoided trouble and was a good citizen of the prison. He learned English very well; he learned Spanish. He was the perfect prisoner; walls were not needed.

The problem with being a perfect prisoner, of course, is that they let you go. He was released and taken back to Arizona. On his first night of freedom, he got drunk and broke the windows out of a store. He then waited for the police to come. He never made it back onto the reservation. They put him back in jail in Arizona. There wasn't a need to take him back to Leavenworth; he wasn't a dangerous person unless he loved you, and he was a very good prisoner.

I really hate this story; I get angry and very frustrated in trying to write it. From a pure writing perspective it should be a good story. You've got tragedy, violence, that whole business. Someone should be able to make a good yarn out of it.

I dislike it because it is too clear. Wallace fits very nicely into and is explained completely by a number of categories. There is no mystery, no subtlety, no complexity. His life is known and predictable with absolute certainty. For me this is not the nature of man. At least it is not how I want him to be.

I could add subtlety, I suppose, and talk about how bright Wallace is— his intelligence, what a waste, that sort of thing. I value these things, but it is not a basis for caring about, for loving someone. And with Wallace the intelligence has become cleverness, a way to manipulate and control, rather than an expression of the spirit.

A Navajo might say that this story has many branches. The problem is that they all lead to the same place. That is the troubling thing about Wallace and his generation; their paths lead to the same point. Whenever there is certainty in life, it involves grimness. Anytime you are sure about the outcome in advance, there is no joy.

As a part of the process of looking for subtlety, I went through the newspapers for the year his wife died. I didn't know the exact date, so I had to go through a lot of newspapers.

There were other stories like his, about Navajo men who had committed a violent crime against a woman they cared about and who then escaped. And many of them were gone for months and months living, according to the reports, in the wild. In part this is a reflection of the Anglo view of Indians. They are wild and their world is wild. And they would also see a man in the wilds as alone. Probably the wilds of the Anglo newspaper were home to the man, and there were other people who helped him.

But these stories reflect another side. A part of these people's past. There was a knowledge of living in the wild, off of the land. It is part of what a boy would have learned fairly early in his traditional education. Again, the basic premise of that education was in paying attention. To watch, listen, smell, feel, taste the habits and the patterns of the world you were a part of.

Anglo education isn't like this. It puts you into a box where, ideally, you are supposed to exclude the world. I remember starting school and being classed as one who wasn't so bright and who couldn't learn; they had given me an IQ test and the score was around 70 or 80. In those days they didn't have special ed or drugs. So they gave me a seat in the back by the window. I was left alone and got to watch the world outside the classroom. I alternated between doing that and trying to drill through my maple desk from the inside with a paper clip that I had made into a drill. After several years of relative peace, they gave me another test, which I unfortunately did well on. They reclassified me as bright. Because of my new intelligence and because they felt guilty, I was put near the front, away from the window. They wanted me to pay attention to the teacher now, rather than the world outside. Later, in a brand new high school built in the late 1950s, they even improved on this. The vast majority of the classrooms had no windows. Nowadays I occasionally teach at a university where the seminar and lecture rooms also have no windows. Anonymous people have put travel posters on the wall—pictures of beautiful places, more abstractions, like the words that pass for ideas in higher education.

It is very difficult not to be impressed with socialization that is based completely on excluding and denying experience, that rests completely on authority—the authority of books, things written on the blackboard, and especially on the person in the front of the room. I remember talking about the fall of the year and what happened to plants, trees, and animals in a room with no windows during the fall of that particular year. To put people in a box insisting that they pay no attention to their immediate surroundings and to call that learning: strange stuff this.

These people who could herd sheep, who knew where water and grass were under all circumstances, and who knew how to live in the wilds began with different ideas on what it meant to pay attention. When you put these people in a box and insisted that they not look out the window, I think that they would watch each other and watch especially the people who had power over them. That would be the world that mattered. They would learn what was expected and how to survive. There is a more accurate truth in watching than in only listening. The rules of the world are not in what people say, but in the complete message. If you need to catch a rabbit in a snare or go hungry, then you need to know what rabbits actually do, rather than what people in authority say that they generally do. And if it is people who are the rabbits or the bears, you need to know about them and how they actually think and behave.

These were the things they learned in school, about what people in authority wanted. And later Wallace, and those like him, learned more of the same in other boxes—the army, jails, the penitentiary.

His father's life had been similar to Wallace's, up to a point. The life history of old men always has certain common themes. From around adolescence to age fifty or sixty, they run wild. The details vary, but usually they drink, always there are women, always there is travel, usually there is violence, always there is deceit. The stories of their lives are the same as those of the heroes/gods in those more ancient stories. Then at some point these men start to believe. Typically there is a particular incident that they remember as precipitating the change—like being at a ceremony, being disrespectful and skeptical, and being taken ill or feeling something happen. And then starting to believe and perhaps starting to pursue knowledge.

Wallace had this story. In his youth he had a cynical attitude toward the traditional religion. He was at a ceremony helping out and he fainted. The singer ministered to him and told him that it was the particular power at and of that ceremony that was working on him. And then the singer prayed a bit more and Wallace felt better. He started to believe and to learn certain things. He was very bright and he learned quickly. He wasn't a saint, but that doesn't seem to be a requirement to be a singer.

But his father would only teach him up to a point. And the question is why no further. What was there in Wallace that made his father reluctant to give him knowledge that would bring power, that would give him control over things.

His father and others saw a flaw, a broken or a missing piece in his character. He was a dangerous man and that wouldn't change.

People debate such things, absolutes about someone's future. Can certain types of people or certain individuals change? Is there any hope? All people, Navajo and Anglo included, have rituals to treat people like Wallace, but no one really believes they will make any difference. So you are left with certainty, absolute knowledge. It is one of the few times that social science really works. You have a man determined by context. A nice lineal cause-and-effect explanation. You can predict with certainty everything about the rest of his life. More than anything I hate certainty.

6
THE CHILDREN

Even before the children died things had been bad. For reasons I never totally understand, I always associate this with the weather. It had rained and rained; the earth was mud and my knees hurt. The high desert of the Colorado Plateau wasn't supposed to be like this. You couldn't go outside because of the wet; you couldn't take even the four-wheel-drive truck anywhere because you would likely get stuck and stay stuck until the ground dried out. So you were in the house, and you were cold, and the cold and the dreariness surrounded you. You hated to go to the outhouse because it leaked air and water, so the urgency you felt in the relative warmth of the house disappeared about fifty feet before you got there.

The families that made up the camp where I lived had been covertly fighting among themselves into this, the third generation. The reasons they gave for the fighting varied. But they did agree that the source of the conflict was wealth. Actually there wasn't very much wealth, which is usually the case when families fight over it, and what there was was supposed to be shared between them. There just wasn't enough to go around and they stayed frustrated and angry with each other. As the weather forced them together, the anger and jealousy that they tried to keep hidden increasingly manifested itself.

The grandfather lived there along with his children, his grandchildren, and a few great-grandchildren. Some would move elsewhere occasionally, to go to school, to work, to marry. But this was home and this is where they returned. Grandfather lived with his second wife, who was about thirty years younger than he.

The old man had been wild and a drunkard as a youth; this is one of the reasons he married his first wife, an older woman. Actually, it is more correct to say that this is why his family decided on this marriage. As he got older he grew wiser (attributes that we assume are paired, but that rarely are). And he became a singer of great renown, a man possessing knowledge and power.

If you are a Navajo and powerful there should also be wealth,[1] not necessarily for you but for your family. Along with this, your family should be safe. Knowledge gives one the ability to provide wealth and protection, and the protection is needed. As a singer, one who intervenes and alters the course of events, you necessarily incur the jealousy and the wrath of others. They try to harm you, and they especially try to harm those who are close to you. The means are primarily spiritual—prayers, songs, or thoughts directed at the singer and his family. A man of power is able to protect those close to him.

But the old man's children thought of themselves as poor, and even before the children died a great deal of harm had come to the family. For quite some time they had doubted their grandfather's strength, but they still had enough respect, or maybe it was fear, not to question it.

On this particular day it was still overcast, but the rain had momentarily ceased. Even though it wasn't the best of days and you had to be a pretty fair mudder, you took the opportunity to go outside. Children, of course, in all societies that don't have television take any opportunity to be out of the house and away from their parents.

The children had been digging a tunnel; the damp earth made this easy. It also made it easy for the earth to collapse. Two of the children, a brother and sister, had suffocated; their cousins, two brothers and a sister, had gotten out, escaped the suffocating death, and survived.

---

[1] As an aside, it is worth noting that people tell stories about singers who "give everything away." That is, they keep no property for themselves. You used to hear stories about this rather frequently. With the pressure, jealousy, and bickering you often see over valuables, this makes a great deal of sense to me.

Everyone needed to find a reason, an explanation for the death of some and the survival of the others. The children who lived said that lightning had struck nearby at the moment of the cave-in, and that they'd seen an old man lurking about. They hadn't exactly recognized him, but they'd seen this shadowy figure. People went and looked and said they'd found moccasin prints. You hear this sort of thing a lot, stories of mysterious strangers, obscure figures. This is how skinwalker stories begin. In a few years people will talk about the moccasin prints changing into wolf prints, and perhaps later of the man being identified and suddenly dying. But some people also had thoughts about the surviving children causing the death of their cousins. It wasn't yet talked about, but the thoughts were there.

I knew these children, particularly the children who died. They came to my house more than the other people. Children are attracted to new things, to oddities like a white man living on an Indian reservation. I gave them books, and my daughter and this boy and girl played together.

Their mother was one of the old man's daughters; she and her husband were in their late fifties. The children who had died were their last born. But it was the children's older sister who had really been their mother. She was in her thirties and hadn't married. This by itself is very unusual in this setting. It was very likely that she never would marry. She had a very bad congenital hip which made it improbable and quite likely impossible for her to have children.

Most middle-class Americans have never seen an adult with a congenital hip disorder. It's one of those tragedies you feel real frustrated and sad about. This is why the pediatrician grabs the baby's thigh and aggressively rotates the hip. He's feeling and listening for a click in the hip joint. If he feels it, it can be fixed. So in the world served routinely by modern medicine, congenital hips don't exist, or when they do, the strong presumption is that someone has made a very bad mistake.[2] On the reservation, they are relatively common among those over thirty.

---

[2] Ken Salce tells me that about 15 percent of congenital hips cannot be detected by physical exam alone.

So these were really her children, her family. She had always been on the periphery; perhaps it was her physical deformity, maybe it was just the way she was. She only really belonged through and with these children. By being their "mother" she was more connected to and had a more normal and central place in the rest of the family and in the community. In kinship-based societies, this is how you belong. They had been her family, and she was now alone and without them. She had been a good mother and, as would any good mother, she blamed herself for what had happened to her children.

It is said that tragedy brings out the best in people and brings them closer together. This may be true somewhere, but I am more used to seeing the opposite happen. What had been bad became worse. What had been hidden, albeit poorly, became visible. The parents of the children who died and the parents of the survivors had been jealous over who had the best of certain kinds of property. People started to think of these bad thoughts as contributing to and even causing the deaths.

For the Navajo, bad thoughts are very powerful things. We think of thought and action, and mind and body as different sorts of things. For the Navajo, they are not separate at all. Bad thoughts are bad actions and they produce more tangible bad occurrences. So the prior jealousy and bad thoughts were taken as the cause of death. And of course the bad thoughts, the sadness and the anger, that had come with the death of the children were a part of and the beginning of another sequence. Things were being said, not just secretly, but they were beginning to be said in the open around other people. Words and thoughts were getting very bad.

Then there was the old man. He was very sad, but there wasn't the desperation in his sadness that was present in the younger people. This, I suppose, is a part of wisdom. I think that wisdom means the recognition of being a part of a grander process, a larger whole, and with that realizing one's own insignificance relative to that whole and one's own powerlessness over that process. He wasn't angry either. I'm not sure why, but I think in part it is because anger is based on the belief that a process is subject to the will of, or control by, man. You get angry because you couldn't or didn't control what happened; you feel it is your fault, that you should have been more careful, or paid closer attention, that you should have known what was going to happen. I think that the old man accepted that the grander process wasn't to be controlled but to be observed and contemplated. Perhaps this was why he rarely performed ceremonies anymore.

But his children and some of his grandchildren didn't have the same equanimity. And a part of their anger was directed toward the old man. Not only were they lacking in riches, but he had not been effective in protecting them. He was not powerful enough; he had not taken proper care of his family. They didn't say this to the old man. But he knew it was being thought and being said. He'd done enough ceremonies among enough different families that had experienced tragedy to know how people thought and what they whispered . Plus, the old man always seemed to know people's thoughts. If you were a Navajo, you would accept the truth of this; as an Anglo you tend to try to explain such things in a more naturalistic way. For me, the old man knew.

A number of the men in the family started drinking heavily. It meant fights, yelling, anger, fear, noise, and visits late at night. It made a time that was unpleasant quite a bit worse. But I suppose it was a distraction, something to momentarily get your mind off the children and provide a focus for the anger. One of the uncles, the oldest, was something of the leader in this. We'll return to him later.

The children were taken to the morgue at the Indian Health Service hospital. Perhaps they had to determine "cause of death"; I'm not sure. The practical reason was that the weather was warm and the morgue was refrigerated. It took several days to arrange a funeral and a burial. Traditionally, Navajos did not dispose of their dead the way we do. So a funeral is always, in large part, an Anglo phenomenon; it never quite fits the context, and in this case it fit especially badly.

The funeral was at a graveyard on a hillside above a beautiful canyon with water and huge cottonwoods, the greenery and water of a desert canyon. This is one of the most splendid places I've ever been. The weather was clear and sunny, and the ground was still soft from the rain. I guess this is ideal if you are in the business of burying people.

There were quite a few people there, around a hundred. The

old man and his wife were absent, and generally there weren't any very old people. It is said about the Navajo that they are afraid of the dead and there is a level of truth in this, especially for the older generation. But in this dislike for corpses I must be a Navajo and so must many of the people I know. We all stood in the sunshine in the desert in the beauty above the canyon. There was an Anglo man there who did what you would call the service; such things are Christian by definition. I should qualify this; they are the worst kind of religion that passes for and calls itself Christian.

He sought me out and talked to me before the burial. My daughter and I were the only other Anglos there so that is probably why. He must have assumed that I was a missionary; he was close. On the reservation away from the towns you are either a missionary or an anthropologist. One zealously tries to bring about a change that matters, the other zealously tries to preserve tradition. Both want things to be different than they are. He told me that "they" had burned down his church; when you do this to a missionary you confirm his basic premise: a good missionary is to varying degrees martyred. They are unhappy without difficulties. Anthropologists, on the other hand, are in the habit of vehemently hating missionaries. You are supposed to feel this anger. The plentiful availability of missionaries (especially Mormons) keeps you from getting angry at natives, or at the tragedies that are part of a less-than-modern environment.

The children were in boxes made of wood; for me there is a horror in small coffins. They are an image I can't get out of my mind even though I avoided looking at them as much as possible. There were lots of plastic flowers on the other graves and there were some standing ready to put on the graves of the children. The missionary spoke. He said that those who were fortunate enough to be baptized would have a wonderful afterlife in heaven, but for those who weren't, bad news in hell. And he went on and on about this. The big finish was that fortunately the children had been baptized. (An aside: maybe this was true and maybe it wasn't. The Navajos I lived with and knew were, above all else, pragmatists. So they wouldn't avoid baptism if it was convenient and if there was some immediate benefit. Similarly, if they needed to lie about it to get the services of someone to bury the children, they would have done that.)

Of course, all of the people present had relatives who had died and weren't Christians. So I was furious, and naturally I was sad. I thought it was the missionary causing this, but it was the situation, and he was just an all-too-convenient object. I told him off, and then I went into the brush and cried.

The final bizarre touch to this whole business was when the brother of the children opened their coffins and the people flocked to see the bodies. I in my cowardly way avoided looking. Afterwards he asked me if I didn't think that the children looked good. He'd more or less been in charge of the arrangements, so maybe it was his way of showing that he'd done a good job. I suppose also that people rush to see what is taboo. We then all took turns shoveling the dirt into the hole.

One other thing happened that was important to me, but maybe to no one else. The mother of the children, whom I didn't know very well, made a point of telling me that she'd put some of the things I'd given the children into the coffin with them. These things weren't much, but she told me how much they'd valued a particular book, a coloring set, and other things. That really finished me off; stoicism isn't my strong suit.

When it was done, we went back to the parent's house. There was a great deal of food for everyone who had been at the funeral. Some had driven several hundred miles. We all ate and talked. I've been to funerals in rural Anglo USA and it's very much the same. The missionary came driving one of those Dodge Maxivans, which shortly before had been the children's hearse. And he was the only person there who was treated less than courteously. No one was rude exactly, but people tended to avoid him and not talk to him.

The children's brother, the one who had done the arranging, asked me what I thought of the funeral. I told him it was fine, but that I didn't care for the minister. He said it was no big deal, they'd just needed his van to carry the bodies. Idealism again demonstrates its irrelevance in a world that demands practicality. I wonder if the missionary suspected that his limited success was a function of the vehicle that he drove. He should have suspected when they burned his church but left the van untouched.

No solutions, other than the disposal of the corporeal aspect of the children, were provided by the funeral. The family members were more divided than ever. The cousins of the children were having problems; it was natural for them to feel guilty and responsible since they'd survived, but their aunts and uncles also felt that they were to blame.

The old man became more and more withdrawn. You'd see him sitting in the sun, quiet, often weeping.

Around this time two things happened. The first took place four days after the children's death. Their uncle, who worked with me, and I were sitting outside the house where I lived. It sat up on a small knoll, a little higher than the surrounding terrain. You could see the old man's house, about a half a mile away, and the children's house, about three quarters of a mile distant, as well as the other family members' houses.

We saw something unusual, unique, something we'd never seen. There were twin whirlwinds, and they danced around each other, danced with each other. They started at the house of the children and then they followed the path to the grandfather's house and then the path to my house. They lingered for several moments at, what seemed like, each destination, and then they went off to the north and dissipated.

When they first came into view, I knew that it was the children. And I also realized that I had been waiting for them. Ten years later, I still know it, and I am still grateful for their visit.

The other thing about this is that it coincides with how Navajos think about what happens after death. Whirlwinds (we usually call them dust devils) are an aspect of the human spirit. It is said that after four days the spirit, or really "the wind that stands within," returns to one of the cardinal directions.

A second thing happened at about this same time. It was decided to have a Native American Church (NAC) meeting in the camp. The old man's youngest son had belonged to the church for about a year. The family didn't like this. For some of those who believe in what they call the traditional Navajo religion, the Native American Church is a newcomer and counter to tradition. This antipathy is less common today than it was, but you still see it. The church is also quite commonly seen as wrong by the Navajos who are fundamentalist Christians. Those who believe in the NAC view it as a return to a more conservative form of traditional religion, one that was originally Navajo, but that was lost for a while. It is also Christian, and this is given a greater or lesser emphasis, depending on the practitioner.

This son had been quite successful since belonging to the church. He'd gotten a job that paid well, he was driving a new truck, and had been able to buy a few head of cattle. It was his children who had survived the cave-in. The parents of the children who died and their brothers and sisters had also decided an NAC meeting was worth trying.

In a way this was a statement to the old man. Here he was the old one, the powerful one, who could no longer protect his family. They needed an outsider and they needed something that wasn't part of the old way, the traditional way that he knew and practiced. But none of this seemed to bother the old man. Pride wasn't something that was very strong in him anymore. He knew his children were angry with him, but you couldn't see this affecting him. I think that wisdom is acceptance.

The meeting took place in the children's home. It was a hogan, the eight-sided, usually log, traditional Navajo dwelling. There were other more comfortable and larger rectangular houses in the camp, but they simply would not do. In addition to being the Navajo home, the hogan is the church, where the religion is practiced both on a daily basis and at the times of the big rituals. During that period and in that area, use of the tepee for Native American Church ceremonies was infrequent. Today it seems that the tepee is coming more and more to predominate.

The old man and his wife went to the meeting, as did everyone else in the camp. There were also quite a few people who lived nearby and other family members who came from quite a distance. One of the things that I remember most vividly is how tired we all were. We were exhausted. The children had died; they'd had to be buried. There was all that preparation along with the sleeplessness that is a part of death that is not your own. People say you stay awake as a part of grief; I think it is more out of the fear that accompanies the acute awareness of your own mortality. We would be up all night in the meeting and would probably not sleep the next day. The effect of the peyote and the meeting can take a while to subside.

The road man, the person in charge of the meeting, was from about one hundred miles away. A little while into the meeting, after the preliminaries, he spoke to the people present. He was very delicate; he didn't mention names or point fingers. He spoke abstractly, metaphorically, even poetically, so that what he said was more meaningful than if he had been blunt. When someone speaks this way, you feel that he is talking to you personally. We all took what he said this way, as directed at each of us individually; there was an intense individual and collective intimacy in the shared meaning of this ritual and as a part of that in the words that he spoke to us.

He didn't speak of the death of the children; he spoke of their mother calling them back. Their mother is the Earth, Earth Woman and Changing Woman, the heart and the essence of the Navajo way. In NAC meetings, this is also a reference to Mother Peyote. Their placement in the Earth had been their return to her. This wasn't a bad thing, although it felt bad to all of us. But it had come about because of events that were taking place on the surface of the Earth, on the body of our mother.

These things were happening between brother and sister and parent and child, the kind of jealousy and thinking that was going on. Their mother had heard these words and been offended and she took the children back to her. These were the kinds of words and feelings that didn't belong between people, let alone in a family. And they were unnecessary; if people led their lives correctly there would be enough of everything for everyone. There was no reason to fight among themselves.

And another thing: there was some thinking, even some talk that the children had done this to each other or to themselves. This just wasn't so. Someone else had been around, been at the place, when it happened. It was someone that everyone knew, that they had known for a long time. It was someone who had been jealous and had bad thoughts against the family for many years. He had been there. But there mustn't be retaliation against this man; that isn't the peyote way. Through the belief in and the practice of peyote, it would be as if a barrier against harm would be built up, the family would be safe, protected, behind this wall. The harm intended against them would be deflected and it would return to and ultimately cause misfortune to the person sending it. But if the ugly thoughts and the jealousy persisted within the family, the barrier would weaken and the ugliness from without and from within would do its work.

Then the meeting went on, and there were songs and prayers and the taking of the sacrament. The message of the road man was repeated many times, in many different ways, and became a part of all of us. And then, late at night or very early in the morning, the children who had died came into the meeting and spoke to us.

They said that they were all right and that they were in a beautiful place: a place with running water, blue skies, plants and game—the dream that desert people have of afterlife. They were happy and at peace. They wished that their brothers and sisters, their parents, aunts, uncles, and grandparents would get along. Then they said personal things to some of the people present. And then they left and said they would not return again.

At dawn the meeting ended and we ate. I went home and tried to sleep, but of course I couldn't. Later that day and over the next several days I talked to the people who had been at the meeting. I was trying to understand something in my terms, which meant that I needed to impose some sort of a naturalistic explanation on what was essentially spiritual. In the world of social science this is what you are supposed to do. You distrust and even deny your senses and impose an always less-than-adequate rationalistic explanation; further, you know that it is inadequate while you are doing it. The paradox in this is that you alienate yourself in order to belong. At those times that you feel things the most strongly, you are placed intensely in between something called the native and your colleagues. At these moments you deny the native by trying to understand him in the language that your colleagues will accept, and you are exquisitely alone in the hope that after your fieldwork you will be accepted.

All of us at the meeting had shared the same experience, but the experiences had not been identical. We'd all heard something a little different in the words of the road man and we'd all had a personal experience of the children that could only be our own, a product of each person's private knowledge of and experience with them. So the experience had been collective, but it had also been personal.

I don't know that I believe in ghosts or in anything spiritual that continues for very long after the death of the body; I just don't know. I do know that a person's presence continues after his body dies. A part of this has to do with his existence in the minds of others. A large part of each of us resides in the people who knew us and who cared about us.

Before we went into that meeting, we needed to be healed. Any resistance to or ambivalence about this was pretty much gone by the time we went into the hogan. The children were still alive for all of us, but this couldn't go on; the cost of keeping them alive was just getting to be too great. And with the acceptance of their death there was a great need for each other, to be a family.

In order to keep them alive, everyone else had to be kept apart. It was necessary to be angry at and to blame each other so that the children wouldn't die. In the process of doing that, everyone became more and more separate, and the more separate they became the more desperately they clung to the children. The isolation grew worse and worse the more their death was denied.

You can see this with people who never get over the death of a parent, or a lover, or a child. Their lives stopped when that person died. And they never again connect with anyone, except to blame them or remind them that they can never replace the one who is gone but eternally present. As in, You will never be the man my father was, or the child that your brother was, or the lover that she was.

Contrary to what happens on the evangelical TV network, healing does not occur simply because someone puts his hands on you and proclaims you well; even if the proclamation is said loudly and in the presence of whatever deity you happen to believe in. Healing instead involves a sequence of events. A healer has a knowledge of the timing of the sequence, the ability to manipulate, ever so slightly, that timing, and an awareness of the factors that matter in the context of healing. This knowledge and ability is what makes one person look like the magical healer and another just a person who tried his best.

This particular road man understood all of this and he understood enough about the particulars of our context to know what to do. The reason that people don't get over a loss is because they keep it vague and incomplete so as not to experience the intensity of what they feel, so as not to lose control of what they have left, their feelings. They refuse to talk about the loss, or they discuss it one-sidedly; they are only sad or only angry and not both. So, in any kind of ritual of grieving, you first have to make the object of grief tangible. You bring the object of the grief back to life and then you bid it farewell; that is what ritual is. And that is a part of what happened here. I think that an understanding of context makes the magical possible. I don't mean to deny the magical nature, but magic doesn't just happen; it requires an intense understanding of the human world to be possible.

And the other part of the process is, of course, those who are left behind, the ones who didn't die. And this is more difficult. There is too much that has happened, there is too much remembered for even the most sophisticated Band-Aid to fix. The road man seemed to create a scapegoat outside the family to externalize the cause and the problem.

But there was more to it than that. When the road man talked about the man outside the family, he wasn't saying that here was an evil person. He was saying that ugly thoughts and feelings and talk were the source of what happened. So for those at the meeting he had created a classic dilemma. They agreed on blaming the outsider, in part because it absolved them and in part because it gave them an object for their feelings. But in the very moment of acceptance, they must also accept their own blame and responsibility for the same sorts of feelings, thoughts, and talk for which they blame the outsider.

Always there is an offer you can't refuse: to place it elsewhere, to put it outside yourself. To have to carry it with you is unbearable, so you gladly make the deal. But by doing so, by placing it elsewhere, the responsibility for those feelings and thoughts that made the other man culpable are squarely back with you. The wisdom of the healer is this: it is only by the acceptance of your responsibility for a tragedy that you can do anything to change those feelings and alleviate that burden. And the healer must, in some way, trick you into this. No one will accept responsibility just because someone says so; it just doesn't happen.

People avoid feeling responsible in two ways. The first is total denial of blame: It wasn't my fault, it was someone else's; or I did everything I could to prevent it. The second way of avoiding the responsibility that you feel is to take all of the blame. This is the more clever strategy, the one we miss. Good people do this all the time; it allows them to continue appearing good by feeling inordinately guilty in a way that others can see.

Their feelings are always on display. Those around them will surely try to convince them that it wasn't their fault, at least for a while, until they tire of constantly hearing it. Either way, it is the nonacceptance of what is truly your own. And the acceptance of your sin is much more painful than these two means of avoidance; the potential gain is that by facing it, you can get better, you can heal. The games go on forever.

In addition to what this externalization of cause did on an individual level, it also produced a change in the family. By putting blame on the particular person, that mysterious stranger the road man was alluding to in the meeting, he was also placing it back in the family but in a different place than it had been before. He took it away from the old man and put it on his oldest son.

The family and that other man had been close some thirty years before, so close that the oldest son married the man's daughter. The oldest son moved into his wife's parents' camp as was the custom. But after only a few days, he came home. His family pleaded with him to return to his wife, but he wouldn't. This was something that people wouldn't talk about very freely; it was one of those secrets, those shameful things that you tried to forget. And since you couldn't forget you tried to hide it. Something else shameful had happened between the couple and between the families, but it was never mentioned.

This had started something between the families: an ongoing process of conflict that was occasionally expressed in angry words but usually was acted out ritually and spiritually. The old man was a singer and so was his adversary, and they used their power against each other, or that is what people said, and they fought for those thirty years in this way. And during this time the family had seen this as the ultimate (although not always as the immediate) cause of the various misfortunes that had befallen them.

And over those years the oldest son reminded them that he was the cause of their problems. But it wasn't only this one thing. The oldest son continually gave them reason to feel this way towards him. He was a drunkard, and when drunk he was violent and a thief. But he stayed around, he lived with the old man and the old man's wife. And when trouble came, they thought of him. They also thought of him during the brief moments when there wasn't trouble as they waited for misfortune to strike.

Of course, depending on how you looked at it, you could have seen his misfortune as having an external cause, something bad was being done to him. But generally this isn't how he was looked at.

So the road man's "cure" was based on the nature and history of the family; it transformed what already existed. The emphasis was placed on a long-standing rival who was an outsider, and this at the same time placed an emphasis on an insider who would always be apart; it emphasized the thoughts and actions of that outsider and, here again, was a commentary on the thoughts and feelings in the family. This was the glue that at that particular moment, and cyclically at other moments like it, diminished the divisiveness.

Momentarily certain thoughts diminished. No one really thought very much about the old man or his powerlessness, or about whether or not the childrens' cousins had done wrong, or whether the other family members had caused harm through their jealous thoughts. Scapegoats don't change reality; they distract one from it and, here, they join people in their grief, their sorrow, their anger. They make the abstract concrete, and in this ritualization they make the sorrow manageable.

But in the death of children the most that one can hope for is to manage, to get by, until the feelings diminish. Their oldest sister, who had really been their mother, was comforted very little. During this process she was for the most part out of control and unmanageable. People will try to tolerate this for a while, but when they are barely making it, they won't be able to put up with it for very long. And after the funeral and the peyote meeting you just want to try and forget, and you avoid the people and things that serve as reminders. She was always potentially there to jog the memory, and people started to avoid her. Momentarily with the death of the children, the rest of the family tried to include her in the process, momentarily she was a part of things. And then she was the reminder of what was, and we started avoiding her. She had been on the periphery before, but she had had the children. Now she was without them and without, pretty much, anyone else.

She'd gone to a Christian church before all of this happened, not particularly regularly or with any enthusiasm, but she'd gone. The particular church was an evangelical mission whose pastor was a Navajo in early middle age. The church was like an old-time Navajo family, or at least what people say these families were like. They lived near each other; they shared property; they did everything with one another; they were this large family of people only barely related by kinship, but who were brothers and sisters, the children of God the father.

They came to her after the death of the children and they spent time with her. So here she could belong, and in belonging to that society she became even more distant from her own parents; they weren't a part of this family in Christ. The old man understood, but she was even more distant from the rest of that family. But she now belonged to the family at the mission, and, more important, she had her own family, her own children back. Because of course they hadn't died at all; they were living everlasting life. How could she resist this? And if she lived her life right, she would join them. Last time I saw her she was making the effort to do just that. For me it seemed terribly empty, betting on an afterlife. I hope that she wins her bet.

AFTERWORD

Not so very long ago I went back to where the children were buried. I wanted to check my memory, and to check some other things, especially whether the graves were kept up. I wanted to see whether or not the children still mattered to anyone. I guess that they did because there were some relatively new plastic flowers there, and some glass jars set into the earth which must have held fresh flowers not too long ago. This is a bit odd; Navajos don't generally like cut flowers. But someone had been there and had been coming there for all these years.

There were two new people in the family plot: the father and an older brother, who had died in an accident while drunk. Their graves were kept up too, but not as well as the children's. I'm sure that it is the older sister who continues to care for her children. She has since gotten married, to another Christian. There are no children. I didn't see her, but I know what that relationship must be like.

I noticed that many children were buried in the graveyard— not infants, but children between two and fifteen, the age of hope and expectations for parents and family. Again this is odd. The only relatively frequent cause of death in this age group is accidents and violence.

I can never make sense out of the death of children, nor can I feel anything other than an immense continuing sadness. Although this seems natural to me, there is a strangeness in it. Why, after all, shouldn't children die like everyone else? My feelings, my reaction, assume that there should be a justice or a fairness in such things, a benevolent force governing things.

The children I had known were buried with possessions that seemed unimportant or trivial, but that made their graves immensely personal. For the boy there was a book, a Navajo autobiography done in the thirties that he liked, given to him, of course, by an anthropologist. For his sister there was a set of colored Magic Markers that she liked to draw with. Putting these in the boxes with the children made their deaths ultra real, as contrasted with the jewelry and the made-up corpses of the Anglo funerals I have attended, which make the deaths so very unreal.

I was looking for an article on something in a quasi-academic journal and came across a brief report written by an archaeologist in the thirties. This was before it had dropped out of fashion to rob graves. In those days you could do it in the name of science. The person talked about two Navajo children's graves she had examined. There were a boy and a girl, both about two, in small pine boxes. In the hands of one was a candy cane, and in the hands of the other was an all-day sucker.

There is something about this that captures one's thinking beyond any sort of objective description. Two-year-olds are so much more real than infants. Somewhere between two and four may be as real as we get. They are completely hope and potential. They can move on their own and get into things and every day they learn and display new things, new words, new looks that make them seem more and more human and very distinct, strongly expressing their personalities. They are happy most of the time, manipulative in getting what they want. They are very alive.

In societies where children die with some regularity, this is the age that you begin to have more hope than fear. If they make it to two, they tend to live and you hope more; you give them names, buy them things. You do a variety of rituals that are focused on creating and establishing their character as future adults and that reinforce their place in society and in a group of relatives.

They die and you put them in a box. What would you put with them? Something they liked, whatever they liked. It wouldn't be much; they don't have much. A doll and a piece of candy they liked. It would be something they sought out when you were in town or at the trading post, something that they knew the location of in the store and would go to and let you know they wanted. And because you were hassled or didn't have money, or because you didn't want their teeth to rot, or because you were an adult and they were children, you would mostly say no. And of course they would be sad and maybe cry or get angry, typical kid stuff. And the next time you'd go through the same thing. With my children it is always gum.

And when they were dead you would remember each and every time you said no, for their own good, so that they would become good adults with things like healthy teeth. And of course they weren't going to be adults so you had done the wrong thing; they were only going to live for two years and you should have given them whatever they wanted.

So you would put their favorite thing in the box with them. Why? You would do it because you had to do something and there was nothing else to do. Like the Neanderthal man who was found buried with the wildflower bouquet in his hands.

I was recently in a remote part of the Navajo world, climbing down a trail that the Hopis came up after having been born of the earth. I was looking for different things that convey the meaning of this place. Places have meaning, and some people can recognize that and create rituals and sacred places to regulate that meaning.

I came around a corner on a narrow ledge and under a small overhang was the grave of a child. The bones were eroding out of the soil. At first you ask why and how; of course there are no answers or, more precisely, there are many answers. But with this, the whole trip, being in this place takes on a certain melancholy. You want to do something, rebury the bones, not have the child washing down the slope in pieces, you want to preserve and keep him and not have what is left of him disappear. Stupid really—he is long gone—but there is an unwillingness on my part to accept that, to accept that a child has died.

There was nothing to do really. I wanted to stay there with him so he wouldn't be alone. But in the moments I was there, his stillness made me feel very alone. And when you are by yourself in a remote place that is full of power and meaning, you don't want to be that intensely existentially aware. In these places you have to perform, do the work so that you survive, and an intense existential crisis can get in the way of this. Such insight is best left for carpeted and heated rooms with electronic distractions.

I left him some gum and moved on.

7

LOTTIE AND CARL

When I was a child, the bums near my father's warehouse spoke to me the loudest. The adults tried not to notice them, but you could see that it didn't work. My father's age mates had been adults during the depression and no matter how rich (and supposedly secure) they got, they remembered that time. It shaped them and their children; they came to believe in hard work, but they also believed in chance and in luck. The message of the bums was that luck could turn, riches and success could vanish. And it could happen to anyone. We thought of these down-and-out people as very much like us, much closer than we think of them today. Some were people that my father had known; he would tell me the story of their fall. Red Skelton would always close his TV show by saying good night to his friends at Third and Howard, the heart of San Francisco's skid row. It was one of those serious jokes.

I worked in warehouses in that part of San Francisco. I'd walk from the train station at Third and Townsend either to Mission Street or to Folsom and Main. I'd take kids' sorts of shortcuts, which translates to mean that they were never any shorter but they were different. The trails led through the vacant space under the freeways and the on- and off-ramps to the Bay Bridge. The bums lived there, under these concrete roofs. They kept the rain off, but it was always dark and seemed cold.

They lived in settlements, subdivisions with houses of cardboard. Ten miles away the more affluent lived in the little boxes (on the hillside) that were the topic of a popular song of the day. Some of the people under the freeways were friendly; they'd say hello, sometimes they'd ask for money, or an extra sandwich from the lunch I was carrying. I wasn't afraid in this; I wasn't especially brave or naive, it was just that they weren't particularly dangerous.

What impressed me the most were the societies and families that these people created. A few women lived there, and they always coupled with a man. Living with the couple was usually another man in the role of uncle or brother or even son. When I walked by in the morning, these families would be sweeping out the cardboard houses or building a fire. They'd accumulate the discards from the warehouses and stores in the area. As with other Americans, these people were acquiring things.

The message to me in all this was the persistence of the social, the need for others, the sense of family. Very clearly this was the nature of man. I didn't like seeing and knowing this. I didn't see it as hopeful or as indicating anything grand about the spirit of man. It was sad: our need for others under any circumstances. The families I knew and was attempting to grow up with were not happy; children see this very quickly and accurately. So I liked to think that living outside society or living alone was an option. But seeing the families under the concrete made me think otherwise; they were very convincing.

There was also a lastingness or constancy to the families I knew. They persisted over and through time, without any change that mattered. There were no divorces; they pretended there were no deaths. The grimness of their togetherness was not just momentary, but eternal.

As I grew older I spent less time in the world, looking at it and trying to make sense out of it, and more time in classrooms, listening to someone talking about what someone else had written that the world was like. I began to forget the world and accept more the categories of experience that we are told describe it.

At some point I professionalized this and didn't look at people and their experience at all, but at groups or classes of people and classes of experience. When I did this as a social scientist, I said that it was to understand; when I did it as a clinician, it was to diagnose preliminary to trying to change the experience, the symptoms, of the other person.

Today the bums of my father's day don't exist. They are the homeless. We should feel closer to these people than my father and his peers felt to the skid row bums. They are very similar to all of us. They are people with families; and the hard times they experience very often are not of their own doing. But instead, we have placed a huge distance between them and us.

We establish this distance through an epistemological trick. We create a category, the homeless, and we gather and then cite data about this category. And then, based on the data, we create programs. These objective descriptions of categories produce a feeling that we know something about these people, while at the same time we don't really have to look at or otherwise experience an actual person or family who is having hard times. We hire others to do it, create agencies and government to absolve us of responsibility. We create distance where there should be affinity. And this speaks to the reality of the times, the ways we have learned to think about others. We now have a class of people and we possess knowledge about that class.

I remember a grand rounds in a hospital where I used to work. There is a patient sitting on a slightly raised stage in front of a small amphitheater. The seats are filled with white, starched people, two of whom stand at the front with the patient, who is robed in a color other than white. For me this made her stand out; to the rest it seemed to make her invisible. On the wall in the front hang the X rays and scans of various sorts, back-lit photographs of the patient.

They are talking about her. No, they are talking about her disease. No, not even that, they are talking about the back-lit pictures of the disease, although they think they are talking about the disease. So they are (at least) two levels of abstraction removed from the person and from what the person is trying to say. And as they talk about those pictures there is no mention or notice of her sitting there. If it were a movie, and I were the director, I would make the person in the wheel chair begin to fade. I would either make her gradually invisible, or I would make her transparent, and as they talked more and more about the pictures (the boys and girls in white call them pictures) the appropriate parts of the transparent and otherwise invisible person would become back-lit and visible.

Invisibility and transparency are different. There is a safety and protection in invisibility. People glance at you no more often than they glance at air, and they are not looking through you really since there is no knowledge of your presence. Transparency is different; it is experienced as having people look through you, as having you not matter or of having your existence be trivial or unimportant.

Like the lady in the amphitheater. She is trying to tell these people something of importance to her. She hurts, or she is afraid of death, or there is something not right with her and she needs to know something about it or to have it go away. The white, starched ones don't listen to this, they look at the pictures. They have taken her message and made it into something else. They are asking about meaning, about what the pictures and the clinical presentation mean; but they are taking her message and making it into something else. They have disqualified her. And in the act of doing that, of translating her message into theirs, they have missed the meaning and missed the opportunity to learn something about meaning in the abstract.

CARL AND LOTTIE

The summer I first went onto the reservation, I kept thinking about those cardboard villages with their concrete skies and the people that inhabited them. It wasn't because the Navajos were poor; I was a student and poorer than they. In fact they gave me the free USDA food they didn't use. You don't really have poverty until someone creates and imposes that concept on someone else. Otherwise, you simply don't have any money.

What brought the past back were the same sorts of things that had impressed me thirty years before, grimly persistent social things. What was strange about this was that I'm sure that one of the reasons I'd left the urban for the rural, and the high tech for the low, was to find something different, to discover something hopeful and less grim. People who actually knew how to have relationships and who valued them.

What I found instead was that the grim messages were harder to ignore than they were in the city. In a city they are confined to places you don't visit, and when you stumble on them you are programmed to ignore, to walk quickly by without even a glance. In the rural they are a part of and mixed in with the things you normally pay attention to; and if you are in the social science business, you are programmed not to ignore, or to ignore with difficulty. You are supposed to pay attention to what makes you uncomfortable and transform it into the understood. You make sense out of it and you can stop being uncomfortable.

There was one couple in particular. I first saw the woman as I drove over a rise that limited her camp, really that bounded her world. She didn't look up as we approached, but she stayed with her task, picking up the small pieces of bone and dust and whatever else she privately saw surrounding the hogan. She had been at this for thirty-five years, so there wasn't much left. She could no longer look at wholes, at landscapes or at skies, she only saw detail and that which was beyond the sight of the rest of us. The larger pieces of debris that had appeared around her house in the last ten years were invisible to her; her focus had become smaller and more private.

She no longer saw what the rest of us knew, took as real. Perhaps she had never shared a world with the rest of us. Somewhere she had decided that if she found the right detail, perhaps the right piece of dust or bone, she would have her answer and her life would change. The rest of us think this way, that if we only find the right answer, the right lover or job or investment, life will be okay. But most of us have learned to camouflage our obsessions. As a people we believe in the rather odd notion that correct answers, good choices, bring quality to life, rather than believing that the approach, commitment, or passion with which we live is what matters.

She dressed the way old Navajo ladies dress—full satin skirt, velveteen blouse, tennis shoes and socks. Spider Woman's white cotton thread for the hair knot. Completely typical.

Combined with the completely odd. Her legs were bandaged in rags, and under the rags were strips of inner tubes that she used as pressure dressings, like Ace bandages made from old tires. She had the same apparatus around her waist. It helped with but did not totally alleviate the pain, she said.

But I think it served another purpose as well, as a reminder of her boundary and of her existence. When she had the pressure on her skin she knew where she left off and the world began. Pain is another reminder of existence, for some people it is their only awareness. Like biting your tongue or pinching yourself to make sure you're there at difficult moments. I hurt therefore I am.

The final element in the first impression was the Parkinson's-like tremor in her hands and her head. We could see this even from a distance as we drove up.

After we were there for a few minutes, Carl rode in on a bony white horse. The middle-aged man I was with looked like he was getting ready to run down the road. He was terrified. My companion knew that Carl was a witch and a werewolf.

Navajos have stories about were-animals; they call them skinwalkers in English. These are humans who wear animal skins and perhaps even take on animal forms. They can travel very rapidly at night and harm others. These stories are told around the fire late at night to frighten children.

The same stories are simplified and told to Anglos, especially anthropologists and missionaries. Just as the adults love to frighten children and the children scream no meaning emphatically yes, so the adults and especially the adolescents delight in the reaction of the priest and the ethnographer. There is disbelief on their faces but they are too polite or too professional to say so. The children shriek and laugh at their own terror; the missionary talks about evil and Satan and is very satisfied in the knowledge that the Navajos too have stories confirming their existence, thus validating his own view of the world. The anthropologist takes notes and feigns respect for what is for him superstition; the polite label he assigns to it is "Navajo belief." He pretends to listen, but he has already dismissed the stories by relegating them to the realm of culture. The teller is describing not belief or culture but a world he knows as true.

Carl personifies these stories. He is the essential skinwalker. The first impression of him, and the one that persists years later, is of a powerful presence. But it is difficult to remember the details of his appearance.

Part of his strength was an arrogance or aloofness. He stood back from the world of humans, creating the impression that he was above or otherwise outside it. He seemed to dominate through indifference. I think that this is what the skinwalker idea is about: someone having a strong essence or core, combined with a relative indifference to external form. Just the opposite of most of us, who emphasize the external, prop up our appearance, so as to hide and distract from the internal doubts or insecurities. Or maybe power dressing for the Navajo is wearing a wolf skin.

The terror of my companion was typical. People were extremely nervous around Carl. It was striking to watch. When I wanted to visit him, the people I worked with would use every excuse to avoid going there. Then they would use a medicine to prevent harm. When they were in his presence, they would pretend to be friendly, but if he had so much as coughed they would have been running down the road.

The fact that Carl was thought of as a witch and/or as a skinwalker wasn't unusual. Navajos say this about anyone except their parents and siblings, and they might even think it or say it about them occasionally. Different extended families have fairly long-standing rivalries that are expressed in terms of witchcraft accusations; it is one way Navajos argue. So this sort of accusation can be one of those grain-of-salt things.

But Carl was different. First off, no one would say anything about him unless they were many miles away, felt themselves ritually protected, and were pressed or were drinking. Second, everyone thought of him this way. Carl was not easily placed into any of the groupings of the community. This was unique, because the factions were nothing more than groups of relatives. He was related to everyone, but only with great reluctance would anyone claim him. Further, he seemed indifferent to the social strife in the community. I guess he was only interested in himself and again this made him odd in a society that was primarily socially and not individually oriented.

People wouldn't look at him directly, nor would they spit around him or use the outhouse in his camp. They didn't want to leave anything of themselves behind that he might use against them. This is one of the ways that the sorcerer accomplishes his magic. Something tangible that represents or is a part of you is harmed, and by means of that you are harmed. Additionally, for the Navajo, words and thoughts are tangible things.

For Carl, external form was something to be played with. This fluidity and changeability implied a certain arrogance about his being and identity that did not hinge simply on the external. Lottie was exactly the opposite. She encased herself in butyl rubber and rags because she was unsure about her own boundary, she was afraid of dissolving, coming apart, ceasing to exist. This attempt to maintain her form was an intensely serious business, not the play it was for him. With the inner tubes, the rags, and the obsessive ritualization of everyday existence, she attempted to maintain her physical integrity. And the maintenance of her physical self was the maintenance of her illness.

People who are alone don't have questions about existence at least not very strong ones; people who are alone in relationships have the strongest, most frightening doubts. Carl and Lottie were alone together; and when she needed to feel less isolated, she would do something to upset him, to penetrate his veneer. When someone is aloof or distant or ignores you, you find ways to get them to react. I make them angry, therefore I am. This is what Lottie wanted and got from Carl. He would try harder not to get upset. The more he tried to stay aloof, the crazier she got.

What is disturbing in viewing this is that we all do it. If we want attention we will give up a part of ourselves to get a reaction. The more extreme we get, the more they pull away, and so on. It always escalates. Maybe in thirty years we will all look like Lottie and Carl, or maybe we will just give it up and watch TV all day.

This couple was frightening and odd in the absolute, not just as members of another culture. For their Navajo neighbors this was expressed as fear of witchcraft. For me it wasn't fear of witchcraft, but of something else, something I find much more terrifying.

The first part of this is the tangible reminder of the grim persistence of the social, back to the cardboard houses with the families. I thought I had forgotten what I knew as a child, but I had simply found enough distraction momentarily to not have to think about it. Another part of this was the hopelessness in what I saw. This was a situation that would never get better. It would always be the way it was during the moments I saw it. Carl and Lottie would each make certain that the other would never change.

But beyond these generalities, what were these people saying? What was their message? What were they communicating? Lottie's strangeness, especially, transcended culture. She made no more sense to Navajos then she did to Anglos. But she got people's attention; a shout with no other apparent meaning.

But this in itself can't be. People learn the language of illness and craziness just as they learn anything else. And idiosyncratic messages are created in an attempt to avoid saying something.

And in avoiding that particular word or symptom or message, the meaning, the part that is left out, is conspicuous. An omission, something that should be there but isn't, is the clearest statement of all, and it is the one that is impossible to ignore. You are always looking for the missing piece, listening for it. The one shoe drops to the floor in the apartment above, and silence. In the house next door the couple fights every night, and one night it is quiet. The sentence without a period

MEANING, PART ONE

CULTURE

In a way, the rest of this is an experiment in the creation, or the removal, of meaning. There are various ways in which Lottie and her symptoms can and have been explained. The question is whether or not these explanations make her communication more or less meaningful. Of course I already know the outcome. The beauty here is that we don't need to ignore the unpleasant messages in the world; we can pretend to listen and excise what matters through interpretation.

The initial attempts at understanding belong to social science. The first of these is cultural, specific to anthropology. Lottie is a Navajo Indian. Anthropology attempts to make sense out of her message by looking at her as a member of that class, or some would say nonclass. It is a little tough to say what it is about Navajos that makes them Navajos. Fortunately her membership in the class has been decided. She has a census number given by the tribe. Of course the tribe is a governmental entity created and imposed by Washington on God knows what basis. But no matter.

Lottie has a very public secret. She had sexual relations with her brother when she was thirteen. Everyone in the community knows this, although it is unclear whether or not Lottie knows that they know.

Incest is universally a very public secret. Always, everyone in the family will seemingly be trying to keep it hidden, and always there is something to bring the family into the public eye. Usually it is a mysterious, very flashy symptom in one of the members that no one quite understands. Like a very good daughter who keeps getting caught shoplifting. When you first see this, it is very puzzling. How can this be? you wonder, and no one really can tell you. Her family, everyone, seems completely mystified. The symptom makes no sense; here again there is the noise, but no meaning. And as time goes on, it usually gets noisier.

Anthropologists, psychotherapists, and Navajos are fascinated by incest, but there are important differences in the quality of their interest. First, when Anglos talk incest they are usually referring to that between a father, a parent-generation male, and a daughter. When an anthropologist or psychotherapist discovers it, he thinks he has an explanation. Navajos aren't so naive. They know that there is nothing that has a single answer or that is unicausal.

For Navajos the concern, almost the preoccupation, seems to be with brother-sister incest. This is curious. The association here is with pathology, on the one hand, especially seizures and insanity. But the other association is with fecundity, the very power of creation.

In the Navajo universe the beginnings of everything are in the primeval man and woman or, more correctly, in an abstract maleness and femaleness. This pair brought life to various equally abstract beings. Wherever you choose to begin, this pair were brother and sister, and of course they embodied creative power.

This power continues today and its expression is in the creation of wealth. Everything in the world is divided into male and female, and everything increases through reproduction. The example that would be the easiest for us to accept is the sheep or any livestock; the more offspring they have, the wealthier one becomes. But other valuables are thought of in the same way. Jewels are described in prayer as increasing through reproduction, as are fabrics or manufactured goods, as is everything else.

Exceptional wealth and power brings accusations of witchcraft. And incest is always a part of witchcraft. Your child or sibling doesn't belong to you; he or she is born for others, to be married to other clans, not to your own. In exceptional wealth and unusual power there is a selfishness, a refusal to share and/or taking too much. It is the same selfishness as with incest, the sexual use of what belongs to others.

And danger is the companion of this power. The danger

comes not from the act itself, but from not having the knowledge to control the power. Inadequate knowledge results in sickness. This illness or other misfortune is not a punishment from the gods for moral transgression. But this is true for any sort of effective knowledge; danger is the other half. Power and danger are twins, brother and sister, two who necessarily follow each other.

Incest is implicit in many of the stories the Navajos have about their gods, or in any religion for that matter. It is talked about symbolically, usually metaphorically, or it is assumed. You have to know something about these stories, often a great deal, and the way they connect to each other before you can see this. I've never been sure whether this was something people kept hidden and secret, or was simply obvious to anyone except Anglo anthropologists.

There is one story though, a part of the chant Mothway, that has brother-sister incest as its very overt theme. The various gods talk about how it would be a good thing if those that were brother and sister have sexual relations. With this, there is a generalized discussion of intimacy and comfort and how nice all this will be. This is one of those fairly universal human themes. The comfort of the womb, the family, and the danger of marriage. But as with all stories having this theme, Mothway goes on to talk about the ultimate necessity of intimacy with others, of marrying those that are unrelated to you.

The story focuses on gods described as butterfly people, but in addition there are other beings around. So these various deities prepared beds and slept with their siblings. They woke up and were embracing each other talking about how good they felt and everything seemed fine. Fires were lit later that day and those brothers and sisters who had slept together flew toward the flame; they behaved like moths. When the fires were put out, they acted crazy, like they were drunk. Some of those who had been incestuous were the beings that animated mountains, and they would look at their sibling and burst into flames. In some accounts this explains the existence of volcanos. Nice association.

At this point they set about trying to repair the problem they have created. And they talk about how to go about it. Interestingly they use knowledge and ritual derived from hunting and from the wild animals. This means that the incest is part of and associated with the power of the wild. A way of thinking about this is that it derives from a time when the people lived by hunting. A time when they traveled about, and when there were shamans who were possessed by various powers. The newer religion superimposed on this is more about domestic things. And the knowledge is learned, not a result of possession. So with incest and its treatment there is this association with extreme power, the wild and the very, very difficult to control.

In Mothway these gods sing over the various incestuous pairs, and they are cured. The way I interpret the cure is that it creates a revulsion in these individuals for sex with their siblings.

In anthropology this is how you go about creating meaning. You find a person or a group doing something odd, unusual, or otherwise interesting and you show how it makes sense. You say this is the sort of thing that Navajos believe and this explains why Lottie is a crazy, shaky lady. We can even interpret her tremor as mothlike; her neighbors in fact make this association. Full-blown seizures would be better (they are more typical for these situations), but the tremor is pretty good. Craziness is also a part of Mothway and of brother-and-sister incest, and Lottie is clearly crazy.

In the act of interpretation we have also disqualified Lottie: we have taken something very personal and we have made it generic, saying "This is the sort of thing Navajos believe." In a way this is true, but it is only half true. Because ultimately what they believe, the belief that rests on top of all the others, is that people communicate in very different, very personal ways. If you want to understand, you need to pay attention to these differences and respect them. You lose the meaning when you group messages under generic pseudocategories.

As a part of this understanding we have used culture to provide a reason, a cause, for Lottie being ill. We can further invoke it to explain her reluctance to seek traditional treatment. The orientation of Navajo healing is etiological. Therefore, the goal of diagnosis is the discovery of that etiology, and the goal of the subsequent treatment is to correct the cause.

The most common form of diagnosis, and the one that would be used here, is hand trembling. This is another one of those very magical, very pragmatic things. The spirit of the Gila

Monster possesses the diagnostician as she sits with the patient. The hand trembler's right hand and arm display anything from a slight to a dramatic tremor. This can be seen as another throwback to the old religion, when the shamans were possessed by the spirits or powers of the world.

But magic that works must also have a very practical component. The hand trembler is known by and knows the local community. So although her diagnostic practice has a spiritual basis, she is an expert on the social world of her patients, as well as being an expert on society generally. Effective healers and cause finders know about the world of man. In understanding their magic, we need to know this above all else.

Hiring a diagnostician is a step in the healing process. Overall, a way to think of this process is as transforming what was very private into something quite public. As one moves from the diagnosis to enlisting financial and other aid for the ceremony to having the ceremony, one is involving increasing numbers of people and making the problem and its cause known to them.

Incest specifically can only exist as a private, secret sort of thing. Making it public creates a contradiction, directly undermining a key element in the pattern that allows it to continue. Rarely was this information an absolute secret to begin with, so the hand trembler's diagnosis often serves to confirm what the patient, family, and extended family suspected all along.

So this woman, the hand trembler, would sit over Lottie inside a hogan. She would hold her hand over her and it would tremble or shake.

At some point the hand trembler would identify a cause or more likely ask certain questions about real-world things that she has seen or imagined symbolically. Sometimes the symbols are traced into the dirt of the hogan floor. The diagnostician is looking for beginnings, not just the beginnings in Lottie's life but the beginnings in the underworld, in the Navajo stories of the past. The prototype descriptions of what animate beings are capable of. Then she looks to the lives of the parents, especially when Lottie and her brother were growing inside the mother. Then to Lottie's past and to her present.

We tend to think of this as we do our own diagnosis, as the search for a single dramatic precipitant, the germ that caused this woman's craziness and her pain. And having discovered that, there will be an inoculation that will destroy the pathogen and make her well. I think this is a mistake, not just in looking at the Navajo but in application to our own world.

The stories provide a template, a standard, through which Lottie's life and the lives of her parents can be ordered and understood. They describe the range of emotions and behaviors that are available to humans; they describe the range of the possible. Everyone in the world has stories like this, about the pattern of the universe. Anglo stories involve molecules, or stories about economic trends, or theories on developmental psychology. But all these stories describe those features of the world that matter, that are relevant and that must be paid attention to. We all try to describe and understand any particular instance in terms of the more general order described in our stories.

The diagnostician, as well as knowing the community, is an expert on pattern recognition. This in fact is the essence of diagnosis, the ability to abstract the common and the general from the details of any particular event. For the Western physician and for the one who listens to spirits, diagnosis is a search for beginnings, the prototype event that caused the current problem.

For the Navajo, committing to traditional treatment is committing to this search, and it is committing to these beginnings being discovered, known, and made increasingly public. You can't lie to gods whose essence is knowledge, nor can you lie to their agents.

A treatment is implied by the diagnosis. These range from the brief use of prayers and herbs to ritual performances that take from one to nine nights. A problem as severe and persistent as Lottie's would involve one of the big guns, a ceremony. The ceremony is an expression of the stories of the people; thus it re-creates the prototype pattern as well as the specifics of the patient's particular situation. Ceremonies are impressive events, and they cost a great deal of money. People may travel several hundred miles to attend them.

The ritual takes us back to the beginning. The beings, who originated in the underworld, return; sometimes they are masked, and they dance and speak and sing as they did then. There are sandpaintings; incense is burned. The whole thing is very magical and very intense. When you write about such things, it is primarily an intellectual exercise, but the experience is primarily emotional, visceral. All of the senses are enhanced to create this experience. The invocation and dramatization of the past bring the sense of connectedness of one's current experience through all time. The healer is working to create this experience on the part of the patient and her family, the sense that something tangible and therefore alterable is occurring.

In all of this there is an affirmation of the patient and of her experience. There is a statement that what she is experiencing, her pain, anger, sorrow, has been experienced before. That such things have existed since there were thinking, speaking beings. In these rituals one does not go directly to trying to alter the patient, but time is spent on listening to her and accepting the legitimacy and importance of what she has to say.

At the same time, the rituals are concrete and practical. Although, as with most other distinctions, this is not the way to look at it. For a person who lives in a religion, there is no distinction between the magical, the clinical, and the pragmatic. They are part of a single whole.

The sheer work involved in organizing a ceremony functions to heal the social problems that are always associated with illness. Herbs and other medicines that Western physicians regard as pharmacologically effective are administered. And the symbolism and re-enactment of the ritual makes an illness that was previously vague and unmanageable into something that is real and tangible enough to be manipulated.

The mere commitment to the ceremony involves another even more public disclosure of what is wrong—not just with the patient but with her family and her extended family, especially those living nearby. It is not like being privately naked and anonymous in the doctor's office.

It also involves getting financial and social help from these same relatives and neighbors. Society, momentarily at least, takes on a new structure. The large group of people work together towards a common goal, the resolution of the problem. The everyday and usually long-standing conflict and strife are put aside and occasionally even healed. This means that Lottie's family would have to be committed to the treatment and accept the consequences of whatever disclosure it brings.

Those who are connected to the ill person would also expect her to get well. Having a ceremony implies a certainty that the the ritual will transform the person from a patient back into a person. As a people, we Anglos do this social part very poorly; we make the fundamental mistake of viewing illness as residing completely inside a person, rather than as being the individual's way of communicating with the world around her.

These same two sorts of things must happen in all healing. First, the vague and subjective is transformed into something very concrete, initially by diagnosing—merely labeling the experience. And later in the healing/transformation process this continues. The more concrete and more tangible you can make the vague, idiosyncratic experience, the more you are able to transform it into something else. This is what ritual is about, making the intangible exquisitely real and then manipulating it. The second thing that must happen is that society must be altered. People must expect the patient to be transformed, and they must participate in the transformation.

For Lottie and for incest, the correct ceremony would be Mothway. People say that there is no longer anyone alive who knows this. I am always suspicious of statements like this, primarily because I have always found them to be wrong. In books on Navajo religion, you commonly encounter such statements; they say that so-and-so was the last practitioner of a particular chant. And then thirty years later, you travel to some part of the reservation and find six people who know it. Or you find the ritual contained within a larger ritual. So you can use a part of this larger one as a substitute. Kind of like generic drugs.

Jerrold Levy, an anthropologist, talked to an older woman who said that she had Mothway performed over her in her youth. She told him a really strange story. And it is difficult to know whether or not it was because she was a strange woman (she was), or if it is a strange ritual. Perhaps the treatment for strange people is strange ritual. The woman and her brother were sung over together, that is, both were patients. At a certain point in the ceremony, a kind of fence of blankets was put around them and they were told to have sex behind the blankets and presumably out of sight of those present, while the chanting continued.

Viewed purely in terms of the logic of treatment, this is very elegant, but I doubt that this would be done in a ceremony. It is too much like the stories of witchcraft, too much like the behaviors that people try to hide. So all in all I think the strangeness of the woman says more about the account. I think this would happen symbolically but not literally; sometimes people confuse the abstract with the concrete.

If Lottie wants to keep her secret, seeking out traditional diagnosis and treatment is not the way to do it. Additionally, if there is a reason for her to continue being ill, the traditional process is also something to avoid, for it will force her to clarify her meaning, to transform her vague and ambiguous messages into ones that are quite clear and understandable. A part of anything not changing is that it is always too vague to grasp; when you think you have it, it becomes something else.

This whole thing, Lottie's story, would make a good article for an anthropologist to write. We've got incest, a crazy, sick woman, and Mothway. Everything fits together very nicely. It is also the sort of story that Anglos like to believe: a youthful victim who is permanently damaged. Fortunately it is not a good enough reason to be sick your entire life. One of the reasons that victims of incest stay sick forever in Anglo society is because of the fascination that the healers have with it. Staying sick because of incest is a way for the victim to keep the healer's attention and to keep people relating to her as a victim.

As we said, Navajos have a similar fascination, but they tend to be a little more practical in their assessment of cause. Lottie's neighbors allude to the incest, but they don't see it as the cause. For one thing it is too remote by itself; for another the secret is too public to hide so rigorously.

And ultimately the fit between cause and symptom simply isn't good enough. She is still sick in a way that Navajos do not typically get ill. And a part of this lack of fit is of Lottie's own creation. She keeps things fuzzy and ambiguous, and by doing that she eliminates the possibility of resolution. To understand this, we have to remember that the ambiguity is in the communication, not in the disease. All illness is idiosyncratic and ambiguous, but we learn to communicate symptoms relevantly and precisely to a healer so that we have a chance to get well. If we muddy it up, the illness continues. Her neighbors are aware of the fact that Lottie is keeping it unclear, and they know there is a more abstract meaning in the ambiguous communication.

MEANING, PART TWO

THE SOCIAL

A second way of explaining, creating, or doing away with meaning in the world of humans is social. Here we don't look at a person in isolation but in relationship to others. And we look at how what she is doing or how she is communicating "works" or functions or fits. This way of looking at things is not owned exclusively by anthropologists. Sociologists do it, as do family therapists, as do others.

We start with Lottie and Carl's relationship, how they fit together to form a single entity, and then look at what that entity communicates to the world it inhabits. Carl controls and intimidates everyone except his wife. When she babbles in his presence, his general distance and aloofness evaporate and you can momentarily see his disgust and his anger. He wants her quiet, but he is trapped. If you are a powerful person and a Navajo, you can't express anger directly. It simply isn't allowed; it shows that you aren't powerful at all. At least one other person can control you by getting you angry.

Carl's whole being is involved with creating and maintaining the illusion of mastery. He is the magician, the shadow figure. If you offend him or anger him he will say nothing, just smile and walk away. But then you will wait for something to happen, and when it does you will know who caused it. Carl's essence is spiritual power, and Lottie says to him through her action and her illness that his power is inadequate. Her sickness is a public statement of Carl's impotence.

Witchcraft is a label that is attached to ongoing relationships that are conflictual and competitive. The adversaries trade volleys of, usually, spiritual power back and forth. Depending on where you stand, one is the aggressor and the other is only acting in self-defense. Who started things is, of course, never very clear, and since these battles go on for years and even for generations, the waters become even muddier. However you punctuate the sequence, if you are labeled a witch, your opponent is trying to harm you. If your knowledge and therefore your power are adequate, he will not succeed. If you have multiple adversaries, there will be multiple attacks.

The man of power is usually not harmed, but often those close to him are. It is common to see members of a singer's family who are seriously ill or experiencing other misfortune. The cause is viewed as the adversary's attacks. But the more immediate and important cause is the failure of the man of power to protect those close to him. Lottie's illness is a statement to and about Carl: "You are not powerful enough," and "What people say about you is true." There is also a suggestion that Carl might be the one more directly causing the illness.

Witches, by definition, care about power. And the struggle for control is the basis of the relationship between Lottie and Carl. People who care about dominance tend to spend time and effort on those they can't control, not on those they can easily master. So Carl stays interested in Lottie, and since most people are more successful at ignoring her, Lottie likes the attention, even if its foundation is rage.

You see this all the time with chronic illness. People always want to control the other person's symptom, usually to make it go away. But the power remains in the persistent symptom. The symptom is all the more powerful because we view it as something that is not subject to will or volition. Therefore there is never resolution. That which is the most out of control is always the most powerful. People are always trying to make an alcoholic stop drinking or cheer up someone who is depressed. The alcoholic or depressed person is thought of as out of control, without power. But through the symptom, he controls those around him, absolutely. The more it persists, the more the powerless demonstrate the impotence of those trying to achieve mastery.

Lottie speaks to a larger audience as well. She makes the universal accusation, "How could you do this to me?" both to Carl and to his adversaries in the community. They may direct their bad thoughts and feelings at him, but she is the one who pays. Some shame and embarrassment for allowing this to happen and to continue were also felt by Lottie's relatives in the community. Partly this was because of their own bad thoughts, but more importantly it was because they were afraid to confront Carl.

Carl was reluctant to have any sort of traditional healing endeavor. He would have to be involved in it. He would be taking the risk of having the finger pointed at him and the opinion of the community corroborated. A part of the community healing that would have to occur before a ceremony could take place involves these long-standing difficulties that Carl has with his neighbors. But if he doesn't encourage a ceremony, the community will also take it as evidence that he is a witch. They will say that he is afraid of being found out, of being discovered. They will also say that he is stingy, too cheap to pay for a ceremony, which is really a part of the same accusation. Witches are, by definition, selfish. They care more about personal wealth than they do about their family.

The hand trembler knows all this, and if she does her job properly, she mentions all these reasons. She may say it very directly, or she may be more abstract or symbolic. You can have a ceremony without complete disclosure, but the treatment will, by definition, be incomplete. You hear this given as a reason in hindsight for an illness getting better for a while and then returning. Incompleteness, a part missing in the diagnosis and/or treatment, is why an illness "keeps coming back."

A true healing, resolution, would involve the past, a transition from being an incest victim to one who acknowledges control or responsibility for her life. Lottie controls, as do all victims, taking no responsibility for their power, speaking instead through their symptoms. It would also involve the context being made well, the community getting together and putting the past aside to effect a cure. And it would involve Carl becoming different. When you mobilize and transform a society in this way, the healing has already occurred. The ceremony is simply the after-the-fact, public statement of what has taken place. It says, "Lottie is no longer ill, so stop treating her this way."

There used to be a psychiatrist from Madison, Wisconsin. His colleagues called him Nutty Carl. For some this was affectionate, for many it wasn't. He was seeing a family from a small Wisconsin town that had a schizophrenic adult son. At a certain point, he held a town meeting where he announced that little

Johnny was no longer crazy and could be expected to behave and be treated like everyone else in the world. Both John and his family had little choice but to change. Their world would no longer tolerate their illness and failure. Nutty Carl must have stolen this from the Navajo; it is exactly the same sort of thing as a traditional ceremony.

I am impressed with the wisdom in this approach. It treats what is essential about man, that he belongs to and communicates in society. If you change how that society acts and, hopefully, thinks, then the one who is sick changes. Simple really. Of course, we don't do this any more; we think it is all inside the person, either biochemical, genetic, or mental. And we keep trying to impose our will on that particular phantom. We have better and better machines to look inside and we think that if we get the right X-ray or scan or blood test, the right photograph of what we cannot see, that we will have the answer. It doesn't matter that we haven't found it. Our particular compulsion, addiction really, says a better machine or a more elaborate test will finally give us the right picture and we will be able to act on it. You can see how this works when Lottie interacts with modern medicine.

MEANING, PART THREE

MODERN MEDICINE

On the Navajo Reservation you find modern medicine in the form of small mission hospitals, occasional private practitioners, and, most commonly, the Indian Health Service. The IHS is free to Indians, and the care is pretty good, although it is not perceived that way. Most Navajos would say that you get what you pay for.

Lottie is a trouble case for physicians in general. She comes to them asking for help. But when that is attempted, she says, by not getting better and occasionally more overtly, that they aren't helping her. Although the details are different, the themes of power and control are still the basis for the relationship. The physician wants to help, to control the illness, the pain, or the patient, depending on your point of view. And Lottie asks precisely for this, but it never works. The symptoms continue. Physicians really hate it when a patient demonstrates their impotence; they despise it when the powerlessness of their paradigm (the medical model) is demonstrated week after week, visit after visit.

Of course they don't say this; they talk instead about the flaws in the patient or in the treatment setting. And the patient's time in the waiting room grows longer. They hope she will leave, although they are probably unaware of this and they certainly wouldn't say it. But she persists like a winter cold or a recurrent unwanted thought; that is her essence. The little bent-up, crazy old lady who excels at the creation of impotent rage. When Lottie enters the exam room, they are embarrassed, in part because of the wait and in part because of their dishonesty. Especially at the hypocrisy of being caring people who are very angry. You are supposed to feel compassion, not anger and rage.

The history of Lottie's treatment by modern medicine is stereotypic. At the back of her chart is a very long "medication list." It lists the drugs that have been prescribed for her over time. Two types of drugs fill the pages. The first and predominant set are the "nonsteroidal anti-inflammatories." The prototype and still the gold standard for these is aspirin; Motrin is another that is now sold over the counter. But there are hundreds of them. Drug companies market these more aggressively than any other class of drug, claiming that the nuances of their particular flavor is the best. Why? Because there is a market. Americans want to feel better without side effects, without cost.

They are typically prescribed for pain that no one understands. Lottie had between thirty and forty of these prescribed to her over a period of time; none will work, or they will work a little but have such severe side effects that she can't take them.

The second group are the antidepressants; again there are hundreds of these. There are two rationales for their use. The one is that her pain is a "symptom of depression," and if you treat that disease, the symptom will go away. The second rationale is that in smaller doses some antidepressants are used as analgesics. Doctors "know empirically" that this works, but no one "yet" understands the "mechanism." I apologize, but doctors actually do talk like this. They can't simply say that they are playing around randomly, trial and error, that they don't have a clue. It is always this pseudorationalistic bullshit.

The time line for each of the meds is relatively brief. She will take them for a while, typically not as prescribed. One way she will vary the instructions is to horde the valuable medicine, using it only when she is desperate. If she used it as prescribed, then she wouldn't have it when she really needed it. At some point, she may discontinue the pills on her own, saying that they didn't work or that they made her sick. And she will ask the doctor for "stronger medicine." For Navajos, and many Anglos, the strongest medicine is a shot. The old general practitioners knew this and would oblige with something like vitamin B-12. Younger physicians, those just out of training, in the beauty of scientific medicine, the dangers of masking pernicious anemia, and the barbarism in the GP's empiricism, will never engage in this sort of chicanery.

And since in Lottie's time the overwhelming majority of IHS physicians are just out of training, they will not resort to these sorts of placebos. They will instead alter Lottie's meds with medicine that they think is real. They will see from the list that she has never been "compliant," that she has never taken her meds as instructed. For physicians the remedy for "noncompliance" is a lecture to the patient on how important it is to take the particular drug as prescribed, perhaps on how it works, while prescribing another drug for the "side effects," and so on. Physicians call this patient education; if something is explained clearly and rationally, people will do it. Strange that this idea exists at all, let alone persists. It never works, never has worked. But more basically these prescriptions and accompanying lectures are about the physician's need to find reason in the world, and to impose it where it is absent or inadequate.

The medicine men go home frustrated on a day that Lottie visits. They are playing her game, trying to convince her to acknowledge their power by taking the drug, and of course she is the master here.

As soon as you see this sort of meds list, you know the story. And you know, as a clinician, that you are in trouble. You are dealing with a hopeless situation. Of course the patient is also dealing with a hopeless situation, but that is another story.

Her chart will also chronicle referrals to psychiatrists, and to pain clinics, if available. None of it will work. Eventually she will be diagnosed as some sort of schizophrenic or other sort of generic psychotic, whatever the current popular hopeless psychiatric diagnosis is. Now something is interesting about this. The medical and/or mental health types don't just say that the situation is hopeless. They obsess and argue about which of the hopeless diagnoses is correct. For example, they will debate the kind of schizophrenia she has, or accept the schizophrenia and debate the presence or absence and kind of characterological disorder. Diagnoses that were fashionable twenty years ago are out of fashion today; so there is always talk of misdiagnoses.

I used to work with a psychiatrist in a community mental health place in Chicago. He would see my patients on occasion. Once in a while, fortunately not too often, he would come up to me after the consultation and he would say, "John, this guy will never be a star."

But what is so bizarre is that medical types don't just say this. They obsess over these truly stupid psychiatric diagnoses. All the labels have the same meaning—none of the people with these labels are ever going to be stars—but the exact label for the particular shade and flavor of hopelessness needs to be obsessed and debated about.

If your particular addiction happens to be control, you resort to illusion when confronted with hopelessness. And this particular illusion is that something is understood and controlled by naming it. The more obsessive you are about labeling and the more detailed the label, the more powerful the illusion.

So far modern medicine treats Lottie as it would any Anglo with the same or with a similar problem, but since she is a Navajo, and since this is the Indian Health Service, there is one more alternative, one other way to label and disqualify her. In the IHS there are staff ethnographers, anthropologists or their equivalent, whose job it is to explain how being Navajo impacts on a particular patient. Such people are thought of as ancillaries and as such they are called in when the real medicine doesn't work.

The anthropological ancillary now helps in reducing Lottie's illness, not to biology or to psychology, but to culture, as we did above. She had an incestuous relationship with her brother at thirteen and this has special meaning to the Navajo, her husband is a witch, and so on. The liberal bleeding-heart physician just out of residency can now reaffirm his basic premise as a caring, sensitive, now even culturally sensitive, person. When he finishes his stint in the IHS and has his medical school loan forgiven, he can go back to his friends in Boston and tell stories about what it was like on the edge of civilization and how much he came to understand.

So Lottie's illness can be classified as belonging to the realm of culture, or to psychosomatics, or to an insanity they can't understand or treat because of culture. Physicians are funny in this way. They pretend to be materialists. But when the patient has an a-material belief system that she believes in more strongly than she does the materialism of the physician, the physician will find labels to disqualify her. Psychosomatic is one, and on the reservation culture is another. If the magic of the physicians doesn't work, they can say that it is a Navajo thing. This is a funny kind of statement. They think of it as respectful, but of course it is simply another way not to take the person seriously.

The entire thing is simply an expression of frustration on the part of these particular medicine men. They are supposed to do something, and they can't. They have the same rage as Carl, and just like Carl they can't express it. They are, after all, caring human beings who don't get angry at patients.

But this is all generic explanation and generic treatment. And Lottie's statement is not generic, but very specific and quite personal. Her symptoms don't fit culture any better than they fit a reduction to biology or to mind or to relationship. Which is to say that you can offer an explanation in terms of all or of none, but you feel uneasy with it. Lottie takes away the levels of abstraction that bring us comfort, our attempts to classify into categories that we think are the same as knowledge. She disqualifies and disallows our disqualifications.

MEANING, PART FOUR

CHRIST

Lottie is a Christian. She belongs to a fundamentalist evangelical church located on the reservation about fifteen miles from her home. Its pastor is a Navajo, and in the traditional scheme of things he is fairly young to hold a position of such importance.

Just as Lottie denies our reduction to the concepts of biology and culture and to categories generally by communicating in a way that is idiosyncratic, so does this church claim that its message is not relative or cultural but absolute and transcendent. They both strike at the foundation of the very attempt to classify. They both claim that their truth is more real than any interpretation.

Lottie and the church are similar in two other ways as well. They are both on the margin of their local communities and they are both quite emphatic and persistent in what they have to say. They are very hard to ignore.

The members of the church are quite adamant in stating that the traditional religion is the work of Satan and that they reject it. But in this vehement rejection, they re-create it. First off, because they imbue everything with meaning. And the symbols are not just symbols, they are real and they are everywhere. As in an Ingmar Bergman movie or medieval Catholicism. When you start labeling something as a symbol or a metaphor, you can no longer appreciate these concepts or understand what the symbols meant to the people who lived within them.

The congregation has also created what amounts to an ideal Navajo traditional society. The members of the church are members of the same local community—they tend to live near each other, socialize with each other, help each other, and so on. They behave as a large Navajo kinship unit should. And just as the traditional religion pervaded people's existence and gave it meaning and structure, so does the church.

The church is very emphatic that what it has to say is absolute. It is *the truth*. It is not traditional, it is not interpretation, it is not cultural, and it is in no way to be viewed as relative. People are very nice about this, but that is how it is. I am not sure why converted Christians are universally zealous. But they always need the badge of fervor.

At a certain point some years ago, the congregation got together and in a fairly dramatic demonstration of faith burnt the accoutrements of the traditional religion. They did this to demonstrate the strength of their faith in Christ and their rejection of Satan. Here again the universal irony of the faithful having to prove that they believe.

At any rate, since everything is a part of the traditional religion and therefore a work of the devil, a lot of things got burnt. It must have been a very impressive fire. Some of the more dramatic items included were jewelry, medicine pouches, and corn pollen pouches. I should state the obvious here: it is a major rule violation to treat these sacred things disrespectfully.

The gods must have been very displeased, because this fire started an epidemic in the community. At one time, I interviewed several hundred people about what must have been several hundred more instances of sickness. And this bonfire was mentioned as at least a partial cause of all the illness.

So of course is it a partial cause, or the cause, or a reason for the exacerbation of Lottie's illness. When asked she denies thinking this, but one has the sense that she is not as firm in this conviction as she claims. Those around her are quite clear that this caused her problem, but of course it is convenient for them to think this and say so. It takes away their responsibility.

The church would of course see it differently. As with all good evangelical Christians, the problem would not be in terms of a traditional wrong, but would be explained, as all things are explained, in terms of a lack of faith on Lottie's part. If she truly believed, she wouldn't be ill. Lottie, you have to make your faith stronger. I know it hasn't worked, and it may have made you worse, but you have to really believe. Just like physicians, they think that if something doesn't work you need to prescribe more of it.

Lottie is a problem for those who believe in a benevolent god who cares about and intervenes in everyday life. If Satan is causing the illness why doesn't the benevolent god do something about it? There are, of course, answers to this question, like Lottie's lack of faith, but the answers aren't very satisfying; if they were, Christians wouldn't need the concept of faith and they wouldn't need to keep propping up that particular construct they call a religion with prescriptions for more belief. If something is true, you shouldn't have to work to believe it; it should be obvious.

By raising this question for members of the congregation, Lottie paradoxically creates a situation where they try to believe more. When you are this sort of Christian, the alternative of not believing, of questioning more, is simply too terrifying; it implies the loss of everything that promises to give meaning. For most, a false promise is better than the void. Not believing simply isn't an option, so the more there are questions the more dogmatic you become. In such religions it is also good to be tested, although they aren't really tests, they are just steps in becoming more zealous. So people like Lottie are necessary for the strengthening of this particular Christian community. But at a certain point the members become annoyed with her, and then they become annoyed at their annoyance (Christians aren't supposed to feel this way) and ultimately at the impotence of their god.

FINALE

Lottie stays ill in a way that can be multiply explained but that cannot be changed. This in itself is remarkable and disquieting. Navajos and Anglos share the belief that if you can discover the cause, answer the question why, then you have power over the phenomenon that results. Everyone can provide a why for Lottie's illness, but no one can change it.

Her audiences differ, but they share the desire for power and control. The way to prove their own correctness, that the world is ordered in a way that gives their own life meaning and direction and that eliminates the terror of uncertainty, is to change Lottie. But she is the only one with any power—the absolute control of the victim, of the powerless. Carl is the fearsome witch whose glance can cause terror, but he can't do away with the statement Lottie makes to the world about his impotence. The church has the power of God to call on and the power of the faith of its members, but God and faith can't protect Lottie from the harm of the traditional religion that is clearly Satan's work. Her neighbors and relatives are supposed to help and to care, but they don't; their hypocrisy and indifference are on display in Lottie. The physician has much more than the power of God or of evil. He is backed by science and modern medicine and all he has to do is make her well or at least better, but he can't.

The anthropologist attempts explanation, pretending that he understands the order in the world of people by defining what it means. This, he says, is cultural; it is the way Navajos are. But of course it isn't. Navajos are any way they want to be. But you can't really base a profession on statements like that.

A part of the persistence and power of any symptom is that the patient has no responsibility for these messages. You couldn't go to her and ask her what she means. Nor could you ask her to clarify a particular aspect of her message. Carl couldn't say, "Are you blaming me for this?" because in the act of asking the question he would have his answer. The physician couldn't ask if she is angry at him, because in the question the reality of his inadequacy is revealed. So people continue to coexist with her, trying to ignore her, trying to avoid her but continually hearing what she has to say.

In our love for understanding and explanation, we eliminate experience by transforming it into something it is not, into something sensible and not too disquieting. A clinician tries to reduce to a diagnosis; Lottie's experience is called schizophrenia or hysteria or both; but clearly these labels are less than either her experience or our experience of her. We are told that a diagnosis brings a potential to change, but that is incorrect. The labels bring control or its illusion to the clinician, but nothing that anyone can change. The change instead is in the clinician; it creates a remoteness from something, someone, he can do nothing about.

Once I watched as the plug was pulled on a fifty-two-year-old woman whose brain had died the week before. She was in an intensive care unit where the only rule is that life must be maintained. All the natives gathered to watch the rule be broken. The woman was separated from the respirator. People don't actually disconnect the plug; they either separate the hose from the machine or they block the hose's connection to the machine while creating another opening to room air. The doctor says, "We'll let her breathe (or try to breathe) on her own." No one at all expects that she will, in fact there is a certainty that she won't. But on occasion they do breathe on their own, everyone is astonished, and all sorts of problems ensue.

We all immediately looked away from the patient and at the cardiac monitor attached to the wall above her bed. At first the beat was normal, then it speeded up, then it diminished, then there were a series of bursts of activity, the heart trying to stay alive without oxygen. The lady gasped, just once, in a final attempt to avoid suffocation. She had no wiring or programs left, but still the one gasp and then the discovery of the absence of that part of her nervous system. The gasp was a surprise, a shock. We looked, just for a moment, away from the monitor and to the woman's face. Disturbing, the doctor had to comment. But then back to the monitor; this is what held our attention. Thank goodness the distraction had not lasted. Then a gradual cessation and after what seemed like a tremendously long time, a horizontal line and a buzz.

The experience of this woman's death wasn't that at all. We could be objective, watch monitors, stay detached. Experience was transformed into an image on a cathode ray tube, another program on daytime TV. After a few minutes someone turned it off and we left. Another version of the transparent woman.

The map and the territory. We could say that the map had become the territory but that wouldn't be right. Because we weren't convinced. We knew at some level that we were missing something important. We knew that we were supposed to feel something more. We still knew somehow that a person was there, and it was her heart that was joining her brain in death.

The very obvious remedy to this is to go back to experience, to let it occur in an unadulterated way. But we don't do that. In fact it simply doesn't seem to be an alternative. We instead try to create more convincing and more lifelike maps. We get so strung-out on this process that we somehow forget the obvious. Like looking away from the cardiac monitor at a dying woman.

Anthropology has its own maps and its own rituals of distraction. When you first start doing something like field-work, you don't know the proper way of going about it. You feel like you are wasting time and missing things. You get very uncomfortable. With some frequency anthropologists go crazy. Some stay that way; most don't. They go back to normal, or as normal as they can be, which is less normal than real people.

As a group, before their occupation became a profession, anthropologists didn't know how to go about discovering any-thing either. So they just went and did whatever it was that they thought they were supposed to do. Some of the results were alive; they said something about people, about particular people and about the person writing the description. Some were unin-teresting and mediocre. In my world the best that you can hope for is to create occasional things that are interesting. But most wouldn't agree. People want a very standard, uniformly good product. I think instead that you end up with a uniform prod-uct; novelty is eliminated. And in the world of ideas, novelty is the goal; you don't want to eliminate it even though the only way of achieving it is extremely nonstandard and wasteful.

To produce a uniform product, a ritual is created. It is like the tests of the physician, but it is called method. Actually it is called methodology. As soon as you have that particular suffix you know you are in trouble. Method is invented, say the members of the profession, so as to make things more standard, more scientific, more accurate. Another way of saying that they want to better capture experience. If you do ethnography right, you can also do it more briefly than did the old-time ethnographers. You no longer have to spend years in the field, you can do the work in the summer between college semesters.

The ritual of method exists, as do all compulsive behaviors, to make the world manageable. The ritual of the clinician or of the social scientist (a term I despise) eliminates people. The clinician eliminates Lottie by making her into something quasi-medical, a list of labels that have no outcome other than to create for the doctor the illusion of understanding. The ritual-ized methodology of the anthropologist is much worse because it claims knowledge as its goal. But the transformation of a difficult but intriguing process into an especially imprecise entity eliminates all possibility of understanding.

The products of anthropology are statements like, "Navajos believe that incest makes you ill in this way," or "A ghost made her ill and she needs such-and-such a ceremony." Anthropologists like to pretend that by saying things like this, by reducing her to their level of abstraction, that they are doing something different and being more respectful than are, in this case, physicians. But, of course, the physician's reduction to the biological and the anthropologist's reduction to the cultural are the same sort of thing. You are taking someone's experience and reducing it to a level of abstraction that makes you think you have power over it. It makes very little difference whether the power sought is called treatment or understanding.

Each time we celebrate our professional ritual, we miss something. We deny and then obliterate a part of the experience. We miss what is being said, the meaning. And when there is a particularly persuasive level of abstraction to power a profession, a great deal is lost.

The most common complaint made about physicians is that they don't listen. And the more one is able to use a ritualized technology, the less one has to attend to and experience the discomfort of the patient. It is important to remember, but totally overlooked, that people seek help because they are uncomfortable, not because they are sick and even less because they have a disease. The ritual of the social scientist is methodology, and the more rigorous it is, the less he hears.

Lottie takes away the comfort provided by the way of thinking, the mind, of the profession. Being denied a convenient explanation, we pay attention, but there is a cost, and that is it takes away the possibility of a cure or even of an adequate treatment. For the treatment of illness is always firmly embedded in a setting and a meaning system that the participants take as real and as deterministic. And the more firmly that you believe in this system, the better it works. Lottie speaks strongly, but she has no choice but to continue speaking.

THE LAST WALTZ

8
THE ROAD

There is a movie made in the early 1970s called *The Last Waltz*. It is a documentary, directed by Martin Scorsese, of the last concert of a band called The Band. It is very funny, although it is not intended to be. But it comes out as being a caricature of the 1960s, rock music, and especially musicians. The humor is in listening to and watching people who are not rocket scientists, and not Mother Teresa, taking the mundane and treating it with pious seriousness.

When I watch it, I am reminded of a group of anthropologists in some sort of public setting, like a meeting or a seminar, talking about fieldwork. There is one scene in particular where one of the musicians is talking about The Road. Says he, "You learn everything from the road." He then elaborates, taking on a posture of seriousness, wisdom, and even wise humor. He talks about the places you go, the sorrow, the joy, the women on the road. "Yeah, they're great," he says, smiling, kind of laughing, making it clear that women especially is what it is about. Then on to drugs and that part of nonexperience. "The road will kill you," he concludes, making the obligatory references to Morrison and Hendrix. "You just have to walk away from it."

Fieldwork is the road, the *tao* of anthropology. Fieldwork would make a poor movie because, if it were accurate, it would depict a lot of nothing, just hanging out, which is what fieldwork primarily is. Hanging around with nothing to do. An awful lot of waiting accompanied by your two companions, boredom and anxiety, two states that you had previously thought were opposed. You get to know trading posts real well, become a devotee of the junk food sold there.

With fieldwork you don't end up on the same road you started on, sometimes there is no road in sight. Often, in a context that requires it, like a book introduction or a lecture, you will explain very rationally and logically the path to your destination, but it is all rationalization even if after telling it many times you come to believe it.

The travel, the movement, rather mysteriously occurs and you are a passenger. There is a word in Navajo, *álílee*. It is used to refer to movement or travel by rapid and often by otherworldly means—by rainbow, sun ray, lightning. You just think about the destination and you are there. Fieldwork is *álílee*. You wake up somewhere with amnesia and invent directions.

I started out rather rigorously studying psychosomatics and illness, and I ended up having conversations with some wise old people about how they saw the world, and what their secrets and the secrets of the world were. I have little actual memory of how this came about, although I can tell good stories about it. But the conversations and the relationships I had with these old people are what matters most about me being there. A part of this is that these people and their ideas brought a change in me, a change in how I thought about and saw things.

At the beginning of fieldwork, I would have dismissed a statement like this as romantic nonsense, which it is; I just don't dismiss it anymore. At the beginning of fieldwork, I would have emphasized the practicality of what I was studying and the good it would accomplish. But the bottom line turns out to be that I care about good ideas and am almost completely motivated by curiosity, which is very impractical.

In order to pursue these ideas you live in circumstances and are a part of events that are different than anything you are used to. And you work and live with some people whom you would be strongly inclined to avoid in any other situation, people like Wallace and Andrew. I don't like drunks and the family difficulties of drunks. I don't like the patterns of use and manipulation that go with the drinking. This is for anyone, not simply Native Americans. But the additional problem for Navajos is that I want them to be perfectly respectable. My problem, not theirs.

In normal circumstances I would avoid Wallace and Andrew. I might be friends with them and be interested in them when they were sober, but not when they drank. And after a while I would find that the two states were part of the same whole, the sobriety and drunkenness blending together. And I would avoid them. But here I lived and worked with them and was friends with them. There is something about this that makes me uncomfortable. There is a feeling of use in being with people you sometimes disrespect and dislike. It matters very little that the use is mutual.

Wallace and Andrew and a few other people were my mediators, my translators. They were able to translate the ideas, to tell me what I needed to know in order to begin to understand. Finding and having this relationship with the translator, mediator, research assistant, whatever you call him or her, is very difficult. You can use very young people; they are the easiest to find, but for a variety of reasons they don't usually work out very well. Often they don't know very much, and in this position they are continually called upon to reveal their ignorance not only to you but to the people they call grandparent. Often their knowledge of Navajo language and culture isn't very good, and it puts them into a really humiliating situation. And they are really of the wrong generation to be politely pushy towards the old people.

The best and the worst people to work with are the forty-five-to-sixty-year-olds. They are the right age to be learning this sort of thing, so it is correct for them to be having these conversations with the old people. And they know the language and a fair amount about the knowledge. But, to overgeneralize, they often have problems including spending the pay that you give them on drinking. So you end up caught between them and their families. You are not just an anonymous employer, you are someone who lives in the community in very close proximity to the people you work with. You pay the man for his work, he disappears for a week, and the wife, the children, and everyone remotely related is upset with you. One of the kids comes over and mentions indirectly and in passing that you might want to give any future money to their mother. Now what?

A friend of mine worked with a man for years and would put his pay towards the trading post account. And this was how the family, my friend, and the man controlled his drinking. This sounds, and is, incredibly paternalistic. But some years later some less paternalistic people paid the man directly and he got very sick from the drinking. He didn't die but is demented and lives on in a nursing home where every day and all day he repeats the only prayers that he can remember. If he stops repeating them, they too will disappear from his consciousness.

Along with the boredom and the relationships, the other very striking thing about fieldwork is the amount of time spent on subsistence activities, things that you normally take for granted, do quickly, and that exist in the background of your life.

We cooked mainly on a Coleman white gas camping stove, sometimes on an old-style but fairly new wood-burning cook stove, sometimes on a fire outside. You need to haul the wood for cooking and for heat. We would drive a distance onto some piñon-and-juniper-covered mesas and gather mainly deadfall. Sometimes we would limb a tree and occasionally cut a dead one down. We used an axe. We didn't cord the wood but would put it up in kind of a vertical tepee, and when we needed fire we chopped up one of the pieces.

We hauled water—in one community from five miles away, in another from about thirteen. You put your water containers in the back of the pickup and then drove to the well, the community water source, located at the trading post, or at schools, missions, the chapter houses. You would wait until the people ahead of you filled up their containers. Usually people used old fifty-five-gallon drums. The worst case scenario was five pickups in front of you with six to ten fifty-five-gallon drums in each. I used surplus powder containers; they held about seventeen gallons. Water is heavy; you notice this when you have to handle more than a cupfull.

Bathing is a chore. Basically you do sponge baths after heating the house and the water. Occasionally you shower at someone's house in a BIA school compound or in a gym. I had a sweathouse that we had built, but that really takes a long time and it is for more than just a physical cleansing.

At the beginning of winter, when the flies were gone, we would slaughter an old ewe and hang the meat in the shed; this gave us meat to eat for a while. Once we slaughtered a goat, but that was awful. She screamed and screamed; it sounded just like a child. I couldn't really eat the meat, kept thinking about how she died. Sheep just lie there and bleed to death without so much as a whimper. Stupid animals really. Summers were harder; food didn't keep, but there was more fresh food about. All very mundane.

There are certain moments that you really look forward to. We had this battery-operated radio and at night we could get one of the stations in the CBS radio network. They had a show called "The CBS Mystery Theater"; it lasted an hour and was narrated by E. G. Marshall. I loved this show; my daughter hated it. She would get scared, but she was proud so she would get angry and cuss me, wanting it turned off. Once they did a Tony Hillerman story, *Skinwalkers* I think; that was really great.

When you are doing fieldwork, you see the difficulty in relationships, the time spent on subsistence, and a lot of the grimness that goes on as getting in the way, as impeding. They are things that you have to put up with and tolerate so as to be able to do the real work, the stuff that matters—talking to the old people and listening to their ideas. Here as with everything else there is a tendency not to accept experience as a unitary sort of phenomenon, but instead to divide it. Generally the division is between the things we want and care about, on the one hand, and the things we put up with or tolerate to get the desired objects, on the other. As with doing work we don't like so as to get money to pursue things and experiences we do like.

But the truth about me and about people like me is that our experience is rather limited; we are awfully naive. Even with something as mundane as subsistence—little connection is seen between plastic meat packages and the death of an animal, wood and heat, water and weight. The experience is always a step removed, more abstract than the thing itself, vicarious rather than actual. It is like going into a wilderness area with a map, paying very close attention to the map, where you are, how to get out, and so on, and thinking afterwards you had quite a fine experience in the wilderness.

Or in being told and in thinking that one is a good citizen if he uses less water. Here conservation is an abstraction based on will power that is supposed to derive from the pursuit of what is morally correct. No will or good intentions are required when you haul water from many miles away; it is the easiest and obvious thing to do.

It is in the mundane activities where you learn to pay attention, to listen. And you have to because there are immediate and tangible consequences if you don't. And with the social, the world of man, it is the same. In the rest of America, we don't have to pay attention, we can retreat to our room and be by ourselves or be alone with electronic distractions. But in living with people in a way that ends up (like it or not) being cooperative, none of this works. In living with, and sometimes within, alcoholic relationships you really learn to pay attention.

There is something else that is a part of this but that is difficult to connect and explain. Somewhere along the line we learn to adapt, to conform, to behave in terms of our reading of other people's expectations. For some, this is in terms of pleasing the other; for others, it is in the form of rebellion. But the expectations of others are the engine, the motivation for both.

In living with these people on the reservation, you also try to adapt. You try to be nice, to be liked, to say correct things. Like "I really respect your religion," or "The government really gave you a bad deal," or "Wasn't Fort Sumner terrible." You think you are being real, but of course you aren't. You are a caricature of correctness—a Doonesbury comic strip. The more you do this, the more people dislike and avoid you. Actually it is more correct to say that they have no interest in you. At a certain point you become desperate and accept the situation as futile. And at that point you operate on that futility, on that desperation, and give up on correctness and just are. In my case that includes such unattractive characteristics as volatile anger and other emotions, and being strongly opinionated and outspoken. The strange thing is that when you stop being a caricature of correctness and start behaving more in terms of yourself, you get along just fine.

The point of all this is that you need the distractions, they are an important part of what you are trying to discover. You need to have the mundane and the necessity of paying attention; you need to learn something about yourself and expressing it; you need to learn what people and what society are like. Otherwise you can't possibly understand what these old people have to say. Otherwise it is only words, only some sort of artifact of something called culture. Not something that is true and that matters.

There are many, many Navajo stories about pursuing knowledge. Come to think of it, I'm not sure there are stories about anything else. Some of these are the stories of a people, the stories Anglos call myths; some are the stories of individuals.

They all involve travel, a journey. In many ways they are like the quest stories of Europeans. The route is never direct and the goal is often unclear or it changes. When you listen to the story there are many incidents that seem like distractions.

For example: My parents were driving me to school in Flagstaff but we had to go by way of Gallup, my sister had some pawn there and we had to make a payment, we also had to sell a rug my aunt had made so as to get the money for the payment. In Holbrook we were real low on gas and didn't have any money, so we had to drive north to my uncle's house, but he didn't have money, but he had gas in his truck but the truck didn't run, so we got the battery from our truck. . . . And so on.

All the stories have these detours, and no one seems able to go directly from one point to the other. It is difficult to imagine what a railroad designed by Navajos would look like. A railroad is probably a totally Anglo idea.

I had spent about a year talking to all sorts of people, becoming more and more confused. And I suppose I was looking for someone to make sense out of the world for me, to explain it to me in such a way that I would understand it (another foolish, romantic dream that I am reluctant to admit to).

Near the end of this year of looking for the wise man on the mountain, I finally found him. I was with Andrew, and we came to this man's house in the spring of the year. He lived, literally, on a mountain. His summer home was a log house by the side of a lake that was in a small meadow in the midst of a ponderosa and douglas fir forest. It is about as beautiful a place as there is to live. It was very exciting to find him and be able to talk with him; you always hoped people like him existed, but after spending a great deal of time looking for them, you kind of gave up hope.

There were the three of us there. I was excited, listening intently to every word while understanding maybe one in ten. And Andrew, who had this great opportunity to learn the holies of his world, was badly hung over, kind of moaning, kind of dozing off, wanting nothing more than to go lie down somewhere. I asked the old man a profound question, I heard a moan with a few words in Navajo which I knew were off the mark. The old man spoke for fifteen minutes while Andrew fell asleep reeking of yesterday's booze. And so it went.

At the time this seemed incredibly strange: the man who belonged here and should have valued this knowledge was more worried about throwing up; the stranger who understood very little and couldn't even speak properly to the wise man was beside himself with excitement.

In those days I thought there was something seriously wrong with this. I think it was because I still believed in culture and categories of thought, not in people and their ideas. So there were Navajos and Anglos, and Navajos were supposed to care about Navajo ideas, that sort of thing. Anglo anthropologists could care about them too, but in a different way, more as markers or artifacts of culture than as thoughts for their own sake.

I just don't see it that way anymore, and this particular man had something to do with that. He had a need to teach. This is complex, but it comes down to him seeing things clearly and in a special way and being very skilled in communicating what he saw. This was his gift. He needed to teach; I wanted to learn.

I was, and to a lesser extent am, a good student of people and of words. I pay attention and I think about things and am a curious sort (ambiguity intended). The old man knew this and that was one of the reasons he talked to me; when people who know things are old, they want to transmit their meaning, what they know to be true about the world, to others. No one wants to die without leaving that valuable piece of themselves behind for others to know and hopefully to pass on to future generations. I was also very brash, very pushy. I wanted to know everything right now. And of course he was in much less of a rush; this was his lifetime, not some multiple choice test with quick answers. So he would chastise me for my pushiness and impatience. But he expected it from someone who was serious about learning.

This is also difficult to explain. There is something rather odd, even paradoxical, about being a learner. On the one hand you are supposed to listen respectfully and remember the past, listen to what was, to tradition or some other conservative body of knowledge. But on the other hand you are supposed to take risks, venture into new territory, and even be slightly arrogant.

The Navajo stories are a part of this past, things to be talked about and remembered, but they are also about how to learn. They talk about young people being warned about certain dangers and being cautioned against venturing to certain places. The young people of course don't listen to the warning and travel to the dangerous place anyway. They manage somehow to extricate themselves from the situation with something they have been taught previously and with the help of others. Or they ask for a certain power and knowledge and are refused, but they come back and either keep asking or resort to some sort of trickery to get it. As the story proceeds, they become wiser and less brash. Pretty much the story of mankind.

The old man I first met by the lake wasn't a singer; he didn't do any medicine. In the morning he would pray with corn meal, he'd use corn pollen and mountain tobacco during the day, and pray again to the twilight. These are the celebrations of life, the acknowledgment of what is. Wise people pay attention; they listen and don't tamper.

This man hadn't always been wise. At one time he had done some sort of medicine, but something had happened. This was something we heard in pieces mainly from others; he would never really talk in detail about it. A part of his not speaking about having been a practitioner was that it was so distant. He had grown older and different. When we first met him, he and others gave his age as ninety-nine.

Once we were talking to him about one of the ceremonies and we asked a question about one of the healing prayers or songs, and he said, "I'm not really a singer you should go and talk to my older brother." It seemed very funny at the moment, but of course he was serious.

So we went and talked to his older brother. The brothers were very different. The older one was shorter, more feeble. He had a fifty-year-old wife, which caused a lot of completely obscene jokes. And she would help him get up, help him walk and move about. He had the difficulty in moving that comes with old age. He used a *gish*, a staff or a cane. Navajos have the same parable as the Greeks about what walks on four legs in the dawn, two legs at midday, three legs in the twilight. The older brother's thinking was clear and good and he knew a lot about the ceremonies, the magic, and healing. But he was without his brother's wisdom, while of course his brother either didn't know or wouldn't act on the healing knowledge. Just two different ways of being.

When we went there to the older brother, I would always bring my five-year-old daughter. She would go to the old man and say in Navajo, "Hello, my grandfather," and to his wife, "Hello, my grandmother." And they would laugh and laugh.

It must have been strange to hear this very blond, very blue-eyed little girl speak Navajo so well to them. What she was good at, what all kids are good at, is the sounds; they may not know much, but they sound like native speakers of what they do know.

We would talk to the old man and his wife would cook for us. And while she cooked, she would talk on and on to my daughter, who would listen and smile. And it went on like that for a while.

Most of the knowledge this man possessed died with him; he had no students that cared about much of what he knew. And at the time, there wasn't much of a market for his particular brand of medicine. There are fashions in what ceremonies are used and the ones he knew were out of fashion. I was a poor student to him. I listened, but I sought wisdom, not technique. And what was special about him was the technique he knew and possessed. If he were an Anglo he would have been a surgeon or maybe a cardiologist. He had that same mind set and character. He would go into great detail on the how-to of a particular part of the chant and I would listen, but not really pursue. Wallace would have been a good student, but he was too twisted to be a singer.

These two brothers had not seen each other for fifty years or so. And there was a story about this that we heard in pieces from different places. Sometimes one of them would reveal a piece, kind of accidentally, but they would never really tell the whole story.

It seems that as young adults they used to live near each other and near their sister, who was younger than both of them. The younger brother had a great intimacy with this sister; probably they were raised in such a way that he watched out for her, or maybe they played together. The oldest brother was cool toward her, not angry or hostile, but seemingly indifferent. It is the sort of thing that happens in families, often just because of a distance in ages. One day she got sick, and her sickness was such that the oldest brother knew the ritual to fix what ailed her.

The younger brother called for him to come over to where their sister was. He didn't come and was called again. He didn't come for three or four days, and by then the sister was dead. The younger brother was of course overcome, and he was full of sadness and fury. He told his brother that he would kill him, that he had caused her to die.

He could have meant a lot of things by a statement like this.

And since such statements never get clarified, they always keep their multiple insinuations. He was first saying that the brother's absence, his not treating her, had caused the death. But the statement also implied that he had more directly caused it. I suppose that everyone needs explanations for inopportune deaths, and as part of that they need someone to blame it on. Today Anglos sue hospitals and doctors. The Navajo stories are about *yeenaaldlooshii*, skinwalkers, and about witches.

Singers are always suspected of witchcraft. If they have the knowledge to do sings, they have the knowledge to harm. People who possess power or the knowledge of how to exercise it are always thought of this way, in any society. The knowledge is both desired and necessary, and it is feared. We have this same ambivalence toward our own healers. We think that they are able to save lives and prevent certain misfortunes, but we also strongly believe that they are capable of great harm either through ignorance, laziness, or simply malice.

In the stories the fee, the price, for becoming a witch or a skinwalker is the death of someone close to you. You cause the death, rob the grave, and give the corpse to the others, usually to be used sexually. Incest is also a theme in these stories. Having paid the price for initiation, you are given the knowledge and the power. This includes the ability to live past your time. You use the life force of the person you killed to perpetuate your own life. It also includes the ability to accumulate riches. These stories are about selfishness, being selfish in a world where the one rule is process. They are about transforming this process characterized by generational continuance into lengthening your own life.

When the older brother was accused, he said nothing. In these sorts of stories, the accused typically responds with silence. The meaning of the silence is the meaning of silence anywhere. It is ambiguous; it can mean whatever you want it to mean. You can take it as affirmation, as denial, as anger, as the silence of someone who is preoccupied, and so on. You could say that he felt the loss, too, that he felt culpable, and that he understood his brother's feelings and perhaps welcomed or even agreed with the attack.

Families have these dynamics that they don't like to acknowledge. People at times feel anger and jealousy, sometimes even hatred, towards each other. Usually it is momentary;

occasionally it persists longer. Or one might have sexual feelings towards a cousin or a sister. Such things happen; they are not as unusual as we would like them to be. In the Navajo world, thoughts, especially recurrent thoughts like this, are very tangible things. And these stories about skinwalkers and witches are an expression of the reality of these feelings. Did the older brother have inappropriate thoughts toward his sister? Probably. Did he go to a witches' coven? Of course not. But then I don't really believe in such things, in organizations devoted to evil. For me, the thoughts and the feelings are real enough.

This is where the contrast between the brothers became more striking. Up until that time, both had pursued the kind of knowledge that allows for the possibility of control, or at least its illusion. They had both studied chants and medicine. And I am sure the younger brother had tried to control his sister's process with what he knew; he had prayed, sung, gotten medicine. He would do his magic and he would look very closely and think or say, "I think she is better, don't you?" The way we lie to ourselves about someone who is dying: lying and knowing that it is a lie. And of course there would be these moments of false hope, and then she would be worse, and then death. And of course he would have done everything to halt her movement from life into death. And he would try, as a part of that, to control his brother, to make him come to them and use what he knew.

So you have each brother pursuing one side of the human coin. The one seeks acceptance (if you can seek acceptance) and the other control. The one accepts his powerlessness over human events, and the other seeks power. The one assumes that his knowledge of what is will always be limited and that if he attempts to control something at one point, there will always be unforeseeable ripples somewhere else. The other assumes that if he only knows more, tries harder, he can force his will onto the world. In acknowledging this powerlessness the one brother begins to look at knowledge and understanding differently, trying to understand how the world works, the meaning of it all, looking at the pattern rather than only focusing on the things that he can manipulate and control.

I think the older brother hadn't come over to where his sister had been ill because he was frightened, afraid that he would be unable to help, that he didn't know what to do. And that was a part of his motivation to learn more, to become a better, more powerful healer. You find this same story with fledgling healers everywhere. In childhood, someone who mattered was very sick or died, usually both. And the healer retrospectively wants to do something about that. He has objectified the process of dying, taken the very personal, say the death of his mother, and made it into the enemy death. Then he battles this fabricated enemy. False concreteness toward the process, misplaced abstractness toward the person who died. He made his mother into the abstract death, and death into the person of his mother. Both are incorrect; both create problems that cannot be understood, let alone resolved. All there really is, is my experience of someone I care about dying. There is no entity "death" to be understood—just a loss to be felt, experienced. There is no enemy to battle; we create it so we don't need to acknowledge our own powerlessness.

The brothers hadn't seen each other since their sister died. We offered to take them. It was real nice to see them together, very pleasant. They joked and they laughed. I took pictures of them together and gave them each copies. They stood for the pictures the way my grandmother and her sisters would stand; they groomed themselves, stood very erect and very still, and looked very formally and seriously into the camera. Before the era of snapshots, portraits were a serious business.

The older one got out of the truck with his wife's help, kind of straightened his body out and saw his younger, one hundred-year-old brother. They both smiled and laughed and embraced. Then they started joking with each other. The one would address the other as First Man, then the other would say, "No, you're First Man." Lots of laughter. The essence of old age is knowledge; the personification of knowledge is First Man. We ate, visited for a while, and then took the old man and his wife back home.

One of the more curious ideas in the world is the notion of secrets. One of the things you do in anthropology is pursue other people's secrets. But why secrets? Why should there be ideas that are withheld and only told with great reluctance, and why are these ideas viewed as having such power? I don't know the answer, but have an idea about part of it. It has to do with how people view knowledge and ideas. There are always two aspects to knowledge: the relatively fixed stories about the past and the new ideas. As a people, we tend more to value the new; as a people, Navajos probably at least start with the old, the stories of the past.

You go to the old people to hear these stories. And you need to hear them many times to remember them and to know what variations can occur, and also because parts of the story are withheld. Most of the old people are slow in sharing certain knowledge; they keep their secrets. It is often said that certain things are shared only when the person is ready to die. A part of this is that once you give your secrets to others, you are no longer necessary in the scheme of things.

If you believe in process and in future generations, then in old age you exist, primarily, as a repository of knowledge. When others know what you know, you are redundant; there is no longer a basis for living. I think when people tell their stories they are ready to die. It is not that they are willing or causing it; they are simply ready. And there are probably mixed feelings. I think I will be sad and frightened at death, but I will feel grateful if there is someone who has learned and values my ideas.

For the one who is learning it is the same. You feel excited and grateful for having the truth of the world revealed to you, but there is the realization that it also foreshadows your teacher's death. You want to say, "Yes, tell me your secrets, but not yet," or "Withhold a little bit so that our relationship can continue." No one who is a student ever has any wisdom.

About a year after the brothers' reunion, I left the reservation. Two months after that, during the winter, the younger brother was coming back from somewhere in a pickup with his grandson driving. The old man was sitting there quietly, erect as he always was. When they arrived at the winter house, the old man was dead. There is more of a story than this, because no one would talk about what happened. I don't know what it is. I don't suppose it matters.

A SLEEP AND A FORGETTING

Gregory Hall is the author of *The Dark Backward*, which was shortlisted for the Crime Writers' Association John Creasey Memorial Dagger, *A Cement of Blood*, and *Mortal Remains*. Married with two children, he lives in Bath.

BY THE SAME AUTHOR:

The Dark Backward
A Cement of Blood
Mortal Remains

GREGORY HALL

A SLEEP
AND A
FORGETTING

HarperCollinsPublishers

This novel is entirely a work of fiction. The names,
characters and incidents portrayed in it are the work of the
author's imagination. Any resemblance to actual persons,
living or dead, events or localities is entirely coincidental.

HarperCollins*Publishers*
77–85 Fulham Palace Road,
Hammersmith, London W6 8JB

www.harpercollins.co.uk
This paperback edition 2003
1 3 5 7 9 8 6 4 2

First published in Great Britain by
HarperCollins*Publishers* 2003

ISBN 0 00 651135 X

Set in Sabon

Printed and bound in Great Britain by
Clays Limited, St Ives plc

June's

ONE

That Saturday, just as Catriona Turville had been about to leave the house for her usual morning run, the postman delivered her sister Flora's suicide note.

As she sat on the bottom tread of the staircase in her navy-blue tracksuit, the bright early Spring sunlight shining through the stained-glass panel of the front door and splashing the encaustic tiles of the hall floor with bars and blotches of red and blue, she wondered, while tying the laces of her new, alarmingly white trainers, how long their pristine cleanliness would survive the dog shit which lay in whorls like enormous worm-casts half-hidden by the long grass of the park, and speculated whether the overweight middle-aged man who had been sweating and panting over the exact same route at the exact same time rather too coincidentally for the previous three days, and who had appeared to gaze longingly after her as she effortlessly outpaced him, would get around either to speaking to her or assaulting her, when there was the clatter of heavy-shod feet on the tiled front path, a shadow behind the glass, and the white envelope fluttered through the letter box on to the coir mat.

She had had no premonition of disaster. She unhurriedly picked up the envelope. Recognising the sender from the

1

small, precise handwriting of the address, she felt nothing other than mild curiosity. Her sister rarely if ever wrote letters. But there could be nothing bad, as otherwise Flora would surely have phoned. The telephone was her preferred method of communication. She phoned Catriona at least twice a week, usually for quite long conversations.

Catriona sat down at the kitchen table to read the letter, intrigued as to what news it could be that needed to be communicated in this manner, and quite glad of a genuine excuse to delay her departure and thereby upset the timetable of her fat fellow jogger.

Minutes later, the trivial concerns and inconveniences of London living brutally thrust back to the far distant periphery of her mental universe by the cataclysmic impact of the news, her body numb, she sat staring at the sheets of writing-paper in her hands, the warm, comfortable room at that moment become as cold and alien as one of the moons of Saturn.

She read the letter yet again, its words already imprinted on her memory.

> *The Old Mill*
> *Ewescombe Lane,*
> *Owlbury*
> *Glos.*
>
> *Friday morning*

My dearest Cat,

There is no gentle way to tell you what I have decided to do directly I return from posting this letter. It will hurt you as it will hurt everyone I love and who loves me. By the time you receive this letter, the sister you know and love will be dead.

I've often thought of killing myself but I've never had the courage. But now I have found the drug to put an end

to my suffering and to give me peace. Now I am afraid
only of the loss of the dear faces which have been the only
things that have kept me sane all these years.

I love you, you must know that. And I know you
love me. But somehow, that love has never been enough
to exorcise the ghosts of the past. Terrible things have
happened to us, the memories of which are with us every
waking moment and in our dreams, though no nightmare
could ever be as bad as the reality.

We have never before spoken of such things, have we?
They have spread their darkness over us so thickly that no
light that we could generate would pierce it. Perhaps if we
had talked, really talked about what happened all those
years ago, things might have been different. But we never
did and now we never shall.

I'm not blaming you, dearest Cat. Your remedy is to
endure the unendurable in solitude, and by your power
of mind to endeavour to forget the unforgettable. But I
have never had your strength. I've decided I can't go on
any longer waking every day to the dreadful things inside
my head.

What I am about to do may seem weak to you, but
it doesn't seem that way to me. I'm about to do the
strongest thing I've done, to seize the remedy for
my agony.

Please come directly you receive this. You must be
here to help my darling Charlotte. I need you to use your
strength for her.

I hope it's going to be like one of those hospital
anaesthetics where everything suddenly blanks out like a
TV screen, except that this time there won't be any nurse
to say, 'Welcome back, sweetheart', a micro-second later.

I've chosen this weekend because it's half-term. Bill
is away in the States at a conference and won't be
back before Wednesday. Charlotte has gone to a

3

study centre in Devon with her school for the entire week.

Now, you must destroy this letter and never tell anyone you received it. Charlotte must never know the secret of our past. It has destroyed our lives. It must not destroy hers.

Goodbye, my dear. As your old Wordsworth says, 'We must grieve not, rather find strength in what remains behind.'

Love, hugs and kisses, my beloved, from your very dearest little sister Flora.

The words of Flora's letter hammered inside her skull as if they were physical blows. For a hideous moment, like a storm-tossed lake of black polluted water spilling over the edge of a crumbling dam, those terrible memories to which Flora referred threatened to sweep away the wall which confined them and flood Catriona's conscious mind. She stood rigid, her eyes closed, forcing her mind to counter this image, as she had countered many others, as if they were spells cast by a magician, battling to keep that filthy tide from engulfing her. Then she was breathing easily. The water in the lake was aquamarine, the sun was shining through the clouds and the massive curve of white concrete, springing majestically from side to side of the rocky valley, was unbreached.

Flora was right. That was how she tried to bear the unbearable. By the constant effort of forgetting. By struggling with her memories in solitude and in silence. And in that silence, she had always assumed that for Flora, the demons had been less tormenting. Now it was clear that she had been wrong. Dreadfully, unforgivably wrong. And now it was too late.

But was it? Wasn't the threat of suicide sometimes a way of forcing hidden matters into the light? Had Flora indeed travelled to the undiscovered country? Would she, could she have done that? What if she had lost her nerve at the last moment? Or what if she hadn't, by accident or by subconscious design, taken enough pills? Maybe she was even now waking up, groggy and sick? Please, let it be so! Let it not be too late to act!

Catriona grabbed the kitchen phone off its hook and jabbed out her sister's number. It rang, and for a few glorious seconds, she imagined a drowsy arm reaching out at the other end, and then a fuddled voice saying, 'Who's that?' and Catriona replying, 'It's me, silly. What do you think you're playing at?'

The ringing tone went on and on. There were several extensions in Flora's house and they would be chirping in unison like an avian chorus in the morning silence. After five minutes she gave up. She had done it. That was the only logical conclusion to draw from the silence. Flora alive would not have allowed that dreadful letter to arrive without warning to unleash its appalling message. She would surely have called, or she would have come to London. At the very least she would have answered the phone.

Almost a day had elapsed since she would have taken the pills. More than enough time to ensure that they would do their job. That was why she had used a letter. To avoid any possibility that Catriona would arrive too soon. Flora would have done her homework on how many she would need to take, and then added a few more just to make sure. From the tone of the final paragraphs of that terrible letter, business-like, organised, efficient, there had been no doubt she had been in her usual state of mind. In that mood, if Flora had determined to do something, she would do it.

The letter had not, though, merely been a farewell. It had been a warning and an injunction. No one must know their secret. More than that, no one must ever know or suspect that there was a secret. The young life of Flora's child must not be blighted further than it must inevitably be by loss and grief. The reason for Flora's death must remain a mystery. But not only for Charlotte's sake. For Catriona's too.

Catriona laid the letter's three white sheets in the empty grate and struck a match. The thin paper blazed briefly. The loops and curls of Flora's handwriting were still dark against the grey flakes of ash when she crushed them to fragments.

It was time to answer her sister's summons. She collected her car key from the hook by the bulletin board alongside the phone, and, pausing only to engage in a hurried search for her shoulder bag, which had unaccountably found its way into the bathroom, and to grab a charcoal grey shower-proof jacket from the bentwood coat-stand in the hall, went out into the agonising brightness of the morning.

At the time she received her sister's letter, Catriona Turville was thirty-eight years old. For the previous five years, she had been the Bloomsbury Professor of English Literature at London University's Warbeck College.

She had commenced her climb to this lofty academic peak at the Camden High School for Girls, where she had been by a long way the most brilliant pupil of her year. Her achievements at the school were, however, not merely intellectual. She had played sports and games with skill and a fierce determination to win, although this did not always make her popular, since her need to perform as an individual frequently took precedence over that of the team. At two sports in particular, she was outstanding: in judo, she had been the most skilful and aggressive student the school had ever had; on the running track she had had no equal. On numerous occasions, there had been attempts to persuade her to compete at a higher level, but she had disdained the blandishments. 'The only person I'm running for is myself,' she replied. Some more perceptive observers might have said that it was from herself that this austere, serious girl was running, but no one had had the courage or the honesty to point this out. Besides, she knew it already.

She had crowned her career by winning a scholarship to St

Hilda's College, Oxford. But it was there that the shadow side of this formidable young woman became evident. Although there were many at Oxford, themselves wealthy or well-connected or merely brilliant, who were fascinated and awed by her, who would gladly have befriended her, or borne her like a trophy to ball or country-house party, or bedded her, she made no close friends even amongst her own sex, and had no lovers, male or female. At some point in a burgeoning relationship, she would shy away, like a wild animal that is suddenly aware it has been tempted to venture too far out of its known territory. Then she could turn a hurtfully cold and indifferent face to someone with whom only the previous day she had seemed to be verging on intimacy.

Intellectually, however, she had no peer. She had continued to dazzle her tutors both with the awesome concision and maturity of her written papers, and with the calm assurance of her bearing. She gained a starred first, the most brilliant of her year. Three more years at Oxford saw her gain her doctorate – on Coleridge and the German Metaphysicians – then, despite the flood of offers to remain, she left the dreaming spires.

Wholly uninterested in doing what others of her generation called travelling – or, as she saw it, the pointless infliction of themselves on the parts of the globe that had already been thoroughly ravaged by colonialism and by its successor, foreign aid – she did nevertheless wish to see something of some other world than that bounded by the High and the Banbury Road. She enrolled as a post-doctoral student at McGill University, taught seminars, which she enjoyed, following which she was offered an assistant professorship. She had liked Canada and the Canadians, but after three years it had seemed increasingly artificial to be teaching English nineteenth-century literature in the context of a country whose language, landscape and traditions were so different.

Offered a number of appointments on her return, she had accepted a readership in the English department at Warbeck, and when one of the two Chairs fell vacant some years later, she had been the natural successor. In addition to an unusually heavy teaching commitment, which she had insisted on maintaining in addition to her departmental duties, she had produced several well-received books, as well as a regular stream of articles and reviews in learned journals. The pinnacle of her professional career to date had been the commission she had received to produce the first complete edition of Wordsworth's poems to have the benefit of the most modern biographical and textual discoveries. The Grasmere Edition, which many lesser minds would have regarded as a lifetime's work, was proceeding with quite extraordinary speed for such a vast undertaking.

Her colleagues in the senior common room were not a little jealous of her combination of intellect and energy. Workaholism is not particularly common in the Arts faculties of institutions of higher learning, where a high rate of production is often regarded as shallow self-advancement. But no one who knew Catriona Turville's work could accuse her of being unscholarly, quite the reverse, and she was also unfailingly generous in the time she would spend assisting a colleague.

Personally, she was regarded as an enigma. In the prime of life, tall, slim and extremely fit, with a mass of jet-black hair surrounding a pale, classically featured face, attractive, even beautiful, she had never been known to have a sexual relationship, or even an intimate friendship with anyone of either sex. She never spoke of her private life, never referred to any personal tastes or preferences for anything other than authors and works in her chosen field of expertise, never invited anyone to her house – never, in fact, disclosed her address or even her telephone number to anyone who had not official authority to demand it.

Rumours abounded, of course – some of the most fanciful and fantastic kind – which she did nothing to confirm or deny, maintaining her habitual composure and calm indifference. Such a woman could not fail to be a target for those members of the university who prided themselves on their irresistibility in sexual matters. Over the years, many attempts at the conquest of this formidable woman had been made, but all, like the Knights in Browning's poem who had ridden to the Dark Tower, had failed ignominiously in their quest.

Owlbury is a village in the Cotswolds, between the endemic shabbiness of Stroud and the despoiled elegance of Cheltenham. Those who like that kind of thing, and there are plenty who do, call it picturesque. The narrow, winding A46 climbs a hill, and becomes an even narrower High Street of gabled, stone houses, their plain facades given austere dignity by the precise fit of the yellow-grey ashlar and the skilful carving of lintels, dripstones, and mullions, their characteristic steeply pitched stone-tiled roofs enlivened as by an Impressionist with splashes of green, yellow, white and orange lichen.

In the centre of this touristic gem is, as might be expected, a parish church, large and imposing, for Owlbury once waxed fat trading the wool of the hugely fleeced sheep known as Cotswold lions that grazed the sloping pastures of the surrounding valleys. St Michael and All Angels has a tall tower, which bears at its summit a gilded weathercock, and on its western front a handsome clock face, below which two quaint figures in the gaudy costume of seventeenth-century men-at-arms strike the hours and the quarters on a bell that hangs between them. It is surrounded by an extensive churchyard, sprinkled with ancient, meticulously clipped yew-trees, in which the rude forefathers of the village, unlike the other inhabitants of the High Street, blessedly enjoy their sleep untroubled by the traffic that grinds its way along on the other side of the lychgate by which they were admitted.

Opposite the church stands The Tiger Inn. Its eighteenth-century exterior cloaks a foundation several centuries older.

In front there is a cobbled yard, from where on certain days of the calendar the unspeakably posh Beaufort Hunt, in its unique dark blue livery, departs in full pursuit of the uneatable. The rest of the year, the impracticably uneven, heritage-listed surface – ladies in high heels beware! reads a helpful notice – is occupied by wooden benches and tables, which on sunny days are crowded with drinkers and diners.

At this relatively early hour, the pub had not yet opened its doors, and the Saturday influx of tourists had not yet arrived. The few inhabitants who were up and about, and who saw the passage of the white, battered, rust-streaked old-model Ford Fiesta as it roared and rattled along the High Street, might have noted that it was being driven at considerably more than the legal speed limit, but that was hardly unusual in these lawless days. Only those who combined curiosity with acute vision would have observed that the driver was a woman, and that her pale face was wet with tears.

Narrowly avoiding scraping a bumper on the stone gatepost as she made the awkward turning through the open five-barred gate, Catriona screeched the car to halt in a spray of shingle, then, reluctant to move, sat staring at the solid stone building that Flora and Bill had turned from a derelict shell used to store farm machinery into what most people would regard as a highly desirable residence.

Eventually, she roused herself, shouldering the car door, which eventually opened with its usual screeching. She swung her long legs over the sill and stood upright, gazing around her. The sun, blocked until now by the rise of the wooded hillside opposite, was just beginning to shed a few feeble shafts of light onto the stone tiles of the dormer-windowed roof, and the air was damp and cold. From the darkness of the trees to one side of the house came the plashing sound of the brook, which replenished the silver mirror of the millpond, in which fronds of green weed floated, like the long hair of a drowned maiden.

The spare key was in its usual place: under the plant pot on the right-hand side of the oak front door. As she touched the chilly phosphor-bronze, she felt a shudder like a mild electric shock: the metal might be the last point of contact with her sister's living fingers.

Her feet clattered on the uncarpeted hardwood treads of the open-work staircase. On the beige cord carpeting of the landing, she hesitated, staring at the veneered door panel of what Bill had referred to, half-ironically, mimicking the jargon of the estate agents, as the master bedroom suite. Flora had riposted tartly, 'Such a pity you have no mistress to share it with.' Flora always had a nose for the pretentious, and was merciless in mocking it.

Had. Was. How easily she had slipped into the past tense.

She stood at the door listening, holding her own breath, hoping to hear thereby the softer murmur of a breath from within. But not the faintest whisper leaked from the gaps by the jambs. The silence coated the whole interior, as if it had been applied like paint. Finally, she exhaled, and the sound, which might have been a sigh, broke the spell. She pushed open the door, closing her eyes as tightly as she had as a small child, shutting out the imaginary horrors of the dark. But this was broad day, and the horrors were real.

She blinked in the sunshine which was now streaming unobstructed through the open curtains of the dormer window. The bed was in front of her, the bedclothes as brilliantly white as those in a detergent commercial.

At first she thought she had been dazzled, or that her brain had simply refused to acknowledge the message from her eyes. But as she drew nearer, and out of the direct line of the blinding rays, it was evident that she had not been deceived: no blonde head lay in a hollow of the bleached cotton fabric of the pillows. They were freshly plumped up, quite undented. The duvet lay flat and smooth, with no tell-tale hump to indicate a body lay beneath. She nevertheless snatched it aside. The tightly stretched sheet betrayed not a wrinkle of any recent occupancy. The bed was, undeniably, completely empty.

TWO

The house whose location Catriona rarely and reluctantly disclosed was, in fact, situated in a quiet street on the southern slope of Muswell Hill. She had bought it with a mortgage ten years before, when she had returned to England to take up her first job at Warbeck.

After years of student residences and communal living, she had been determined to have a place of her own. She was fed up of having to dodge damp underwear hanging from the shower-rails in shared bathrooms, and tired of rows over the responsibility for chores, damage, and the apportioning of household bills. Most of all, she was utterly sick of the constant presence of other personalities, other egos, and their intrusive interference with her own. God, how pleasant it was to come down in the morning into her own kitchen and not find in it some bleary-eyed fellow, a boyfriend, no doubt – how she hated that juvenile, mealy-mouthed word boyfriend! – slumped at the table over a mug of coffee, the stereo blaring the rock music she hated. How good it was to be able to read a book or a journal without being interrupted or distracted by a flatmate's inane whining about being in love or not being in love. She was finished with all that.

From the start, she had loved her house, and for several years she had spent every spare moment doing it up. The weekend she had moved in, she had discovered in the hallway the original geometric and encaustic tile floor, quite intact under multiple layers of filthy linoleum. With a thorough cleaning and a lick of polish, the golds, azures, terracottas, blacks and reds had glowed as brightly as they must have done a century before. It had seemed, as she sat back on her heels to admire her handiwork, an omen. Underneath the tacky accretions of hardboard, chipboard, vinyl and laminate was the living form of the original Edwardian house. Its identity was occluded but not destroyed. It was her role to coax it once again into the light.

In the following weeks, she had exultantly hurled into a skip the cheap kitchen cupboards, the tacky DIY-store fitted wardrobes, the nylon shagpile carpets, and the other hideous sixties and seventies rubbish with which the place had been smothered. In the months and years afterwards, she had combed junk shops and reclamation yards in search of replacements for the features that had been destroyed. Every weekend had been spent in overalls and headscarf with almost manic effort: scrubbing, filling, sanding, painting, papering, tiling. She had reinstated fireplaces, matched and repaired plaster cornices, architraves and dado rails. She had hung doors. She had laid York stone paving in place of the cracked concrete that had covered the rear terrace. She had spent hours of frustration supervising slow-moving and sometimes recalcitrant workmen in those things such as plumbing and electrical wiring which she had not the skill or knowledge to tackle herself.

Such work is never finished. There were some little corners that still needed attention. Some larger items – a really nice Welsh dresser, for example – she had not yet been able to afford. And some of what she had done in the beginning itself needed freshening or retouching. But a veritable transformation had undoubtedly been achieved, through imagination and ingenuity and good taste and sheer hard work. She admitted that her house would never be an architectural masterpiece, but at least she now inhabited a place that was more true to its essential nature than when she had acquired it. But in making it something of what it had once been, she had not wanted simply to recreate some historically accurate but sterile original, in the manner of a museum-piece. Although she read books and magazines on house restoration and decor avidly, Catriona was not a purist or a sentimentalist in her refurbishments. There was no question but that her house was one occupied by a woman born towards the end of the twentieth century, who embraced many of that century's most significant cultural artefacts. Her tastes and her habits, not those of some long-dead Edwardian, animated it. Her identity and personality permeated it. The house had regained its own dignity, but at the same time, in every way, it reflected its owner's sense of her own self.

Sometimes, of an evening, she would kneel on the hearthrug in front of the beautiful cast-iron fireplace in her sitting room, watching the glow of the coke in the grate, and reflecting on the way she and her house had developed together, the process by which their relationship had grown and deepened over the years. Every square centimetre of its surface was known to her, as intimately as some might know the body of a lover. Every night-time creak of floorboards, every rattle of a sash, every moan of wind in the chimney, every gurgle or vibration of pipework were the familiar marks of the house's physical presence. It was at these times that her mind seemed in suspension, about to dissolve in some greater whole, and a soft warm blanket of peace seemed to be laid upon her shoulders by some beneficent household deity.

On the day after she had received her sister's letter and made the desperate journey to Gloucestershire, as she sat in the kitchen of her house, her half-eaten breakfast toast and a mug of cold coffee before her on the pine table, Catriona took no such heady pleasure from her surroundings. The early Sunday morning sun streamed in through the French windows, casting on the polished floorboards the nodding shadows of the Albertina roses that climbed the rear wall and, in the garden beyond, a quartet of chaffinches squabbled cheerfully around the bird feeder. These were sights and sounds that usually elevated her spirits and reminded her of the childlike joy in the commonplace so well imitated by Wordsworth:

> The birds around me hopped and played,
> Their thoughts I cannot measure,
> But the least motion which they made,
> It seemed a thrill of pleasure.

This was normally her favourite time of the day, but for all the brightness of the morning, to her it might have been as adust and dead as a field of newly cooled lava.

Flora's letter had exploded like a terrorist car-bomb in a city street. The familiar shapes of buildings were reduced to windowless, blasted hulks. And, as the smoke gradually cleared, there was the sound of screaming, a dreadful abandoned wailing that seemed as though it would go on for ever.

Like a member of the emergency services, she had rushed to Owlbury to perform the duty with which Flora had entrusted her: to bury the dead and comfort the living. But now she was herself a confused and bewildered bystander, her ears ringing, her senses numbed, groping in a void. How could she bring aid and comfort, when she did not know the name of the grief? She had gone prepared for a funeral. Should she rather erect a cenotaph? Where, where, where was Flora? Had she taken fright and run away? Would she eventually return? Why had she then not contacted her sister to tell her of her change of heart? Why had she left Catriona to suffer the hell of receiving the letter? Catriona's head throbbed with the possibilities and the responsibilities heaped upon her.

In the midst of her hurt and distress, like a chronometer unperturbedly continuing to tick as a storm raged around the vessel that carried it, with ceaseless accuracy providing the data that located it on the trackless ocean, the logic centre of her brain continued to function. It had been that highly polished, reliable instrument – the mechanism that had enabled her effortlessly to surmount every scholastic hurdle from school through to university, and to take the glittering academic prizes beyond – which had taken over the previous day, when she stood stunned, staring down at the spotless whiteness of her sister's bed, in the calm order of Flora's bedroom.

She had almost fainted. The room had blurred as she pitched forward. Putting out a hand to the bedside table to steady herself, she was dimly aware of the thud as the bedside lamp fell over and onto the floor. Recovering herself, she stared at the room. Flora was not in the bed, the logic machine told her, therefore she must be somewhere else. Somewhere, in this room, in this house, will be a clue as to where that place is. Furthermore, if she had indeed abandoned her attempt at suicide, if she had thought better of it and gone away to reflect, then she would have needed clothes to wear, and the more she had taken, the longer she would have intended to stay away.

Opposite the bed was a range of built-in glazed wardrobes, the cottage panes obscured by pleated chintz drapes within. She yanked open the doors, pair by pair. Flora loved fashion and had so many things. Within, there were rows and rows of garments – skirts, dresses, blouses, tops, slacks – on proper wooden hangers. Flora disdained the wire type, the gift of inferior dry-cleaners, with which her sister was content. There were shelves on which sweaters were neatly folded, racks on which shoes were precisely arranged. The last cupboard was Bill's: suits and shirts, jeans and trousers in no particular order, shelves crammed with bundled jerseys, and, on the floor, a jumble of shoes, trainers, tennis rackets, cricket bats and golf clubs.

Catriona gazed helplessly at Flora's open cupboards. There were no obvious gaps in the ranks. She had no idea what might be missing, and hence what her sister might be wearing. Bill would certainly not have a clue. Charlotte might remember some of her mother's more striking things. But the last thing, surely, that Flora would have gone off in – if she had indeed done such a thing – would have been a glamorous outfit?

One by one, Catriona pulled open the drawers of the tallboy. As she did so, her action released faint traces of Flora's perfume, which hung like a ghostly presence in the still, warm air of the immaculate bedroom. Arranged as if in descending physical order, there were silk scarves, carefully folded bras, neat piles of pants, tights and socks. There was no sign that a substantial number of items had been removed, but there was, as with the clothing, no certain way of finding what, if anything, had been taken. Would even Flora have known how many pairs of knickers she owned?

On the dressing table, cosmetics and scents were tidily arranged, as were the old fashioned silver-backed brushes and mirror which had been their maternal grandmother's.

Nowhere was there a note – a hint, even – that anything dreadful might have happened or been contemplated here. The whole room spoke of the order in which Flora habitually lived her life. There were no nighties thrown carelessly over the backs of chairs, no crumpled underwear hanging from half-opened drawers, no magazines and newspapers strewn over the floor, no higgledy-piggledy pile of unread and half-read books teetering on the bedside table. The only note of chaos, the fallen lamp, had been imported by Catriona.

Hearing in her mind her sister's click of disapproval, Catriona bent to pick it up and set it back in place.

Then suddenly she froze, staring at the empty top shelf of the bedside cabinet. Flora's existence depended on order, and the fundamental principle of order, as she never ceased to remind her disorganised sister, was that one should know at any given time where one kept one's important things.

The most important thing for Flora was her bag. Her plain, soft black leather shoulder bag was kept on or by her person at all times. Even in the house she carried it from room to room as if, Catriona sneered, it were the U.S. president's legendary briefcase containing the codes to launch a nuclear war. In turn, Flora scoffed at her sister's habit of leaving her own handbag hither and yon, and having – at least twice a day – to engage in a frantic search for it or the items it contained. Its location, along with the location of umbrellas, handkerchiefs, pens and keys were among the few things which Catriona could never remember.

When Flora was in bed, the bag, repository of her information and memory systems, remained in its allotted place on the top shelf of her bedside cabinet, so that when she woke up she had only to stretch out a hand immediately to access her bulging Filofax; change purse; wallet containing never less than one hundred pounds in twenties, tens and fives; credit cards; cheque book; paying-in book; building society pass book; house keys; car keys . . . Car keys!

She ran down the stairs, yanked open the front door, and, without stopping to close it, charged across the shingle to the detached stone double garage. The up-and-over door was locked. Cursing she ran back into the house, to the board in the kitchen where the spare keys lived. She grabbed the bunch neatly labelled 'Garage' and hurtled back to the pale green metal door. She inserted the small chromed key and twisted it in the lock. There was a squealing sound mixed with a metallic rumble as the steel panel began its ascent.

The smell that drifted out as the door opened was of damp concrete mixed with faint traces of oil and petrol. There was none of the scent she had feared, the acrid reek of exhaust gas.

Within, to one side, stood a red VW Golf, two years old, and as shining clean as you would expect Flora's car to be.

She dashed over to it and wrenched at the driver's door. It was locked. Her head thrust close to the spotless glass of the side window. She could see, with overwhelming relief, that the interior was completely empty.

Other than the car, the garage contained a ride-on motor mower, three bicycles leaning against the rear wall, and a slotted metal shelf unit containing tins of paint, a plastic container of motor oil and a small metal tool box. Bill was not the type for hobbies, and even here Flora had been a dedicated enemy of clutter. Catriona thought of the garage which gave on to the lane at the back of her own house. An ancient rickety affair of timber and corrugated iron, it was stuffed from floor to ceiling with junk. Her car lived on the street.

She had returned to the house relieved but still confused. Wherever Flora had gone, she had not taken her car, and could not therefore be traced by reference to it. The cavernous spaces of the Old Mill's principal rooms were as equally, blandly uninformative as to the fate of its chatelaine.

In the kitchen, sparkling granite work-surfaces, gleaming high-tech laminate cupboards up to the ceiling and shiny stainless steel appliances reflected only Catriona's own pale, puzzled, anxious features. There were no unwashed pots. No jars or packets left out. The dishwasher was empty. The rubbish bin contained only a clean plastic liner. In anyone else, Catriona for instance, this absence of clutter and detritus might have seemed abnormal, but for Flora, this hospital-like functionalism was quite usual. Catriona had often joked with her sister that the Old Mill was the only place where one might literally eat one's dinner off the floor.

Even beside the huge American fridge-freezer, at the table that Flora used as a sort of housekeeper's desk, where there was a cordless telephone and a pin-board on the wall, there was no sign of anything other than routine domesticity. The message pad was blank. The cards stuck on the board were of tradesmen and local services. There were typed lists of numbers of friends and acquaintances. A copy of Charlotte's lesson and homework timetable. A school bus schedule. Exactly what one could find in any bourgeois household anywhere in the country.

The other downstairs rooms – the vast, double-height, galleried sitting room; the dining room with its antique mahogany table at which Flora and Bill had given their elaborate dinner parties; Bill's study with its bookshelves containing weighty scientific tomes, series of periodicals and digests, its shut-down computer and the satellite receiver and television on which Bill could watch sport from round the world, round the clock – they were also all clean, tidy, and orderly.

Only in Charlotte's dormer-windowed bedroom on the top floor had there been anything approaching disorder. But even there, amidst the spilled stacks of CDs and the books scattered on the floor, the daughter was enough like her mother for it to show far more than in most girls her age. The single bed was neatly made. Her soft toys stared down in an orderly row from the top of the tallboy. The books on the shelves were in alphabetical order by author. On her desk, pens and crayons were gathered together in a jar. Her computer had been shut down. Underneath the combined TV and VCR stood a labelled row of videotapes.

It had been only as she stood in the doorway of this room – full of the expensive tools of modern materialist culture, yet redolent of that vulnerable innocence which even the most outwardly mature and sophisticated child carries at their heart – that Catriona's tears began to flow. How, if the worst had happened, could she break it to Charlotte? Would she ever recover from such a blow? Desperately she had hoped that Flora would return, that this was only a passing episode.

In that hope there was some justification. The only clue as

to Flora's intentions that had emerged from Catriona's search of the Old Mill was that Flora appeared to have taken her handbag. The dead need no luggage. If Flora had walked out of her house, in whatever clothes she stood up in, intending to go through with her suicide, but wishing to end her life in the countryside she loved, perhaps even with the fatal drug at that moment coursing through her veins, then surely even she would have regarded herself as free from the need to burden herself with earthly possessions. She could have gone without even a handful of coins to pay the ferryman across the infernal river. She would not have needed her handbag.

As she stood in the hall, ready to leave, Catriona stared up into the shadows where the staircase climbed. Aloud, she begged: 'Please, Flora. Wherever you are. Please come home.' But the silent empty house had absorbed her words, returning not the faintest echo.

For four days, she went about her normal life. The iron discipline ineluctably imposed by her rational nature caused her to function with her usual efficiency, and in fact she took a kind of pleasure in her ability to subdue the turbulence of her feelings beneath a mask of confidence. Morning, afternoon and evening, on every one of those days, she had telephoned the Gloucestershire number in case Flora should have returned. Every morning she had waited, in excruciating suspense, for the arrival of the post. Every evening, the first thing she rushed to do when she got back home was to check her answering machine.

For four days of grief and bitterness, she had considered what to do. Should she get in touch with Bill at his conference? If so, what should she tell him? The truth?

And what was that? Flora had threatened suicide, no, had stated in so many words how and when she was going to kill herself. That much her letter made plain. But then he would inevitably want to know about the contents of the letter, about Flora's reasons for taking this extreme step, reasons about which hitherto he knew nothing. She could not, would not explain those to him. Whether to do that had been Flora's choice, and she had chosen not to share her past – and thus her sister's past – with the man with whom she shared her life, sparing him the anguish and the burden of that knowledge. Catriona, who shared her life with no one, had never been faced with that decision, had determined never to be faced with it. She could certainly never contemplate breaching a twenty-four-year wall of silence to Bill of all people, a man to whom she was not in the least close, whom she neither liked, nor trusted.

But the truth was also that there was as yet no body. And without a body there could have been no suicide. And without a suicide, there could only be an absence. But what was the nature of that absence? Had Flora thought better of what she had intended and simply gone away in distress? Would she return in a manner that made it clear that the idea of suicide was merely an episode, a fugue that had passed? In that event, the content of the letter was in the nature of a trust which it was incumbent on Catriona not to break, certainly not to a man who might react with anger and bitterness, a man who might reject her if he knew.

There was another explanation: that Flora's departure was intended to be permanent. That she had deliberately abandoned Bill, Charlotte and Catriona. That somewhere she was adopting a new identity. That in that new life, she would no longer be Flora Jesmond, née Turville, but someone else entirely. Catriona shuddered at this thought.

Would she, could she have done that? Catriona then really would be entirely alone in the world. Alone with the dreadful memories, which from time to time, as if from the depths of a still lake, attempted to rise like the kraken.

What most tore and worried at her as she contemplated the situation was that what had happened, what appeared to

23

have happened, was not the act of the sister she had thought she had known. Like an eruption, the events of Saturday had overlain with alien matter all her familiar features. But, on reflection, that was not the right image. The ash and rock of a volcanic explosion buried and obscured. Saturday's cataclysm had revealed. It had shown Catriona a different Flora, a Flora who was more like Catriona herself.

She was stunned by this epiphany. Her image of her sister, from earliest childhood, had been founded on the concept that they were polar opposites – in appearance, in everything.

Little Flora was the blondest of blondes, and wore her hair either in long and luxuriant straight tresses, or wound and plaited into complex braids and chignons, from out of which her bright complexion shone like a sun. Young Catriona's abundant black hair had a naturally stiff and awkward curl, and it surrounded and hung in tangles over her face, obscuring her pale features, like streaks of dark cloud across the moon. Flora was a neat, clean and tidy girl. Catriona was constantly rebuked for her personal habits; she cared not a fig for clothes or cleanliness and her room was always a mess. Flora was animated, effervescent, social, loving parties and company. Catriona was quiet, dour, shunned society, and hated social gatherings. Flora had had boyfriends and admirers by the dozen. Catriona was aloof and cold, and scorned any boy who came near her.

As they grew up, Catriona even as she loved and cherished Flora, was inclined to patronise, even to have some measure of contempt for her younger sibling's character, regarding it as less interestingly complicated than her own. Flora, she decided, lacked intellectual or emotional depth. She did not read the kind of books that Catriona read; she did not think about the kinds of issues which her sister constantly pondered; she did not respond to the power of literature or the arts generally, with one exception: she did like some music. This taste, though, was another area of difference between them.

Flora loved folk songs, genuinely traditional or in the style of Bob Dylan and his followers. The better to enjoy these, she taught herself to play, or rather, in her modest words, strum the guitar and sing along to it. On several occasions, the endless repetitions of 'Mr Tambourine Man' or 'Blowing in the Wind' provoked Catriona to fury, the only occasions when they had had real rows. Catriona's prejudice – and perhaps her jealousy, as she could not herself play a note – blinded her to the fact that Flora actually had some real talent, which she later exploited to her advantage.

This ability was the only one that had given Catriona the least pause, however. In everything to do with school, the elder had been far and away the champion. She had been the keenest and most driven of scholars, top in every subject, whilst Flora, with no sense of shame, had bumped along at the bottom of her class, a cheerful, unaffected presence who regarded the classroom activities as a distracting irrelevance compared to the important things in life: personal grooming and appearance, physical health and fitness, make-up, and fashion.

Not that she had been a troublesome pupil, far from it. She had always been polite, helpful, and, ultimately, uninterested. The only thing the school offered in which she could have excelled was drama, where she proved, like her sister, to have a natural talent as an actor. Typically, though, although she loved costumes and dressing up and being a presence on the stage, she found plays boring, the learning of words tedious; yet another aspect of education which held no interest. As soon as she was able to leave school, she left, with only a few paper qualifications.

Her first job was as a junior dogsbody in a travel agency in the West End. In no time at all she had revealed a flair for the work. Her people skills were good, she was told. She was being groomed for management. But Flora had had her own ideas. She had saved her money assiduously, and one fine morning, just after her eighteenth birthday, she resigned from the agency, but not before she had bought a clutch of budget air tickets. For the next year, she travelled the world, seeing the exotic destinations that she had spent her days selling to customers. She took her guitar, and worked bars and clubs and cafes en route, or busked in the streets.

On her return, her travel bug had not left her. She had applied to British Airways and been accepted for training as a flight attendant. Catriona remembered, guiltily, the scorn with which she had greeted Flora's proud announcement. She knew now what she hadn't known then: that it was actually incredibly difficult to get onto the training course, still less to pass it with such élan as Flora had managed.

By that time, Catriona had her starred First and was beginning her doctoral research. The fact that her sister was an air hostess was not something she wished to broadcast amongst the sage and serious feminist community of St Hilda's College.

Flora had flown for several years. Then she had met Bill Jesmond and married him.

That was the first thing her sister had done which Catriona had found did not accord with her view of Flora's character. However, this going against type did not raise her opinion of Flora, rather the reverse. Bill was the last man in the world Catriona could have imagined any lively, attractive young woman wishing to marry. He was a tall, rather gangling and awkward man. Though he was only thirty-five and his chestnut curly hair bore no hint of grey, he talked and behaved as if he were at least ten years older. He was undoubtedly brilliant, possessing a string of chemistry degrees from the Cambridges in both England and the United States, but, despite this intellectual achievement, he was, as a personality, unspeakably dull.

As Flora was always at pains to point out, their relationship did not begin as a plane-board romance, but in New York's Central Park, by the skating rink. Flora was with another girl who had come in on the same flight, and Bill, a researcher for a multinational pharmaceuticals corporation in Cincinnati alone during a business trip to the city, hearing their clear English voices with a pang of nostalgia, had overcome his natural reserve to engage them in halting and diffident conversation.

They had lived in the States for three more years, where Charlotte had been born. Then Avalon Corporation, Bill's employer, had taken over an English company, and he had been the obvious choice to return to head its research department, based at Wychwood Court, a country house, formerly a girls' boarding school, near Cheltenham.

At Catriona's first meeting with her brother-in-law, Bill made no secret of his male chauvinism. A woman's brain, in his view, was not suitable for academic work, and besides, he regarded literature, the focus of her interests, as unworthy of sustained intellectual attention by anyone, male or female. Poetry, novels, plays, he thought of as lightweight entertainment for an idle hour or two. Art and sculpture were merely forms of decoration. His main pleasure outside his work was playing and watching a variety of sports.

Bill had straightaway picked up the habit of addressing Catriona through Flora, referring to her as 'your sister'. 'Would your sister like another cup of coffee?' 'Is your sister coming with us this afternoon?' He avoided situations in which they would be forced to converse together by themselves. If they were left together in a room, he would immediately mumble an excuse and find something to do in another part of the house.

Her visits en famille were consequently infrequent and rather a strain. She preferred to keep in touch with Flora by twice or thrice weekly phone conversations. If Bill took the call, he did no more than grunt a greeting, then she would hear him yell out to Flora, 'Your sister's on the line!'

In fact, the few weekends Catriona did spend in Gloucestershire were only tolerable because Bill was out for much of the time, either jogging around the countryside to keep fit, or playing cricket, tennis, squash or golf. Even at weekends, he would go over to the laboratory for hours at a time, pleading that an experiment needed attention or that results needed to be run through the computer in time for the return of the technical staff on the Monday.

Flora seemed to accept this workaholism. He was hardly ever around to share bedtimes or to read stories or simply to have fun with his daughter. Flora, in contrast, was devoted to Charlotte. She seemed to enjoy the demanding but dull routines of motherhood. Physically strong, she used to joke that, after having four hundred adult babies to cope with on an international flight, only one real baby was a piece of cake. She would spend hours playing with her, or taking her to the local playgroup.

To Catriona, this signified that her sister's individuality had been further compromised. Flora had ceased to be an independent person. She had dwindled into a wife and was now further diminished into a mother. When Charlotte had gone to school, Flora had taken a part-time job, but it was not a real job, not a job like the Bloomsbury Chair of English Literature at Warbeck College in the University of London, which Catriona herself occupied with such distinction.

For years, Catriona had persisted in her belief that she and Flora, attached to each other though they were, and willing on occasions to share their differences – Flora would read a book that Catriona recommended, Catriona would allow herself to buy an outfit or some underwear of her sister's choice – remained the opposites she had always regarded them as being.

For years. Until Saturday. The day that had changed everything.

On Wednesday evening, the phone was answered. But it was a male voice. Bill's.

'Catriona?' He had never called her Cat.

'Hi, there Bill! Good trip? Sorry to disturb the joyous reunion, but I'd just like a word with the lady of the house!' As she spoke, watching her knuckles whiten as she grasped the plastic handset, she was conscious that the false, nervous joviality was so uncharacteristic that even the insensitive biochemist might suspect something was wrong.

But when he replied, his voice had in it only the habitual note of irritation, emanating, she believed, from his conviction that no tiresome mortal had the right to interrupt the deep thought processes on which the future of the human race might depend. 'Actually, she's not here, although she knew quite well I was coming back today.'

She was trembling now. Breathing deeply, she waited before replying, so long that Bill demanded impatiently, as if the connection had been lost, 'Are you still there, Catriona?'

'I haven't heard from Flora since last week. I've phoned several times and got only the machine. I've left messages. It isn't like her not to return calls or to be out so often. I had the impression she might have gone away.'

'Now you mention it, there's no sign of her having been here at all, not for some time. It isn't that the house is tidy. It's always that. But even Flora leaves things out occasionally, and there's nothing of that sort. And I looked in the fridge just now and I noticed there's none of the salad stuff she normally eats. As if she hasn't been shopping recently. Which reinforces the idea that she's away. So do you have any idea where she might have gone?'

'No, none whatever.'

'She never mentioned anything like that to you, even as a remote possibility?'

'No.'

'You're quite sure?'

'Of course I'm sure!'

'Why did you happen to ring up just now?'

29

'I wanted to speak to her, of course!'

'Look, Catriona, if I find out that you and your sister have cooked this up to put the wind up me, then I shall be very annoyed indeed. Now I'm going to make some calls. To friends locally. Her boss. See if they know anything.'

Seething with fury she slammed down the phone. The bastard had accused her of conspiring with Flora in some petty act of spite. Had the two of them had a row? Or was this the normal state of their marital relations? Had Flora simply walked out on him? In Catriona's view she would have had ample justification. But why the terrible letter? Why drag her sister into their private quarrel?

Later that evening the phone rang again and she snatched it up.

This time Bill's voice had a more conciliatory tone; from that unusual state, she judged with a sinking heart that he, the great unflappable, was worried.

'I've exhausted all the possibilities I can think of and there's no trace of her. Nor did she say anything to anyone about going away. I'm letting you know that I consider that I have no alternative but to report her absence to the police.'

'The police? You think you need to do that?'

'I really think I do. Now I've had the chance to look around the house, there are some other puzzling features. Her car's still in the garage, for example. I've never known Flora take the bus or use a cab ever since we've lived here. Why would she start now? Her handbag has gone, but there's no sign of anything in the way of clothing being missing, though she had so much that it's hard to tell. The overnight bag and make-up bag she always used are still here. I've looked in the loft and none of the suitcases are missing.'

'If Flora's simply gone off on her own for a few days, won't she be annoyed to find herself the subject of a missing persons inquiry?'

At this, his usual truculent tone returned. 'Frankly, Catriona, if my wife and your sister has been so damned insensitive as to walk out on her family without a word of explanation to anyone, without having the consideration to leave so much as a note as to her whereabouts, then she needs to be made aware of the effects of her behaviour. I don't care if she's annoyed. We'll find her first, and worry then about whether she's embarrassed. Besides,' and here there was almost, to her amazement, the trace of a sob in his voice, 'we have to face up to the possibility that something, something serious may have happened to her. She can't have had just an accident. I've called the hospitals round here that have emergency departments: Gloucester, Bristol, and Cheltenham. There were no unidentified casualty patients or victims of accidents.'

'Something serious? What do you mean?'

'Isn't it rather obvious? It's desperately upsetting but we can't yet rule out the possibility that she might have been attacked or abducted. I don't want to think these things, but it seems to me they have to be considered.'

'But is there any indication of something like that having happened?'

'Here? None whatever. But it could have happened while she was out. You know how much she likes rambling around the countryside. But we could speculate endlessly and quite pointlessly. That's why I'm going to the police. They have the resources and the knowledge to do what's necessary.'

'What about Charlotte?'

'She's not home until Friday. Besides, if Flora does turn up, there may in the end be nothing to tell her.'

Catriona sat unmoving staring at the phone for long after he had rung off.

In the light of what Bill knew, the action he proposed was entirely logical. He was, after all, a scientist. A disappearing spouse was no different from one of Newton's billiard balls. If she had moved, some force must have acted upon her.

All appropriate means should therefore be taken to identify that force.

Was she right to deny him the data concerning the nature of the force that might have acted? Was she concealing vital information for her own selfish reasons? If Flora did not return in the next few days, would she then be bound to reveal all she knew? Her gorge rose at the very thought of that idea, of broaching that taboo with such a man.

Did he in fact even care what had happened to his wife? Had the marriage been a mere shell with no kernel of love or affection? There had seemed at some points to be in him more anger than concern, as if he felt that Flora had been playing some kind of game with him. But the contemplation of her abduction, injury or even death had shown a little more of his vulnerability, and a little was a great deal in a man of his generally dispassionate nature.

And Flora, this new Flora whom she hardly knew, was she really playing some sort of attention-seeking game? At that, Catriona found that she too could feel anger and resentment, mixed with her anxiety and grief. And wasn't suicide itself the ultimate piece of attention-seeking, the easy, the coward's way out? Wasn't that why she herself had shunned it? How could Flora have vanished in this fashion, leaving such emotional wreckage in her wake? Was it desperation that caused it, or cruelty – a desire to wound and to punish? Each thought was like a further stone added to the cairn of desolation in her heart. How could she have been abandoned like this, full of a grief that could neither be assuaged with knowledge or purged by death?

THREE

There were eight of them in the seminar room, six women and two men, varying in age from Mary O'Shaugnessy, a sixty-five year old grandmother, who hailed, as she said, from Cork via Kilburn, to Kenny Bridges, a plasterer in his mid-twenties, who always arrived straight from his work, carrying his canvas bag of tools, and wearing a dusty donkey-jacket, the capacious pockets of which bulged with well-thumbed volumes of poetry.

Such a range of ages and stages is typical of Warbeck College. It admits only mature students to its undergraduate degree courses. Established by a wealthy Victorian philanthropist specifically to educate only the working man and woman, whose access to the established routes to education had been denied by the necessity to earn a living, this mission continues, even though the concentration of resources on such a class of individuals no longer accords with modern educational notions.

Undergraduate courses at Warbeck were still taught mainly in the evenings, hence the college's motto, *Sub Stellis Discere*. Catriona, a night owl, without commitments of partner or family, was ideally suited to this nocturnal existence. Further-more, she had chosen Warbeck, when she had had the offer of other more obviously prestigious institutions, because she had been so impressed by the atmosphere of discipline and dedication she had found, and which resonated strongly with her own disposition. There was no sense that standards had been relaxed here. Quite the reverse. The students who embarked on such a rigorous combination of work and study had to be tough as well as bright. It seemed as though it would be a privilege to teach them.

After ten years, she had not lost that initial enthusiasm. She felt genuine warmth that evening as she regarded her nineteenth-century literature class. They were a good year, but then there had been no bad ones. Every intake displayed the same qualities. She admired them enormously for the families they raised, the consuming work they endured. She was touched by their belief that knowledge was the holy grail of life's purpose. She was moved by their humility in seeking it, their often despairing agony in the quest, and their wonderful faith in her as the teacher who would aid them. She was the crone by the wayside who whispered the solution to the magic riddle, or told of the secret entrance to the ogre's castle, and whose reward was to see them emerge triumphant, the fair prince or damsel clasped in their arms.

And emerge triumphant they did, on the whole. They studied in every spare moment, making up for the time they had lost through lack of opportunity, in youths ill-spent, or better spent than in the pursuit of academic honours. Without exception, afterwards, they wrote wonderful letters of gratitude and thanks, praising her for what they themselves had achieved. When had she ever been thanked before she came to Warbeck? They made the ordinary students she had taught elsewhere, fresh from school or from some pointless circumnavigation of the less comfortable parts of the globe seem spoiled and immature.

Not the least good thing about Warbeck students was their punctuality. They arrived a polite few minutes before the specified time. They didn't breeze in halfway through. And they were always prepared, with the right text, which they had read and thought about in advance.

Of course, there was always the exception that proved the rule, and tonight's group contained the biggest exception of all, in the unruly shape of Alan Urquhart. He was late again, of course.

She took off her watch and set it on the table in front of her. It was time to begin, whether or not the massive Scot had managed to get himself here.

She said, 'Good evening, everyone. This week's text, as you know, is Wordsworth's *Ode. Intimations of Immortality from Recollections of Early Childhood*, begun in the Spring of 1802, when Wordsworth and his sister Dorothy were living at Dove Cottage, Grasmere.' There was a rustling as eight copies of the *Collected Poems*, in various editions and states of repair were opened at the poem, when the door creaked ajar, and a large red face appeared in the crack.

'Och, late again. I'm really sorry, Catriona.'

'Yes, we've already started.' But she could not help accompanying the disapproving words with a smile. It was impossible to be truly annoyed by the endearingly bear-like figure.

He squeezed his large frame around the table into the only vacant chair, which happened to be directly opposite her. His arrival produced a certain amount of coughing and shuffling and scraping of chairs as the women at each side of him budged along to make room for him. There was another pause while he fished around in the very battered leather briefcase for his Wordsworth and his notebook, which he dumped onto the table higgledy-piggledy, so that the notebook slid off onto the floor and had to be retrieved with a great deal of bending, heavy breathing and more chair-scraping. Finally, from an old-fashioned hard spectacle case lodged in the breast pocket of his suit jacket, he produced a pair of rimless reading glasses which he settled upon his great beak of a nose, tucking the ear-pieces into the mane of grey hair around his face, in which could be faintly discerned the fleshy tips of his red ears.

Catriona took a deep breath and said, 'Well, then, who's going to begin?'

Marilyn spoke. 'This Wordsworth. Was he a Buddhist?'

She was a thin-faced woman in her thirties, with lank mousy hair, who wore long, floral print dresses and baggy cardigans. She had a nasal twang which indicated an antipodean origin. At the beginning of the course, Catriona had found her intensely irritating. Her wincingly gauche, uninformed and beside-the-point comments delivered in her whiny voice had set Catriona's teeth on edge. But, gradually, she had come round. Marilyn was not stupid, merely ill-educated. Whatever outback apology for a school she had attended had left her in complete ignorance of the most basic aspects of English literature and history, making the Canadian students Catriona had taught seem prodigies of knowledge in comparison. This realisation had shamed her. Marilyn was more stunningly uninformed on her course of study than any student Catriona had ever come across, but her role as a teacher was to cure that defect, not to despise it or be embarrassed by it.

And Marilyn, to give her credit, worked hard and learned quickly. Catriona had learned something, too. Marilyn's oddball remarks, viewed without the prejudice of received academic wisdom, occasionally had the effect of a liberating insight.

So, the typical Marilynism yoking Buddhism, which she undoubtedly did know something about, with the poetry of Wordsworth, which she didn't, which a few months ago might have made Catriona inwardly squirm, seemed on that evening, fresh and interesting.

One of the essential qualities in a teacher, Catriona had also learned, is to know when not to answer the student's question. A factual answer can kill the lively thought that gave birth to the enquiry. So she didn't reply dismissively that of course Wordsworth wasn't a Buddhist, which was the strictly correct answer, but which, like all strictly correct answers, was actually quite misleading.

'A Buddhist? Perhaps you'd like to expand on that observation, Marilyn.'

Marilyn flushed. 'Well, like this bit here.' She quoted:

'"Our birth is but a sleep and a forgetting:
The soul that rises with us, our life's star,
Hath had elsewhere its setting,
And cometh from afar."

'I mean, what he's saying is that we've had another life. You know, Buddhists believe that you're reincarnated. You come back to the world, to samsara, they call it, over and over again.'

Catriona smiled, 'Until you become perfectly enlightened. Yes, I think Marilyn has a point. Do we agree that there is a sense here of having come from elsewhere, and of forgetting what has happened in that previous existence?'

Urquhart, who, as usual, was shifting in his seat, fiddling with his pen, and from time to time blowing noisily through his nostrils like a spouting whale, gave the hacking cough which announced he was about to contribute.

'Ay, there's a similarity. But surely the difference is that Wordsworth is saying that our souls come direct from God, "trailing clouds of glory do we come From God who is our home." That's not the same as saying you've been a wee mouse in your previous existence.'

Marilyn had her mouth open, ready to protest about this travesty of her philosophy, but Catriona could see that there were several other members trying to catch her eye. The ball was rolling, and she didn't want them to be side-tracked into an argument about Buddhism.

Joyce spoke. She was a dark, well-dressed woman in her forties, who was apparently the personal assistant of an extremely big cheese in the City.

'Aren't we getting rather ahead of ourselves here? Surely the first stanzas are about Wordsworth's losing his poetic gift. He can't see things as he used to as a child: "Where is it now, the glory and the dream?"'

'Yeah. Old Wordsworth's got this thing about his childhood, an't he?' said Kenny. 'Always going on about how happy kids are. "Thou child of joy, Shout round me, let me hear thy shouts, thou happy shepherd boy!" I don't think he grew up where I did, that's all I can say. Any shouts of joy from me, my old man would have given me a clip on the ear, and told me to fucking shut it!'

There was a little uneasy laughter, and Joyce could be seen to make a face at the obscenity. She and Kenny had had a confrontation about what she called his gutter speech a few weeks before, and the row was still simmering.

'So, does anyone else agree with Kenny? Does Wordsworth idealise childhood?'

Gradually, the whole group was persuaded to contribute, and once more Catriona was struck by the subtlety and perceptiveness of their responses. Unlike the normal run of students who were still too near being irresponsible children themselves, these people had taken many hard knocks and felt in their own lives the loss of faith, and the possibility of being reconciled to that loss which the poet was describing. They also, most of them, had children of their own. They had experienced that wrenching love first hand, they had seen their own children and grandchildren change from careless beings to ones bent under the 'inevitable yoke'.

Then, as the two-hour session neared its end, Mary O'Shaugnessy, who had been watching Catriona with a calm, shrewd blue eye, addressed her directly. 'And you yourself, Professor Turville? Where do you stand on the childhood issue? Did you as a child see things "apparelled in celestial light"? Or do you "grieve not, rather find strength in what remains behind"?'

Throughout the seminar, Catriona had been steeling herself. Of all poems to have to teach at the present! She had considered whether to duck it, but that would have been unprofessional. The 'Intimations Ode' was a key text in the study of the poet. She had been particularly dreading the mention of this line, dreading the memories it would evoke. She had hoped that her scholarly detachment would carry her through.

She tried to speak, but her lip trembled so much the words would not come. She felt the tears starting at her eyes, and through her blurred vision saw nine faces fixed on hers in various expressions of concern and astonishment. She fumbled in her bag for a tissue, then took refuge behind it. She blew her nose, and wiped her eyes.

'I'm sorry, a little touch of migraine.' She glanced down at her watch. With relief she saw that the time was up. 'Thank you, all of you, for your usual stimulating company.' As she gave out the tasks for the next meeting, she was pleased to observe that she had regained control of herself.

She bent her head to her bag, intent on putting away her books and papers as they said their farewells and filed out. When she looked up, it was to see that the room was not empty. Alan Urquhart hovered by the door, nervously swinging the battered leather briefcase like a schoolboy, as though he couldn't decide whether to go or to stay.

She was slipping on her coat when he made up his mind.

In contrast to the chaotic state of the rest of him, his speech could be, when he chose, as formal and precise as a dominie's.

'I am wondering if you are all right?'

'Yes, of course. It was just a touch of migraine, as I said.' She slung the bag on her shoulder, and smiled brightly. 'It's gone already.'

'I wonder if you'd care to join me for a drink?'

She turned her direct gaze on his keenly observant blue eyes.

'Thank you, but no.'

He held her scrutiny. 'I'm quite harmless. Nothing to be afraid of.'

'I'm not refusing out of timidity.'

'Och, so it must be my own lack of appeal.' He said this lightly enough, but she saw the weight of genuine disappointment as he shrugged his huge shoulders at the rebuff, turned, and shambled towards the door.

Normally, she had no compunctions about the curt rejection of would-be suitors, but on this occasion, to her surprise, she felt an unwonted pang of guilt at her brusqueness. 'Wait, Alan. I'm sorry. I didn't mean to be rude. It isn't that I . . .'

He paused with his hand upon the handle, his hesitation a sign that hope sprang eternal. He turned towards her, his expression inviting her to continue.

'I mean it isn't anything to do with you personally. It's just that I don't . . .'

'Drink with students? Is there some rule or other?'

She liked neither her own unaccustomed hesitancy, nor the fact that he had attempted to finish her sentence for her, a male social habit she found intensely irritating.

She replied in what was almost a snap, 'No, of course there isn't a rule.'

'Except for yourself, maybe?'

Though she made no response, she could not prevent the flush that rose to her cheeks at the pointedness of this remark.

They descended together in the lift in silence. In the entrance lobby, he asked, 'Can I give you a lift anywhere?'

'No, thank you. I walk to the tube at Russell Square.'

'It's late. Would you like me to walk with you?'

'No, I'll be quite all right.'

He raised his bushy eyebrows. 'You're sure? It's no bother.'

'I'm quite sure. I walk that way every night of the week.' She smiled, intending condescension – this overweight, unathletic man could surely have nothing comparable to her own proficiency in various martial arts! – but she could see from his reaction that her expression had not achieved the chilliness at which she had aimed.

It had been raining and the pavement gleamed with an amber sheen under the street lamps. As she reached the end of Malet Street, on her left the great tower of the Senate House, which bore on its reinforced floors the weight of the university library, loomed black against the glow of the sky like a vast Egyptian pylon. For a moment she had a definite urge to look back at the figure of the Scotsman heading in the opposite direction, but she fiercely resisted the impulse and walked on.

Since her childhood, work had been her joy and her refuge. After clearing a mountain of paperwork relating to her departmental duties, instead of taking a break, she turned with relief to the rough notes she had made for her next article in *The Journal of Nineteenth-Century Studies* '"*Strange fits of passion I have known": Erotic themes in the poetry of Wordsworth.*'

Her article argued that the poet's entire *oeuvre* was deeply permeated by the erotic. Even in the most well-known, well-loved, often quoted poetry, there is a sexual element that has never been fully acknowledged. In 'I wandered lonely as a cloud', an apparently innocent tribute to wild natural beauty, frequently recited by primary school children, there are powerful erotic undercurrents.

It is usually assumed that the ultimate source of the poem is a visit to Ullswater in April 1802, recorded in her *Journal* by Dorothy Wordsworth. The daffodils which grew in a belt along the waterside are there vividly described '& seemed as if they verily laughed with the wind that blew upon them over the Lake'. But an earlier incident in Wordsworth's youth may also be relevant to the text. On a visit to Lake Como, the poet observed a group of local girls dancing. In his *Descriptive*

Sketches, he refers to them as 'fair dark-eyed maids' engaging in 'Lip-dewing song and ringlet-tossing Dance'. These explicitly sexual verses were excised by Wordsworth from his later published editions. A full reading of the poem needs to take into account both these incidents involving lake-side beauty.

The daffodils which the poet sees when wandering 'lonely as a cloud' are a 'crowd', a 'host', 'a jocund company', words usually applied to people in a social gathering. Like the nubile young women attending a ball in a Jane Austen novel, they are dancing. They toss their heads in sprightly dance. The word 'dance' and its derivatives appear four times in this short twenty-seven-line poem. They outdo the sparkling waves with their dancing. Their petals are 'fluttering' as if they wore ball gowns.

But dancing can signify not only an ordinary social courtship ritual. Peasant dances are frequently connected with celebrations of growth and fertility: weddings, harvests, births, the Spring. Dancing by women in a secluded place is suggestive of arcane ritual – of witchcraft, of invocations to the Goddess of the Wood, to the great Mother Goddess, of Bacchic rites.

The daffodils are not merely yellow, but golden. It is the only colour word in the poem, and colour words generally are very rare in Wordsworth. By drawing attention to the golden colour of the daffodils, the poet invokes the sensual connotations of gold: Shakespeare's 'golden lads and girls'; the sun and the heat of growth and generation, the ripeness of corn and harvest; personal adornment and luxury; the lure and glamour of sexuality; Aaron's Golden Calf; the golden shower by which Zeus impregnated Danaë; the golden apples which the virgin athlete Atlanta could not resist; Cleopatra's barge, 'of beaten gold'; Blake's 'bow of burning gold' and 'arrows of desire'.

The poet is 'lonely as a cloud'. He is a solitary male observer with a high viewpoint from which he can observe but not be readily or closely observed himself. He is a voyeur. The word 'gazed' is repeated, to emphasise the passivity of the observer. Finally, having feasted his eyes, he departs.

The show has brought wealth to him – a further hint at the gold of the daffodils, an inner satisfaction. The nature of this wealth is elucidated in the final stanza. In vacant or in a pensive mood – what a modern might describe as a meditative or trance state – the poet has a vision, or fantasy of the feminine daffodils. He has an inward eye which gives him bliss. In this pleasurable state, he fantasises that he is dancing with them.

By his richly suggestive language, Wordsworth creates the essence of the male voyeuristic experience. If the daffodils are nubile young women, like the bathers covertly observed and depicted later by Renoir and Cezanne, then the poet's vision of bliss is a masturbatory fantasy which he enjoys on the privacy of his couch. Wordsworth's poem celebrates a peak experience of intensely sexualised natural beauty.

The innocent, child-like eye with which the poet appears to view the beauties of the natural world has thus its shadow side. Behind this modelling of the child's vision lies the adult's predatory sexual desires.

'Spare me a minute, Catriona, darling?'

It was a rich mellow male voice, a voice that was reputed to send shivers up the spines of any woman who heard it. But in Catriona, it merely provoked irritation, particularly as she had been so absorbed in her work and hated to be interrupted. Looking up, and instinctively and protectively sliding a blank sheet of paper over the closely written pages of the fledgling article, she had been about to retort that no, she couldn't spare even thirty seconds, when she saw that, without waiting for her reply, the owner of the seductive instrument had already slipped inside her office and closed the door behind him.

She swivelled her chair around to face him. 'What do you want, Michael?'

He was a tall man, wearing expensive but tasteful, not quite formal, but not entirely casual clothes. These, together with his fashionable haircut and smooth manners set him apart from the majority of the male members of the college, whose dress sense and social skills were on a scale between minimal and non-existent.

Michael Harwood, Professor of Cultural Studies, a Chair sponsored by Channel Six, a newish television company already well-known for the lavish nullity of its cultural output, could afford to affect the garb and patter of the well-paid denizens of television and the higher journalism because it was in this world in which he spent most of his time and energy. It was rumoured in the college that he did not even have a university degree, or that, if he did, it had been awarded by some white-tile institution in the Midlands that had become a university only by administrative fiat, and therefore did not count. Harwood was not in the least fazed by his lack of academic respectability. He regarded his nominal colleagues, by and large, as boring sad-hats, grubbing for meagre worms in the scholastic sand, while he surfed the surging ocean waves of the wider world.

'A warmer greeting, seeing as how I have a very interesting business proposition to put to you.'

'I'm already quite busy enough, thank you.'

'Hear me out. You may change your mind. I've been asked to front a high-profile arts review programme on my sponsoring channel. We're looking for a new face to do the literature side. I think you are that face.'

'Me? On television? You're joking.'

'On the contrary. You're exactly the right type. Youthful, successful, energetic, brilliant. And also, if I may repeat what I've told you on many other occasions, you are an extremely beautiful woman. You could be a star. You're wasted here.'

'I like my work. I do not like television. I do not want to be a star, even assuming your view of my potential were correct, which it isn't.'

'Please at least consider it. I've got some publicity stuff with me, showing the scope of the programme. Have dinner with me, and we can discuss it in more detail. I've found this superb restaurant – in Crouch End, of all places. I've managed to get a table – which hardly anyone can.'

'No, thank you. Now I have some urgent assessments to do, so would you please leave me alone?'

'Oh, for God's sake, Catriona! I'm offering you fame and probably fortune. Don't turn it down without even thinking about it. Have dinner with me, at least. I'll run you back to Muswell Hill afterwards.' He laid an imploring hand on her forearm.

She instantaneously snatched her arm away, as if his fingers had been white-hot irons. 'Don't touch me! And how did you know I lived in Muswell Hill?'

He was taken aback by the sudden fierceness in her tone. 'Why, you must have mentioned it in the common room on some occasion or other.'

'No, I didn't. I never do.'

'All right, then I may have looked you up in the phone book.'

'I'm ex-directory.'

'For God's sake, Catriona! Why are you behaving as if I'm some kind of threat?'

Her full mouth was set in a tight hard line. 'Because that's how you're beginning to seem. You've got hold of my address from somewhere in the college records. I don't hand it out to all and sundry.'

He shrugged, and grinned lop-sidedly, an expression which he believed, with some justification, was guaranteed to succeed even with those most resistant to his charm. 'So what if I did? I can't help being fascinated by you. You're the kind of woman a man would commit far worse crimes for than sneaking a look at a file. Have dinner with me, please.'

'The answer's the same now as it always has been. If your

idea is that dangling this television thing in front of me like bait will make me more receptive to your blandishments, then that's worse than unforgivably insulting, it's crassly stupid. If you continue to pester me, then I shall make a very public complaint about your behaviour to the provost, who, as you know, has as one of her aims the eradication of sexual harassment from the college. Now would you please leave my office.'

She swivelled her chair back to face her desk.

Harwood was unused to being turned down in such a contemptuously forthright manner. A man whose life has been dedicated to the cultivation of his own personality guards this tender plant jealously against its being trampled upon. His handsome face twisted in a sneer. He strode to the desk and leaned over her, his sweating palms flat on the polished surface. He hissed in her ear. 'You may look like a million dollars, but you get your kicks out of saying no, don't you, you frigid bitch! Humiliation is what you get off on. You need to see a fucking therapist! You've got real problems!'

She felt a quiver in her spine, as if the insult were a dart that had struck her between the shoulder blades. For a moment, she was tempted to round on him, screaming at him, 'Yes I have! And there's no therapy on earth to cure them!'

Into the silence came a soft rap at the door, as welcome at this tense point in the drama as the knocking at the gate in *Macbeth*.

'Come in!' she called out loudly. The panel swung open a fraction to reveal not the drunken porter of the play, but an entirely satisfactory substitute, the large red face of Alan Urquhart. The Scotsman took in the presence of the other man, and his proximity to Catriona. 'Och, I'm sorry, Catriona! I didna realise you were engaged. I'll come back later.'

'No, it's all right! Come in, Alan!'

'It's none but this wee bit essay to hand in. I have it right here.'

The Scotsman, his grubby cream trenchcoat draped over his

arm, began to fumble in his scuffed leather briefcase with one hand, while grasping it insecurely in the other. Inevitably, the case slipped to the floor, spilling its contents. Urquhart lowered himself to his knees and proceeded to gather his scattered books and papers, cursing under his breath as he did so.

Harwood, who had moved swiftly away from the desk at the Scotsman's irruption, watched this display of clumsiness with unconcealed distaste and impatience.

At length, the big man had scooped his study materials together in an untidy heap, from which he extracted a thin folder. He stood up, dusting down his crumpled trousers, and held out the file to Catriona.

'I'm sorry it's late.'

'I'd expect nothing less from you, Alan,' she replied gravely.

Harwood said, 'Look, Mr . . . Professor Turville and I were in the middle of a meeting.'

'Urquhart's the name. I'm just on my way.'

Catriona said, abruptly, 'Actually, Michael, we had dealt with the matter, hadn't we?' Her slate-blue eyes stared coldly at him as she spoke. 'Hadn't we?'

Harwood shrugged. 'You can always change your mind,' he said as he left, slamming the door behind him.

Urquhart raised his bushy eyebrows, but said nothing, though he did not fail to notice that Catriona's normally pale features had gone deathly white.

'I'm sorry I butted in like that. If I'd known . . .'

'Frankly, I'm very glad you did.' She paused, then, before she could prevent them, the words were slipping from her mouth as beads from a broken necklace. 'You asked me to come for a drink with you the other evening and I refused. Why don't you try again?'

He held open the door of the pub for her. It was busy but not crowded. Although, to her relief, she could see no one she knew from Warbeck, who might have gleefully reported to all and sundry that she had a secret lover, she was already regretting her uncharacteristic impulsiveness and somewhat puzzled as to its source.

When the barman produced their order, she got out her purse to pay for her Perrier.

He started to object. 'Don't be daft. A bit water . . .'

'No, I insist.'

He checked the expression on her face, then shrugged.

He carried the drinks over to a table by the window. He waited whilst she seated herself on the upholstered bench seat, then lowered himself gingerly on to a small Windsor chair, which his bulk overlapped all around.

'Good health!' Urquhart drank deeply from his pint, while she sipped at the cold mineral water.

There was an uneasy silence. She noticed that Urquhart was squirming uncomfortably on the chair, causing it to creak under his weight. She felt at a loss for the right words. What indeed were the right words in this altogether unusual situation? Invariably, when she had one-to-one meetings with students – or with colleagues, for that matter – there was a topic for discussion, or an agenda. What was the agenda of this meeting she had so rashly set up? So, to hide what felt like, but could not possibly be, nervousness, she resorted to safe banality.

'Are you enjoying the term?'

'Aye, I am that. It's been a struggle to keep up with the reading, but it's worth it.'

'I've always admired Warbeck students for their dedication to study.'

'Dedicated! You make me sound like a monk! But it's true I'm not beating my brains out for any motive of worldly gain. I gave up on that years ago. Literature has always been a passion, but I'd never had the opportunity to pursue it. It was my unrequited love affair until I came to Warbeck. As a young man I even tried to write poetry.'

'Do you still?'

'Och, no! And what about yourself?'

'No, I never even dreamt I could create. I'm a scholar, a harmless drudge, searching for the gold of a text's true reading in the muddle of manuscripts and previous editions.'

He swallowed more beer and she sipped the ice-cold water, the bubbles burning her tongue like acid. Sooner or later, the conversation would move from these polite tributes to more personal acknowledgements. He might allude to her appearance, his feelings of attraction towards her, and that was when, in the time-honoured jargon, she would make her excuses and leave. But she was wrong. When he spoke again, it was with a whimsical air.

'I'm thinking from your name there's some Scots in you,' he said, raising his bushy eyebrows, still dark brown in contrast to the grey of his unruly hair.

Startled by this, she managed laughingly to repeat the formula she had rehearsed ready for such enquiries. 'That was a romantic fancy of my very English parents. Robert Louis Stevenson was a favourite of theirs. I was born here in London, as a matter of fact.'

'RLS! Isn't that strange now! I had the fancy as a wee boy that my parents had *Kidnapped* in mind when they picked my name. Even though I knew full well that they regarded the reading of anything other than the Guid Book as sinfu' indulgence. Aye, I passed my childhood pretending I was the incarnation of the dashing Alan Breck Stewart, wi' his silver buttons and his bonny sword-play. But nobody kenned that. And now I'm overweight and drink and smoke too much, it sounds ridiculous I could ever think it!' He paused and his already pink complexion turned a darker shade. 'I'm sorry. I shouldna rattle on so.'

As he spoke, he had been worrying the edge of a beer mat with his thick fingers. His sprawling body trembled with nervous energy.

49

'Why don't you go ahead and have a cigarette, Alan? You're surely not holding back on my account?'

'My mother dinned into me I was never to smoke in the presence of a lady. But since you've so kindly given me permission . . .' He rummaged in his pocket and produced a squashed pack of Marlboro and a Zippo lighter. 'I've tried to give up so many times.' He inhaled deeply, coughed, then turned away to blow out the smoke behind him. 'But booze and fags are a traditional occupational hazard in my line.'

'Really? So what is your line?'

'Don't you know? My entire CV's on a college file.'

'Those files are confidential.'

'Ha! They must be the only files in history that are. And I should know. I'm a professional snooper. A member of the fourth estate. A journalist.'

'And what do you write about?'

'You're going to laugh.'

'Of course I shan't.'

'I've sat at most desks in my long but not particularly distinguished career: crime, sport, politics; even, when I was a good deal younger, a stint as a foreign correspondent – in West Africa, of all places. But at present I report the Royals. There, all is revealed. I said you'd laugh! No, don't apologise. Most people do. Either at the incongruity, or the naffness, or both. But there's no obligation on us Court hacks to dress like flunkies, thank God, and it may be naff, but the Windsors sell papers, like it or not. Some of the broadsheets have tried from time to time to avoid the goings on at the Palace, but they come back to it in the end.'

Suddenly, it seemed as if fate had intervened to give her the opportunity to share the grief that gnawed at her. To share it, moreover, with a man. And with a man who, it could not be denied, was evidently attracted to her. But nonetheless, a man in whom she felt there was a deep well of kindness and sympathy. She said, quickly, rushing out the words before the moment passed, 'I'd like to ask you something. Have you ever in that varied career written about a missing person?'

He took a long pull from his glass, draining the remains of the pint it had contained. He stared at her, his blue eyes keen amid the creases and folds of his haggard features, a living sentinel staring from the battlements of a grand but ruined tower, bright with shrewd interest, as he sensed the beginnings of a story. 'Indeed, I have written about such matters. But is this a general enquiry, or is there a specific reason for asking?'

'Nearly two weeks ago, my younger sister Flora disappeared without warning from her house in Gloucestershire, leaving, without a word, her husband and her teenage daughter. There's been no communication from her and no trace of her ever since.'

'I see. I'm so sorry. That is a dreadful thing to have happened. So, would you like my opinion on what might have happened to her?'

'Yes, if you're willing.'

'Of course. But first, I'll need another one of these.' He stood up and collected his empty foam-flecked beer-glass.

She shook her head at his nodded enquiry towards her own tumbler, the thin slice of lemon curled sadly round a half-melted cube of ice at the bottom.

She watched his broad back as it ploughed a path to the bar-counter. Already the impulse was leaking away, leaving behind a sick feeling. For a moment she contemplated flight, but that would have been juvenile and abject. Then he was back, a fresh pint in his huge fist.

He sat down again, with elaborate care, but even so, the table rocked as he nudged it with a knee, causing him to steady the glass with both hands.

He drank deeply, snuffling through his nostrils as he did so.

'So tell me about Flora.'

Briefly, she recounted the basic facts of her sister's life:

her career with the airline, her marriage to Bill, family life in Owlbury.

'We used to speak two or sometimes three times a week, for hours, sometimes. Bill would complain about the phone-bill, in my hearing, almost as if he expected me to contribute to it. Although, to be fair, it was mainly her who called me and she talked while I listened. I used to think that Flora told me everything about the smallest aspect of her life. I realise now that she may have told me the small things, but there must have been some big things she didn't mention at all. I spoke to her last on Thursday three weeks ago. It followed the usual pattern of our conversations. Flora was complaining about how difficult it was to deal with Charlotte, my niece. How she was grumpy and insolent, dissatisfied, bored – the usual adolescent problems that I was heartily glad I didn't have to deal with. I didn't hear from her on the following Saturday, so I rang her myself, and got no answer, not even from the machine. I rang her again on Sunday, several times, but still no answer. I was slightly worried, but then I thought, as it was half-term, she might have gone away – though it wouldn't have been like Flora to forget to mention it to me. I kept on ringing from time to time with no reply, until on Wednesday evening I got Bill, who had just returned home.'

Like a train going over points, she inwardly felt a bump in her narrative as she crossed back to the main line of the truth, but the version she told was so convincing that it almost seemed to substitute in her memory for what had actually occurred, drowning the sound of Flora's voice reading her letter, and blanking out the vision of the empty bed and the unsullied whiteness of the sheets.

There was no change in her inflection, and Urquhart gave no sign of having noticed anything amiss, but listened intently as she proceeded to tell him the rest of what had occurred.

'Her husband said there was hardly anything in the fridge.

No fresh food. Flora was a strict vegetarian. She ate a lot of salad, raw food generally.'

'So if there was none of that kind of thing, it would indicate some preparation on her part? If she were planning to leave, she wouldn't have bought provisions?'

'Bill checked with the bank and the credit-card company. Flora drew her usual one hundred pounds in cash from the Lloyds Cashpoint in Cheltenham on the previous Thursday. The card account showed she shopped at Waitrose in Cirencester the same day. That was also her last day at work. She worked only Mondays to Thursday lunchtimes. She used to buy her vegetables from a growers' co-operative that have a stall in Stroud on Saturday mornings. Bill rang them and asked whether they'd seen her, but they said they hadn't.'

'You'll have checked the hospitals?'

'Yes, Bill did that. And he went through every number in the desk diary in the kitchen, in case she'd seen or spoken to anyone, a tradesman or workman, during the period she went missing. He's very thorough.'

'She and Bill. Had they had a row? Did they have a troubled relationship?'

'That's possible, given the way Bill was when I spoke to him, more angry and resentful than upset. But Flora and I had an agreement that we didn't discuss her marriage. She knew that Bill and I didn't like each other.'

'But do you think she might have been having an affair?'

'Again, it's possible, but I had no hint of it. Perhaps Bill may suspect she was. That might explain his attitude. But if she had left him for someone else, she would surely not go off leaving Charlotte without even a word? Whatever complaints Flora might have had about her, I know she loved her daughter deeply.'

'Forgive me for asking, but had she any reason to consider committing suicide?'

'Suicide?' Her voice was quite steady. 'Absolutely not.

Flora was, I would say, completely lacking in that kind of mentality.'

'Was she seriously ill or taking medication?'

'No, definitely not. Flora had scarcely had a day's illness in her life. And she didn't in any case believe in taking drugs, only natural remedies. I often wondered sometimes how this affected her relationship with Bill, given that he works for one of the world's largest pharmaceutical companies.'

'So her disappearance is quite out of character? She's never left home before?'

'Never. I know from what I've said that Flora seems to have every reason for suffering something of a mid-life crisis. An attractive woman, trouble with her daughter, possibly trouble with a husband whose belief system she doesn't share. It's a recognisable psychological response, isn't it? To flee from everything that gives you grief. But I've never thought of Flora as having the capacity to behave like that. She's never been neurotic. Even when we talked about Charlotte, she was calm and rational, sympathising with the child's problems and coming up with ways of dealing with them. It certainly wasn't the reaction of someone who was preparing to jump ship because they couldn't stand life on board.'

'So did Bill go to the police?'

'Yes. He went to Stroud police station and filled in a form with Flora's basic details. She would be given a W/M number – that means Wanted or Missing, but I expect you know that – and entered on the Police National Computer. They also said they would "ask around", whatever that means. I got the impression they'd have been more interested if she'd been a lost dog or cat.'

'It's their usual procedure. I suppose you do have to look at it from their point of view. Thousands of people go missing every year, in similar circumstances. Without definite evidence of a crime or of someone's being in danger, there's no role for them. People are free to come and go as they choose. The authorities have always been wary of behaving as if that weren't the case. They can't look for her, as they don't know where to look. You see Flora, as an adult of sound mind and body – not a child or an elderly person, or mentally ill or handicapped – is not, in the jargon, "vulnerable". Even the fact that she has a child doesn't influence that. Charlotte is too old for them even to consider bringing the case within their criteria. It would be very unusual, if hardly unheard of, for a woman to walk out abandoning a baby or a very young child, at least without some kind of warning, but the older the child becomes, the more common it is, unfortunately. The police are also aware that of those missing thousands that people in my profession are forever quoting, as if there were somewhere a legion of the lost, the vast majority quietly return and get on with their lives. If they'd mounted a full-scale search for them, they would have been wasting their time and resources on people whose absence has merely been a protest, or a way of clearning the air, or a way of calling attention to a problem, or simply a misunderstanding. In those cases, when they feel better they come back. The problem is that people are far more likely to report an absence than a presence. Consequently, the police statistics don't record those who have returned.'

'But there are some who don't return?'

'Yes. There are undoubtedly many who vanish deliberately and permanently without trace, possibly to start a new life in a new town or even a new country. Although, as I've said, it's difficult to be sure about the numbers. But in many of those cases, there is usually some indication of why they disappeared – a hopeless personal situation, a financial scandal, or a serious criminal charge pending, like Lord Lucan.' He paused, his face grave. 'In the rest, I'm afraid to say, there is at least the suggestion of foul play, even if there's no direct evidence, as in the business some years ago of that woman estate agent Suzy Lamplugh who left her office to meet a client and was never seen again.

'I wrote an article once about a middle-class housewife, not unlike your description of your sister, who vanished completely. There was no indication that she was unhappy or disturbed, quite the reverse. In that case, however, her disappearance had occurred during a sequence of appointments in London which she had arranged herself for the day she went missing. She kept the first ones, but failed to keep the rest. In her case, the police strongly suspected she had been abducted and murdered, but without a body, and without any reliable last sighting, or any indication of where to begin looking for her, they had no basis on which to proceed with a full enquiry.'

'But that's the most unlikely eventuality of all, isn't it?'

'Yes, murder or abduction by a stranger, particularly when there's no demand for ransom, is very rare, fortunately. And in this case there's absolutely no evidence of anything of that nature. I have to say, though, that that's sometimes the case. It's an area where you need the instincts of a good detective, someone who's a psychologist, who's prepared to act on instinct, not just a run-of-the-mill plod. Now I've been mixing with policemen since I was a wee cub reporter in Glasgow, following every drunken brawl I could find on Sauchiehall Street in the hope it would turn into murder or GBH. The police like that kind of crime. One drunken yobbo glasses another, surrounded by their mates. The yobbo bleeds to death. That's the kind of murder they can understand. But a puzzle where half the pieces are missing, where there's no body, forget about it! But, fortunately, as I said, that kind of case is incredibly rare. From what you've told me, I think it's far more probable that your sister has some problem that no one knows about. She's either run away from it, or is trying to deal with it on her own.'

'So is there anything to be done?'

'Other than waiting and hoping? She has to be living somewhere. She has to have the means to live, so that means getting money and spending it. Perhaps if she's been planning this, she's opened another bank or credit-card account. If she is known to be missing, and can be recognised from a photo and a description, someone, somewhere may see her. Publicity is the best thing. Have some posters printed and circulate them as widely as you can. If the local paper hasn't picked up the story already, then make sure they do. I've come across quite a few of the local hacks in that part of the world through reporting on the doings in Royal Gloucestershire. I could have a word in a few ears if that would help.'

'Frankly, I'm not sure it would. As a matter of fact, Bill is against any publicity at the moment, and for once I agree with him.'

'For why?'

'If Flora has had a crisis, then the fact that it had become common knowledge in the community might inhibit her return. And there's Charlotte to consider. Other children at school can be horrid in those circumstances.'

He shrugged, apparently easy at her sharp response to his suggestion. 'Och, you may be right at that. And how is the wee girl taking it?'

'Apparently, not as hard as might be expected at the moment. On the surface, at least.'

'You can never tell with children. Their minds don't work in the same way as those of adults. I should know. I've had three of my own. Two sons and a daughter, all grown now and gone. Scattered to the four corners of the earth, like wild geese. The USA. Australia. Hong Kong.'

His battered, kindly, shrewd-eyed face regarded her. The loneliness, the desire for further intimacy was plain in every feature. In a moment he would ask her was she married? Had she ever been married? Probably, if he was at all switched into the college gossip circuit, which, given his profession, he almost certainly was, he knew the answers already. So, it was, a little later than usual, time to go. But on that evening,

57

oddly, disturbingly, something was prompting her to stay in the warm, unthreatening glow of the Scotsman's benevolent personality. But go she still must, as she always had to.

She forced herself to rise. She stood, hesitating. Then she slung her bag on her shoulder like a rifle. 'I have to leave you now. Thank you so much for listening to me.'

He struggled to his feet, and began to say, 'Anything else I can do, you have only to . . .'

But Catriona in a few strides had reached the door, through which she stepped without a backward glance.

FOUR

She examined the room yet again, checking to see whether she had, despite her scrupulous preparations, missed anything vital. The brass-framed bed, with its new gleaming white duvet faced the two narrow rear windows. In the alcove between the chimney breast and the back wall, she had placed a small Edwardian mahogany writing table, recently rescued from a roadside skip and carefully restored. On the other side was a narrow wardrobe, the door of which had a pleasant marquetry pattern. By the bed was a small bookshelf with a lamp and a digital clock-radio. On the far side, near the door, was a chest of drawers, also in mahogany.

The spare room had always been just that. Spare in use and spare in furnishing. The only person to sleep in it – indeed, the only person who had ever been invited to the house – had been Flora, and she had stayed only a handful of times, the occasions on which Bill had been persuaded to do a weekend's child-care. The last time had been about six months before. They had eaten out, gone to the theatre, the cinema, and in between they had slummed about the house, feeling gloriously lazy, and no shadow had come between them.

She had tried to say no when Bill called to ask her if Charlotte could stay the weekend. He had to go to a conference in

Brighton, which he couldn't get out of as he was reading a paper. Charlotte's best friend Alice was away on a family visit to her grandmother. So, in the circumstances, there wasn't any alternative. Catriona had felt bullied into agreeing, angry with herself at her weakness in submitting to the bullying, and guilty at her uncharitable attitude.

In two hours, Charlotte would arrive. Bill was dropping her off with her stuff on his way. The idea of her niece staying in her house, even if it was only for the weekend, the thought of a child's unpredictable personality disrupting the carefully assembled structure of her life, was making her feel nervous, almost to the point of being physically sick.

At nearly thirteen years old, Charlotte was not quite what you could any longer call a child, exactly. She had her mother's blonde colouring and willowy figure, but her intellectual development had from her earliest years been overseen by her father. From the beginning, he taught her to think mathematically. Even as a toddler, she had been encouraged to count the things which made up her world. 'How many ducks on the village pond today, Charlotte?' 'Fifteen, Daddy.' A pause and a wrinkling of his brow while he checked. 'I make it fourteen.' A delighted chuckle. 'There's one gone under the water, Daddy.'

He taught her figures to remember and disgorge as a kind of party game. She could recite the metric equivalents of imperial weights and measures, and vice versa. He taught her the times tables, then mental arithmetic. At the age of four, she was a computer adept. Not surprisingly, she was already a star at her school, Stag End Comprehensive in Cirencester, where the formidable Linda Rice, a trustee of the Prince's Trust and the government's favourite educationist – after a stint in which she had turned round the ailing Waterbury School in Oxfordshire – had recently become Head.

How could this prodigious child of the future and her spinster aunt, lover of old books and dead poets, ever hope to reach any common understanding? Even when her niece was small, Catriona had never found it easy to communicate with her.

'Auntie Cat, are you a witch?' she had asked at six.

Bill had chuckled. Flora had been shocked and tried to hush her daughter into silence.

Catriona had been amused. 'Why do you think I'm a witch?'

'Because you always wear black.'

This was not invariably the case, but often enough to prove that the child had good powers of observation. She had thought of replying in the words of Masha in *The Seagull* that she was in mourning for her life, which was as good a reason as any, but it would have been unfair to load that on her niece. Instead she had said simply, 'Because I'm a black Cat,' thinking that for one who never made jokes it was quite a good one. But instead, Charlotte had stared at her with eyes round with suspicion and fear.

The bell rang. Catriona, engaged in the last-minute preparations of their meal, hurriedly wiped her hands on a paper towel and ran out of the kitchen to open the front door. Charlotte stood on the step. She wore blue jeans and a white top tightly stretched over the buds of her breasts.

'Hello! Come in!'

She stretched out her arms to give the girl a hug, but there was no mistaking that the thin shoulders remained stiff and unresponsive.

Bill followed from the car, carrying a bulging nylon sports hold-all.

Charlotte pulled out of the embrace and stood in the hall, staring up and around at the pictures and framed prints, tapping her fingers to some kind of internal rhythm on the newel post, her white-trainer-shod foot idly kicking the bottom step of the stairs.

'I'll show you your room!'

Led by Catriona, the three of them trooped upstairs. Bill dumped the bag on the bed, then went over to one of the windows and stared out, his tall, heavy body partially blocking out the evening sunlight.

'Hey, Charly, you can see Ally Pally from here.'

'What's that?'

'Alexandra Palace. It's a famous London landmark. Where television started. That should make it appeal. Come and look!'

She clumped to his side. 'What a sad-looking dump.'

'Nothing looks interesting to you at the moment, does it?' her father responded with asperity.

The girl swung back abruptly into the room, glancing around without enthusiasm. 'Is there a power point?' she demanded of her aunt.

Catriona did her best to maintain her initial note of bright enthusiasm. 'Yes, of course! There are doubles on each side of the bed and another here by the fireplace.'

Her niece nodded curtly, then proceeded to unzip the hold-all and lug out of it the black rugby-football shape of a portable CD-player. She banged the machine down on the writing table. Catriona tried not to wince as the hard plastic grated on the polished surface.

Charlotte rummaged further in the bag and removed a stack of CDs in shiny plastic cases, the covers of which featured young blonde-haired women, who looked similar and may indeed have been the same person, for all Catriona knew.

These were slammed down by the CD-player with the previous disregard for the french-polishing.

Bill was looking at his watch. 'I ought to be going. You know what the bloody traffic's like at this time.'

At the open front door, he bent to give his daughter a peck on the cheek. 'See you Sunday. Don't give Catriona any hassle.' He raised a hand in farewell to his sister-in-law who had hung back by the stairs. 'Bye, and thanks.'

The girl and the woman, left alone, stared at one another.

'I expect you'd like to unpack?'

Charlotte consulted the lime-green fashion watch she wore. 'There's this programme starting. Where's the telly?'

'I don't have one, I'm afraid.'

The girl's heavy brows contracted and her face twisted in a look of fury. 'You haven't got a telly? I knew you were weird, but not that weird. Why didn't you say? We could have brought mine.'

'I'm sorry. I didn't think of it.' It was true. Television didn't figure in her life. She had a sudden vision of Charlotte's bedroom in Owlbury, crammed with electronics. She should have thought of it. But would she then have done anything about it? Probably not. 'You'll be deprived only for the weekend. And there's so much else that we can do in London,' she added, with more than a touch of irritation. She might have had a blank over the wretched television, but she had picked up a copy of *Time Out* and marked some of the places they might visit together.

'Such as what? We came here on a trip in the Juniors and it was really boring. Traipsing around museums and going on about history all the time.'

'I'm sure we can find something to interest you.' She said this with more conviction than she felt.

'Oh yeah?'

Catriona decided it was time to assert some kind of authority in her own house. 'We'll discuss that later. Supper will be ready in a quarter of an hour. I suggest you go up, sort out your things and wash your hands.'

The girl turned and ran up the stairs. The bedroom door slammed, and after a moment the pounding beat of rock music played at high volume filled the house.

Catriona thought of saying something, thought better of it, sighed and returned to the kitchen. She had the impression that children of her niece's age lived on hamburgers and chips or similar, but she had no intention of cooking such stuff. Instead, relying on the belief that a growing child would be hungry enough to eat whatever was put before it, she had decided to make the kind of thing she would have eaten if she'd been alone: in this case a bean casserole with rice and green salad.

The food, which smelt delicious, was simmering ready on the hob. She laid the pine table for two, set in the middle a cut-glass vase in which she placed a few stems of early blooming roses from the garden, then called up the stairs.

'Supper-time, Charlotte!'

Charlotte flopped down on the indicated chair and stared at the table.

'This is posh.' She indicated the flowers. 'These from your boyfriend?'

Catriona smiled, with an effort. 'No. Only from the garden.'

The girl regarded the plate set before her with an expression of outrage. 'Yeuch! Christ, you're a veggie. I might have known. I can't eat this slop. Isn't there anything else?'

'No. I thought you might like it.'

'Well I don't. Haven't you got any real food? I was really fancying a pizza. Haven't you got one in the freezer?' Interpreting the look on her aunt's face, before Catriona could reply, she continued, 'Yeah, right, of course, you don't have a freezer. OK, what about a sandwich? You do have some bread and cheese?'

Suppressing her anger, Catriona – whilst Charlotte stood by, offering more sneering criticism: 'Have you only got that kind of bread? And no cheddar?' – made her a couple of sandwiches.

The girl ate ravenously and slurped from her glass of orange juice – this was one thing which appeared to be acceptable – whilst opposite her Catriona picked at the cooling mess of beans. She had almost no appetite, but she forced herself to eat.

It would be a sign of humiliating weakness for her to reject the meal as well.

As she mechanically forked a few grains of rice into her mouth, she was aware that Charlotte was, in between noisily chewing savagely torn-off mouthfuls of her sandwich, watching her both attentively and speculatively, as if she were waiting for the right moment to ask her something.

Finally, she asked it.

'Cat, what do you do about sex?'

Her aunt stopped eating, her mouth suddenly dry. As naturally and unhurriedly as she could, she put down her fork and took a sip from the glass of mineral water at her elbow. She thought she had prepared herself for the sex question. But it had arrived in an unexpected and particularly unwelcome form. Charlotte was not asking for information about changes in her body, or whether you could get pregnant from kissing a boy, or other such uncontroversial matters. This charmless, ill-mannered child was asking, in a tone of hardly disguised contempt, about Catriona's own sex-life.

She temporised, searching for an appropriate, safe, non-committal formula. God, this was what being a parent was like, forever at the inquisitive whim of a junior member of the Gestapo.

'How do you mean, do about it?'

The girl tossed her dark, greasy hair impatiently. 'What do you think I mean? You're not married are you? So, have you got someone regular you have sex with?'

Catriona decided the best tactic was to answer the question exactly in the terms it was put. 'No, I don't have anyone I regularly have sex with.'

Charlotte pursed her lips. 'Then do you have a different man when you feel like it? And how often is that? Every day, every week?' She paused, her lip curled in a sneer. 'Every month? Every year?'

To her annoyance, Catriona could not prevent herself from

blushing, with both anger and embarrassment. It was clear that this little bitch's prurient interest would hardly be impressed or satisfied with anything less than a record of constant promiscuity. For a moment she considered lying, then, realising that it could rebound upon her if, as likely, it were retold by Charlotte to all and sundry, she resisted. She started to say, 'Look, I don't think you quite understand how adults relate together, I mean . . .'

Charlotte's eyes flashed with irritation. 'I don't want to know about your stupid relationships. I asked you how often you had sex, got that? How many men? How frequently?' Again, she paused; again, the sarcastic look appeared. 'Or perhaps you don't get it at all? Perhaps no one fancies you. I know Bill doesn't. So do you have to make do with just playing with yourself? Is that how it is? Sad old auntie Cat wanking herself off in her single bed?'

Suddenly, she'd had enough. She snapped, reverting, in her temper, to playground abuse. 'Shut your mouth, you nasty little cow! Mind your own bloody business!'

She got up from the table, collected up her plate and scraped the unfinished food into the pedal bin. She yanked open the dishwasher door with unnecessary force, making the dirty crocks inside rattle together, and jammed the plate into one of the racks.

When she turned back into the room, Charlotte had gone, and the music, louder than ever, was booming down the staircase.

'Charlotte?' She tapped again lightly on the door.

A muffled voice from within said, 'Go away!'

'I think we should talk. I'm making some breakfast. Sausages.'

'Not stinking veggie sausages?'

'No, real, one-hundred-per-cent fat, gristle, cereal, monosodium-glutamate and maybe-even-a-little-bit-of-meat sausages.'

'All right. I'll be down in ten minutes.'

She looked much younger that morning in her pyjamas – Mickey Mouse patterned, which were totally genuine, she explained, as they'd been bought on a family trip to Disneyland Paris.

'Mum loathed it, but Bill was like a kid himself. I've never seen him like that. Most of the time he's so uptight about his work and that, but he went on everything. Course, the old dad was still there underneath, 'cos when we were doing Space Mountain, which is a really, really scary ride, he was like, "We're getting I calculate more than one g here", while everybody else was screaming their heads off.'

She demolished the plateful of sausages, fried egg and baked beans and tomatoes while she talked.

Catriona had risen early and slipped out to the Asian supermarket at the end of the street. There she had stocked up with the sort of food that Charlotte would eat.

'That was a great breakfast.' She paused. 'I was out of order last night. Sorry.'

'No, I'm the one who should be sorry. I'm supposed to be the grown-up. I shouldn't have said those things. I shouldn't have got so angry.'

'I shouldn't have gone on about, you know.'

'It isn't, for me, the sort of thing I can talk about very easily, particularly not to someone I don't know very well. There are private things which I like to keep private.'

'Yeah, particularly from some snotty-nosed kid.'

Catriona smiled. 'That's not how I think of you. At your age, you're coping with a lot of growing up at once. It's painful. And then there's everything that happened lately on top of that.'

'But I was still rotten to say those things. Perhaps I'm not a nice person. Perhaps it was because of me that Mum went away. Perhaps I was so awful she couldn't stand being around me.'

Catriona was on her feet in an instant, rushing to her niece's side of the table. Crouching down she enveloped the child in a hug, drawing the blonde head against her bosom. 'No, Charlotte, you mustn't ever say that. I'm absolutely sure it had nothing at all to do with you. Your mother loved you more than life itself. She would have done anything for you!'

'Anything but stick around! Anything but want to be with me! She must have hated me underneath, whatever she said, otherwise she would never have left. Now you hate me too. You must do after all those things I said. I didn't mean to be so nasty.' She struggled to raise a tearful face. 'Those things I said, I don't want you to think I'm a bad girl. We talk about things at school, that's all. About . . . our bodies and how they make us feel and what it might be like to . . .'

'I know, I know, I understand. Of course, it's absolutely natural and normal to be curious. I was more upset than I would have been because of how I was feeling about your mother. Both of us are under a lot of pressure. It comes screaming out of us.'

'She used to get mad at me.'

'Everyone gets angry sometimes.'

'Not just angry. Once she said I'd ruined her life. That she hated me.'

There were tears glinting in her eyes as she spoke.

Catriona was astonished. She'd always regarded Flora as the perfect mother, the mother she could never have been: endlessly patient, calm, unfazed by mess or stinks, practical and, more than anything, loving.

'I'm sure she never meant it Charly. Everyone says things they don't mean from time to time.'

'She meant it. I could see it in her eyes. I thought she was going to hurt me. I could see that she thought she was going to hurt me. Then she sort of pulled back.'

'Why was she so angry, Charly?'

'It was about the uniform.'

'What uniform?'

'Her uniform. From when she was with British Airways. It was about a year ago. We'd been doing some stuff at school about careers. I mentioned that my mum had been an air stewardess and that made the boys start sniggering and going Phwoarr! Though I could see that they were actually a bit impressed. She was out when I got home, so I went into her bedroom and took the uniform out of her wardrobe. Just to look at it. I'd seen it hanging there in a plastic cover. I couldn't resist putting it on – first the skirt, then the blouse, jacket and hat. They fitted me quite well, because I'm tall for my age. I was prancing about in front of the mirror, feeling quite glam, and thinking of all the exotic places Mum had been to, when she came in. I hadn't heard the front door, so I was quite surprised. I wasn't expecting she'd mind, because I used to try on her things all the time. But when she saw me in the uniform she went absolutely ballistic. She practically tore it off me. Like I said, I really thought she was going to hit me. More than that. I thought she was going to murder me.'

The recollection of the incident had made the child go quite pale.

'That was when she said I'd ruined her life, that she hated me. I could see that she meant it.'

'Perhaps at the time she did. Having children is a huge event in people's lives. It changes everything. Perhaps Flora had ambitions that none of us knew anything about. Ambitions for a career in the airline. It wouldn't have been easy to combine that with being married with a family. When she saw you wearing the uniform, it brought it back to her.'

'Like I was a sort of symbol of what she had lost?'

'Yes.'

She nodded slowly. 'Yeah, I think I can understand it a bit more. So you think she loves me as well?'

'I'm sure she does.'

'Have you got the life you want, Cat?'

The question took her unawares. Suddenly it was as if their roles were reversed. The tall, slim, willowy girl-woman was staring at her with her penetrating blue eyes, displaying a calm wisdom beyond her years.

'I'm not sure anyone gets exactly what they want or expect. But I think I have as much as most people. A job I like. My own house.' She smiled in an attempt to lighten the atmosphere. 'A wonderful sister and a beautiful, charming, intelligent niece, both of whom I love dearly.'

'You're not married, though. And you don't have children of your own.'

'I'm only thirty-eight! Not due for the scrap-heap yet.'

'But you've decided not to get married, haven't you? If you were really wanting to have kids, you'd be working on it now. We did stuff about eggs and that in human biology. But you've not even got a boyfriend, have you?'

Catriona started to feel uneasy again. 'I think I've said, Charlotte, that I don't want to be quizzed on my personal relationships.'

'Yeah, right, sorry. But I'm not asking in a crude way now. I'm just asking why you don't want children of your own?'

'For a start, I'm not in a position to! As you've pointed out, I don't have a man, never mind a husband. Secondly, I don't think I'd make a very good mother.'

'I think you would.'

'It's generous of you to say that, but I don't think so. I'm much too selfish. I have my work, and my house. I don't need anything else.'

'Your house is amazing. It's like you've thought about every bit of it. The right picture here, the piece of sculpture there. I used to think Mum was house-proud, but with her it was a matter of keeping everything clean and tidy. You've put so much of yourself into your house, haven't you? Maybe that's why there isn't much left over.'

* * *

'So what did you like best?'

'The sloth bears, definitely. They were so cute with their big claws and friendly faces. I would love to have brought one home.'

'It would fit well in your room, wouldn't it? And we could let it out in the garden for a run.'

'And we could feed it on vegetable scraps. We could throw them out from a bucket at meal-times, just as they did today!'

The child's eyes were bright as she involved herself in the fantasy. The sulky, withdrawn, early teenager had for the moment disappeared, and someone far more unaffected and likeable had taken her place. The zoo, suggested enthusiastically by Charlotte, had been a great success. Catriona, who didn't care for animals, but was nevertheless uncomfortable with the morality of keeping them in captivity, had been uneasy about the visit. To her surprise, she had relaxed enough to enjoy herself, laughing like a child at the antics of the monkeys, who certainly did not behave as if they were incurably depressed. Only the elephants, trudging around their bare concrete pen, seemed melancholy and out of place. Had they, though, ever seen the savannah of Africa? And if not, did their genes still cry freedom as they stared out over the safety ditch that separated them from their grinning, yelling, waving human admirers?

They walked back over Regent's Park. The Spring sunlight cast long shadows over the grass. In the rose garden, the unopened flower buds on the bare bushes were yellowed, shrivelled and battered by the recent rain, like Brussels sprouts at the end of winter.

They were enjoying what seemed like a companionable silence when Charlotte said, 'When Mum comes back, you won't tell her about this afternoon, will you?'

'Why ever not?'

'She wouldn't approve of our going to the zoo. She hates zoos. She says they're degrading both to animals and people. There was a dreadful stink when I was in the Infants'. The

71

school trip was to the Cotswold Wild-Life Park. Mum wouldn't let me go and I cried all night, because my friends were going to laugh at me. I thought you might have known, but when I suggested it and you said OK, you obviously didn't. But perhaps I ought to have said something. Only I did so want to see London Zoo.'

Catriona paused before replying. She hadn't known about Flora's aversion, though perhaps she ought to have, as it was certainly consistent with her sister's general philosophy. Would it have made any difference if she had known? Charlotte, torn between the loyalty of the child to her parent, and her own stirrings of curiosity and independence, was clearly concerned at the subterfuge she regarded herself as having perpetrated.

Eventually, Catriona said, 'You might have mentioned it before, but you have mentioned it now, and that's brave of you to own up. And maybe it wasn't such a bad thing, because you've had the opportunity to make your own mind up about the subject. Your mother will respect the fact that, at your age, you need to do that. So how do you feel about zoos now?'

'I think Mum's right in some ways. It isn't natural, is it? to be so cooped up, not for the larger animals anyway. But some of the species might have gone extinct by now if they weren't kept going by zoos, and then nobody would have a chance to appreciate what they were like, which would be a shame. I'm glad I've seen those special white leopards.'

'It's complicated, isn't it? I think you should discuss it with your mother when she comes back.'

Even as she said it, she thought how false it sounded. As if Charlotte and her mother would immediately fall into a discussion about the morality of keeping wild animals if Flora did come back! What was the point of pretending like this? Sooner or later, Charlotte would have to be told that it was unlikely that her mother would ever return. She was not a stupid child, far from it, so she must at some level know this. Then again, perhaps it was hope that was supporting

72

her. Truth would merely kick away the crutch on which she leaned, and what good would that be?

'There wouldn't be any point in that. Mum will never change her mind in the least bit. Once she has an idea, that's it. Zoos are just one thing. There's vegetarianism, recycling, conserving energy, having to use eco-products. She won't hear a word against any of them. That's why I got upset with you over the food. I had huge battles with Mum over what I liked to eat and I couldn't stand having to go through it again with you.' She grinned. 'Luckily you gave in quicker.'

Catriona smiled in return. 'Strong opinions weakly held, that's me.'

'Besides, you're a veggie, but I bet you don't go in for the rest of the stuff that Mum does. The meetings, the protest marches, the posters.'

'No, I don't have any interest in activism. I hadn't realised that Flora did.'

'Yeah, course. Green Party, Greenpeace, Friends of the Earth, CND, Animal Rights, you name it, she was into it. Out every evening at meetings some weeks she was.' She paused, a bitter twist to her mouth and a surprisingly adult look of world-weariness on her face. 'Sometimes I used to say to her that she was more keen on saving the planet than caring for her own daughter.'

'And what did she reply?'

'She got really mad. I told you how scary she can be. She said she had as much right to her own life as I did, and that I had everything anyone could possibly want. And besides, there were important issues in the world that needed people strong enough to fight for them. Well, she's certainly strong, is my Mum. And a fighter. She even got arrested once. Did you know that?'

'No, she never told me.'

'No, I bet. It was a demo about GM crops which got ugly when they started trashing the field. Mum wouldn't talk about

73

it afterwards, but a boy at school said that his uncle, who's a policeman, said that she was dead lucky not to get done for assault. She went for a copper with a spade, and it was only because he dodged quickly and wasn't hurt, and she was a woman – and a good-looking one, not a battle-axe in a boiler-suit – so that he thought his mates would laugh at him, that she was let off with a caution.'

'So she must have had friends, acquaintances in these various organisations?'

The girl shot her a swift and suspicious look. 'What do you mean, friends?'

'What do you think I mean? People with whom she shared common interests, people she liked, people she rated.'

Her niece was shaking her head. 'Mum may be a bit loopy, but she isn't so stupid as to think that the Stroud veggie and sandals community contains a single person within it with any more chance of saving the world than a crippled hamster. As for . . . well, she had a bit more taste there.'

'More taste where?'

But Charlotte was, irritatingly, pretending she couldn't hear. 'Look, there's a van over there. I could murder an ice-cream.'

The last night, Charlotte called in to say goodnight. The child's body, which in daytime activity seemed so powerfully present and alive, seemed small and shrunken under the covering of the single sheet in the big bed.

'Mum used to read me stories when I was little. About rabbits and hares and badgers and moles and water rats, living cosy little lives in burrows and hollow trees. And I'd imagine that my bed was a burrow, and I'd snuggle down, and I woke up to find it was morning before I ever realised I'd been asleep. I felt so warm and safe. Now I lie awake, and I know that there aren't any burrows to hide in. The Wild Wood isn't a place you can avoid. It's everywhere.'

'I'm afraid it is.'

74

'That means that everywhere you go, there are things waiting to attack you. You can't trust anybody, can you? Not even people you thought would never let you down?'

'You've had a bad experience lately, one of the worst it's possible for anyone to have. You feel let down, abandoned, betrayed. But there is still hope and trust to be found in the world. You have to believe that.'

'Is there? Where do I start to find it? Can I trust you?'

'Yes.'

'Would you be someone I could always rely on, no matter what? Would you promise it? Would you promise as long as you live never to let me down?'

She hesitated before replying. 'That kind of promise is very difficult to keep. A lifetime is, I hope, a long time. Circumstances might intervene. I might be too sick, or too old one day to help you.'

'But if it were in your power?'

'If it were in my power.'

'Will you promise me then? That as long as you live, if it's in your power, you'll never let me down, that you'll always be there for me?' The child's small hand grasped hers and she gave it an answering squeeze.

'I promise.' The words seemed to echo in the darkness of the room.

She remembered the night when she, hardly more than a child herself, had sworn never to have children, never to be a mother. And unlike so many solemn oaths uttered by children in the dead of night, Catriona had kept hers. Now here it was, broken in spirit.

The child sat up suddenly, threw her slim arms around her aunt's neck, and pressed her full warm lips upon hers.

'Sealed with a kiss. Thank you, dearest Cat.' She sank back against the pillow, as if exhausted by the effort the forging of the new bond between them had cost. Drowsily, she continued, 'I wish I'd made Mum promise, instead of just assuming. If I'd made her promise to send for me if she ever went away, then she would have had to. Instead of which she's too busy to think of me. Too busy fucking Frank.'

It was as if a cold finger had touched her spine. 'Who's Frank, Charlotte?' she asked as casually as she could.

'Frank Churchill. He teaches some art classes at our school. His daughter is there, too, a couple of years ahead of me. That must be how Mum met him. A real poser. Everyone knows he has it off with just about every attractive woman he bumps into. And he's a big-head about his sculpture. About how he's received a new commission, which he's working on in his studio. Sounds posh till you know it's a poxy rat-hole. Actually, he spends most of his time drinking with a load of other layabouts in the Fleece in Stroud.'

'And you think that he and your mother are . . .'

When the girl replied, her voice had become husky, as if she were going to cry. 'Yeah, course. Don't you know? Didn't Mum ever tell you? Frank is definitely her boyfriend. She's gone off with him, it's obvious.'

'But why do you think that? Did she tell you? Your mother never ever mentioned this Frank to me. What's more, she never even hinted that she had a . . . that she was seeing someone.'

'I found out by accident. One afternoon, our class was in Stroud doing a project on industrial archaeology. It was her day off, so I was surprised to see her. She seemed very much in a hurry, so she never saw me. She went into the old woollen mill off the High Street, the one that's been turned into arty-farty workshops. She was using a key to unlock the door. That's the same place that God's gift to women Churchill has his studio in. When I asked her casually where she'd been that afternoon, she said she'd been shopping in Ciren. Why else would she be going into his studio, with her own key? And if that wasn't the reason, why lie to me about it? So I wasn't surprised at first when she skipped. I thought that after a bit, she'd want me to join her. But time's gone on and she obviously doesn't. I really miss her, Cat. If she loved me she'd miss me. If she loved me, she'd come back for me.'

FIVE

Unlike the surrounding villages, such as Owlbury, gracefully unified by the famous yellow-grey Cotswold stone, Stroud had the air of being haphazardly put together from a box of bits left over from building various other places. There was a plate-glass fronted parade of shops from a nineteen-sixties new town, a Victorian pedimented assembly rooms from Glasgow or Leeds, a brick building society headquarters which had strayed from a by-pass somewhere in the Midlands, and a terrace of Georgian town-houses that might have been transplanted from Bath.

Catriona had visited the town on one other occasion, with Flora, on an expedition to buy some sort of herbal remedy for a childish ailment contracted by Charlotte. Catriona had often teased her sister on her devotion to homeopathy, herbalism, acupuncture, reflexology and other such alternative therapies, for which the town was notorious.

Afterwards they had had tea in a restaurant which rejoiced in the name Demeter's Pantry. 'So how does Bill stand on complementary medicine?' she had asked Flora, somewhat disingenuously.

'About where you'd imagine a loyal employee of Avalon Laboratories would stand,' she had replied, tartly. 'He thinks it's all, to quote his elegant phrase, "a load of eyewash."'

'I thought,' continued Catriona, impelled more by mischievousness than by any real interest in the subject, 'that modern medical opinion was tending not to regard such things so dismissively?'

Flora snorted. 'Maybe there is some enlightenment in some quarters. There are some GPs who also offer homeopathy, for instance. But drugs companies exist by selling drugs. They're never going to promote a drugs-free therapy, for obvious reasons.'

'But I bet they monitor such things, nevertheless. Surely if their research indicated that some of these treatments really worked, they'd have to take account of that in some way?'

Her sister had laughed derisively. 'Honestly, Cat. For someone who's such a brainbox, you're awfully naïve sometimes. It's those ivory towers you've inhabited for so long. Look, there's research and then there's research. For instance, you do research into Wordsworth. You discover a previously unknown manuscript. It contains, what? I know, a pornographic poem, yes, as explicit as anything in Rochester. What do you do?'

'I'd suspect immediately it was a fake!'

'OK. Apart from checking its authenticity. If you were satisfied it was genuine, you'd publish it, wouldn't you? With all the usual critical apparatus.'

'Of course. It would be as though a Force-Eight earthquake had hit Grasmere.'

'You wouldn't say that, as the blessed Wordsworth's pure reputation as the poet of daffodils and misty mountains would be sullied, the manuscript should be suppressed?'

'Of course not! I'd be fascinated that the sensuality that is latent in his work had fully emerged in some private moment. It's such an intriguing idea, Flo!'

She laughed. 'Cat, you're a genuine scholar, a sea-green incorruptible. No one's paying you to keep Wordsworth safe for generations of GCSE students. You're not in hock to the Lakes poets industry, preserving their heritage of clean-living and mountain-walking for the coach parties that flock to worship at the shrine! But what if you were?'

Catriona smiled. 'I see what you're driving at, you devious woman. You mean, there are some scientists who might fudge their findings to preserve the status quo.'

'Precisely. That's what scientific research is for. To prove that what you, or rather the person who is paying you, would wish to be the result, *is* the result. Genetically modified crops? Absolutely safe. BSE? Absolutely not transmissible to human beings. Mobile phones? No problem. It happens over and over again. Until, that is, the weight of the evidence is such that even the scientists in the pay of the governments and the big corporations can't ignore it or argue it away any longer, and then, of course, there's a need for yet more research into ever-more expensive drugs to cure – or preferably to alleviate, there's more profit in alleviation – AIDS, or vCJD, or any of the other horrid plagues that their masters have inflicted on us in the first place.'

Catriona had been genuinely taken aback by the hornet's nest the discussion had stirred. She had never heard her sister speak so passionately, and yet so cynically on a matter of this kind. She told her as much.

And Flora had said, 'I've been interested in these things for a long time. You just haven't noticed before. I read a newspaper – a real one, *the Guardian*, not the *Daily Mail*. I listen every night without fail to the midnight news on Radio Four. I'm a member of Greenpeace and Friends of the Earth. I read books, too – not novels but serious stuff on the environment. For years you thought of me as just an empty-headed blonde. The air-stewardess factor, wasn't it? You always thought my job was a joke. A glorified waitress, you said once. Remember those awful sexist adverts years ago for that airline? "I'm Flora, fly me!" I'm Flora, fuck me, more like. Well, it wasn't like that. Not for me. I never had the time to fuck a passenger, never mind the inclination! At various times, I delivered a baby, I gave heart massage, I dealt with a fire in the galley. I was on two flights on which there were full-scale emergency landings: sirens, fire-tenders, chutes out, the works. I wasn't ever hijacked, but that was a real and constant danger. And every time we took to the air, someone was sick, someone was drunk, someone was a pain in the arse, some unaccompanied minor needed a mummy to hug. Oh yes, and I had to serve drinks and meals non-stop!'

There had been defiant fire in her blue eyes as she had drunk up her tea, and a decisive clink as she had set down her cup.

'Excuse me, are you Frank Churchill?'

The tall, sunburnt, middle-aged man with greying chestnut hair, wearing a leather jacket and standing at the bar in the crowded, smoke-filled pub, turned around at her light touch on his shoulder. She could see from the way he paused to look her over, his eyes widening and his smile deepening, that he was a man who was accustomed to appraise a woman in the manner that in, another century, he might have assessed a horse. The only difference was that he did not grab her jaw to examine her teeth. But he did not trouble to disguise the fact that he was mentally running an appreciative hand over her withers. 'Yes, that's me. And who are you?'

'My name is Catriona Turville. I'm Flora's sister.'

She spoke the latter words softly, only loud enough for him to hear the words. He hesitated for a long moment, as if he hadn't heard, or perhaps as if he'd heard only too well. Then he nodded casually at an empty table in the far corner. 'Why don't we sit down over there? It's a bit more private.'

A few heads turned as he ushered her away from the bar, his arm on her shoulders. She itched to shake off the unwanted guidance, but to do so would have drawn more attention to them. Nonetheless, she could hear vaguely sala-cious murmuring from some of the other drinkers as the two of them crossed the floor together.

'Don't let them bother you,' he said as they sat down.

'I won't,' she assured him.

'Can I get you anything?'

'No, thank you, Mr Churchill.'

'It's Frank. No one calls me Mr Churchill. Too prime-ministerial. Though family legend has it that we are a cadet branch of the Marlborough dynasty. On the wrong side of the blanket, of course.'

'I'm not here to discuss your family tree.'

Unmoved by her rudeness, he took a swallow from the pint glass, then set it on the stained deal table before him. 'So, what are you here to discuss?'

'Please don't waste time by pretending ignorance. I've already told you, and, by your reaction, you've already acknowledged being told. Flora, as I'm sure you are aware, has disappeared. You, more than anyone, have a reason to know or to suspect where she might have gone. You were, by all accounts, having an affair with her.'

'By all accounts? Whose?'

'Are you denying there was an affair?'

He grinned, settling back in the Windsor chair. 'Define the word affair, and maybe I'll be able to answer you.'

'Do please stop prevaricating, Mr Churchill.'

'Frank, please! Flora told me that her sister was a high-powered academic at London University. A professor, no less. So surely, as a scholar, you can see why I want to define the terms we're using? What I mean by the word "affair" might be quite different from what you mean. My affairs,' he grinned, 'might not be the same as your affairs.'

Struggling to control her desire to walk out of this squalid drinking den, and to escape the sordid situation in which she was involving herself, she forced herself to reply. 'A temporary sexual liaison between two people who are not married to each other.'

'Very good, Professor Turville!' He tapped fingers against

palm in ironical applause. 'What I particularly like is your inclusion of the important word temporary. Permanence is a word I shy away from these days, having at some trouble and a great deal more expense recently freed myself from the marriage from hell.'

'So it's over? Is that why you show so little concern about Flora now?'

'I have trouble showing my emotions. It's something I'm working on with my therapist.'

He was so deadpan, she found it hard to decide whether he was being serious. Her confusion must have showed.

'I'm not kidding you. Therapy is the principal local industry. Everyone round here has a therapist. Even roughnecks like me.'

'You're not a roughneck are you?' she responded tartly. 'You're quite clearly an educated man. As well as an exceedingly cynical one. Women are like buses to you, aren't they? You miss one, there's another along in a minute.'

He flushed, and for a moment his laidback expression seemed to disappear, then he gave a slight shrug of his broad leather clad shoulders. 'I don't know what planet you've landed from. You seem to know nothing about human relationships. Just because a man and a woman have no intention of building a cosy nest together doesn't mean that they don't mutually respect and honour each other. Which is more than most married couples do, in my experience.'

'But your respect and honour hasn't resulted in any action on your part, has it? You haven't denied you knew she was missing. You never came forward. Didn't you have the least concern about what might have happened to her?'

He sipped the beer reflectively. 'Of course I did hear about her. The whole town knows, even though it was kept out of the *Stroud News and Journal*. It was precisely because I was concerned about her that I didn't come forward. If her going away was simply a temporary aberration, then I didn't think

83

it was a good idea to get involved. It might have complicated matters. And at first I thought she might have simply needed a break. But the longer she's been missing, the less sure I am about that. I have absolutely no idea where she might have gone, though. She's left me in the dark as much as apparently she did everyone else. But from the way you're behaving, you obviously suspect that I know more than I'm admitting. You may even think I had something to do with her disappearance?'

'It had crossed my mind, as a possibility, when I learned of your existence.' She stared at him levelly, watching his reaction. 'It would no doubt occur to the police, too. Which may be another factor in your decision to keep quiet about your involvement with Flora. Don't the statistics show that murders are most often committed by spouses or lovers?'

He returned her gaze unblinkingly. 'You don't have a very flattering impression of me, do you? First of all I'm the callous, womanising wrecker of a happy marriage. Then I've not only bedded your sweet, vulnerable sister, but done her in into the bargain.' He spoke with his habitual insouciance, but beneath she detected a harder edge. 'I think it's about time we stopped this nonsense. Let's start by getting a few things straight. Most importantly, in the highly unlikely event that she is in fact dead, I certainly played no part whatsoever in her demise.'

She shrugged in acknowledgement. 'You may be a lady-killer, but I don't see you as a murderer.'

'Thanks a lot! But as for the rest, I have to admit I did lead you on at the beginning of our conversation. You were so aggressively sure about my relationship with Flora. That pissed me off. But things have got serious. I'm telling you now, whatever the source of the accounts of my relationship with your sister that have led you to seek me out, they are dead wrong in a crucial respect. Flora and I were not lovers. We were not even particularly friendly in an intimate personal sense. That was precisely why I chose not to come forward.

As you've just demonstrated, people have nasty suspicious minds. Flora, if and when she returned, wouldn't want that to add to her other problems.'

'I don't believe you. Flora was seen going into your studio. For what other possible reason could you and she have been seeing one another?'

'I don't know what your academic discipline is professor, but I certainly hope it isn't the study of law, otherwise I shall start to believe the newspaper reports about declining standards in our universities. For a start, the fact that she was seen going into my studio is not proof of anything. Did your informant trouble to mention whether I was in fact inside the said studio? Or that I entered it subsequently?'

Catriona felt the warm beginnings of a blush. How could she have let this man put one over on her like this? Was he telling the truth, or was he a skilful and inveterate liar? Whatever he was, he was making her look a fool.

Churchill grinned at her obvious confusion. 'The truth is that whoever peddled you this yarn was acting, at the most charitable interpretation, out of error, and at the least charitable, out of malice. There are plenty of people who might well take the latter course. This is a small town, Professor Turville. I'm not always so solicitous as I might be about what I say in public and whom I might offend in consequence. Maybe someone decided to get back at me this way. But to continue with my analysis of what this person claimed to see. Even if I were inside my studio waiting for your sister to arrive on the occasion in question, there is another reason why she might have been calling on me than to engage in acts of sexual intercourse – pleasant though that might have been, as she was undoubtedly an attractive woman. Not as beautiful as you, of course.' He dipped his head in the semblance of a bow.

At this obviously insincere flattery, she resolved her expression into its coldest and most penetrating. 'What other reason?'

'Flora didn't want me for my body; she wanted me for my art.'

'Your art? Flora was interested in your sculpture?'

'You don't have to sound so surprised. I'm actually quite good, but I haven't yet entirely succeeded in convincing the philistine world of this fact. Flora was interested in my work but, more precisely, she herself wanted to do some sculpture. She engaged me as her tutor.'

'Flora wanted to learn sculpture?' The incredulity was patent in her tone.

'Yes, is that so surprising?'

'Frankly, it is. I never heard her express any interest in art. Was she any good?'

'Good? A person who wants to create, who desires to put something of themselves into a piece inevitably creates something good, in my opinion. Everything else is technique, which can be learned. Some artists are more technically skilled, but they don't necessarily produce better art. Flora was very enthusiastic. I gave her a key to the studio so that she could work there if she wanted on the days I was away. I have to teach to earn a living. Two days a week at the college in Cheltenham. One day at Stag End Comprehensive in Cirencester. My daughter is a pupil, as is Flora's, as I'm sure you know. That's how I met her. My daughter is a couple of years older than Charlotte, but they were both in the same school play. An adaptation of *Jane Eyre*. Charlotte was young Jane, and Lizzie was the teacher who befriends her.'

'Miss Temple,' Catriona responded automatically.

'I was talking to my ex-wife Pat in the interval – in public we're civilised – and Flora joined our conversation. The next day Flora called me and asked me if I would be willing to take her on as a student.'

'Had you ever done that sort of thing before?'

'No, no one had ever asked me. Though historically, it's

hardly uncommon is it – the master and the pupil in the master's studio.'

'Is that how you saw it? It played to your vanity?'

His easy smile once more deflected her rudeness. 'I suppose it did.'

'You didn't think it was a kind of code? Flora asking herself up to see your etchings?'

'That may have crossed my mind. I took the view that if she wanted it to happen, it would happen. And contrary to what you might imagine about me, I respect what women want. I like them too much not to. I'm not a seducer. I don't need to be.'

'And Flora never invited you?'

'No, I've already told you. She never once made any flirtatious gesture or any reference to her sexual need. She was entirely concentrated on exploring her artistic sensibility. You find that hard to believe, don't you? You don't think your sister was capable of a creative urge which needed to be satisfied? I thought you were close. It makes me wonder how close you were.'

'You've a bloody nerve, haven't you?' In her anger, her voice rose, attracting the attention of the other drinkers. She reflected with annoyance that no doubt they were now watching with interest the interview between good ol' Frank – what a one he is! – and this dark stranger. 'You've no bloody right at all to comment on what you think may be my relationship with my sister!'

'You're even more lovely when you're angry!' he said, feinting to dodge the imaginary blow she might have aimed at him. 'But you're right to be so. I shouldn't have said that.'

There was a softness in his tone which almost convinced her that the contrition was genuine.

'No, you shouldn't have.'

'So, do you believe that Flora and I enjoyed a merely professional relationship? There are such things between men and women.'

'I know that. Of course there are.' Her voice broke slightly and the icy reserve which she had been holding around her like a shield seemed to crack and melt. 'I'm sorry, Mr Churchill. I've been terribly rude. This thing has made me very tense. I don't mean to be so abrasive.'

He shook his head. 'You don't need to apologise. I'm renowned for my thick skin.'

'I do need to apologise. I've been horrible to you. I don't know you and yet in the space of half an hour I've managed to accuse you of dreadful things. I feel so confused. Perhaps, as you said, I don't know Flora as well as I thought I did. How well does one know anyone? What you've told me seems so out of character from the sister I knew. As does the fact that she has apparently walked out on her life. There may be some link between the two.'

'You mean she may have gone off to Tahiti like Gauguin?'

'It sounds fantastic, but the truth is that she must have gone somewhere. Do you think she was really bitten by the art bug?'

He shook his head. 'No, I don't. She was a diligent explorer, but I wouldn't say she was totally absorbed to the extent of wanting to drop everything else. But why don't you form your own view? Her things are still in the studio. Come along and see for yourself. It's just round the corner.'

'Here we are.' He had stopped in front of a pair of massive double wooden doors set in the facade of a huge stone building. 'Mugford's Mill. Part of the glorious heritage of the Stroud Valleys. Once it churned out West of England broadcloth by the mile. Now it shelters a post-industrial community of artists.'

He unhooked a bunch of keys from his belt, and turned it in the Yale lock of one of the boarded panels, pushed it open and flicked a light switch on the inside of the jamb. There were other doors in flimsy partitions on either side where the original ground floor had been split into individual workshops. Opposite the entrance was a wooden staircase, lit by a single bulb hanging from the shadows above on a long flex.

He led the way up the creaking treads. On the first landing, he unlocked another door. 'This is my place.'

There was a large space lit by grimy, small-paned transom windows set high up. The bare boards of the floor above were supported on thick wooden beams.

He waved an arm around. 'Work in progress.' It looked like nothing so much as a scrap-yard. Rusty slabs of iron were stacked against the walls. There were painted metal panels which had once been the body parts of cars. Shiny chromium bumper bars were supported on shelf brackets. The centre of the room was taken up by a gigantic bench formed from enormously thick baulks of blackened timber supported on square steel posts bolted to the floor. On the bench were several heavy steel vices of various sizes, an array of tools, and the hooded mask and wand of an oxyacetylene welding apparatus. Alongside stood a bank of black painted gas cylinders.

He grinned at the expression on her face. 'It's funny how people assume that sculpture is still marble and bronze. But art moves on.'

She pointed at a complex arabesque of shining polished steel which rose from the floor like a frozen waterspout. 'Is that what you're working on at present?'

He nodded. 'What do you think?'

'I like it.'

'It's for the corporate offices of a software company. The spiral follows the Fibonacci sequence of numbers. It looks natural, but is in fact digital.'

'You're actually quite traditional then. Wasn't Greek art highly mathematical? "The lineaments of a plummet-measured face", as Yeats described it. And the art of the Florentines? And perspective. Think of Piero della Francesca.'

He inclined his head in irony-tinged respect. 'Flora told me you were an intellectual.'

She smiled. 'I'm a scholar, an academic. Don't you know that there are no intellectuals in England?' Before he could reply, she glanced swiftly round the room. 'Where are Flora's things?'

He pointed. 'That's her corner.'

On the bench top were a number of figures formed from grey clay and now dry and hard. They were like the matchstick men drawn in childhood, but even a cursory glance showed that they had an indefinably sinister quality. Catriona shuddered and averted her eyes.

Churchill observed her reaction. 'Disturbing. Powerful, aren't they? I was surprised when I saw them. It made me realise Flora was, underneath, quite a different person from her public face. All that brisk efficiency must have cloaked a mass of personal insecurity. She wasn't willing to discuss the meaning of them. And that one wrapped up in cloth she wouldn't let me see at all. Refused point blank – she was really angry.'

He was clearly hoping that Catriona would suggest unveiling the shrouded figure, but she did not. Nor did she respond to his perceptive characterisation of the missing woman.

'This was the last thing she was working on,' he said, pointing to the object alongside.

Standing on a length of wide-bore flanged steel pipe, which raised it to working height, was the bole of a tree. Flora had begun to work the natural lines of the wood, polishing the protruding nodules, deepening and refining the fissures. While in no sense was there an attempt at anthropomorphism, a feeling of twisting vitality had begun to emanate from the object. It had an altogether healthier feel than the figures.

'I'm amazed. I never knew she could do this sort of thing, or that she even wanted to.'

He shrugged. 'It may sound a romantic cliché, but I believe

the capability is in everyone. If there is a desire for expression, there is a capacity to express.'

'I think also you're a good teacher.'

'I prefer the word facilitator.'

'Yes, I can see why. When I teach, I try to remember that I'm still learning too. That I don't know everything. What's happened just now is an excellent reminder of that. I feel I've learnt more about Flora as a result. But,' her voice, despite her efforts to control it, faltered, 'but it still doesn't help me find out what happened to her.'

'I've remembered something. There's a holdall here with some of her stuff in it. Her tools and the overalls she wore. You might like to look in case there's anything else. It's there, underneath the bench.'

With hands that trembled, she pulled out the battered blue British Airways flight attendant's bag and yanked back the zip.

On top was a white smock, clay-smeared but neatly folded. She lifted it out and set it on the floor beside her. At the bottom of the bag was a canvas roll tied with its own tapes, which contained, slipped into pockets within, a variety of chisels and gouges of different sizes, and a decorated metal tube which, from the printed logo, had once contained a bottle of Bushmills Irish whiskey. She pulled off the lid and slid into her palm a variety of smooth wooden sticks, like paintbrush handles, with pointed, flat or spatula-like ends, or fitted with metal loops. Judging from the residues adhering to them, they must have been used for modelling clay. There was also a sinister-looking piece of wire with a wooden handle at each end which looked exactly like a garotte.

She held up this object to Frank Churchill and he laughed at her expression.

'Ist nicht for ze strangling of enemies of ze Tausend Jahre Reich,' he said in an excruciating Hollywood-German accent. 'Is for the cutting of clay.'

The holdall contained nothing apart from these items. She ran her hand around the inside, looking for pockets in the lining. But there were none.

She sat back on her heels.

'You're disappointed?'

'Yes.'

'You'd hoped to find something?'

'Yes. If this new enthusiasm for art was an element of some change in her life generally, some shift that might have caused her to flee, then I was hoping there might be some clue to other aspects of it, which in turn might suggest where she's gone.'

'We can search the rest of the place, if you like?'

She shook her head. 'No. If she had wanted to keep something here, she wouldn't have wanted you or anyone else to come across it by accident. It would then be evident that it had some significance. The first rule of hiding something is not to make it look as if it's been hidden.'

'The purloined letter principle?' He grinned at her look of surprise. 'I read books as well.'

'I'm glad to hear it. Yes, I believe that if there had been anything here, it would have been in this bag.'

She stood up. 'I'm sorry I wasted your time, Mr Churchill.'

'You keep saying that! Frank! You don't have to apologise. I want to help. If there is anything else, you only have to ask.'

'Thank you.' She pointed to the holdall. 'I'd like to take this.'

'Of course.'

She hesitated. 'I'd like the clay models, too, even though I find them disturbing and I can't look at them too closely at present. They represent an aspect of Flora I never knew.' She smiled. 'The tree trunk should, I think, remain here. With you.'

He nodded, quite solemnly. With speed and delicacy his large, powerful hands wrapped the fragile objects in newspaper and packed them securely in an old cardboard box.

She slung the bag over her shoulder and he carried the box out to her car; she had parked near the pub. They stowed the items in the boot.

She held out her hand. 'I was wrong about you. I have a bad habit of thinking that I know everything. Goodbye, Frank.'

He smiled. 'I was fond of Flora. If I can help you any further, call me. Call me any time. Here, keep this. You never know.' He handed her a white business card through the open window.

'You never know,' she agreed as she glanced at the card, which read

FRANK CHURCHILL
2 MULBERRY LANE
WOODCOMBE
GLOS.

Then she let in the clutch and drove away.

She didn't want the unsettling clay figures in the house, so she carried the cardboard box and the holdall to the ancient garage at the end of the back garden. It was used only as a glory hole, being too narrow even to accommodate the Fiesta comfortably, added to which the double doors that gave onto the rear lane were in no fit state to open without falling to pieces.

She put the box on a dusty shelf and was about to dump the holdall on the floor when some instinct made her decide to check it through one more time in case there had been something she had missed under the earlier scrutiny of Frank Churchill.

One by one she removed each item it contained. Again she searched the tool roll and the old whiskey-bottle container. Still nothing except what she had seen already. She stared into the interior of the holdall, bitterly disappointed that it contained no secrets. Then she noticed that the vinyl bottom of the bag, which she had assumed to be fixed to the canvas, was in fact a loose insert of plastic-covered board.

She slid her fingers underneath its edge and tugged it free. Beneath was a yellow padded envelope. She lifted the flap and tipped the contents onto her lap. Several dozen glossy colour snaps spilled out, some sliding off her jeans-clad thighs onto the grimy concrete floor. Quickly she gathered them up, wiping off the dust from their shiny surfaces with a handkerchief.

Many of them featured Flora. They were taken outdoors, and in the background were various touristic locations, amongst which Catriona recognised Berkeley Castle, the Royal Crescent at Bath, Gloucester Cathedral and the Roman Villa at Chedworth.

There were several, however, in which another woman featured, with a background of the same locations. She was tall and dark-haired, possibly slightly older than Flora, with a tanned face that was strong and handsome rather than pretty. In many of the photographs she wore jeans and a T-shirt, in others, a pair of slacks and a blouse. These must have been taken by Flora. The two had clearly been sight-seeing together.

There were also several in which the strange woman appeared alongside her sister, with an arm around her waist or across her shoulders. Presumably these had been taken either by some unconnected third party, a fellow tripper persuaded to the task, or by using a shutter-delay mechanism. In all the photographs, both the women looked happy, smiling and relaxed. Two girls out on the razzle. Eating ice-cream, munching apples, being themselves. Thelma and Louise.

Catriona sat on her heels, oblivious of the discomfort from the hard surface beneath. She stared at these images with surprise and more than a touch of jealousy. Who was this woman? It was evident that she and Flora were close friends; it appeared they shared their days off and had done on a number of occasions. The camera must have been the friend's. Flora had never possessed one, nor had she ever been keen to be photographed. The friend must have given her copies of the developed prints, which Flora had then hidden away in the holdall.

But why hide them? And why had Flora never mentioned this person either to Catriona or to her husband? That must be the case, as Bill had been quite adamant that Flora had no close friends, only acquaintances amongst neighbours and parents at Charlotte's school. He had certainly not known of the existence of the relationship with Frank Churchill – he would have been enraged. He would never have believed that it was platonic. Catriona was sure there would have been a row about it if he had found out, and she would have heard about it herself.

The relationship with this woman seemed to fall into the same category of secrecy. Why otherwise had Flora kept the photos at the studio? If she had told Bill about her, then there would have been no need for this elaborate concealment. If Bill had known of her existence, he would assuredly have mentioned it. If he had not been told about it by his wife and subsequently discovered it, then it would have been adduced by him as another reason to believe Flora had been leading some kind of double life from which he had been excluded.

She held up the envelope, and felt inside it to see if it contained anything else. Her fingers closed on another paper within. Drawing it out, she saw that it was an ordinary white envelope, the flap of which was unsealed. She slid out its contents and gasped. There were several sheets of plain A4 paper on which photographs had been printed by a computer printer, the original images sourced from a digital camera or taken as stills from a camcorder.

Catriona felt the heat of a blush spreading over her face and down her neck. She was embarrassed by nudity, even her own, and these photographs were frank in their erotic, not to say pornographic, celebration of nakedness.

As she stared again and again in shock at each of the prints, she saw that the place in which they had been taken was unmistakably Frank Churchill's studio. In one, Flora, unclad save for a pair of high-heeled shoes, sprawled prone on a rug, a rose between her teeth, one leg raised provocatively. In another, the mysterious friend, displaying an enviably firm figure and unblemished skin, sat astride a chair, copying the pose of the iconic photograph of Christine Keeler. In another, Flora was contorted into a yoga position that left nothing to the imagination. There were several others of a similar nature, blatant in their sexuality.

But the ones that riveted Catriona's attention, which made her catch her breath, were a series which showed both women together, naked on the same rug on which Flora had been taken in reclining pose. But not just sitting. A sleazy journalist who got hold of such pictures would describe the particular positions they were in as explicitly passionate.

It was clear that Flora and the unknown woman were not only good friends who spent days out together. They were lovers.

The offices of Marshall's estate agent's were in the High Street. As she opened the plate-glass door, a young man who had been leaning back in his chair, apparently studying with great attention the design of the acoustic tile ceiling, snapped to attention and rose to greet her.

'Good afternoon, madam! Do please take a seat.'

She sat down in front of the shiny veneered desk. The estate agent made a show of shuffling together the few files that lay on its surface.

'How can we help you?'

She hesitated, then blurted out, 'I'm Catriona Turville. I'm Flora's sister.'

At that his expression changed. He no longer wore the false welcome of the young sales executive, but a look of genuine interest.

He extended his hand. 'I'm Phil Howard. Does this mean there's some news?'

'No, I'm afraid not. She's still missing.'

He shook his head. 'We were completely amazed when her husband told us what had happened.'

The outer door opened and a tall, extremely well-dressed red-haired woman came in. She was carrying an attaché case, the image of the successful career woman.

Phil Howard jumped to his feet and bounded over to her. 'Anne. This is Ms Turville. Flora's sister.' He turned back to Catriona. 'Anne Marshall, my boss.'

They shook hands. The estate agent put her case down on one of the empty desks. 'The office feels so empty without Flora. That was her place.' She pointed to a desk with a large flat-screen computer monitor. 'She insisted that we get those liquid crystal displays, long before they became so common. It was expensive, but she could be very persuasive. She even tried to make me get rid of my mobile, but you have to draw the line somewhere. We do miss her so much, don't we, Phil?'

'Dreadfully.'

She nodded, her mouth tight. She looked as if she might burst into tears. 'Yes. It's awful, that empty desk. When she left that Thursday lunchtime, she seemed not to have a care in the world. As I told Mr Jesmond, she never gave the least hint that she wouldn't be back on Monday as usual. She was the most completely reliable person I've ever worked with. She was never ill, never late. Never forgot anything. Always professional. That's what I just can't believe – that she'd have left us without a word. It's so unlike her. Now it's been nearly a month, and I can't help worrying that something awful may have happened . . .' She faltered.

'You're obviously fond of her,' said Catriona, gently.

'Yes. She was always kind and thoughtful. It's so dreadful to think that she may have been . . .'

This time the tears did come. She turned back to her desk, opened a drawer and took out a handful of tissues.

Phil Howard smoothly intervened to cover his boss's indisposition. 'She was so good with clients, on the phone or in person. House-buying and -selling's a pretty stressful time, as I'm sure you know. She had the knack of calming people down, putting them at their ease. She never had a bad word for anyone, and no one ever had anything but praise for her.'

Ms Marshall had by now recovered her composure. 'I hope I'm not upsetting you by saying that when we heard the news, although Mr Jesmond was at pains to emphasise that there was no sign of . . . of foul play and that the police were not treating it as a criminal investigation, we did try to think whether there had been anyone we had dealt with who might have, well, developed an unhealthy interest in Flora. She was, after all, a very attractive woman. Everyone in the profession remembers the Suzy Lamplugh case. But there had never been the least suggestion of anything like that.'

Catriona nodded. 'You don't have to apologise. It's something that has obviously occurred to all of us. As a matter of fact, the reason I came to see you today is to ask you about someone she might have encountered in the course of her work. I've found a photograph amongst Flora's things of a woman neither I nor Bill, her husband, recognise, but who seems to be an acquaintance.' She opened her handbag and took out the photograph she had brought with her. 'Do you happen to know this person?'

The elegant red-head held the oblong of glossy paper in her manicured hand. 'I think so.'

She handed it to her colleague. 'Phil?'

He studied it carefully, then said, 'It's the woman who wanted to sell her mother's property in Owlbury. She was her POA. It was Ellie's matter.' He handed the photograph back to his boss, who returned it to Catriona.

'I could say that anything to do with our clients is confidential, but I think in the circumstances that would be very pedantic and inappropriate. If this woman can shed any light on what might have happened to Flora then I'm prepared to take the risk of being criticised. Though I'm sure you'll be discreet about how you found her?'

'Of course.'

'Her name is Hazel Marchant. As Phil said, she came in about a year ago, I recall. The old lady had gone into a nursing home, and it had become obvious that she wasn't ever going to return to her house. My colleague Ellie Masters dealt with it. She's on holiday at present.'

'Did you know that she and Flora had become acquainted?'

'No, I didn't. Did you, Phil?'

The young man shook his head.

'Perhaps Ellie knew about it.'

'I'd really like to speak to Ms Marchant. Do you have her address and phone number?'

Ms Marshall turned to her desk and expertly clicked a few computer keys. 'Here's the file. Hazel Marchant. 35A Empire Court, Empire Road, Cheltenham. I'll give you her phone number, too.'

Empire Court was an upmarket development of modern apartment blocks, set in meticulously maintained gardens. Catriona parked her scruffy car in the parking area between a Mercedes and a brand-new BMW.

At the glass entrance doors, she pressed the buzzer of 35A, which was labelled MARCHANT. There was no reply. There had been no reply when she had phoned before she left Stroud, and no answering machine either. She had driven here in the hope that Hazel Marchant would have returned home by six-thirty. But clearly she was a late worker. Reluctant to return to London without having satisfied her need to meet her sister's lover, she impulsively stabbed the black plastic button against 35B, RICHARDSON. After some delay, an elderly-sounding male voice answered, 'Who is that, please?'

She spoke slowly and distinctly into the chrome grille of the speaker panel. 'My name is Catriona Turville. I want to talk to your neighbour Hazel Marchant. When does she usually get home?'

There was a silence, then in the background another elderly voice, this time that of a woman, could be clearly heard demanding, 'Who is that, Johnnie? The paper boy's already been.' Johnnie was heard to reply, 'It's someone, a young woman I think, asking for Hazel.' 'Hazel?' came the voice of the woman sharply. 'Are you sure? I'd better speak to them.'

'Are you still there? Why do you wish to see Miss Marchant?'

'She's my sister's friend. It's rather important.'

Again there was a silence, then the woman's voice spoke again. 'It isn't right to explain what's happened through this awful device. You'd better come up.'

They were waiting in their doorway as she came up the stairs, clearly rather anxious, obviously ready to shut the door in her face if she failed to pass the respectability test.

The wife was a tall woman, well-dressed and still hand-some, despite being probably in her late seventies. He was even taller, gaunt and rather frail, but ramrod straight, some years older than his wife, immaculately dressed in a lovat tweed suit, at his neck the dandyish flourish of a paisley bow-tie.

The woman looked at her with the searching scrutiny of one used to deciding whether a person was or was not the genuine article.

'What did you say your name was?'

'Catriona Turville.'

'And you're a friend of Hazel?'

'No, my sister is her friend.'

She must have decided that Catriona had passed whatever test had been mentally applied because she said, 'I'm Leona

Richardson and this is my husband Johnnie. You'd better come inside.'

The large combined sitting-and-dining room had a French-windowed balcony and looked down upon the wide, tree-lined suburban thoroughfare of Empire Road. It was furnished with some extremely good pieces: genuine antiques, noted Catriona rather ruefully, not stuff like hers, picked up in junk shops or out of skips. People like the Richardsons didn't do that. They inherited.

'Do sit down. Some tea?'

'Thank you, but please don't trouble.'

'It's no trouble. Would you do the honours, please, Johnnie?'

The elderly man went out of the room, and presently the sound of tea things being assembled could be heard on the other side of the wooden serving hatch.

Leona Richardson leaned forward and spoke in confidential tones. 'Do I take it that you did not know Hazel?'

'No, I'd never met her.'

'I see, then what I have to say will come as less of a shock than it might have, although that will not apply to your sister if she has not already heard the news.'

'What news?'

'I'm afraid Hazel is dead.'

For a moment, she thought she had misheard.

'Dead?'

'Yes. I'm very sorry to say that she is.'

The return of Mr Richardson, bearing a tray, which he set down with elaborate care on a Sheraton side-table, interrupted their conversation. It was only when she was equipped with a fragile china tea-cup and saucer – the Richardsons were clearly not mug people – that Mrs Richardson ventured to enquire, 'Have you been trying to contact Hazel for long? You never suspected anything was amiss?'

'It's a little complicated to explain, but I never knew of her existence until recently.' She paused. 'My sister is . . . has had

101

an emotional crisis . . . and . . . left home. I've been searching for her amongst her friends. I found a photograph of a woman who I am given to understand is Hazel Marchant.' She took the somewhat dog-eared snapshot out of her bag and showed it to Mrs Richardson.

The elder woman raised her eyebrows slightly at the reference to Flora having left home, but made no comment, concentrating on the image of the smiling woman at the Royal Crescent. 'Oh yes. That is certainly poor Hazel.'

For a moment she seemed overcome by emotion. 'Oh dear. What memories such things evoke. Hazel was always so charming and kind to us, far more than you would expect a neighbour to be. We used to say, didn't we Johnnie? that if we had had a daughter we should have hoped that she was like dear Hazel.'

Catriona was touched by the affection, but recalled the nude and provocative photographs of Hazel which would have surprised and probably shocked the Richardsons. She was aware of the irony. With good-hearted but conventional neighbours such as these, no wonder the gay woman had chosen to keep her other life a secret.

Mrs Richardson rather reluctantly handed the photograph back to Catriona.

'Please, I'd like you to keep it,' she said, returning it to the bony but elegantly long-fingered hand.

'That's very kind. We were regretting only the other day, weren't we Johnnie? that we had no picture to remind us of her.'

Catriona felt in her bag again and took from it the leather photograph wallet in which she kept her favourite picture of Flora, sitting in the garden of Palace View Road, her blonde head framed by Albertina roses. 'This is my sister, Flora. Did you ever see her here visiting Hazel?'

Mrs Richardson studied the picture. 'So attractive, and although you have different colouring, one can see the likeness. But I do not recognise her. Johnnie?'

''Fraid not, my dear.'

Seeing her expression, Mrs Richardson said kindly, 'You must be disappointed not to be able to find any news of your sister.'

'Yes, terribly. I was hoping that Hazel might know where she is. But she must have died suddenly. Was she ill? Or was it a car accident?'

'No, a fall. On Cleeve Hill, a favourite spot for ramblers. She appears to have slipped down a steep slope onto rocks. There are many such places, and every year there are accidents, but not usually fatal ones. Poor Hazel was unfortunate.'

'How did it happen?'

'No one knows. There seem to have been no witnesses. It was indeed a great shock to us. We had been away from home for a few days on a short holiday. Before leaving we had asked Hazel as usual to draw the curtains and turn on the lights in the evening. Burglaries are so common even in Cheltenham nowadays. We used to do the same for her. We each had a spare set of keys. When we came home, we were surprised to find the post on the doormat. Hazel would normally have collected it up and put it on the hall-table. We thought that she must have forgotten our little arrangement. That evening we read the dreadful story in the newspaper. One was used in the war to seeing the names of people one knew among the lists of the dead and the missing in the press, but it was shocking to see in peacetime the name of such a relatively young and healthy woman. It was, I repeat, a most dreadful shock.' She paused, took a lace handkerchief from the sleeve of her cardigan and dabbed her eyes. 'Do forgive me.' Recovering herself, she said, 'We have kept the cutting, if you would care to read it? Johnnie will get it for us. In the second drawer, darling.'

The old man got stiffly to his feet and crossed the room to the handsome mahogany tallboy.

'Rambling,' he grunted as he returned. 'Don't see the point of it myself.'

Catriona took the sliver of newsprint he handed her.

VICTIM OF BEAUTY SPOT TRAGEDY NAMED

The woman found dead on Cleeve Hill yesterday at the foot of a rocky gully near the summit was today named as Hazel Marchant of Empire Road, Cheltenham.

Ms Marchant, who was forty-one, and an independent financial services adviser, with an office in the town centre, appears to have fallen to her death while taking an afternoon stroll at the popular local beauty spot. Police have appealed for anyone with any further information about the matter to contact Cheltenham Police Station.

A coroner's inquest into the incident will be held.

As she set the cutting down on the occasional table in front of her, she noticed the date at the masthead. Hazel Marchant had died only a week before she had received Flora's letter. The news of her friend's death must have been burning in her sister's mind as she wrote those dreadful, despairing words.

SIX

As she made the turn through the open gate, Catriona saw her niece outside the garage, throwing an orange basketball through a hoop screwed to the beam above the door.

The Fiesta squealed to a halt. Charlotte stopped her game and, holding the ball under her arm, sauntered over to the car.

Catriona pushed open the creaking driver's door and swung her legs over the rusty sill. 'Why don't you change this rubbishy old banger for something decent?' the girl said by way of greeting, kicking the worn front tyre.

'It's perfectly sufficient for my needs. Hello, by the way.'

Charlotte did not reply, but bounced the ball on the gravel.

With a swiftness that she saw to her pleasure surprised the child, Catriona intercepted the ball and bounced it back across the drive to the garage, where, with an elegant pirouette on one leg, she flicked it up and through the hoop. She caught it on its return, repeated the action, then tossed the ball back to Charlotte, who was gazing at her in amazement.

'Hey, I didn't know you could do that!'

'You don't know everything about me. When I was your age, I could play any game. I was Victor – or was it Victrix? –

Ludorum at my school. Now please go and tell your Dad that dull old Auntie Cat is here.'

The girl gave a quick grin and disappeared around the back of the house. She was wearing white shorts with a stripe and a white sports shirt with some kind of logo. She seemed to be even taller and leggier than when Catriona had last seen her only a couple of weeks before.

Charlotte reappeared from behind the garage, followed by her father. He was carrying a garden fork, which he put down against the wall.

'Hello, Catriona.'

'Hello, Bill.'

''Ullo Bill, 'ullo Ben. 'Ullo little weed,' said Charlotte, her voice contorted into a passable imitation of the Flower-pot Men.

'Charlotte, why don't you go and get on with your home-work?'

'Because, Father dear, I've already completed the same. But don't worry. I'm quite aware that you wish to exclude me from your conversation with dear Aunt Catriona.' She scooped up the basketball, crossed the drive to the garage and carried on with her game.

In the kitchen, there were dirty plates scattered on the worktop, and unwashed saucepans piled in the sink. The waste-bin was full to overflowing. The entropy of the domestic universe that Flora had always sought to deny was reasserting itself.

Bill poured mugs of coffee from an electric filter machine.

'She's twigged something's up. When I said that you were coming to lunch today, she gave me one of her knowing looks. She's well aware that you and I wouldn't be meeting for the pleasure of each other's company.' He stared at her defiantly, as if inviting her to deny the truth of this statement. 'So we don't have to waste time on politenesses and pleasantries. You can tell me straightaway why you wanted to see me.'

Much as she didn't like or respect this man, Catriona was still reluctant to hurt him. 'It's about Flora, obviously. I didn't want to tell you over the phone.'

'You've heard from her?'

'No, I'm sorry. It isn't that. It's something I've discovered about her. Something you will find painful.'

His face creased into a kind of sneer. 'She's having an affair, isn't she? Now she's comfortably shacked up with the fellow she's shagging and she's sent you to get my daughter away from me.'

The crudeness of his language and the anger it betrayed appalled her. How she hated having to be in this position. But what choice had she got? She couldn't remain silent about what she had found out.

'Yes, I'm afraid she was having an affair. But not in the way you imagine. And, as I just told you, I don't bear any messages from her. I haven't heard from her.'

His eyes were wide and glaring, the aggression blazing out of him. 'So what kind of affair is it that I can't imagine?'

'It's an affair that was over before she disappeared. Nothing I've found out about it suggests that Flora had any intention of leaving you for this person. So there was no question of her wanting to take Charlotte away.'

'You knew about this, didn't you? You've known about it all along. So why has it taken so long for you to tell me? Were you waiting for the right moment to gloat over the pain it gives me? Why are you telling me about it now? To see me squirm while you pour the poison in my ears?'

'Bill, I know you think the worst of me, but believe me, that was never my motive. I thought long and hard about it, but I decided in the end you ought to know. I think it has a bearing on why Flora is missing. That's why I decided you had to know. But please believe me, I knew nothing of this until a few days ago. You have my word of honour that I did not know before Flora's disappearance.'

'You don't seriously expect me to believe that Flora never said anything to you? Never let slip the least hint? You nattered to each other on the phone for hours every week. You knew, you must have known! You probably encouraged her! My God, you were always a bitch to me, Catriona. You were always trying to turn Flora against me.'

The maudlin turn in his voice, on top of the other emotions churning within her drove her to fury. 'That is a damned lie! We never discussed you or the state of the marriage. It was one of the agreements we had. We didn't want that coming between us.'

'A likely story!'

'It's the truth. I know nothing about how relations stood between the two of you.'

He glared at her as if he still thought she was lying. Finally he said, 'You definitely haven't heard from her?'

At some level he must still think that she knew where Flora was; that they had colluded on her disappearance.

'No! How many more times do I have to tell you! I haven't heard from her. What the hell are you suggesting? That I've got her hidden at my house?'

'All right, if you didn't hear of this affair from Flora, how did you find out about it? How can you be certain that there was an affair? Have you spoken to the man involved? Who is he? Tell me who he is. I need to know. I have a right to know.'

'Bill, please. I know you're upset. But I don't think it's helpful to go into the details. There's no doubt that Flora was having an affair. It isn't relevant with whom. What is relevant is the effect its ending would have had on Flora. You see the affair didn't simply come to an end. The person, the lover, died, in a tragic accident. Only a week before Flora disappeared. Flora would have been devastated by that. Quite devastated enough, perhaps, to wish to take her own life.'

'You think Flora has committed suicide?'

'I think it has to be faced as a possibility.'

'Because of this lover's death? On that reading, she would have been depressed, disturbed, crazy with grief. I never saw any sign of that, did you?'

'No. But everyone reacts differently to strong emotions.'

'I find it impossible to believe that a state of mind as intense as you suggest was undetectable.'

'Undetectable!' she burst out. 'We're talking about Flora's feelings, not a chemical reaction!'

'I'm quite aware of what we are discussing. And so far, I have no evidence other than your say-so to prove the existence of this so-called doomed love affair. You say Flora did not tell you herself. So how did you find out about it? How do you know it drove Flora to kill herself?'

She felt her warm certainty cooling under the assault of the man's icy logic. What indeed did she know of the affair, beyond those photographs of physical passion?

Aware of her hesitation and uncertainty, he did not wait for her reply.

'Your problem, dear sister-in-law, is that you read too many of the wrong kinds of books. You're soaked in tales of romantic passion, of doomed lovers, of blazing emotions. But you yourself have no passion at all. You don't actually understand what makes flesh-and-blood people tick. You know nothing of emotions first hand, nor do you have any understanding of real psychology, the sort of psychology you can measure and test. You sneer at all that. You think your bloody poets have all the answers. Now I don't know anything about poetry, but I can't escape remembering some of what was dinned into me at school, and there's one line of Shakespeare which goes something like, men have died and worms have eaten them but not for love. You've picked up some idle gossip about Flora from somewhere and turned it into the grand romantic passion that you've never dared have yourself.'

She strove to keep calm. There was no point in responding

either to his insulting remarks concerning herself or his misinformed comments about literature. The devil shouldn't quote scripture if he has not even the most elementary knowledge of the Bible.

'I'm sorry, Bill, but there was an affair. My reading of it is that Flora may well have been suffering from depression as a result of its ending. I suppose we may have to agree to differ. But you must prepare yourself for the worst.'

'You don't know anything about Flora, do you? If there was an affair, I know exactly why she went in for it. I would have thought at least she might have had the guts to tell me about it herself. But oh no. She really wants to put the knife in. She wants to make sure I suffer, by having you be the messenger of the bad news. She's determined to pay me back.'

She stared at him. Yet again the scenery of the play had changed. 'To pay you back? Are you having an affair?'

'Not any longer, if you could ever call it an affair in the first place. It was about a year ago. A woman chemist on secondment from the States. It lasted a few weeks, then she went back to Chicago. End of story. But just before it was over, Flora found out. She was late-night shopping in Cheltenham one evening and she saw us drive past while she was queuing for a space in the Regent Centre car-park. Sod's law in operation. I didn't see her, so I spun some yarn about having to work late at the lab. I was contrite. She was furious for a while. I thought it had blown over and she'd forgiven me. But she was just biding her time for her revenge.'

It was evident that Bill's contrition, like that of many adulterers, related not so much to the commission of the deed but to the fact that it had been detected.

'All right, so she wanted to get her own back. I can understand that. But she could have confined it to between the two of us. Why did she have to leave, and inflict the pain on Charlotte? How could she just walk out on her with never a word? And where the hell has she gone?'

Despite the aggression and anger that clearly burned in him, he was sinking into a mawkish self-pity that revealed how insecurely based was his trenchant analysis of Flora's motives.

But could he be right? Could Flora have leapt into the arms of Hazel Marchant as a way of particularly hurting and humiliating her self-consciously macho husband? Would she have taunted him with the superior love-making skills of another woman? But the fact was that she had not, and she had not given him the least hint of the matter. Did that mean that she had changed her mind? Had she embarked on the affair with retribution in mind, then become swept up in emotions she had not hitherto understood?

How would Bill react if she told him Flora's lover was a woman? Would Flora's affair with a woman count less in his mind than an affair with a man? Or would he be disgusted by it? She herself found it hard to cope with.

And what of Charlotte? Was she old enough to understand such matters? And if Flora had not committed suicide, then why had she written as she had, and where was she now?

Suddenly the air in the kitchen seemed stifling, and behind Catriona's eyes the first stirrings of a migraine began to wriggle. She needed air, fresh air and light.

'I'm going to take a walk,' she announced, and stood up, adding, in the unlikely event he was about to offer to accompany her, 'by myself.'

Charlotte was still practising at the hoop as, her feet crunching on the shingle, Catriona made her way out through the gate. She paused and breathed deeply. Emerging into the lane, she heard a sudden movement in the hedgerow that divided it from the Old Mill property. It was akin to the involuntary scuffle into deeper concealment an animal would make when disturbed, but, even to her urban ears, it was clear it was on a scale that no animal in the English countryside could achieve. Someone, not something, was hiding there.

She stopped dead, resting one hand on the rough stone of the gatepost, listening, waiting to hear whether the noise would be repeated. Then, slowly and deliberately, she walked down the lane to the spot from where the noise had seemed to come.

The clipped line of beech was thick with bright green leaves, a solid screen for the garden beyond. From the blue sky above, there was the drone of a plane. Perhaps it really had been a big bird. A pheasant. Then, from the within the hedge, she distinctly heard a twig crack. That was no pheasant.

'Whoever's in there, would you please come out? You are trespassing on private property.' This combination of overt politeness and implied threat delivered in Catriona's clear, cool voice had an immediate effect. The scuffling noise she had heard previously was now resolved into the sound of feet on dead leaves. The branches before her face shook, and then parted to reveal the hooded figure of a man.

As she stepped back in alarm from the verge onto the metalled roadway, staggering slightly as she did so, she caught a glimpse of a pale face, its lower half shadowed with dark stubble, its eyes averted, avoiding hers, one arm raised – not to deliver, but to ward off either the sting of the beech twigs that scraped against the thick cotton of his camouflaged combat jacket, or an anticipated blow. It was immediately evident from his cringing half crouch that he presented no danger to her, but was entirely intent on his own escape. Still bent double, he scuttled rather than ran past her.

Recovering her balance and her presence of mind, she reacted swiftly and, she reflected later, in the circumstances, rather foolhardily. She shot out a long arm and grabbed at the fleeing figure, but her hand ineffectually brushed the shoulder of his padded coat as he raced by. As he hurtled up the steep lane, she gave chase.

Her steady long-legged stride easily outpaced him, despite

the evident panic which propelled him. At the bend where the lane turned into the final ascent to the village, she caught up with him, and this time when she reached out to grasp his collar, her fingers dug in firmly and she held on. Catriona was strong and had no difficulty in arresting his flight and dragging him back to face her.

'Hey you! Not so fast!' She tightened her grip on the greasy grey-green material. He was, she estimated, about thirty or so. Shorter than her, and apparently lightly built, he might nevertheless have gained strength from desperation, and in a fight he could well have hurt her. But although he was squirming uncomfortably in her custody, he made no real attempt to wriggle free, still less to force her to release him. He continued to hang his head and avoid her gaze. His demeanour was the sullen submission of a small boy caught scrumping.

'I weren't doing nothing. Let me go,' he muttered. His voice was a childlike whine.

'You were spying on the house. You were going to come back later and burgle it!'

'No, honest, not me! I wouldn't ever do that!'

'What were you doing then?'

'Nothing. I told you!' His rolled his eyes from side to side, his tongue licking his pale lips like a frightened cat's.

'I think we should let the police decide about that.'

At the mention of the word police, he grew visibly more terrified. 'No, not them old police. I hate them. They hassle me and move me on and say rotten things about me. But I don't do no harm. You ask Charly. I was looking out for her, like I always do, but specially now since her Mum got took to hospital. In an ambulance. Her Mum's nice. She gave me lemonade once, not white pop but real lemonade, thick and greeny, what makes your mouth go all wrinkled up. We sat in the kitchen and we had cake too. Home-made cake with black fruit and red cherries. I had six cherries in my piece. My mum never makes cake. Please don't send me off to them police. Please.'

113

Hardly listening to this stream of nonsense, she was wondering what on earth she should do with this pathetic creature, whose physical under-development was clearly accompanied by mental deficiency, when there was the sound of running feet.

She turned to see Charlotte, her long blonde hair flying in a streamer behind her, her face twisted up in fury, charging towards her and her captive.

'What are you doing to him?' the girl yelled. 'Let him go! Can't you see you're scaring the shit out of him!' She took hold of the hand that was still hooked firmly into the man's jacket and prised it loose. Then, holding his arm and giving him a little shake, she said, 'Malcolm! It's all right. No one's going to hurt you.'

With a nervous glance, he edged away from Catriona, so that Charlotte was between them. Charlotte glowered accusingly at her aunt. 'You've gone and terrified him!' It was as though the wretched fellow were a rabbit or a guinea pig.

'He was skulking in the hedge by the house! I thought he was up to no good.'

'So you crashed in and did your martial arts thing on him! Catriona Turville, champion of the Neighbourhood Watch vigilantes. Except, dear aunt, this is the country, not London.' She moved closer. 'For your future information, this man is a friend of mine.' She glanced quickly back to her subject and gave him a reassuring grin. 'He looks out for me, don't you, Malcolm?'

Lowering her voice, she whispered, 'You're supposed to be intelligent. Can't you see he's, you know?'

Bill's attention had obviously been caught by the sound of their voices, because now he too appeared, jogging up the lane towards them. 'Would someone mind telling me what's going on?' He caught sight of the man in the combat jacket. 'You! You've been told to stay away from here!'

Malcolm, his face once more full of fear, began to sidle away from the taller man. As he realised that no move would be made to detain him, his pace quickened into his scuttling run. All three watched as he dashed up the lane and out of sight around a bend.

'Oh, well done, Daddy! I'd just got him calmed down. You must feel really proud of yourself, scaring him all over again.'

'Not particularly. He's a feeble enough specimen. But he knows damn well he's been warned off hanging around here. The creep must have been watching you just now when you were playing basketball. I don't think you realise how you look, you know, in your shorts . . .' He tailed off, embarrassed.

'I know exactly what you're getting at and he's not interested in me in that way in the slightest bit. You should meet some of the real creeps at my school. They'd win gold medals for creepiness, always trying to look up my skirt and making crude remarks. But you won't want to hear that!'

'Well, whatever you say, a man like that, spending his time hanging around young girls. We don't know what goes on in his mind.'

'We certainly know what goes on in yours!' retorted his daughter. 'Malcolm's completely harmless. He wouldn't ever hurt me.'

'You can never be sure of that. He could turn, just like that. Like a dog.' He snapped his fingers. 'The police certainly take that view. I shall have a word with the inspector in Stroud, the one who cautioned him after that last incident. See if they can't do something more than that.'

'No!' The word came as a scream. 'No! You mustn't do that! He's terrified of the police. They'll hurt him! No, you mustn't! Promise me you won't!' She grabbed his shoulder and started to shake him with a violence that visibly alarmed him.

He threw off her hand. 'Control yourself, Charlotte! You're not a two-year-old!'

'You control yourself! You're the one with the dirty mind!

115

Leave Malcolm alone! And if you don't, you'll wake up one morning and find that not only haven't you got a wife, you haven't got a daughter either! Mum saw some sense at last and cleared off. You're not going to tell me who my friends are. I shall see who I want when I want. And when Mum sends for me, I shan't see you ever again!'

Lunch was a silent affair. Father and daughter were not speaking, and neither of them addressed any remarks to Catriona. Charlotte bolted her food and went upstairs to her room, from which loud music was soon blaring.

Bill had been drinking red wine throughout the meal and the bottle was almost empty. He tipped the last dregs into his glass and knocked it back. Catriona had never seen him drink so steadily and concentratedly before.

'It's fun being a single parent. It's bad enough having to deal with the things that Flora used to handle, without the addition of this bastard Thornton on top. If I do involve the police again, Charlotte will go off the scale. You've seen how she can be. But it's got to the point that I don't know what else to do.'

'Has he actually threatened her in any way?'

'He certainly has! That's why he was cautioned by the police and told to keep away from here. He tried to abduct her in his van. Luckily the deputy head of the school realised what was happening and stopped him. Charlotte, of course, took his part and denied there was any problem. So the police had to let him go. We had a blazing row about it afterwards.'

'I know you're concerned with Charlotte's safety, but this man seemed harmless enough today. He was much more frightened than frightening.'

'He's not normal, though. He's a grown man, and yet he spends his time playing with children. Go down the village rec any fine evening, and he's there playing football with the younger kids. When the older youths turn up, he clears off.'

'It sounds to me as if he identifies with children. He's possibly around that mental age himself.'

'But he is a man, physically. He drives a van, holds down a kind of job. As far as I'm concerned he's a pervert.'

'Wanting to be with children isn't necessarily a perversion. Are all teachers perverts?'

'Some of them are! It's fine for you, isn't it? You can have the luxury of your liberal ideas. You don't have this creep hanging around your house. It isn't your daughter who's at risk.'

'No, she isn't my daughter, but she is my sister's child. If I thought she were at risk, I should agree that some action should be taken. What was Flora's attitude?'

'She felt sorry for the wretched fellow. Treated him as if he were really a child. I came home one afternoon to find the three of them sitting round the kitchen table drinking lemonade. We had a row about it afterwards. I thought she had behaved with stupid naïvety and I told her so.'

'I expect that went down very well.'

The big man's face went a dull red. 'This is my house, and I do in it what I damn well like. And that includes keeping out of it demented riff-raff like Malcolm Thornton.'

'It's funny you should mention the lemonade party. He was going on to me about it himself. He said something else as well about Flora. That she had been taken to hospital in an ambulance.'

'Ha! It's he who needs to be in hospital.'

'You don't think there's anything in it?'

'In what? In Malcolm Thornton's head? No, I don't, except stuff neither of us want to know anything about.'

'You don't think he might have seen something? When he was hanging about?'

'He may have seen fairies at the bottom of the garden for all we know. The fellow's a loony. Who knows what it was he saw or when? For God's sake, you're as naïve as your sister. This man has some kind of fixation with my daughter. He needs to

117

be locked up. I've made up my mind that if he sticks his runny nose onto my property again, I shall call the police, whatever my precious daughter has to say about it.'

'Charlotte? Can I have a word with you?'

Almost drowned by the insistent beat of the rock music, the girl's voice came faintly from the other side of the door. 'What about, as if I can't guess?'

'Your father is very worried about your relationship with this fellow Thornton. He's concerned for your safety.'

'Yeah, right.'

'Please let me in. I'd like to talk.'

There was no reply, only the hideous bellow of the music.

'Please open the door, Charlotte. This is where we came in a couple of weeks ago, remember? Talking on opposite sides of a closed door.'

There was a sniff, which might have been the beginning of a chuckle, the noise stopped, then the door opened. Charlotte waved an ironical arm. '*Entrez!*'

She sprawled prone on the bed, kicking her heels together in the air. Catriona removed various items of outer and underwear from the armchair opposite and sat down.

'What's he been saying then?'

'He's very worried about this man.'

'He doesn't know shit. He's so prejudiced. Just because Malcolm isn't going to win a Nobel Prize, Dad thinks that makes him into some kind of danger.'

'No, it isn't only that. Your father told me there had actually been quite a serious incident only a week ago. Apparently, he tried to make you go with him in his van, and he was arrested.'

'Malcolm tried to make me? Is that what Dad told you? He was there, of course, Mr Know-All! Actually, it was that Miss Waterstone's fault. She's one of the deputy heads. She's such a bitch. She started it.'

'All right. Why don't you tell me your side of what happened?'

'It was at going-home time. I get one of the school buses. They stop in a lay-by outside the school gates and there's always a scrum. This time some of the boys started pushing and shoving, and then they started fighting, so no one could get near. The teachers waded in to sort it out, but we had to wait. I hate getting the bus. Mum used to pick me up sometimes. But Dad never does. He has to work, and that's far more important, isn't it? Anyway, I'm standing there with my friend Alice, and we're like, This is really boring. Then I saw Malcolm driving past in his van, and I waved and he stopped. He asked us if we wanted a lift. Alice said she wasn't allowed to accept lifts from strangers, and I said he's not a stranger he's a friend. Malcolm got out of the van, and held the door open for me like he was a chauffeur and I was just getting in when stupid Miss Waterstone rolls up – she is so fat! – and goes in her, I say, my man voice. Do you know this man, Charlotte? And I say, course I do, he's Malcolm from the village. And Malcolm gives her a grin and says, I'm Malcolm. Then old Big Bum gives him one of her looks and says, I think I've seen you here before, loitering outside the school. She turns to me and goes, Please get on the coach, Charlotte. And I'm like, No I'm getting a lift from my friend, and she says, No you are not. So I started getting into the van. And then, would you believe it, she grabs hold of me by the arm and starts to hoik me out again. Then I started screaming at her to let go, and Mr Fitch the PE master appears and starts being all macho and Oi you-ish to Malcolm. Malcolm of course is dead scared and gets into the van and tries to drive off. Then some of the boys from the village hear what's happening and they gather round in front of the van so it can't move and start making fun of Malcolm. And then, would you believe, a panda car drives up and two coppers get out and they're like, "'Ello 'Ello 'Ello, what's going on 'ere?" And Miss Waterstone says she's caught a man trying to abduct one of her pupils. And then they grab Malcolm and stick him in the panda car and drive off. By this time, I'm screaming my head off and no one's listening to me. I get took to Mrs Rice and I have to wait until they get Dad to fetch me. And then they all tried to make me tell the police I was being molested, but I wouldn't do that either.' She banged the mattress on either side of her with her fists.

'But you didn't explain any of this?'

'What's the point? He wouldn't listen. He's decided that Malcolm's a perve. But he isn't. Why can't he just be like he is and everyone leave him alone?'

'In these sorts of situations people act for the best motives. They see the safety of a child as being the most important thing.'

'That doesn't give them the right to pick on someone for being different, does it?'

'It doesn't give them the right, no. But it explains why they do it.'

'Well, I think I've the right to pick my own friends.'

'Sometimes it isn't easy to see who's a friend and who's an enemy. Even grown-ups make mistakes about that. Your teachers and your father, if they are in error, are erring on the side of caution. You must understand that.'

'You've seen Malcolm. Do you think he's going to murder me or something?'

Catriona hesitated, then said, cautiously, 'I've only seen him on one occasion. He didn't give me the impression of being dangerous, but the men we're talking about, the men who prey on children, often seem very plausible. They pretend to be kind, to gain their victim's confidence. Sometimes, sometimes . . .' She tried and failed to control the tremor in her voice. '. . . sometimes, they can be the person you least expect, the one you most trusted.'

Charlotte appeared not to have noticed her aunt's change of mood, lost in her own emotions. She thrashed her legs with impatience. 'I'm not stupid! Of course I know about "those kinds of men"! Everyone's been going on about "those kinds of men" since I was in primary school! Don't take sweeties, don't accept lifts, don't get near if a car pulls up alongside you. Yell, run, tell! I know all that. But I've known Malcolm for years. All the village kids know him. He doesn't pretend to be like he is to get off with me, he is like that! He looks out for me. He thinks he's protecting me! If Mum were here, she'd tell you he was all right. If Mum were here . . . but she isn't, is she? She got sick of me.' She started to sob.

Catriona sat on the bed and held her while the tears flowed. Eventually, Charlotte stopped crying and thrust her wet hair out of swollen eyes. 'I expect you'll get fed up of me soon too.'

'No, I won't. I promised, remember?'

'Yeah, 'course. Perhaps you did that because I bullied you into it. Because you thought you had a duty to, or felt sorry for me, something like that?'

'No, I said it because . . .' Catriona's hesitation was that of a twig at the crest of a waterfall; a second later the words were out. 'Because I love you.'

'Even when I'm rotten to you?'

'Even then. "Love is not love which alters when it alteration finds, or bends with the remover to remove: o no! it is an ever fixed mark."'

'I like that. That's true. I still love Mum even though she's gone away without saying where.'

'I love your mother too, just as you do.'

'I wish we could find her.' She dropped her voice to a whisper. 'You'd say, wouldn't you, if you knew where she was?'

'Of course I would.'

'And if there were any remote chance of finding her, if you had the least clue, then you'd try to find her, wouldn't you?'

'Yes, I would. Of course I would.'

*   *   *

A cracked and peeling wooden signboard reading 'Walter's Yard – Car Breakers' pointed off the Stroud road, a couple of miles out of Owlbury. A steep, unsurfaced track led downhill past fields high with unmown grass into the former quarry. A high steel mesh fence with double steel gates shut off the entrance. On the other side, a red tow-truck, a flat-bed trailer, and a couple of vans were parked on a concrete hardstanding. At an oil-stained bench in front of a low asbestos-roofed brick building, the door of which bore a sign reading OFFICE, a large man in a dirty white T-shirt and even dirtier jeans was hammering at some rusty metal. By his side, apparently oblivious of the noise, slept a large shaggy-haired black-and-tan dog, one of whose remote ancestors might have been Alsatian.

Behind the hut, stretching back to the high, scrub-topped cliffs of jagged stone, were the cars – or rather the multi-coloured shells of cars, washed up on this stony beach. In this graveyard, the corpses were not buried but left out in the sun to be picked at by automotive scavengers, in the way that vultures and kites dealt with human remains in a Tibetan sky burial. The passion for waste that distinguished the industrial world meant that this repository was full to overflowing. In places, the cars, battered by and then arranged as at the whim of some giant infant, were stacked in huge unsteady-looking piles. Over them towered the fretwork jib of a crane, from the cable of which dangled the massive steel disc of an electromagnetic hoist.

As she climbed from the car, the air was heavy with the treacly smell of oil, which mixed oddly with the scents of the meadows surrounding this intrusive chunk of modernity. The man, red-faced and sweaty, had ceased his hammering, looked up at the sound of the Fiesta's engine, and wandered over to open the gates.

'You looking for a new silencer for that, lady? Won't pass your MOT without. We got one if'n you're interested. Fit him too, if you've got a few minutes.'

'I was looking for Malcolm, if he's around.'

'Malcolm? He's around all right. Only he don't often get visitors.' He grinned. 'Not like you, anyway.'

He turned to the scrap-yard and bellowed, 'Malcolm!' The sound echoed around the ivy-hung rocks.

'There he is. Like a monkey, ain't he? Good thing those Health and Safety Inspectors can't see him.'

The spare figure of the young man appeared, crouching like some woodland sprite on the dented bonnet of a semi-flattened blue Mondeo, at the summit of one of the tottering heaps of vehicles. He looked down, a scared expression on his face.

'It's all right,' she called up to him. 'I just want to have a word with you. Nothing to worry about.'

He hesitated, then climbed down, using the glassless windows of the car bodies as hand- and foot-holds, with an ease and grace that astonished her. She thought back to the shuddering, cowering figure she had seen at the Old Mill.

He grinned awkwardly, not meeting her eyes. 'You're the lady who grabbed me at Charly's house. You said bad things about me. But Charly told me afterwards you were cool.'

'I was wrong when I said those things. I'm sorry. I didn't realise then you were Charly's friend.'

'I got took away in a police car. Ford Escort S 632 VFH.'

'I heard about that. Charlotte was upset about what happened to you.'

He nodded. Then he said, 'That policeman, the one who hit me. Number 604. He said as how I would get put in prison if he caught me again. If I so much as look at her, he said. I told him how I always looked after her, and that's what she wanted. Then he hit me and called me bad names, and the other policeman laughed.' He hung his head. 'I was scared and I went and weed myself. And they laughed even more.'

'That's outrageous. They had no right to do that to you.'

'You won't tell Charly will you? About me wetting myself. I don't want her to know that.'

'I won't tell her.'

'But you can say how I'm still going to look out for her. Just like I always did. Those old policemen can't stop me.'

He gazed directly at her as he said this, and in his pale blue, vacant eyes, there was a glint of something like fire.

She was set to say that that wouldn't be a good idea, that that would get him into trouble, but in his air of stubborn dedication, there was something honourable, some force not to be denied. So she said, 'Good for you! I'd want to do the same.'

He blushed with pleasure at this acknowledgement. He kept on staring at her as if he hadn't properly seen her up to now.

'You're a friend of Charly too?'

'I'm her aunt. Her mother's sister.'

'Her mum. She's nice. Not like her dad. He always shouts at me. "Get out of here, you!"' He had uncannily captured the exact timbre of Bill's braying voice. 'Her mum, she gave me a drink once when I was hot. Lemonade. Home-made. You can tell it's home-made when it makes your mouth go squeezed together. And a piece of cake with icing on. My mum never makes cake. She's always sick.' Momentarily downcast by the thought of his own mother, in a moment he was grinning again. 'Are you really her auntie? You don't look old enough to be an auntie.'

'I am though.'

'I've got something to show you.'

He beckoned her to follow and ran on ahead, skipping from side to side like a boy along the narrow path between piles of rusting motor panels.

She hesitated, then shrugged to herself. The boss had returned to the hut and was once again hammering away, but he would still be within earshot. Besides, she could not imagine that this child-man presented any threat to her.

124

He had made a kind of den in the back of an old Transit van which, lacking wheels and an engine, lay canted over at an angle in a patch of rank grass. There was an easy chair with the stuffing spilling out, a torn piece of carpet, and a small varnished bookcase, much scratched, in which were a pile of dog-eared magazines and a few paperbacks with creased covers and cracked spines.

'That's my library!' he said pointing at them with pride. 'Charly gave me them. I've read them all hundreds of times.' He grabbed one at random. 'Listen. "*Swallows and Amazons* by Arthur Ransome Chapter One The Peak in Darien Roger aged seven and no longer the youngest of the family ran in wide zigzags to and fro across the steep field that sloped up from the lake to Holly Howe the farm where they were staying for part of the summer holidays."' He paused and grinned. 'At school, they said I couldn't read, but I could. I didn't let on, see. Walter's got these books about cars. I've read them all. I know them all. Like that old "Highway Code". I had to learn that 'fore they'd let me drive. Walter has these cards too.' He paused, closed his eyes momentarily and then started to recite: 'Citroen Xantia 1997 Silver Insurance write-off. Purchased Eagle Star 3.2.01. SORN 8.3.01. Engine number 65474339 . . .'

She stared at him. He was a walking stock catalogue.

'Malcolm, I came to ask you something. When I . . . when I saw you at the Old Mill, you told me something about Charly's Mum. Something important.'

At first she wasn't sure he'd understood, so vacant was the expression on his face. Then he abruptly dived to the back of the van and began rummaging about in some cardboard boxes.

He emerged clutching something in his hand. 'Look!'

'What is it, Malcolm?'

'Hers. To give back to her.'

It was a dark-blue velvet woman's slipper.

'Charlotte's?' It hardly seemed the kind of thing a child would wear.

'No, not hers. Her mum's.'

She shivered as he said this. 'Where did you get it, Malcolm?' she asked hoarsely.

'It fell off her foot when those men I told you about were taking her to the hospital. I picked it up off the grass when they'd gone.'

'These men. Can you describe them?'

'They were ambulance men. 'Cept one of 'em were a woman. They wore them green uniforms. She was on a stretcher under a blanket and her feet were sticking out. They put her in a white ambulance. I was watching, see. It was a Saturday morning, really early. Charly had gone on a school trip to somewhere called Devon. She told me to look after her Mum till she got back. When she got back, I said to her, How's your Mum doing in the hospital? and she gave me a funny look and said she was OK and would be home soon. My Dad got took to hospital, but he never came home no more.'

'The ambulance, Malcolm. Was there any writing on it which said it was an ambulance?'

'No, but it must have been one because it had ambulance men in it.'

'Can you remember anything else about it?'

He screwed up his face and closed his eyes. Then without opening them he began to recite, 'White Mercedes-Benz. Registration number R 641 VFH.'

She scrabbled in her bag for the note-pad she always carried, hurriedly writing down the details.

'What you've just told me is very important, Malcolm. Thank you. Would you be willing to tell someone else what you've told me?'

'I'd tell Charlotte, 'cept I already told her her mum's in hospital.'

'How about a policeman?'

He shied away as if he were going to strike her. 'No, no. They'd lock me up and hit me again.'

'No, they wouldn't, because you'd have someone with you to look after you and make sure they didn't.'

'I won't talk to no more police. They hate me.'

'It's very important, Malcolm. You see, when Charlotte's mum was taken to hospital, the people who took her forgot to tell anyone which hospital they went to. So, you see, we don't know where she is.'

His pale blue eyes gazed stubbornly at the floor of the van.

'Would you tell a policeman if Charlotte asked you?'

'I might.'

'Where the heck are we going, Cat?' asked Charlotte irritably as her aunt practically bundled her into the Fiesta. She drove down the road away from the school, then swung off left down a track under the cover of a small wood, stopped and turned off the engine.

Catriona reached a hand to the back seat, and handed Charlotte the blue velvet slipper.

'Whose slipper is this?'

'Cinderella's.'

Charlotte was not in a good mood. Catriona had interrupted a conversation she had been having with some good mates, and, on top of that, Miss Big Bum had stuck her nose in, quizzing her aunt about who she was like she was in the Gestapo, and lecturing her about how schools couldn't let their pupils go off with anyone without proper authority, 'particularly with regard to a recent occurrence'.

'She is my aunt, OK! I do know my own relations, thank you!' Charlotte had insisted, to her own embarrassment and the amusement of the bystanders.

'Charlotte, please. This is very serious. Please look carefully at the slipper.'

'Hey, what's this about?' The child's jaunty tone had turned immediately fearful. 'Where'd you get this?'

'Please tell me whose it is first.'

'It's Mum's of course! You've found her! She's been hurt. No, she's dead!'

Catriona gripped her niece tightly around the shoulders. 'No, she is not dead. I have no reason to believe she has been hurt. But things have moved on, Charlotte. She didn't run off with Frank Churchill. I went to see him.'

'You went to see Frank!'

'Yes. And I'm satisfied that, wherever she is, she is not and has never been with Frank Churchill. You were mistaken about her having an affair with him. So I'm afraid you have to face up to the fact that your mother is not going to call you one day soon and invite you to join her in her new relationship.'

It was brutal, but she felt it had to be said. Charlotte stared at her for a moment, then her face crumpled, and the tears began to flow.

'If she's not with Frank, then where is she?' she sobbed. 'Where is she? Why did she leave?'

'That's what I've been trying to find out. And your friend Malcolm may be the only witness we have to what may have happened.'

'Malcolm!'

'Yes. He claims he saw your mother being taken away by some men he describes as ambulance men. Though they weren't driving an ambulance, only an ordinary white van. While they were carrying her out of the house, they dropped this.' She pointed to the slipper. 'It's definitely your mother's?'

'Yes, I remember buying it from Cav in Cheltenham not all that long ago.' This reminiscence brought on further tears.

As she hugged the weeping child, Catriona felt her own tears rise, tears which up to then she had refused to shed.

She brushed them away, saying in a business-like tone, 'Well, now. You can imagine what we have to do. Malcolm talked to me, but he won't talk to the police. Not unless you persuade him it's the right thing to do.'

'The police? They hate Malcolm and he's scared to death of them. They won't believe him.'

'That is a possibility, but we have to try.'

'Dad will freak out when he finds I've been talking to Malcolm again.'

'I'll deal with that.'

'Back again? With company too,' observed the man Walter in surprise as he lurched up to the gate, beer-gut hanging out over the leather belt of his jeans. 'Change your mind about that old silencer?'

'We've come to see Malcolm,' said Charlotte.

Walter shook his head. 'Well, you're in for a disappointment, missy. He ain't here.'

'Where is he?' demanded Catriona.

'That I don't rightly know. He comes and he goes. You can't set your watch by our Malcolm. Just after you left, he said he was going out and out he went in that old van of his. I don't interfere, you see. He's not what you call a regular worker. I took him on as a favour to his dad who was a good mate of mine. He's got his uses, has Malcolm, even though he's a bit light in the top storey. More reliable than any computer is that memory of his.'

'So you don't know where he went.'

Walter shrugged. 'Here, there, who knows?'

Disappointed, they returned to the car.

'Where to now, Sherlock?'

'Home.'

'We could try Malcolm's house.'

'I think we'd be wasting our time. I've frightened him off, haven't I?'

'Sounds like it.'

Half an hour later, she watched the girl's slim figure in the short navy skirt, white shirt and white ankle socks, long blonde hair fluttering behind her, as she ran lightly with the vibrant energy of youth across the drive, paused to unlock the door, turned to wave briefly, then disappeared within.

Catriona was woken by the sound of the door buzzer. Blearily she stared at the figures of the digital clock. Seven-thirty. The buzzer went again, and continued as if someone were leaning on it. She shrugged into her dressing gown and went down into the hall. On the stained-glass panel were the shadowy shapes of two heads.

'Who is it?' she called out.

A woman's voice replied through the letterbox, 'Professor Turville. My colleague and I are police officers. From Stroud police station. We'd like to talk to you about your sister, Mrs Flora Jesmond, please.'

Catriona showed them into the sitting room while she returned upstairs to dress hurriedly in jeans and T-shirt.

The man, who'd introduced himself as Detective Sergeant Bussage, was standing staring out of the window, apparently at the house fronts on the opposite side of Palace View Road. The woman, Detective Constable Lacey, was sitting on the sofa consulting a file, which she closed quickly as soon as Catriona came in.

'How can I help you?' Catriona sat down in the big wing chair by the fireplace.

Bussage withdrew from his observation post at the window and joined his colleague on the sofa. He leant forward, his legs apart, his elbows resting on his knees. 'Last Monday, madam, you made a statement to a colleague at Stroud police station concerning certain information that had come into your possession which you believed related to the disappearance of your sister, Mrs Flora Jesmond. You also handed in a slipper which you alleged was one of a pair belonging to Mrs Jesmond.'

'Yes, I did. I'm delighted to see that you're following it up. So, have you interviewed Malcolm Thornton?'

'Before I come to that, perhaps I can clarify the basic facts of the situation? Your sister was reported as missing to the police by her husband Mr William Jesmond approximately one month ago. Since then, she has neither contacted nor been seen by any of her family or friends. Is that your understanding?'

'Yes, of course.'

'When did you last have any contact with her?'

'I spoke to her on the telephone on the Wednesday. Then I called her again the following Saturday. When I had no reply, I rang again several times over that weekend. There was no reply and the answering machine was off, so I couldn't leave a message. I thought she might have gone away for a few days, though she hadn't mentioned anything of that sort to me. I became slightly worried. I called again on Wednesday evening and Bill, her husband, who'd just returned from his business trip, told me she wasn't at home and he had been about to call me to ask if I knew where she was. That was when we both realised that something was wrong. It was completely untypical of my sister to leave home at all without mentioning it to anyone. If there had been some emergency, she would have left full details of where she was and how she could be contacted.'

Both the police officers were staring at her, their faces expressionless. For the first time, it occurred to her that they had not shown her the least sympathy. They hadn't even been very polite.

Bussage asked, 'So the last time you had any contact with your sister was when you spoke to her on the telephone on the Wednesday?'

'Yes.'

'What did you talk about?'

'She was worried about her daughter, Charlotte. She had been difficult. In the way that pubescent girls are difficult.'

131

'Would you describe your sister as being depressed by this behaviour?'

'No. She was concerned. But there was no way she would have walked out on Charlotte because of the way she was being.'

'What would you say were your feelings towards your sister's husband, Dr William Jesmond?'

She almost gaped at him. 'My feelings towards Bill? What on earth has that got to do with Flora's disappearance?'

'Would you describe yourself as fond of this gentleman?'

'Fond?' She started to laugh. 'I see what you're trying to find out. But the idea that Bill and I should have formed any kind of attachment, and that Flora might be jealous enough about it to make her want to walk out is quite incredible. I can't stand him, and he has similar feelings towards me. Ask him if you don't believe me.'

'We shall,' the detective sergeant replied without a glimmer of amusement.

Irritated by this turn of events, Catriona said, 'Can't we get back to the important point, the information I gave you about what Malcolm Thornton saw? Have you interviewed him or not?'

Bussage appeared not to have heard. 'So, there is no reason you are aware of why your sister might have left home suddenly?'

'None.'

'And you yourself had no contact with her after the telephone conversation you have described.'

'No.'

'You did not attempt to see her after that date?'

'No, again.'

'So I turn to the statement you made at Stroud police station last Monday. You state that you were told by one Malcolm Thornton that he saw your sister being taken away in what appeared to be an ambulance?'

'Yes, although it couldn't have been an ambulance because Bill checked all the hospitals. That was the first thing he did. But you know that. I gave you the registration number of the vehicle Malcolm saw. But for the tenth time, have you managed to interview him?'

'We did interview the individual concerned, but he failed to corroborate the matter. He denied knowing anything about Mrs Jesmond's being taken away in a white van. We showed him the slipper referred to in your statement. He said he had never seen it in his life before.'

Catriona shook her head with frustration and annoyance. 'But you had the number of the van! Didn't you trace it?'

The woman constable consulted her file. 'A vehicle of that description, a white Mercedes-Benz, belongs to a company called Cheltenham Transport Services. It is not an ambulance and has never been used as such. Furthermore, according to that company's records, on the date in question, a Saturday, the van was off the road being serviced.'

'So does that mean you don't believe Malcolm Thornton's story?'

Bussage made a face. 'He might at one time have seen that vehicle with that registration number. When or where he might have seen it is a different matter. But whether he did or whether he didn't, I'm afraid that without having the information from – so to speak – the horse's mouth, the statement you made remains what the law calls hearsay. It is in fact not that individual's account, but yours, Ms Turville.'

'So I could have made it up! But what about the slipper? I didn't make that up.'

'The slipper is certainly evidence, but evidence of what? Without a statement from this Thornton – who by all accounts is not what you would call the most reliable type of witness – there is no evidence as to where the slipper was found, nor as to whether the other one of the pair was being worn at the time by Mrs Jesmond.'

'So you are implying that I made up this information? I can assure you I didn't. My niece Charlotte was with me when I visited the yard.'

'On that occasion, I believe you failed to contact Thornton?'

'Yes, I told your officer that. Surely you could ask around in the village whether anyone else saw the van?'

WPC Lacey once again consulted her file. 'In view of the potential seriousness of the allegation, the Owlbury community police officer did make some inquiries at the houses on Mill Lane. There were no reports of any white van on the day in question, but, as it happened, a gentleman recalled that he had seen another vehicle in the lane that same morning, at about nine-thirty. He's sure about the date because he recalled that it was the morning of the day he had a visit from his daughter. He remembered the vehicle because it was driving down the lane at considerable speed. He was out walking his dog and he claimed he had to jump into the hedge to avoid being run over. He went on to say that the vehicle turned into the gate of the Old Mill. It was then that he recollected that he had seen the vehicle there on other occasions, and knew the owner by sight. The vehicle he described was a white Ford Fiesta, in poor condition, with a K-registration prefix.' Lacey paused. She and Bussage were staring at Catriona once more in their increasingly unfriendly and indeed suspicious manner. Then the woman continued, 'He stated that he believed the owner of the car was Mrs Jesmond's sister, a tall, dark-haired lady from London.'

Bussage said, 'I noticed earlier that a K-reg., white Ford Fiesta is parked on the street in front of this house. Is that your vehicle, madam, and would you care to comment on this report?'

'I am the owner of the car outside. However, I think perhaps your informant was confused by the incident. Whatever vehicle drove down the lane that morning, it was not my car and I was not driving it.'

'You're quite certain that you paid no visits to Owlbury on that weekend, or on any subsequent day prior to Mr Jesmond's return?'

'Quite certain.'

'You do realise, madam, that we are dealing here with a serious matter. It's obviously in your interests, and the interests of the missing person, that you co-operate fully with our enquiries.'

'Of course. Though if you'd started these enquiries when my sister disappeared, you might have made more progress by now.'

The detective sergeant remained stony-faced at this sally. 'You have nothing further to add?'

'No, I haven't.'

SEVEN

The morning was glorious. Already at seven a.m. the sun was warm on Catriona's shoulders as she locked her front door and jogged slowly down Palace View Road and into Alexandra Park.

It was the first time she had run since she had received Flora's letter. The fact that she had woken early, conscious of how sluggish her body was beginning to feel without exercise, showed that, although the fact of her sister's fate still weighed upon her, a kind of adjustment was taking place.

As if in response to the lightening of her mood, the city itself seemed to have dressed in its brightest colours. The overnight breezes had cleared the blanket of smog, and from the eminence on which sprawled the vast pile of Alexandra Palace, the distant towers of the City and Canary Wharf glittered in the sunlight, as if they were the magic turrets of a far-off Camelot. London – old, dingy, crumbling, the raddled Empress of a defunct Empire – was once again 'the flower of cities all'. Welcome too was the absence of the man who had been shadowing her on previous occasions. In the interim, he must have given up his vigil, or perhaps he had had a well-deserved heart attack.

She ran well and easily that morning, hardly slower than the times she had been achieving before her lay-off. She returned home, showered, breakfasted on muesli, soya milk and black coffee, then walked to Bounds Green where she took the tube to Russell Square. She spent the morning and afternoon in the British Library, working on the Grasmère Edition, leaving around six-thirty to make her way on foot to the college, where she was due to lecture that evening.

The present home of Warbeck College is a board-marked concrete edifice in the Brutalist style, which had, in the sixties, despite protests from conservation groups, replaced the Portland stone Art-Deco building in which it had been housed since the early thirties, and which in turn, but without any protest, had replaced the original early nineteenth-century stock brick house in which Alfred John Algernon Warbeck had started his Mechanics Institute. A shadowy engraving of this property still hung in the provost's office, like a ghost haunting the scene of its murder.

'Good evening, Mr Alfred,' Catriona solemnly addressed the large oil portrait of a severely countenanced Victorian gentleman who gazed out witheringly over the sterile expanse of the lobby. The tradition of this salute to the college's founder – if something which had started as a joke could be called a tradition – had begun about five years before, when one of the more irreverent of the younger lecturers, having discovered that the worthy Mr Warbeck had made his considerable fortune from the sale of drapery at his emporium in the Holloway Road, had taken to greeting his likeness in the manner in which he had imagined the shopkeeper was accustomed in his days at the counter. This had become established among staff and students, appealing as it did to the love of the facetious and the eccentric which is never very far from the surface in institutions of higher learning. It is not quite up to the standard of being able to exhibit in a glass case your onlie begetter's skeleton, dressed in his own clothes, as if prepared for a country walk, as UC periodically exhibits the mortal remains of Jeremy Bentham, but it is a nod in the right direction.

'And good evening to you, Richard,' she added with a smile as she crossed the lobby to the lifts.

The porter, who had almost as venerable an air as the philanthropist, did not, however, respond in his usual friendly fashion, which was odd, given that he was one of her most loyal admirers.

''Evening, Professor Turville,' he mumbled, without raising his eyes from the copy of the *Evening Standard* opened on his desk.

She was still pondering what she might have done to upset the old man as she came out of the lift on the fifth floor.

'Professor Catriona Turville?' A woman in a charcoal chalk-stripe business suit had stood up from a chair in the corridor immediately she appeared.

'Yes.'

'I'm Detective Constable Ruth Francis of the Metropolitan Police. I'm afraid I have some bad news.'

Her heart started racing as the adrenaline of relief flooded through her. One way or the other, she would know.

'Flora! You've found Flora!'

'I think it would be better if we went to your office, Catriona.'

With hands which shook almost uncontrollably, she took the key from her bag and attempted to insert it into the lock, but the metal merely skidded across the polished veneered panel. The policewoman gently relieved her of it, and unlocked the door.

'I think you'd better sit down.'

Catriona sank into the upholstered swivel chair by the desk. The dark-haired young woman sat opposite her in the armchair used by students receiving tutorials. Her grave demeanour left no room for doubt.

Catriona thought she had long been prepared but, sick at heart, the tears welled, as she watched the white face of the policewoman opposite. Wanting to say something to encourage the young woman, her tongue stuck in her mouth like a crust of dry bread.

Not much more than a girl, DC Francis was obviously affected by her task. Her dark eyes carried a sadness she could not conceal. But when she spoke, her words were not the words Catriona had expected to hear. They were words far more terrible, words from a more hellish nightmare than even she had ever imagined.

'I'm afraid that this is not about your sister, Catriona. It concerns your niece, Charlotte.'

Predictably, the tabloids had a field day.

BEAST OF THE BEACON: MAN CHARGED

Malcolm Thornton (27) appeared at Stroud Magistrates Court yesterday charged with the murder of thirteen-year-old Alice Peters and the attempted murder of her friend Charlotte Jesmond (12) at Owlbury, Gloucestershire, last Wednesday. Thornton, a short, slightly built, dark-haired man, dressed in jeans and a grey sweat shirt, appeared in court only for a matter of minutes and did not speak except to mumble confirmation of his name and address. No application for bail was made by his solicitor. The accused man was remanded in custody to Gloucester prison pending his trial.

Thornton lives with his mother and elder sister in a council house in Owlbury. He works at a local scrapyard. Neighbours describe him as 'a bit of an oddity' who had been warned on a number of occasions about his unhealthy interest in young girls. He was recently cautioned by the police for an incident involving Charlotte.

A prominent member of the local community told our reporter that he believes that if Thornton's behaviour had been taken more seriously by the authorities the tragedy on the Beacon might have been avoided.

A steel bar, believed originally to have formed part of the axle of a motor vehicle which may have been sold for scrap, was found beside Charlotte. It is thought to have been the murder weapon. A blood-stained combat jacket is understood to have been recovered from Thornton's house. These and other samples taken from the scene are undergoing forensic examination.

The picturesque Cotswold village of Owlbury, popular with tourists for its antique shops and tea-rooms, remains stunned by the tragedy. The lane leading to the Beacon, the local beauty spot where the frenzied attack on the two girls took place, has been closed to vehicles.

Charlotte, who has not yet recovered consciousness after suffering horrific head injuries in the attack, remains in intensive care on a life-support machine. Her father Bill (47), a senior research chemist at Avalon Laboratories, is maintaining an anxious vigil at her bedside. The parents of the murdered girl were too distressed to talk to reporters, but Alice's uncle, Ronald Peters (36), a well-known local farmer, called yesterday for the reinstatement of the death penalty for child-killers.

Both girls attended Stag End Comprehensive School in Cirencester. Pupils and teachers there remain in a state of shock. Headteacher Linda Rice (40) told reporters that they had lost one of the best and the brightest, and prayers were being said for the recovery of Charlotte.

On inside pages: *The picnic which ended in tragedy*. 'I found those little girls and I'll never be the same again.' A pensioner speaks of the afternoon walk that has shattered his life. Psychologist Charles Young on *The Men Who Prey on Our Children*.

Gloucestershire police revealed at a press conference today that Malcolm Thornton (27) has been questioned concerning the mysterious disappearance of Flora Jesmond, the mother of twelve-year-old Charlotte, one of the victims of the horrific attack that took place last week on Owlbury Beacon. Thornton has been charged with the attempted murder of Charlotte and the murder of her friend Alice Peters (13), and is remanded at Gloucester Prison.

Attractive thirty-six-year-old blonde former air stewardess Flora, (pictured above) who worked as an administrator at a Stroud estate agency, vanished from her luxury converted water mill home in the Cotswold village of Owlbury last month. Despite extensive enquiries, she has not been seen since.

Thornton is alleged to have been seen acting suspiciously in the vicinity of the Jesmond home on a number of occasions. Only a matter of weeks ago he was cautioned by police concerning an incident involving Charlotte. Detective Chief Superintendent Alec Marshfield told reporters that Mrs Jesmond's disappearance was being treated as suspicious and that further enquiries were being pursued.

Charlotte remains in a coma at Gloucestershire Royal Infirmary, where her condition is said to be stable. Doctors are as yet unable to say whether the young girl, who received serious head injuries in the frenzied attack, will make a full recovery or remember any details of the incident.

Her father Bill (47), top research scientist at Avalon Pharmaceuticals, who has not left her bedside since the attack, is still too distressed to talk about the incident.

Bill had actually told the reporter to fuck off and die. He was staying in the hospital, his face haggard, hollow-eyed with lack

141

of sleep. He ate scarcely anything but stared fixedly through the glass observation window of the intensive care facility, watching the slight figure on the bed, her head covered in a white helmet of dressings, surrounded by tubes and wires and monitors.

When Catriona had arrived trembling at his side on the evening of that dreadful day, he had turned to her and said, 'I hope you're satisfied now. I hope your precious liberal principles are satisfied.' Then he had turned away and not addressed another word to her.

Bill was right to blame her. It was her fault. She had promised to be there for Charlotte and had instead betrayed her. She should have warned her against that psychopath Thornton, and yet she had implicitly condoned the relationship. She had used her influence over Charlotte to pull her further into the clutches of that maniac. She had pitied him. She had been taken in by his air of vulnerability. She had believed his fantasy about the abduction of Flora. Now it was all too likely that he had been responsible for the death of her sister. The police certainly believed that. It only remained for him to confess where he had hidden her body for them to charge him with that murder also.

No one knew quite when the steep-sided, flat-topped hill, which rises some 200 metres above the village of Owlbury, was first called the Beacon. Certainly, long before its flames, one link in a chain of fiery gems, had blazed the coming of the Spanish Armada, though the Rector of Owlbury's account of that day in a letter to his brother at St John's College, Cambridge, had been the first recorded use of the name.

Archaeologists had established that 3000 years or so ago men had fortified this spur of the Cotswold escarpment with earthworks and ditches, had there sacrificed to their strange gods, had fought their enemies, had tilled their crops in the fertile valley below, had lived and died. Then, as the land grew peaceful, there was no longer any need to cluster for fear of slaughter on the high ground. The ancestral hill grew quiet and deserted, a place for children's games, lovers or melancholy wanderers. Only in times of trouble would the people gather there to receive and send a defiant signal across the darkened land.

When Bill and Flora bought the Old Mill – then in a derelict, ruinous state – Charlotte had been a toddler in nappies. Catriona had been, at twenty-seven, regarded as one of the brightest academic stars of her generation, having just returned from Canada and about to take up her Readership at Warbeck, a prestigious appointment for one so young. She had spent the weekend camping out with the family, had jogged over the Beacon on each morning and, intellectually curious as always, had bought in a local crafts shop a slim volume entitled *The History of Owlbury*. She had read it before going to sleep that night and, like everything she had ever read, she remembered it perfectly, even ten years later.

On several subsequent mornings, when she had spent those infrequent weekends with the family, in rain or sun, frost or fog, she had run up, round, across and down the Beacon.

On this day, however, she walked, slowly, as if every step cost her an effort, as if she were crippled or suddenly aged. And as she walked her gaze lighted on every detail of the way, her eyes hungry for every scrap of leaf or fragment of stone, as if every molecule of which the hill were composed had become incandescent with meaning.

The path rose in a zigzag up the hillside, a well-trodden emerald line of verdure like a strip of stair carpet over the dry unkempt whitish grass of the rough pasture. Halfway up was a small wood, with a wooden stile set into the drystone wall. The path turned to traverse the slope under the gloom of the trees. To her left, she could catch glimpses, fretted by branches, of the straggle of yellow-grey stone and stone-tiled houses which was Owlbury.

The sounds of everyday life rose on the still, warm air from the village 300 feet below. A lorry engine roared as it negotiated the winding A46 out of the village. Dogs barked, there was the slam of a car door, the sound of a mother yelling at her child and the child's screaming response. But here on the hill, there was no one. The inhabitants of Owlbury had shunned the place, had forbidden it to their children, and the narrow winding lane signposted from the main road had been closed by the police to discourage sightseers' vehicles.

She knew intimately the events of that day, from the whispered accounts of the progress of the investigation from the various police officers who sat discreetly in the corridor adjoining the intensive care ward, starting on that dreadful first night when it seemed as if the Beacon would claim its second sacrificial victim of the modern era, from the newspapers, and from the television. She read and listened to every word spoken or published, as if they were analgesics which would somehow blank out the hopelessness, the grief and the guilt.

Charlotte and her friend Alice had followed this path. Bill had taken Charlotte over to Alice's house in the village when he left for the laboratory earlier that morning. The two girls had played music together in Alice's room, then they had asked Alice's mother if they could take a picnic up the Beacon. She had readily agreed, as it was a fine day and she had thought the exercise would do them good. Local children had played on the Beacon since time immemorial. In a world anxious to the point of neurosis about the care of its young, there was no tradition in this village of its being unsafe to venture up the hill in broad daylight on a glorious day of high summer.

The girls had not started directly on their walk, but had gone first to buy a couple of cans of soft-drinks at the Post Office Stores. The till roll showed that the purchase had been made at 11.52. They must have gone straight from there to Beacon

Lane, as they were seen by Elsie Chambers, a retired secretary who had been tending her garden about five minutes before noon – she remembered the time because she'd checked her watch to make sure she didn't miss a TV chat show which began at twelve – only a matter of minutes after they had left the shop. Beacon Lane begins as a metalled side road on which fronts a scattering of houses, then turns after a few hundred metres into an unsurfaced track leading to a farm tucked away in the lee of the hill. Just before the farm, the public footpath, indicated by a finger-post at a stone stile, branches off up the steep slope to the Beacon.

The picnic was carried by Charlotte, in a rucksack slung over one shoulder. The meal, which was never consumed, consisted of cheese and pickle and ham sandwiches, fruit and biscuits, a can of Coke for Charlotte and a can of Seven Up for Alice. The police had retained the rucksack as evidence, but, having meticulously recorded, fingerprinted and photographed the contents, had obtained permission to dispose of the perishable items.

The path mounted through the wood, the side of the hill gradually becoming steeper, until it finally emerged on the bumpy green-mounded plateau, full of briar-filled dips and hollows, which was the summit. This was where Charlotte and Alice had come to eat the picnic that they never did eat on that day in high summer when a young life had ended.

Alice had been attacked first. Traces of her blood had been found on Charlotte's clothing, having been transferred by the murderer's hands or clothing or by the murder weapon. The pathologist's report referred to several, possibly as many as ten blows to the head with a heavy instrument, probably the steel bar found at the scene, which was believed to be a motor vehicle component, but investigations were continuing. Charlotte must have heard or seen what was happening and tried to escape, as she had been found in a bramble-filled hollow a hundred yards away on the other side of the Beacon. Although it was suggested that such had been the assailant's intentions, there was no evidence of any sexual assault. Charlotte had been struck several heavy blows on the head with the bar as she ran, rendering her unconscious. It appeared that the murderer may have believed that the child was dead, and had then fled the scene.

The girls' screams had been heard by several people in the village. All had said that they thought it was kids larking about on the hill, a common phenomenon in the summer holidays. It had not been until at least four hours after the girls had last been seen that Arnold Matson, a local old-age pensioner walking his dog, had come upon Alice's body. He had run down the hill and collapsed on the floor of the Post Office Stores. A police patrol from Stroud had been on the scene fifteen minutes later, and had identified the dead child from the name tag on her blouse. Alice's mother, out of her mind with shock and grief, had blurted out that her daughter had been with Charlotte. When the police found her, half-hidden in a bramble-filled hollow, they had thought that she was dead, so dreadful were the injuries that she had suffered. It was evident that even the stolid chief superintendent in charge of the televised press conference was moved by his account of how one of the officers had noticed that the child was still breathing. Charlotte had been flown to hospital by helicopter. After emergency surgery, she had been put on a life-support machine; she had remained in a coma ever since.

Despite the slowness of her pace, Catriona was hot by the time she reached the top. She pulled off the cotton jersey she wore over her sleeveless T-shirt, and let the breeze, cool as always even at the height of summer on these miniature English mountains, play on her exposed arms and shoulders. To the north-west, the wooded edge of the Cotswold escarpment – a surging wave petrified by time – extended into the hazy distance like the blue-remembered hills of Housman's land of lost content. Before her was the crater-like summit of the

146

Beacon, a flat saucer-like depression, the size of a playing field, surrounded by grassy humps. On these mounds, whitish dusty scars of tracks had been worn down through the thin clay soil to the limestone beneath by the passing feet of ramblers, and by the tyres of the mountain bikes that children brought up here, before careering in wild glee back down the steep slopes.

In the centre of the grassy, scrub-and briar-covered plateau, a large area remained cordoned off by blue and white plastic tape wrapped around metal stanchions hammered into the turf. On the tape, block capitals read in endless repetition: POLICE LINE DO NOT CROSS.

Catriona, suddenly as out of breath as if she had run the entire way up the slope, sat down on a patch of brownish grass. There had been no rain for over a week, and the ground was hard and dry.

She had spent the last week in tormented anxiety keeping vigil at the hospital, or dozing fitfully in the spare room at the Old Mill where she had decided to stay until Charlotte was out of hospital. Although she had still not regained consciousness, the patient's condition had stabilised. Hope once again was beginning to flower on the blasted bush of grief. Catriona had felt compelled to come here to the Beacon, to see it once more, to experience the memories it enshrined, once good and now evil, because she knew she would never again return here.

She gathered from comments made by the nurses – he was still not speaking to her – that Bill, who was staying in a friend's flat in Cheltenham, was already making plans to sell the Old Mill, to move away entirely. To start again with Charlotte in a new place. The desire to be somewhere other than he was, to be someone other than he was, burned from his eyes. He was like a man ravaged by a mortal sickness.

She could imagine that, like a mantra, he was repeating to himself his own version of the guilt and regret that tormented her. That he had not been more available to his daughter, that he had not tried to understand her; that he had not appreciated her as she was; that he had never told her often enough that he loved her. Now that lively, insolent, headstrong, lovely girl had been replaced by a being as deathly pale and silent as the marble effigy on a tomb.

The doctors said that Charlotte's abundant blonde hair had saved her. She had worn it up that day, coiled on the back of her head in a complex braid secured by pins which her mother had taught her to do. That and the fact that she had been running away from the murderer as he struck at her, so that the first blow, the blow that felled her, had been only glancing.

It had been a tragic mischance that on the day of Alice and Charlotte's picnic, no one else had apparently been here at the precise time they had arrived. The ancient redoubt had slumbered undisturbed in the heat. There had been stories in the newspaper of other youngsters having played on the Beacon that morning, then, before the antique men-at-arms struck the hour of noon on the complicated clock of Owlbury Parish Church, had become bored or gone home for lunch – the lucky-to-be-alive passenger who missed the plane which crashed type of story; the story which showed, perhaps, that for some people, a divinity really did shape their ends. Why one twelve-year-old and not another? Was anyone grist to the random mill of providence?

But once it had emerged, in the hours after the discovery of the crime, that the second victim of the attacker had been Charlotte Jesmond, it was clear that the finger of death had not, in fact, pointed by chance. The local police and everyone in the village needed no further evidence to identify the perpetrator. The blood-letting had roused their instinctive knowledge of the wicked one in their midst, the one to whom they had foolishly and mistakenly allowed such tolerance and clemency. They knew to whom the evil should be attributed.

Malcolm Thornton, the slouching, shambling, grinning, mentally retarded young man, who spent his spare time

148

playing childish games of football and cricket and rounders with the children of the village until they grew too old to tolerate him, and whose devotion to the Jesmond child was notorious, had, like a dog turning on the former object of his affections, finally snapped. His admiration for the pubescent girl, clearly not normal in a man of his age, had turned to savage lust. Her friend had merely been an obstacle to be got out of the way, before he could enjoy his evil pleasure with the child.

It was quickly discovered that the suspect had not turned up for work at Walter's that morning. The police had immediately sent out a county-wide alert, and, anxious to be seen to be acting expeditiously in such a high-profile case, announced on the six o'clock news the name of the man they wished to interview. In the meantime, no one noticed that the man himself had quietly returned to his own home – it had seemed too obvious to look for him there – until a neighbour saw his old van parked outside the council house he shared with his mother and sister, both of whom were still out at work.

In former days, perhaps, the villagers would have gathered in a posse, seized their victim and strung him up on the hanging tree. In more enlightened times, most inhabitants of Owlbury remained peaceably eating their teas in front of the television; only a few neighbours gathered outside the house, shouting, throwing stones, and breaking the windows, until the police finally arrived, in three squad cars, six Transits, and an armed response vehicle, to quell the incipient riot and arrest the one terrified man within.

Even in the feverish atmosphere following the murder, motive did not prove opportunity. It was necessary to show that Thornton had been on or near the Beacon that day at the appropriate time. And there the police were initially in some difficulty.

Questioned as to his movements, Thornton had refused to say anything. Then, when the seriousness of his position had been made clear to him by the solicitor engaged by his family to represent him, he claimed that he had gone over to Stroud to buy a birthday present for his sister. This explanation was immediately dismissed as a fabrication by the police: his sister's birthday had been two months previously; he was unable to say where he had parked, which shops he had visited or what he had been intending to buy; nor could he produce anything he had bought. The fact that the claimed alibi was untrue showed only that Thornton had something to hide about his whereabouts. It did not prove that he was in Owlbury. His mother confirmed that he had gone out in his van in the morning, but assumed he had gone to work as usual.

Soon, however, two witnesses came forward whose evidence was sufficient to remove any doubt that might have lingered in the minds of those investigating officers who resisted the general hysteria, and who distrusted their colleagues' technique of arresting the suspect about whom they had a gut-feeling and beating a confession out of him.

Jim Green was the gardener at Owlbury Court, a large Victorian mansion owned by a businessman who visited it only on occasional weekends, the carriage drive of which gave on to Beacon lane. He told the police that he had left his work-place on foot that day to go home for lunch to his cottage in Church Row. He had seen, as he emerged from the driveway, a man who, from his general build and from the distinctive hooded combat jacket he wore, he believed to be Malcolm Thornton, whom he knew by sight. He was heading quickly up the lane towards the footpath up the Beacon. He said that he knew it was just after midday, because, a scrupulous time-keeper, he had checked his watch before knocking off, and it had taken him a minute or two to put away his tools. His route home lay back along Beacon Lane to the High Street. He had not seen the two girls on the way.

So if Jim Green could be relied upon for the time, and there were plenty of people in the village to aver that you could set your watch by his movements, the two girls would have passed the gates of Owlbury Court a few minutes before the gardener had finished his work. Thornton, therefore, would have been behind them, and at the pace at which he was said to be walking would soon after have caught up with them. If there had been any doubt that Thornton had been in the vicinity of the Beacon that fatal midday, Jim Green's statement removed it.

The other witness was Nellie Hampton, an old-age pensioner, partially crippled by arthritis. She spent a good deal of time in the front window of her small bungalow on the council estate where Thornton lived. On the morning in question, about nine o'clock, she said she saw a shabby white van drive into the close and park on the road in front of her house. She recognised the man who got out as Malcolm Thornton, whom she had known 'since he was this high.' Thornton looked around in what she thought was a shifty, guilty manner, before slinking off down a path that led directly into Ewescombe Lane, at the bottom of which lay the Old Mill.

From these two accounts, it was clear what had occurred. Thornton had pretended to his mother that he was driving to Walter's Yard, but instead had parked the van out of sight round the corner and walked down Ewescombe Lane to the Jesmonds' house. He had seen Charlotte go out and had probably followed her to Alice Peters'. He had then hung around until the two girls came out, had possibly overheard them discussing their intentions, or, more probably, guessed what they were going to do from the rucksacks they carried.

He followed them up the Beacon, and it was there that his long-suppressed desire for Charlotte burst out uncontrollably. Determined to slake his lust on the girl, he had first callously eliminated her friend and companion, then pursued his victim. Physically unable to perform the rape he had contemplated, he had in shame or anger left her for dead.

Tests on items and samples found at the murder site or

recovered from Thornton's van or his room in the family home provided incontrovertible forensic evidence to support the now well-established scenario of the shocking crime. The murder weapon was a steering bar from a Ford Mondeo, and had very likely derived from one of the wrecks at Walter's Yard. The bloody fingerprints on it were Thornton's. An imprint in the dusty ground near Alice's body had the same pattern as the trainers worn by Thornton, and those trainers also revealed traces of mineral dust from the limestone rock of the Beacon's summit. Thornton's jacket, which had been found hidden behind the wardrobe in his bedroom, had bloodstains on the cuff and on the hem, some of which were of the same blood-group as that of Alice Peters, the rest matching Charlotte's blood-group. Bloodstains on the knees of his jeans, which had been found in the stolen supermarket bread carrier that the family used as a laundry basket, told a similar story. A long blonde hair on the collar of the jacket was Charlotte's. Traces of saliva on Charlotte's T-shirt revealed Malcolm Thornton's blood-group. Salty residues on this item were thought to be connected with the attack but were not readily to be explained.

As Catriona sat on the dry grass of the Beacon, she remembered what she knew of Malcolm Thornton – from the day she had found him crouching in the hedge of the garden of the Old Mill, to their bizarre meeting in the old van at the scapyard.

How she wished she had followed her first instinct, to turn him over to the police. But she had allowed herself to be swayed by Charlotte's angry defence of that apparently pathetic individual. And, after the incident at the school, how dismissive the child had been at the idea that Thornton could have intended her harm. Poor child. For all her apparent sophistication, she was dreadfully ignorant. She thought she knew about sex, on the basis of a few school lessons, and the sniggering gossip of her school-friends. But she knew nothing of its dark and primitive power, the ability it had to metamorphose, like a virus, from harmless diurnal existence in one host to a raging pathology in another. How it could turn a man from a cultured human being into a monster. Catriona knew. She knew only too well.

In the village, it was apparent that either the summery weather or the tragedy or both had drawn the visitors, mainly grey-headed pensioners or early retirees, who had appeared in unusual numbers for a weekday, filling the carparks, crowding the forecourt of the Tiger Inn, and strolling along the High Street to gaze in the windows of the antiques and craft shops.

She twisted the heavy steel ring of the lychgate and walked up the gravel path between the yew-trees to the entrance door in the south porch. She hesitated a moment before opening it.

The click of the suffolk latch was like a pistol shot in the silence. Inside, despite the heat outside, it was chill and damp and musty, as a church was meant to be. And empty.

Catriona was not a Christian. Even as a child, the Bible had seemed to her riddled with inconsistencies and contradictions. She had the child's instinct that the kind of intellectual floundering and emotional blustering to which adults were reduced when she asked her simple, piercingly logical questions – If God was good and all-powerful and all-knowing, why did bad things still happen? If human sacrifice was evil, why did we worship a God who sacrificed his own Son? – was a sure sign that they didn't, actually, know any more than she did.

She had gone up to Oxford a convinced atheist and nothing had happened since to change that. This did not mean that she thought that religion or religious belief were unimportant. Far from it. Christianity imbued Western literature. Its mythology and language permeated every poem, every play, every novel. She had to know, and did know the Bible better than the most devout Christian. It was an essential handbook to her life's work.

The Bible, but not churches. They were a different matter. She disliked their atmosphere of gloom, their morbid preoccupation with death and decay, their crude art and their mawkish iconography. She never visited a church, only excepting weddings or funerals, the public rites of private lives.

But now she had come here, as she had come every day since the attack, driven by the logic of Pascal's famous wager: if there was a chance that God did exist, it was only sensible to put your money on him. She sat in the dark wood pew, staring down at the blue and yellow hand-woven tapestry hassock on the red tiled floor.

Then she prayed, as she had prayed before, in a whisper, like a child: 'Please God, if you do exist, have mercy on poor Charlotte. Don't let her die.'

She was reaching for the suffolk latch of the heavy, oak-planked door, when it suddenly swung inwards, thudded into her, and rebounded. A woman had been shoving it open with her shoulder, as her hands were encumbered with a white plastic bucket, mop, and sweeping brush. Unbalanced by the return swing, she slipped down the step, then fell backwards, sitting down heavily on the hard floor. As she did so, her cleaning equipment clattered to the floor, the bucket bouncing and rolling, sending its contents of cloths, brushes and plastic bottles of cleaning products skidding over the polished tiles.

'Sorry!' they exclaimed simultaneously.

Catriona reached out a hand to help the woman, quite a young woman, to her feet. She winced as she stood up, rubbing her jeans-clad rear.

'I say, are you all right? You went down with a bit of a bang. You didn't hit your head?'

She put up a hand to push back the strands of curly dark hair which had fallen over her face. 'No, I'm fine. Probably have a nice bruise on my bum tomorrow, that's all. Not as

154

bad as falling off a horse, though. It was my own silly fault. I shouldn't have come charging in like that. There are usually tourists in here at this time of the year.'

'Actually, I'm not a tourist,' replied Catriona, as she bent down, reached under a bench and retrieved a container of bleach.

'It's OK, you don't have to do that!' protested the young woman as she dropped to her knees to help her. Between them, they gathered up the rest of the things and restored them to the bucket.

The task completed, Catriona stood up and dusted off her hands, and made as if to continue her departure.

Her companion was still crouching on the floor, looking up at her with frank curiosity, as if she were taking in her appearance properly for the first time. She was aware no doubt, that, even if this tall, elegant woman were not a tourist, nor was she a local.

Then the healthy, outdoor glow of her cheerful, slightly chubby face faded suddenly, as if she were suddenly stricken with nausea. 'Oh my God. I recognise you. You're Charlotte's aunt.'

'Yes. I am. How did you know?'

'I've seen you before in the village. And Malcolm. He told me about you.'

'Malcolm? You're a friend of Malcolm's?'

She shook her head. 'He don't have any friends. I'm his sister, Sam.'

'Oh, I'm so sorry for you. And your mother.'

Instead of a graceful acknowledgement of what Catriona had regarded as a gesture of magnanimity – she would bear no grudge against Thornton's family, as some in her position might well have, the young woman became visibly angry.

'Are you indeed? Well, thank you very much. But I don't need your bloody sorrys. Nor does my ma. It's poor Malcolm who needs any sorrys going. He's the one who's suffering right now. God knows what they'll do to him in that prison, and he ain't even been tried yet.'

Now it was Catriona's turn. She felt her face flushing red, and it was all she could do to stop herself from clouting the girl.

'I hope they do make his life a misery. But it can't be miserable enough for me. I felt sorry for you because I know how I'd feel if my brother were a monster. I didn't realise that you'd not give a damn about the dreadful things he'd done.'

Malcolm's sister was on her feet, almost squaring up to the taller woman. 'Is that what you think? That I don't care about what happened to those two kids? Of course I care. It's because I care so much that I know our Malcolm didn't do it. I'd know if he had done it. He'd never have been able to hide it from me. So I know he didn't. He's innocent. And that's what I care most about. That my brother is in prison right now accused of a crime he didn't commit. And there ain't no possibility of a fair trial. He's been found guilty in every paper in the country. He's going down. And even if there ain't no hanging, he'll die as sure as if there were. Malcolm can't survive in prison, not with what they say he done. They'll kill him in there. No one's going to stop them.'

The vehement certainty radiated from her. Catriona shook her head sadly. Poor girl, hardly more than a child herself. It was the only way she could cope, wasn't it? By denial. It was obvious, wasn't it, that the only way to cope with such a thing, if you couldn't forget it, was to deny it? If her brother were innocent, she would never have to face the consequences for herself of what he had done. There was nothing she could say. She turned to go, her hand reaching for the latch.

'No, you can't go now. You've got to listen. Please! I know you're suffering. That poor little scrap of a girl! But Malcolm didn't do it. I know he didn't. I know he didn't.'

Sam had subsided onto the bench beside the door as she

spoke, the fire gone out of her face and her voice, her lips trembling, her eyes shining with tears.

Catriona felt her former surge of indignant fury subsiding, and her original compassion for the younger woman returning. Gently, she said, 'I know it's hard for you to bear. He's still your brother, despite everything.'

She raised her head, her face blotchy with weeping. 'Yes, I know that whatever else he is, he isn't a pervert and a murderer. He would never have hurt those little girls. Not a hair on their heads. Particularly not Charlotte. You see, he loved her. Not like a man loves a woman. Malcolm don't know anything about that. He's like a little boy where that's concerned.'

Catriona stared at her in genuine amazement. 'But the point is he was obsessed with Charlotte. I know that myself. I saw him for myself, hanging around outside her house, watching her. I blame myself for not doing more about it.'

'I know what he used to do. He'd drive past the school when she was waiting for the school bus to arrive and then he'd follow it in his van all the way back to Owlbury. And a year or so ago, he pinched some flowers out of a garden and gave them to her, and a bloke saw him do it and shopped him to the police. The community copper took him on one side and said he wasn't to threaten her no more. It takes a policeman to make out that giving someone a bunch of flowers is threatening them. And then just recently they reckoned he was trying to abduct her when all he was doing was offering her a lift! Do you know what they did to him in the station when he got took in that time?'

Catriona's irritation burst out. 'Yes, I know all about that! But he's a man of twenty-seven, not a love-sick schoolboy! Charlotte is twelve years old! Surely you see that his behaviour wasn't normal?'

'I never said Malcolm was normal. I'm not stupid, you know. My brother isn't like other blokes his age. But just because he's simple doesn't mean he's a killer. I tell you, I'm twenty-four, and in all that time I have never heard tell or ever known my brother to do anything that you could regard as violent. He never even hit me when we were children. We never quarrelled, you know, because you could do anything to him and all he'd do was grin. He was that soft, you could get him to give you anything. He stayed that way. Like Peter Pan, he just never grew up. He always liked playing with children. Football and cricket on the field every night in the summer with the young kids of the village. There was never any suggestion of anything bad about it. You could have asked that of anyone round here and you'd have got the same answer. Not now, of course,' she added bitterly. 'Now they hardly give me the time of day. Now they say they always thought he was an oddity and that something was bound to happen. But that's afterwards. No one would have said that before, I guarantee.'

Catriona sighed. 'Please, Sam, I can see how upset you are. I don't think this conversation is helping either of us. What I said about your brother may have sounded cruel and vengeful, but it's all I can feel at the moment. Every time I look at my niece, I see the way she is and I remember the way she was. Whatever you say about his character, there's not a shadow of doubt your brother did that to her. I've heard all the evidence the police have got – it hasn't all been made public. He not only has no alibi, he was seen heading in the direction of the scene of the murder at the time it is believed to have happened. Everything else points at him. The murder weapon found on the Beacon was a bit of a car which he could have got from his work. It had his fingerprints on it. Blood with a DNA match for both Alice and Charlotte was found on a jacket of his which he'd pushed down the back of the wardrobe in his room. How do you explain that? I know you want to believe he's innocent, but everything points at him.'

'I don't know. I don't know. I don't know about any of it. All I know is that our Malcolm wouldn't have, couldn't have done such a thing. They beat him up, you know. They reckoned that he'd tried to escape and bashed himself against the door of his cell. But they did it. That big ugly superintendent from Stroud. Parkinson's his name. He tried to get him to confess, and smashed him with a knuckle-duster when he refused. I tried to get the papers interested when Malcolm told me, but they'd got him convicted the minute he was arrested and didn't want to know. But despite that, and the threats and the promises that it would go easier on him if he owned up and didn't make the little girl come to court, he hasn't never said a word. Innocent people have confessed after all that, haven't they? But Malcolm hasn't never said a word. He was out of his mind with grief, you know, when he found out. That's all he could think about. How Charlotte was nearly dead.'

'I know that innocent people have confessed to crimes under duress. But it doesn't follow that someone who refuses to confess in those circumstances is innocent. Now I really think I should go.'

Sam remained slumped on the bench, her cleaning impedimenta abandoned around her. As Catriona pulled the heavy door fully open, into the musty atmosphere came a waft of hot, dusty-smelling air.

The young woman raised her head. The tears were gone, and in their place was a look of stubborn defiance.

'Whatever you say, and whatever everyone else says, I know I'm right. Malcolm didn't do those terrible things, but someone else did. Someone who wanted Malcolm to take the blame.'

EIGHT

'Hi there, Cat.'

'Hi there.'

Charlotte was sitting up in the big white hospital bed. A saline drip bag hung from a stand, its transparent tube taped to the back of her hand. A trolley containing a mass of electronic monitoring equipment stood alongside.

Her face was pale, but her mouth was set in the familiar determined line. 'I'm bored. They won't let me read or watch TV or even listen to my Walkman. They won't let me look in a mirror, though I know I've got a great big bandage on my head. I've felt it. Does my face look horrid? Have I got awful scars?'

'No, no scars. You look beautiful.'

'Huh! You're just saying that. I can't even get out of bed to go to the loo because I've got wires and tubes sticking into me everywhere. And I mean, everywhere!' She giggled.

'It must be very uncomfortable.'

'What happened to me, Cat? Why won't anyone tell me? They say I had a bang on the head, but I don't remember! I don't remember anything. Was it at school? Or in a car crash?'

'You mustn't worry about that. The important thing is to

concentrate on getting well. You've had a shock, and that means your mind is blank about some things.'

'When can I see Mum again?'

Catriona, startled, spilt tea onto her lap. She put down the cup and saucer and mopped herself with a handkerchief, not daring to look the child in the face.

'Charlotte, don't you remember? Before you had the bang on the head, your mother was . . . she'd gone away.'

The child screwed up her face with impatience. 'I haven't completely lost my marbles,' she snapped. 'I do remember that. It's not the sort of thing you'd forget, is it? But she's come back. I've seen her. So when can I see her again?'

'She's come back?' Catriona forced herself to remain calm, to keep the incredulity out of her voice. 'When did you see her?'

'Here in the hospital. They must have let her help the nurses, because she had a uniform on. Knowing Mum, she probably showed them the first-aid certificates she got when she was with British Airways, and insisted she knew what to do. It must have been before I woke up properly. I was all woozy and floaty, and she was bending over me saying she loved me. Then she kissed me on the forehead. But I haven't seen her since. Ask her to come back today.'

'Charlotte, this is awfully hard for you to understand, but when people have what you've had, a terrible bang on the head, then it makes them go into a state like dreaming. And, just as in dreams, things seem to happen and seem very real. I think that's what happened to you. Because your mother isn't –'

'No! It wasn't like that! It wasn't like a dream! She was there! I know she was.'

Catriona felt her lips trembling and the tears forming at the corners of her eyes. 'Listen to me, Charlotte,' she insisted gently. 'Your mother is still missing. I can't pretend otherwise to you. You have to accept that.'

'No! I won't. I won't! I tell you she was here! I know she

161

was!' She paused. 'When you dream, do you ever smell things? Do you ever dream smells?'

Astonished, her aunt reflected. 'I've never thought about it. But I don't believe I do. Dreams don't smell.'

'That proves it then! I smelt her! Mum has always had a lovely smell. Not the scent she put on, but the way her skin and her hair smelt when I snuggled up to her. I smelt that when she bent over me. And I felt it when she kissed me. I didn't dream that! I couldn't dream that!'

The irony was that Catriona had been so sure that the child would reach the same conclusion she had over the last dreadful week.

It had seemed inconceivable that any mother could leave her child to suffer in the way Charlotte had suffered. The thought had been expressed often enough in the media since the incident. The horrific incident on the Beacon, one more in the dreadful catalogue of crimes against children with which the Western world excoriated itself, had received the widest possible publicity. Wherever she might be, Flora could not have avoided hearing of the tragedy that had befallen her own child in her absence.

There was only one inescapable conclusion to be drawn from her continued silence. Flora was dead.

The telephone was ringing in the hall as Catriona let herself in through the front door of the Old Mill. She dropped her bag and hurried to grab the receiver. Since she had been staying there, the phone had rung constantly. Friends and acquaintances of the family, most of whom she did not know, had sent their love and sympathy, and latterly, their joyful relief at the miraculous recovery. For the first time in her life, Catriona had welcomed the chance to share emotions with strangers.

But on this occasion, the voice of the woman on the other

end of the line had the hesitancy of one to whom the telephone is not a regular method of communication, accompanied by the slow burr of a genuine Gloucestershire accent.

'I want to speak to that Mr Jesmond, the one what had the poor little girl that was attacked. I got something important to tell him.'

'I'm afraid Mr Jesmond isn't here at the moment.'

'Can you get him then?'

'Not really, he's away from home.'

'Only it's very important, see. I got to speak to him.'

There was something earnest in the woman's awkward tones that made Catriona think she wasn't simply an eccentric well-wisher.

So she said, 'I'm Mr Jesmond's sister-in-law, Charlotte's aunt. If you were to tell me what it is, I could give him a message.'

There was a pause as the woman on the other end reflected.

'Sister-in-law? You'd be on the mother's side then, the one who was missing in the paper, her sister?'

'Yes, I'm Mrs Jesmond's sister. But why are you . . .'

'I can't talk on the phone. You don't know who might be listening in. But I got to tell someone.'

A frisson of anticipation made Catriona shudder. 'What have you got to tell someone?'

'About her who's missing. You see, I seen her.'

He was already there, in the café in Stroud where they had arranged to meet, his great bulk squashed uncomfortably into one of the plastic chairs, a styrofoam cup in front of him on the formica table.

He stood up as she approached.

'Hello, Alan. Please sit down.'

'Can I get you anything?'

'No, thanks. I appreciate your being here. I needed someone to be with me, to be a . . .' She tailed away lamely. She had

163

been going to say witness, that she didn't want to be caught out again as she had last time with Thornton, but that now seemed in the circumstances too cold and exploitative of this man's good nature. So she added, quickly, using a word she had scarcely ever had the occasion for, 'I needed a friend.'

He started to mumble his self-deprecating appreciation of this acknowledgement, but she stopped him with a raised hand. For a moment there was silence between them.

He said, 'I heard of course what happened to the wee lassie. A dreadful, dreadful business. I phoned you at the college, when I heard, to say how sorry I was, but they told me you were down here. I gather now she's on the mend. Kiddies are strange beings: so fragile and yet so tough.'

'Yes. Charlotte will be coming out of hospital soon. Bill has found a flat in Cheltenham. He says he won't go back to the Old Mill. But before it's all over, there will be the trial to get through.'

'Does she remember what happened?'

'No, but that may change. No one has yet told her about Alice. Or that it was Malcolm Thornton who attacked her. That will be very hard on her.'

'I read that the police were beginning to finger this Thornton fellow for –'

'Flora's murder? It seems bizarre, but what has already happened seems incredible. I was so sure that she was dead, but now . . .'

'Now you're hoping that this mystery woman will provide the answer to the riddle. I have to warn you that this may be a complete wild-goose chase. There are so many cranks about. She may say she has proof that Flora was abducted by aliens.'

'She didn't sound like that at all. Just rather ordinary. Anxious, but ordinary.'

He looked at the gold watch on his red hairy wrist. 'We'll soon find out. Shall we go?'

*   *   *

'I'll wager that she's our subject.'

The small woman, her permed dark hair streaked with grey, wearing a three-quarter-length beige mac, sat where the caller had agreed she would sit, on the bench nearest the gate in the gardens adjoining Stroud's parish church.

'Mrs Arrowsmith?'

The woman regarded Catriona warily before admitting her identity.

'I'm Catriona Turville. You spoke to me on the phone. This gentleman is Alan Urquhart. He's a friend of the family.'

She smiled uneasily. 'Pleased to meet you.'

'Perhaps we can sit down?'

They sat down on either side of her, both towering over her. The Scotsman's bulk practically concealed her from the casual glance of any curious passer-by, though on this mid-week morning the gardens were largely deserted, apart from a couple of elderly men with dogs, and a few mothers with strollers and toddlers and bulging plastic Tesco bags.

For the first time, Catriona began to heed Urquhart's warning and suspect this might be a waste of time. What could this drab, late middle-aged woman know of Flora?

'Mrs Arrowsmith. You were very kind to phone me. I gather that you may have some information about the whereabouts of my sister Flora.'

The woman was, Catriona observed, not merely anxious or nervous. She was scared. She even glanced over her shoulder. 'I shouldn't rightly be here. If they knew I was talking to someone outside about what goes on in there, they'd sack me on the spot. It's one of the rules. "Patient confidentiality", they call it. I had to sign a paper. It's not much of a job maybe, but I was glad to get it and I'm keen to hang onto it. If ever it got back to them it was me that told you, then I'd be out of there so quick my feet wouldn't touch the ground.'

'You can speak to us in absolute confidence, Mrs Arrowsmith,' Catriona assured her. 'So, where did you see my sister?'

Mrs Arrowsmith seemed hardly reassured by this rashly given commitment. She continued to speak in little more than a whisper, and huddled even closer to the massive figure of the Scotsman, bowing her head low. Catriona had to move along the bench so that she was virtually leaning over the woman in order to hear her.

'I work at this place called Willowdene as caters for old people who can't do for themselves. It's what they used to call a nursing home, but it calls itself a residential home for the elderly. I got took on as a care assistant. I'm not a nurse or anything like that, but I did use to look after Mum before she passed away. Then when my George was taken from me – he always did have a dicky heart, God rest his soul – and he not having any pension, I had to find work. Not easy at my age, who's not worked in a job for twenty years. Then I saw this advert in the paper. They didn't seem to mind that I didn't have no paper qualifications. I have to serve the old people their meals and help the ones who can't manage by themselves – cut up the meat for them and so on. Then there's getting them dressed in the mornings and undressed at night. And washing, bathing, helping them to go to the toilet. It's hard work. It's not the sort of glamorous thing you see on the telly, but it makes their lives a bit easier, poor souls, and seeing them like that reminds us where we shall all come in the end, I always say to myself. You have a bit of a chat and a bit of a laugh with them as well. Just because the flesh may be weak, it doesn't mean that they're not all there. Far from it, some of them. They keep their minds really active in there, not like in some places I've known. There's lots for them to do. All kinds of study things, books galore. Computers. They're learning languages, some of them, put me to shame they do with me speaking only the Queen's English and that not very proper. Mind you, some of them are a bit too active for my liking. One famous occasion, two of the men playing chess had a real ding-dong. A proper fight. I never did see the finish of it, because that Mr Roper the security guard appeared and I got hustled out, but there was blood, and both were in the sick bay for weeks after. Yes, it isn't as dull as you might think. Like I say, my job's what some would call menial, but I've got to like it. I'd miss it if I didn't have it.' She paused, staring at both of them defensively.

Catriona who had been itching with impatience during this recital, said, 'Mrs Arrowsmith, you were going to tell us about . . .' At this she felt a sharp tap on her shoulder. She looked up and saw Urquhart wagging a thick finger of admonition at her, which he then laid upon his lips.

If Urquhart shared this impatience, he in no way showed it. He seemed to hang on Mrs Arrowsmith's every word, nodding and grunting to himself, apparently quite content to listen to her the entire day. This, thought Catriona, must be the result of years of journalistic experience, the patience to wait for the vital nugget of information to be unearthed that would justify the hours spent in searching it out. And of course, there was every reason to let her get to the point in her own way. If he prompted her too much, she'd either clam up or he would simply be putting words into her mouth. But what on earth was the point?

'My dear madam,' pronounced the Scotsman grandilo-quently, 'I think that those poor souls must think you're an angel from heaven. My late mother, God rest her soul, was in the care of a similar institution, and I well ken how much she valued those wee attentions of a kindly body such as your own self.'

Mrs Arrowsmith's pinched, pale features coloured with this praise. 'Like I said, sir, I do what I can. And I think those old people appreciate it. Not that them in charge do.' She sniffed. 'That Sister Monaghan. Just because I do the mucky jobs, she thinks I'm stupid. Must do, else I wouldn't have seen what I did see.'

'Sister Monaghan?'

'She's the manager. The big boss. Sister Oonagh Monaghan SRN. A right Tartar she is. Woe betide you if you get on the wrong side of her. She has a fiery Irish temper.'

'But what . . . ?' Catriona started to blurt out, her impatience quite getting the better of her. Immediately, she felt the surreptitious pressure of Urquhart's outsize suede brogue upon her foot, and she reluctantly took the hint.

Ignoring Catriona's interruption, he said, 'Aye, you're a sharp one, right enough. Arrowsmith's a good name. We're all ears for the rest of your fascinating account.'

Mrs Arrowsmith seemed reassured, even flattered by this observation. 'It was about six weeks back. A Saturday. About seven-thirty in the morning. I works weekends when I can because the pay's better, and I haven't got no social life I'm giving up,' she added wryly. 'I'd just been seeing to Mrs Wright – she's over ninety and incontinent, poor duck, but bright as a button. I just come out in the corridor, and what I saw knocked me out. A new patient had been wheeled in through the entrance on a trolley. There was an ambulance man, a big chap I hadn't never seen before, but along with him, pushing the trolley, was Sister Monaghan as well.'

'An ambulance man!' Catriona couldn't restrain herself. Despite Urquhart's warning looks and gestures, her excitement drove her on recklessly. 'How was he dressed? What did he look like?'

'Well, in them green overalls they wear. But he had a peaked cap on, low over his eyes, so I couldn't see much of his face. But he was a big chap, like I said. And he wasn't from the company we normally use. I know all them fellows. He could have been from the Ambulance Trust, that's the NHS. He was wearing the right kind of uniform.'

'You said Sister Monaghan was with him? Did you have the impression she had been in the ambulance?'

'That was the really odd thing. Normally, she doesn't concern herself with the day-to-day matters. She only gets involved when the medication is administered, and then she does that herself, her being a qualified nurse. But on this occasion, she was not only fussing over the new arrival like we had the Queen Mother come to visit, it were obvious she had been out with the ambulance to go and get her. That was absolutely unheard of. I knew if she'd gone out of her office to collect a patient, it couldn't be no ordinary one. Who have we got, then? Royalty? I said to myself, though that were my little joke, but she was flapping around so much.'

'Was she wearing green overalls like the ambulance man?'

Mrs Arrowsmith regarded her curiously. 'No, she weren't. She was wearing what she always wears, her sister's uniform. Why should she be wearing anything else?'

'Did you see the v . . . the ambulance they came in?'

'No, I didn't.' A note of irritation had crept into Mrs Arrowsmith's complacent tones. 'That were parked outside, of course.'

Urquhart said smoothly, 'Do continue the story, madam. We hang on your every word.' He accompanied this with a fierce nod at Catriona over the woman's shoulder.

'So where was I? Ah yes, I were in the entrance watching the new patient brung in. I were curious and I hovered in the background, and of course they took not a blind bit of notice of me. Sister Monaghan were flustered. She rushed in front of the trolley to open the door of the room at the far end of the main corridor. Now that room is only used for patients who get took with something infectious, flu or scabies. It's like an isolation ward, and there hadn't been no one put in there for a while. I'd never heard of it being used as ordinary accommodation, and I knew for a fact that we weren't quite full at that minute, several of the old folks having passed on quite recent, God bless their souls.'

'So it was quite unusual for anyone to be placed in the room straight away?' repeated Urquhart.

'Like I said, I were surprised. I were even more surprised

when the trolley passed by me, and I saw the face of the person on it. She were not much further away from me than I am from you now. She had bandages round her head and an oxygen mask over her mouth. But I could see her forehead. It was pale as milk, and there was hardly a wrinkle there. And what's more, there was a wisp of hair escaping from under the bandages and it were blonde. Real blonde, too, you can tell. Now some of the old folks who retain a bit of their vanity do dye their hair, but you can't dye white hair to blonde and look real like that hair did. I was that surprised. I said to myself, that just isn't an old person.

'I stood there staring as they wheeled her into the room. And the ambulance man came out, but Sister Monaghan stayed in there. I got a grip on myself then, because I felt quite shook up, but I had the funny feeling I'd seen something I didn't ought to have seen. So I beetled off and found something to do, but the rest of my shift I kept wondering what was going on and whether I had imagined it.'

'But you hadn't.'

'No, I hadn't. And I hadn't imagined neither that the ambulance man weren't from the company we normally use, and he weren't from the NHS ambulance service. The next day, I asked casual-like one of the senior assistants about who they'd got in the isolation room, and she said she'd heard it was someone really well-off, because she was completely bed-ridden and needed twenty-four-hour nursing, and that Sister Monaghan was the only person who was to deal with her.

'But I couldn't help being curious about her, because of what I'd seen. I noticed that Sister Monaghan went in every afternoon about three o'clock with the drugs trolley, after she gone round the rest of the residents. So I got into the habit of being in the corridor opposite the room. So I could see in when she opened the door. Like I say, I'm the kind of person you don't notice. She was careful to slip through the door quickly with the trolley and shut the door behind her, though. After a couple of days, she must have felt more relaxed. She pushed open the door, and was about to wheel the trolley through, when one of the assistants came up to her really scared saying that a patient was vomiting uncontrollably. It caught her off guard. She left the door open while she went off to deal with the matter. I saw my opportunity and nipped inside the room. I must have been mad. I was risking getting the sack, being as I was disobeying a direct instruction from Sister Monaghan. But what I saw in there gave me a real turn. I was right. She weren't no old person. She was a young woman. In her thirties, maybe, and that's still young as far as I'm concerned. She was asleep, her beautiful face as white as the pillow she lay on, as still as if she'd been carved out of marble.

'I knew then it wasn't right. I got really scared and got out of there pdq. Only just in time too, because Sister came charging back, looking flustered and angry. She's usually either like that or icy calm. I suppose she'd remembered she'd left the door open. By that time, I'd gone round the corner towards the day room. I was feeling jittery all over. I had the feeling something was going on. But I didn't know what, and I didn't know what to do about it. If I went to the police, they might treat me like an old biddy who'd been seeing things – or they might make some inquiries at the home and most likely drop me in it. I couldn't risk losing my job. So I tried to pretend to myself that maybe she was there for a proper reason, because she was sick and the home was the best place for her to be looked after, and there weren't nothing funny about it. And I just about convinced myself that that was happening when the other thing happened which meant that that couldn't have been the case. And that set me worrying again, till I was near ill with it. And it was then I saw the story in the *Sun*, about that poor young girl being murdered by that mad fellow, and her friend beaten half to death. And then on the telly that evening, they showed a photograph of her mother what had gone missing. That face sort of leaped up at me off the screen. It was the face of that young woman what had been in the home. I knew it straight off. And I knew that what had been going on in the home wasn't right, and that I had to do something about it.'

'You're absolutely certain it was Flora?'

'I am. I'll never forget that face on the pillow.'

'But what was the other thing which happened? Is she still being kept at this home?' She was ignoring Urquhart's renewed signalling for her to be silent, wishing she could shake the truth out of this infuriating woman.

Before she could say any more, the Scotsman intervened in his rumbling bass. 'That must have been quite a shock to you, seeing the picture on the telly screen, and realising that this missing woman and the patient in the home were one and the same?'

'Oh, it was, I can tell you. It knocked me all of a fluster.'

'You were in a wee bit of a quandary. You wanted to tell someone about this woman, but you needed your job.'

The small woman gave him a look of gratitude. 'That's right. I didn't know what to do. Like I said, I'd drop myself right in it if I went to the police, and they probably wouldn't believe me anyhow, seeing as they seem to have decided that this fellow who killed the little girl has done away with her mother as well.'

'So you decided to contact Mr Jesmond?'

'Yes, I got a friend who does for a lady in Owlbury, and she was saying how she knew where the Jesmonds lived, at the Old Mill in Ewescombe Lane. So I looked the number up in the phone book.'

'And that was a very sensible and, if I may say so, a very brave thing to have done. Now you'll be realising that this lady here is very anxious to get in touch with her sister. You'll have seen how worried she is. So we need to know what happened after the day you saw this young woman asleep in the bed.'

'Well, it was a couple of days later. When I arrived for my shift, Sister Monaghan was in the worst mood I'd ever seen,

172

and I've seen some bad ones. She was as white as a sheet and the expression on her face – well, if looks could kill, the entire staff would have been stone dead. Everyone went round talking in whispers, and it wasn't long before I gathered what had got Sister Monaghan's goat. The new patient had gone.'

'Gone?' echoed Catriona, her voice high-pitched with tension. 'What do you mean, gone? Do you mean she was d –'

'No, not that. In our line of business, people dying is normal, not that you ever get used to it, particularly with the ones you get attached to. No, this was much more unusual, unheard-of, in fact. There were all kinds of rumours flying around, but I managed to get the handyman they called in to repair the damage down to the canteen for some tea.'

'Damage?' Catriona almost screamed. Urquhart's brogue was practically crushing her foot, but she couldn't remain silent. Fortunately, Mrs Arrowsmith was lost in her own world of reminiscence.

'Damage to the window. It had got smashed. With a metal chair, he reckoned, and a hefty blow at that, being that it was double-glazed toughened glass. She'd wrapped a sheet round the chair, to muffle the noise, but even so it must have made quite a bang. Sister Monaghan had words with the night staff that left them looking like they wished they'd never been born.'

Before Catriona could intervene again, Urquhart said with massive calm, and a cheery twinkle, 'So, I gather from your excellent explanation, Mrs Arrowsmith, that the new patient had smashed the window and escaped?'

'That's right. Who ever heard tell of that? I mean it's not like we were a prison, were it?'

'He was telling the truth! He did see her abducted! No matter what the police say, it can't have been he who murdered her. Because she isn't dead! Don't you see, Alan! She isn't dead!'

He was looking at her strangely as he fumbled a cigarette

out of the crumpled packet in his trenchcoat and lit it with his battered Zippo lighter, coughing as he inhaled deeply.

'Hold on now! I don't know what you're saying. Who said she had been abducted?'

'Malcom Thornton! The man who attacked Charlotte. I came across him when I visited the Old Mill. Then I went to see him at the scrap-yard where he works. He told me he had seen Flora taken away in an ambulance. He had been hanging around the Old Mill, as was his habit. He saw her taken away on a stretcher by two people wearing paramedic uniforms, a man and a woman! That's why I was so keen to find out as much as possible about what the man looked like! God, that Arrowsmith woman was driving me absolutely mad!'

'Aye, I thought you'd blown it at that point. You have to give these loquacious old biddies their heads. If they can't tell the story in their own way, then they can't tell it at all. But you never mentioned this yarn to me beforehand,' he added with a hint of reproach in his tone.

'Until now, until I heard what appeared to be an independent corroboration of his story, I'd stopped believing it. Malcolm Thornton is in Gloucester prison accused of murdering one child and attempting to murder another, my niece. He's hardly, on the face of it, a reliable witness. The police certainly didn't regard him as such, even before the Beacon murder, and the suspicion that he might have murdered Flora.'

'You told the police?'

'Yes, I made a statement.'

'And did they follow it up?'

'Thornton refused to speak to them. He's had a bad time from them in the past. He's scared stiff of them, with justification. I tried to get Charlotte to speak to him, to persuade him to repeat what he told me, but he did a bunk. Then Bill found out what was going on, and went crazy. Now, of course, after what's happened – to Charlotte, I mean – he blames me.' She turned to him, tears in her eyes. 'I never thought that that could happen. I've spoken to this Thornton. I thought he was harmless. I really did think that!'

'I understand that. Of course you did. And maybe, in fact, you were right. The facts look bad for this laddie, but it wouldna be the first time the boys in blue had picked the wrong man. I thought it myself when I read the accounts in the papers – wicked, prejudicial things, whatever you feel about the horrific nature of the crime. It's a recognised technique the police have, you know. Arrest the local nutter. Which means sometimes the fellow who's a bit odd, a bit light on the top storey. Beat a confession out of him if you can. Fit him up if you can't. This Thornton fits that pattern. But the implication is that, if he didn't do the Beacon murder, then he would have no motive for lying or inventing a story about what might have happened to Flora.'

'So you think that he might not have been the attacker? Despite the facts? Despite the forensic evidence?'

'Facts? How many facts do you know for absolute certain, Catriona? As for forensic evidence, I've taken that with a big pinch of salt ever since the convictions of the Birmingham Six. I may sound cynical, but I speak from some experience.'

Willowdene, approached from the A46 by an asphalt drive which wound through overgrown laurels, was an Edwardian Cotswold stone mansion flanked by single storey flat-roofed wings constructed in the depressing sixties ticky-tacky of plate-glass and panels. On the concrete slab terrace were several wickerwork steamer chairs, in which reposed elderly persons, tucked up in grey blankets, in various stages of alertness. The ones who were awake regarded the two newcomers with interest.

Urquhart yanked at the brass handle of the bell beside the heavy wooden double doors. A dull clanging sounded within. After a few moments, a plain middle-aged woman, dressed crisply in a nurse's uniform, her dark hair severely scraped back in a bun under her cap, appeared on the threshold.

'Can I help you?'

The Scotsman cleared his throat, then rumbled, 'May I please speak to the person in charge of this fine establishment?'

'I am Sister Monaghan SRN, the manager.'

'I have an elderly relative, an aunt, who is unfortunately no longer able to look after herself. Having heard your establishment recommended, I wondered if it might be possible to view the facilities, and to discuss your charges and the availability of a place.'

'Who was it who recommended us?' enquired the nurse, in a sharper tone than one might have expected her to use towards the relatives of a potential client.

'An acquaintance in the social services department of the council,' replied Alan blandly, without missing a beat. 'I was pleased to be informed that the home complied with all the necessary regulations.'

'Naturally we do,' responded the woman, without any increase in affability. 'But I'm afraid you were misinformed as to the admissions policy. Under the terms of our governing trust, we accommodate only life-long residents of Gloucestershire.'

'Madam, that fits my aunt's case precisely! She was born and bred in Gloucestershire. In Minchinhampton, as a matter of fact.'

The nurse stared at him, her dark eyes narrowed in what was unmistakably disbelief and hostility. 'There are other criteria at the discretion of the trustees. A formal application has to be made.'

'Would you kindly inform me as to how I can initiate the formal admissions procedure?'

'Applications have to be made in writing, to the secretary of the trustees.'

'And who is the secretary?'

The nurse took an impatient breath. 'I am. I should warn

you that the trustees meet only every six months, and their last meeting took place quite recently.'

Alan fumbled in the inside pocket of his jacket, produced a battered spiral-bound notebook and laboriously wrote down this information. The nurse continued to regard him with disdain.

Having completed his task and restored the notebook to his pocket, Alan enquired cheerily, 'Thanks for that. Now, I don't suppose we might be able to have a quick look around? Seeing as we're here?'

'I'm sorry, but that will not be convenient.'

She did not, observed Catriona, appear to have a shred of regret at this announcement.

Without more ado, Sister Monaghan withdrew and closed the door in their faces. There was an audible click as the key was turned in the lock.

'I don't mark that nursie verra high on public relations,' commented Urquhart as he drank his tea. They were back in the same café they had met in four hours previously. Four hours which had left Catriona even more disturbed and confused than before.

'She was an absolute bitch. There's no doubt she could have abducted and imprisoned my sister. And God knows what she was going to do to her if Flora hadn't escaped! I shouldn't have let you persuade me to leave. I'd have beaten the truth out of her!'

'As I recall, I didna persuade you as much as drag you away. You were all set to start pounding on the door and screaming your head off. The woman already had suspicion written all over her. She was probably watching us when we were scrapping like barnyard fowls. There was nothing you could have done. She would never have opened the door. If we'd tried to force an entry, she would have called the police. In the extremely unlikely event that we had managed

177

to persuade them that there was a good reason to search the premises, they would have had to obtain a warrant; in that time, she would have made sure that any records or trace of Flora's presence would have been removed, if that hasn't already been done. All this, of course, assumes that she was ever there in the first place.'

'So you think Mrs Arrowsmith was making it up? And what about Malcolm Thornton?'

'I think, for the moment, we have to treat both accounts separately. They may be nothing but two coincidental fantasies, albeit told for different motives. Malcolm Thornton we've discussed. Under Mrs Arrowsmith's dim exterior there may be a woman with a vivid imagination, bored out of her skull with her life, and desperate to inject into it a wee bit of drama. Also, there's no love lost between her and the manager of Willowdene. When she read about the murder on the Beacon, and then the account of Flora's disappearance, she may have put two and two together and made five. Whichever it is, she's made it quite clear that she won't talk to the police or do anything which might result in her losing her job. That possibility seems to be a mite too dramatic for her.'

'But do you really believe she could construct such an elaborate fantasy?'

'Aye, I think she could. But then again, there are aspects to her story which do ring true. I reckon the odds are fifty-fifty, which is quite good in my business. I'd certainly go after a story that had a half-chance of being true. But I wouldna break down any doors for it. The woman she saw and the incident with the broken window may have nothing to do either with each other or with Flora. We have only the old biddy's word for it. Which brings me to the main problem I have with the story as she told it. If Flora was in Willowdene, if she did escape, what I can't understand is why on earth didn't she head for the nearest police station? That would have been the obvious thing to do. At the very least, wouldn't she have contacted you or her family? If there was an escape and it was Flora who escaped, where the devil did she go?'

'She might have been recaptured and taken somewhere else?'

'That's possible, but we're talking about an old people's home, not the Mafia! They don't have the resources to comb the countryside looking for a fugitive. And nor do we. The only people who can do that is the police. And they won't because there is no credible evidence.'

'So we're back at square one? There's nothing to be done?'

'Och, no. I never said that. What I said was that there was nothing to be gained by busting in like Arnold Schwarzenegger. We have to think it through first. Let's assume that our Mrs A. – and your friend Malcolm – are not fantasists and that your sister was abducted and taken to Willowdene. On the face of it, that is a very unlikely scenario.'

'I think we're wasting time. While you're turning it over in your mind as leisurely as if you were Sherlock Holmes with a three-pipe problem, they could, on your analysis, be hunting Flora down! I don't care what you say, I'm going back there and I shall insist they let me in! I'll beat the truth out of that Monaghan woman if I have to.'

'For Godsake, calm down and think, woman! If they had been holding Flora against her will, they're not going to admit it to you. I don't believe you're the kind of person who'd torture someone, whatever was at stake. You'll simply end up in a great deal of trouble. If they have got Flora again, then she won't be taken back to Willowdene. The only clue we would then have as to her new whereabouts would be if we could discover why and by whom she was taken to Willowdene in the first place.'

There was reason and intelligence in what he said. She leant back on the bench of the booth and closed her eyes, trying to think as clearly and calmly as Urquhart was apparently able to do. Her brain was like mush, so stirred up was she by the emotions the journey had provoked – hope, anger and finally despair.

Out of the swirling fog in her mind, a clear thought finally emerged.

She spoke it aloud. 'OK. Let's concentrate on Willowdene. If Flora was really being imprisoned there, then it can't be what it appears to be, can it?'

'Go on.'

'What I mean is, that what has happened to Flora was done with the full knowledge of the management, i.e. the appalling Sister Monaghan. Little Mrs Arrowsmith was an innocent party, and so I imagine are most of the care staff. But that Sister Monaghan is clearly in whatever it is up to her neck. For her to be so easy about imprisoning and drugging against her will a fit and healthy young woman must mean that that sort of thing is not at all unusual for her. She was hostile to us from the word go. She had no reason to believe that we were looking for Flora, although that suspicion may have dawned on her in the course of our meeting. But her first reaction to us – potential clients, for all she knew – was to get rid of us as fast as she could, and not bother that she showed herself to be a complete gorgon in the process. I don't know anything about such places, but I can imagine they'd go out of business pretty quickly if they had someone like Sister Monaghan fronting the place.'

'Aye, and if it isn't a proper residential home, then what is it?'

'Exactly. You tried to scare her by floating your alleged acquaintance with the social services, and she didn't bat an eyelid. So she must think that she's cast-iron in that direction. But if their real purpose is illegal or even criminal, then surely there must be some vulnerability, some trace of whatever it is that they're up to. If we can find out what that weak point is, then we can work on it.'

'You're right. And I can see how to start. A basic principle

180

of journalism elucidated by Deep Throat, the mystery source for Bernstein and Woodward, the hacks who brought down Nixon.'

'What principle?'

'It is, my dear: Follow the money.'

The doorbell rang as she was eating lunch in the kitchen of the Old Mill.

She stared in astonishment. On the doorstep was Sam Thornton.

'I want you to listen to me. I want you to help me.'

The young woman sat at the table in the kitchen, her hands cradled around a mug of tea. 'You probably think I'm completely stupid coming to see you. But it has to be you. What I want to know, no one else can tell me.'

'This is about Malcolm, isn't it?'

'Yes, of course.'

'I really don't think I'm the right person for that.'

She sighed. 'I knew you'd say that. You do think I'm stupid. Don't you? And I suppose I am in your terms.'

'Sam. I never judge anyone on false concepts of intelligence. I do understand how isolated you must feel, how hurt and how confused this whole business has made you. But there must be someone else you can talk to?'

Her round face under the fringe of brown hair had set in a stubborn expression. 'Well, there isn't. Mum's completely gone to pieces, not that she was much use before. She's drunk all the time now. And everyone else in the village has made up their minds, not that there's much there to make up. But everyone says you're really clever, and that must mean that whatever you feel about something, your mind still sort of works on it so you can see that there might be another side. So if you, in your position, could listen to me and think there might be something in it, then that'll back up what I think. Do you see what I'm getting at?'

'Yes. You want me to be a devil's advocate in reverse. If I believe what you have to say, it will convince others.'

'I knew you'd understand.'

'All right. What is it you want to say?'

'I went to see Malcolm in prison this morning. It's awful in there, you know. The warders all hate him. You can feel the disgust and the hatred coming off them like body heat from a horse. He's frightened to death. He doesn't understand what's happening to him. The other times I've been to see him, he's just sat there, staring at the table-top. I kept asking him to talk to me, to tell me what he's thinking. I told him over and over again what they're saying he did, and all he replied was that they should ask Charlotte, that Charly knew everything. Well, finally today, I got through to him. For the first time, he looked at me properly, and it was like the curtains had been opened in a room. He said, "I thought she was dead. That's why I ran away. I was frightened. The other girl was dead. She wasn't breathing."

'I said to him, "You mean you were there, Malcolm, on the Beacon?" He said, "I knew they were going for a picnic. I saw them come out with a rucksack. Then they went into the shop to buy drinks. I thought, I bet they're going up the old Beacon, because that was one of Charly's favourite places, so I went off up there. That Alice didn't like me. She used to say nasty things about me. But that was only what other nasty people said to her. Charly liked her so I knew she must be nice underneath. I had to look out for Charlotte like she said I should. But I didn't want nasty Alice to see me. I walked really fast and it was hot. I waited at the top but it was hot and I must have had a little kip. It was the screaming what woke me. That and this noise like someone chopping wood. I ran and ran. And there was Alice. And her head was nothing but blood, and she wasn't breathing and I was sorry. And I yelled out, 'Charly! Where are you, Charly!' And there was more screaming. I saw her and she fell on the ground and she was being hit. So I yelled back,

'Stop it!' and when the person saw me, they stopped hitting her and ran away down the other side. I thought she was dead too. I knelt down and she wasn't breathing and her face was white and her hair was all covered in blood. She'd been hit with this iron bar. It was there on the ground. I picked it up and it was off a Mondeo, a front steering bar part number 725430. Then I just got frightened and I ran and ran and hid. Then when it was tea-time, I got the van and went home and then they were smashing the windows and then the policemen took me away and hit me, and said nasty things to me. They said I killed Alice and hurt Charlotte, that she was in the hospital and then I knew she hadn't been dead and I should have looked after her and that she'd be cross with me if she found out, so I didn't say anything, not even when they hit me in the tummy."'

Sam's eyes were shining with tears. 'All he could think of was that he hadn't looked after Charlotte. That he'd let her down. He wasn't thinking about himself at all. He was thinking about her.'

She pressed her head in her arms on the pine table-top and sobbed uncontrollably.

Catriona stared at the weeping figure, her mind reeling with the matter-of-fact horror of Malcolm's account of what had happened on the Beacon.

'The man who did this. Did Malcolm get a good look at him?'

The young woman raised her red and puffy face, her cheeks imprinted with the pattern of her woollen sweater. 'I asked him that, of course. What he said was, "He were wearing a jacket like mine, Sam, with a hood and everything. It were just like mine. Wasn't that funny? He looked just like me. Except when he ran away, the jacket fell open and I saw that he had chests what wobbled. He weren't a man, Sam. He were a woman."'

'A woman? A woman?'

'That's what he said. I asked him if he was sure and he said that he was because she had wobbly chests.'

'A woman wearing a jacket like Malcolm's.'

'Yes, that's the point, isn't it? If they were seen, from a distance, they would look just like Malcolm. And the car part. It's the sort of thing that Malcolm might be expected to have. It wasn't an accident he got blamed for this: it were planned that way.'

'If what he told you is true.'

'You mean, you don't believe it?'

'Sam, you have to be prepared for something. Unless Malcolm will repeat that story in exactly the way he told it to you, in the presence of his solicitor and preferably a policeman as well, it won't even be accepted as evidence. It doesn't matter whether I believe the story. It doesn't matter even whether it's true. Unless Malcolm says it, the law says it doesn't even exist.'

'What, they'd like say it was me who made it up, to get Malcolm off?'

'Yes. And even if Malcolm said it, they could say that he made it up.'

'Is that what you think? That I made it up? Malcolm couldn't have made it up. He hasn't got it in him to do that. You've seen him, you know that. So you must think I did.'

'I didn't say that I did. I said that I thought other people might.'

'So you do believe it?'

'I think that whatever you say, you're a bright girl. You could well have made up a story about Malcolm following the girls, finding the bodies, getting blood on his clothes by kneeling down, picking up the iron bar. You could have made it up because I told you the first time I met you the forensic evidence the police had against your brother.'

The young woman's face distorted in anger. 'You're saying

I'm a liar! You won't believe anything except it was Malcolm what did it!'

Catriona held up her hand. 'Please, Sam. Let me finish. I think you could have made everything up except the end. The identity of the killer. I don't think anyone knowing the facts would have made up a story in which the killer was a woman. And that bit about the wobbly chests sounds the sort of thing that Malcolm would have said.'

'You do believe it!'

'It does explain some things which the official version doesn't. For instance, Charlotte's injuries were serious, but the killer hadn't struck her so many times as he had poor Alice. That's why Charlotte will make a complete recovery. If the killer were interrupted, as you say Malcolm claims, then that would account for Charlotte's escape. But the main objection to the story, no matter how well it fits the facts, seems to me to be one that a prosecutor would pursue relentlessly. If your brother was not responsible for the attack, then someone else was.'

'Course. That's obvious.'

'But don't you see, Sam? In that event, it becomes a very different kind of crime. The police, as a result of their dealings with him, regard Malcolm as a pervert.' She held up her hand as she could see that the young woman was about to protest. 'I know how you feel. I'm not making any judgement. It's simply a fact that the police interpret his interest in children, and young girls in particular, as perverted. Furthermore, to them, as what happened on the Beacon involved two pretty little girls, despite the fact that there is no evidence that either Charlotte or poor little Alice were molested in that way, the motive of the attacker must be sexual. So the obvious thing to do when a sex crime is committed is that you grab your local actual or potential sex maniac. Remember that dreadful stabbing on Wimbledon Common a few years ago? The police went after a man they were convinced was guilty, largely as a

185

result of what is called his psychological profile. The profile said he could have done it. So they tried to entrap him into a confession. The problem with the profiling technique is that there are probably any number of people who might, psychologically, have had the ability to commit particular crimes – and they can't all be guilty! There was no evidence that the Wimbledon suspect was in any way involved. The result of this kind of thinking is that the investigators become bogged down in a circular argument. The crime was a sex crime because it was committed by a sex maniac and because it was committed by a sex maniac it must be a sex crime. What you've told me, if it's true, alters the picture very considerably. If the attacker was a woman, then it's very unlikely there was a sexual motive. But what possible reason could there be for such a vicious, brutal attack on two innocent children? Surely only a maniac would do such a thing.'

'Why are you looking at me like that? I don't know who did it. All I've been saying is that Malcolm didn't!'

'But the form of defence begs that question. You're not saying that Malcolm was two hundred miles away when the murder was committed, and that you can prove it. You're not saying that he was unable to climb the Beacon because of some provable physical infirmity. To give evidence in court to support his story, he'll have to admit he was there on the Beacon at the exact time that the murder was committed. And then he'll go on to allege that the killer was a woman! Can't you see the effect that will have on a jury? The prosecution will have produced psychiatric evidence that the motive for the crime was sexual. Malcolm will say, yes, I was there, but I didn't do it, and produce as an alternative the most unlikely candidate to have committed that particular type of crime.'

'I thought you said that what he was saying sounded convincing!'

'I said that, from my point of view, the fact he had come out with such an unlikely story, and described it in the way

186

that he might have observed it, made it credible. I didn't say it would convince the twelve people who need to be convinced. Frankly, I don't think it will. I don't think a defence lawyer would even advise your brother to give evidence.'

'So you're not going to help me. That's was what all those words meant, wasn't it? Push off, I couldn't care less! You're like the police. As long as they pin it on anybody, they're satisfied.'

Tears shone in her eyes and her bright outdoor complexion was dulled.

'I'd better go.' She didn't move, however, but remained sitting at the table staring into her empty mug.

Catriona felt her forehead beginning to prickle with the symptoms of a migraine. She couldn't help but feel sorry for the girl, but at the same time the flimsy story could hardly have been more incredible. And if the shambling, grinning Thornton really had done those dreadful things, then it was right that he should be punished as severely as the law allowed. But that was allowing her emotion to take over. Facts, stick to the facts.

She said slowly, 'Let's think of the murder in another way. It must have been committed on impulse. The girls hadn't planned to go there until late in the morning. If the murderer is this mysterious woman, she must have been watching Charlotte and Alice. But hang on! If she is the attacker, then she can't have acted entirely on impulse, because she went to some lengths to blame it on Malcolm, by wearing similar clothing and using as a weapon an object that he could easily have obtained. That rules out the possibility that this woman is a psychopath from elsewhere who was merely hanging around the village. That would be fantastically unlikely anyway, but such a person would never have had the local knowledge to frame Malcolm. She had therefore planned an attack in advance, but she couldn't have known in advance that it would take place on the Beacon. She wouldn't know that they were planning to go on the Beacon until they started off in that direction. But Malcolm did! Malcolm told you he went off in front of the girls.'

'Yes. Because he didn't want Alice to see him.'

'But Jim Green the gardener said he saw Malcolm going up the Beacon when he came out of the gates of Owlbury Court after knocking off at twelve! Yet the woman who saw the girls – Miss Chambers, I think she was called – said that she saw them about five minutes before twelve. How far is it from Miss Chambers's house to the gates of Owlbury Court?'

'About fifty metres. No distance at all.'

'So the girls must have passed the gates of Owlbury court some minutes before Jim Green came out. He said he didn't see them on his way down the lane. But he did see Malcolm. But Malcolm said he went up the Beacon in front of the girls! Now nothing I know of Malcolm makes me think he could have worked out how lying about his movements might help him. So we can assume that's exactly what he did. So Jim Green couldn't have seen Malcolm. He must have seen the mysterious woman dressed in similar clothes to those worn by Malcolm!'

'I see what you're getting at. If Jim could remember something about the person he saw that wasn't like Malcolm, then it would help, wouldn't it?'

'It's a big if. But it would. It's only a tiny crack in the case against Malcolm, but it's a start!'

'Cat, you're absolutely brilliant!'

She shook her head. 'No, if I were brilliant, I would be able to work out why anyone but a madman would have the motivation to attack two innocent little girls. But the person who planned the attack can't have been mad. There must have been some other motive. But what the hell could it be?'

Suddenly, she sprang to her feet, as a new thought struck her with its own hammer-blow force. 'My God, why have I been wasting time talking about this. Where's my handbag?'

she wailed, desperately searching under the piles of papers and files with which the kitchen table was littered.

'Here. Is this it?' Sam held up a large square black patent-leather bag.

Catriona grabbed it, slung it on her shoulder and dashed towards the door.

'What's the matter? Where are you going?'

She didn't pause to reply, so Sam scrambled to her feet and ran after her.

NINE

As she swung the Fiesta, tyres screaming in protest, through the gates of the Royal Gloucestershire Hospital, Catriona saw half a dozen police patrol cars parked haphazardly by the entrance, their blue lights flashing.

'Oh Christ, no!'

Braking only at the last moment, she almost ploughed into the back of one of the pandas. Kicking open the rickety door of her car, she sprinted towards the glazed revolving door.

Her passenger drew a deep breath, still shaken by the terrifying drive at insane speeds, first down narrow country lanes, then hurtling through red lights on the suburban streets of Gloucester, the old car's engine howling and its suspension crashing sickeningly over every pothole, the driver's pale face taut and her mouth a bloodless line, as she repeated to herself over and over again like a mantra, 'A promise is a promise. I won't break it again.' Seeing Cat fast disappearing, Sam hurriedly extricated herself from the car, and followed her black-clad figure as she pelted across the paved internal atrium of the hospital, her dark hair flying like a streamer behind her, watched by astonished visitors seated at tables in the café.

Sam ran after her. She had thought she was a fast runner, but Catriona ran like the wind. When Sam caught up with her, she was struggling in the grip of half a dozen uniformed police officers, who were restraining her with some difficulty.

'Let me go! Take your hands off me!' she was shouting. 'I have to see my niece Charlotte Jesmond! It's vitally important I see her! She's in danger!'

'Cat, please!' Sam shouted in return. 'Calm down! You'll get hurt!' She told hold of Catriona's sleeve and shook it.

The wide doors to a side ward at the end of the corridor opened. A young white-coated doctor came out in company with a man in jeans and a waterproof jacket whom Catriona recognised as D.I. Bussage.

The detective stared at her in surprise. 'Professor Turville!' He gestured to the officers who still had hold of her. 'All right, you can let her go.' She shook herself out of their grip, pulling down her top and smoothing back her disordered hair.

The policeman regarded her without warmth. 'Now, madam, perhaps you'd care to tell me what you're doing here?'

Catriona heated up a quiche and made a salad. They ate in silence. Sam mechanically shovelled in her meal with unselfconscious heartiness. The older woman covertly observed the younger. Twenty-four, she had said she was. With her fresh open face and naïve manner, she seemed much younger. Perhaps spending her life with horses had saved her until now from the ageing effect of the messes that human beings make of their lives.

Her food demolished, the young woman pushed back her plate.

'That was great. Did you really make the pie yourself?'

'Yes.'

She shook her head with amazement. 'I can't even boil an egg. As for Mum, she used at least to be able to throw some bangers in a pan, but not any more. I'd starve if I didn't get a lunch at the stables.'

Catriona did not respond to these banalities but carried on eating.

'So what are we going to do now?' demanded the younger woman.

Her companion laid down her knife and fork and regarded Sam with her slate-blue eyes. It was evident that under their calm gaze Sam felt uncomfortable.

'You don't have to glare at me like that.'

'I don't care for the presumption in the use of the first person plural.'

'Sorry?' Sam's mouth fell open in incomprehension.

Catriona sighed. 'I didn't like your saying "we".'

'Why not? I thought you were going to help me. I want you to come with me to Malcolm's solicitor.'

'No, I'm not going to do that. I think it would be entirely the wrong thing for me to do.'

'But why? I thought you wanted to get the bastard who hurt your niece?'

'The fact is that the main suspect for the Beacon murder remains your brother. I don't think it's appropriate for me to involve myself in his defence.'

'What? You said yourself that his only defence was to find the real murderer. You went through it with me only a few hours ago! You came up with this brilliant idea. But you've got to help me go on with it!' Her voice was beginning to break and tears were forming in the corners of her brown eyes. They were wide innocent eyes like those of an animal.

'I haven't *got* to do anything! You came to see me this afternoon wanting my help. I've helped you to the extent that our interests coincided. Now you must pursue the matter on your own.'

'But you know now that Malcolm is innocent! Why are you pretending he might still be guilty? If you didn't believe what I told you, then why did you go haring off to the hospital? The only reason for that was that you thought whoever had attacked Charlotte would come back for another go! They might think she would remember what happened. And something had happened, hadn't it? Otherwise why were all those coppers around? They hustled me out when they found out who I was, but they said something to you, didn't they?'

'I don't want to talk about it. Now I think it's time you went home. I'll run you back in the car if you like.'

'Don't bother! I can find my own way!' She was crying in earnest now, the tears trickling down her plump cheeks. 'I thought you liked me! I don't know why you've started to be nasty to me. I thought I knew the kind of person you were. With horses, you know when you're dealing with one with a bit of a mean streak, you sense it. I never had that feeling about you.'

'I'm not a horse.'

'I know you're not a horse! Stop making fun of me! I'm no good with words. You know what I meant! What I feel about horses, I feel about people.'

'I wasn't making fun of you. I'm actually very touched at your faith in me. But as for your knowing the kind of person I am, I don't believe you do. I don't want you to be disappointed.'

'I don't think you could ever really disappoint me! Forget what I said just now. I got upset.' She stopped speaking, hesitating over what she was going to say next. Then she burst out, 'I think you're the most wonderful person I've ever met! You're so clever, so beautiful! I suppose it isn't surprising you don't want nothing to do with me. I'm nothing am I? Nobody.'

'Oh Sam, Sam! Of course you're not nobody! You're an attractive, caring, courageous young woman.'

'But you don't want to be friends with me? You don't like me?'

'Do you mind if I ask you something personal, Sam?'

'No, 'course not. Ask away.'

193

'Have you a . . .' She screwed up her mouth as she spoke the word, but in this context there was no acceptable alternative, '. . . boyfriend, at present?'

She blushed. 'No, I haven't. And I don't want one neither!'

'Why's that?'

'I don't like boys. I haven't ever gone with a boy, not me!'

'That's how you feel at present. You don't feel that boys, men represent what you find most admirable. But, soon, sooner than you think, your feelings will change.'

'Oh yeah? You think I'm just a kid, don't you? You think I'm not grown up! That I don't know my own feelings!'

'I think you're an attractive young woman who should and will enjoy the company of young men.'

'Oh, you do, do you? How do you know that? Why are you talking to me like an old-fashioned agony aunt?'

Catriona paused, and then said slowly and deliberately, 'I may be making a complete mistake, but I think you may have developed certain feelings for me. I want you to know that I respect those feelings, but I don't share them.'

Sam had gone quite pale. After Catriona had finished speaking, she was silent, then she stood up to go. 'I'll let myself out.' She bent her head down to Catriona's. 'All right. You don't want me. But you need someone. You should let someone love you.' She laid her warm lips gently on the older woman's cold cheek. Catriona, trembling as she sat on the kitchen chair, dimly heard the front door bang.

The doctor had said, 'She's resting now. I really don't think we should disturb her.'

'But she's all right?'

'She's absolutely fine.'

Catriona, dizzy with relief, brushed the hair from her face with a trembling hand. 'But what happened?'

The white-coated medic shot a swift interrogatory glance at the bomber-jacketed young detective.

'I'd prefer to ask the first question, Ms Turville. Which is, why did you come here at this particular moment?'

This was no time to explain the complicated process of reasoning which had launched her rescue mission. In the circumstances, mumbo-jumbo was quicker than logic. 'I had a premonition. That Charlotte was in danger.'

'Woman's intuition, eh?'

For a moment she was tempted to give a stinging retort to this chauvinist put-down. But she refrained. 'I suppose it must have been. And it was right, wasn't it?'

Bussage put his hands together in front of his face in a gesture like prayer and blew through them.

'At about three-thirty this afternoon, one of the doctors on duty making one of his routine rounds entered Miss Jesmond's intensive care facility and saw a nurse he did not recall having seen in that ward before bending over the patient. She seemed startled when he came into the room. Engaging her in conversation, he noticed that her security tag was of a different type from the one used in the hospital. In the corridor outside, he challenged her about this. Whereupon she pushed him hard, knocking him to the ground and ran off. By the time the security staff arrived, there was no sign of her.'

'What about Charlotte?'

He smiled. 'She's a character, your niece, isn't she? A real little trooper. She is in no doubt about this strange nurse. She says with complete certainty that it was her mother.'

'Could it really have been Flora?' Urquhart enquired, as he leaned his bulk against the granite parapet of the Embankment. Below them, the tide was at its ebb, leaving a rim of mud and shingle. Beside them towered the ironwork of the Hungerford Bridge. At their backs the ceaseless traffic ground slowly towards Westminster. Above them clattered a police helicopter. 'Sweet Thames! run softly . . .' Earth had a great deal to show more fair.

She pulled her windblown hair out of her eyes. 'When Charlotte told me of being cared for by a Flora look-alike dressed as a nurse, I thought she was hallucinating, part of the effect of her injuries. Now I'm not so sure. Flora could certainly have passed herself off as a nurse. She was always keen on drama and dressing up at school. She knew about medical matters from her first-aid training with the airline. And in those big hospitals, people come and go without anyone taking much notice. Why she chose to do it without revealing herself, I just can't fathom. But it's conceivable she could have been there watching over Charlotte. Or guarding her.'

'So you think Flora suspected that Charlotte was in continuing danger?'

'Yes. I've told you what Malcolm Thornton's sister told me, and my analysis of it. If Malcolm isn't the perpetrator, then the motive for the attack and the nature of the attacker changes very considerably. The improvement in Charlotte's condition has been splashed over the newspapers, so what happened yesterday may have been planned because her assailant feared Charlotte might identify them, or at least be clear that they weren't Malcolm.'

'So Flora decided to lurk in the hospital in case anyone tried anything? But if that's the case, it simply emphasises the main problem I've always had with this business. The fact that if Flora was abducted and taken to Willowdene, and then subsequently escaped, as per Mrs Arrowsmith, why did she not simply return, to accuse her abductors and bring them to justice? What she seems to have done is to have gone into hiding. And the only possible reason I can think of for that course of action is that she was scared her abductors would come after her. She must have been frightened for her life.'

He was staring out across the river at the stunted concrete tower of the Royal National Theatre, the grey hair swept back over his ears, his Roman nose in profile. 'And the only reason for that is that she must know something about them or their activities that they are absolutely desperate not to have revealed.'

'But Willowdene is an old persons' residence! Not a Mafia family!'

'As for that, shall we consider it when you've heard what I've discovered about the place? When you've – as it were – tasted the fruits of my investigations.' He opened his spiral-bound notebook. 'And what ripe and sticky fruits they are, crawling with all manner of noxious insect life.

'Willowdene is a private company. Willowdene Residential Homes Limited was formed in 1990, with the objects of establishing and managing residential homes for the elderly. The company secretary is our friend Sister Monaghan, and she is also one of the directors; of the other four, one is an accountant in Stroud, whose firm is also the company's registered office, one is a Gloucestershire county councillor, and the other two have addresses here in London, but I haven't been able yet to track them down. All the shares are owned by another private company, Xilro Holdings, which in turn is the subsidiary of Valdon, an investment trust registered in Liechtenstein. Convoluted, but not actually illegal, so far as I can see, though not quite what you'd expect for an old folks' home. Willowdene the property was purchased the year the company was formed, according to the Land Registry. I checked with local estate agents and found one who handled the sale. The building had been a former boys' prep school, which had fallen on hard times. The purchasers paid what in those days was a substantial sum – at least a million, according to my informant. On top of that they had to spend a substantial amount refurbishing and equipping the place to meet the various regulations. And then there was the problem faced by every business start-up: cash-flow. There are staff to recruit and pay before you even open your doors to paying customers.'

'That seems a lot of money to have to find.'

'Exactly so. Where did it come from? Follow the money, I said. In the case of Willowdene it's not so easy. There is an entry on the charges register of the Land Registry title of the property, and a fixed and floating charge at Companies House on the company's assets to Ferrec Venture Capital. None of my acquaintances on the City desks of various newspapers know anything about this outfit, and we're still checking. The address is no more than a brass plate at a small firm of solicitors in EC1. There are various alternatives as to what could lie behind this: money-laundering by a criminal organisation, or an investment by a legitimate business that does not want to be directly linked to its investment. In either case, an old folks' home in the Cotswolds is an odd choice.

'So, we have a business which started out with substantial borrowings. You would imagine that they would wish to max-imise their occupancy rates, and hence their income. But not a bit of it. They are very choosy about their clientele. They don't, for example, take referrals from the social services, preferring to select their own. As there is a growing demand for residential places, that wouldn't necessarily be to their disadvantage, except that they rarely recruit to their full capacity. On top of that, their fees are fairly low, compared to the average for the south-west.'

'At least they're not exploiting vulnerable elderly people. If it weren't for what we suspect about Flora, it would appear they were quite a caring set-up.'

'That is what anyone who looks at Willowdene is supposed to think. But who does ever look at it? I found out something very odd about the Willowdene clients. I was trying to get a profile of the residents because I had a sort of feeling it might tell us something. So I went back to the register of deaths for the registration area in which the home is situated. I made a note of the name and date of death of anyone whose address was given as Willowdene. Then I checked back to the local newspaper. The *Stroud News and Journal* is an old-fashioned rag which reports deaths and funerals in substantial detail. It was clear from the former Willowdene residents that they all had one thing in common. No children, or other close relatives. Mainly, they were widows or widowers without children, or spinsters or bachelors. It was too clear a pattern to be a coincidence.'

'You mean the home was selecting them on that criteria?'

'Precisely. Which is why the charming Sister Monaghan had no hesitation in making sure that I was never likely to lodge my ailing relative at Willowdene. The last thing they want is stroppy relatives checking on their old folks' progress.'

'But why?'

'The implication must be that something is happening in the home that they don't want outsiders to be aware of.'

'Is it something to do with wills? Are they forcing their clients to leave their money to the home?'

'And then bumping them off? I had that thought, but there is no suggestion that there is an unusually high death-rate at the home, nor is there a pattern of residents dying soon after they arrived there, which might be the case if that kind of fraud was being perpetrated. Nor do the wills themselves, in the samples of the ones I checked, bear any suspicious pattern of similar beneficiaries. It isn't that.'

'So what is it? What could possibly be at stake at Willowdene for such extreme measures to be used to defend it?'

'I don't know. Money, possibly. That's always a likely motive. Monaghan makes a comfortable living out of Willowdene. She doesn't want anyone to take that away from her. Flora might have obtained possession of some information which could get the home closed down. Sister Monaghan's hand might have slipped again. That might have been serious enough for her to risk silencing Flora. But why then did Flora not make it and the attempted cover-up public when she had the chance? Without your sister as a witness, we have no evidence of wrongdoing. And, on the face of it, the old persons get a good deal. They live as long, if not longer than other members of the community, in an establishment which seems to be a model of its kind.'

'And actually, we have only Mrs Arrowsmith's word that it isn't.'

'That and our own observation of the woman who runs it. Monaghan gave me the creeps and I'm not easily spooked. So I did some research on Sister Oonagh Teresa Monaghan. Born Belfast on 12 May 1959. Trained at the Royal Belfast Infirmary. Qualified SRN 1980. Came to England where she did a further qualification in geriatric medicine at University College Hospital. Then worked in various residential homes in the south-east before becoming the manager of Willowdene Residential Home when it was founded in 1990. An unexceptionable, indeed rather successful career progression, you would think? Well, there is one incident which probably does not feature strongly on her CV. In 1989, she appeared at Winchester Crown Court charged with grievous bodily harm. An elderly patient at a home in Southampton had received, it was alleged, a severe beating at her hands. In the course of the trial, various other allegations of ill-treatment were made against her. In the end, however, the jury – no doubt composed of people who had had dealings with difficult elderly relatives and who thought there but for the grace of God – accepted her explanation that the patient concerned, who had objected to the prescribed drug that Sister Monaghan had been attempting to administer, had fallen from the examination couch on which she had been lying. Notwithstanding her acquittal, she resigned her post and left the area. Testimony in support of her medical abilities was given by one David Anderson. M.B. B.Ch., who was described as the physician of several patients at the residential home concerned, and who therefore had an intimate knowledge of its procedures.

'Now, I was, for no verra logical reason, intrigued by this gentleman. So I looked him up in the various sources publicly available, as well as the various sources available to me which are not. So let's turn our attention to him. David Charles Anderson. Born London 26 February 1951. Trained Guy's Hospital Medical School. Qualified 1977. Worked as a registrar at Hayeswood Hospital in Hampshire which has a substantial intake of geriatric patients. He wrote a thesis on some aspects of disease in elderly patients for which he was awarded a diploma in geriatric medicine. Then, after five years, he went back into general practice, in a city surgery in Southampton. Several patients of the practice were residents of the home where Sister Monaghan was the ministering angel, and this is presumably where the two met.

'After the trial, Anderson sold his partnership in the Southampton practice and moved to the Cotswolds: Stroud, to be precise. There he practises to this day, a popular and valued member of the community. He owns a property in the town which houses his practice; the rest of it is let to tenants. He himself lives in some style in a house in Ampney Crucis, with swimming pool and fitness suite. He rides to hounds with the VWH, and enjoys the life of a country gentleman. He drives a Bristol, which is an unostentatious but nevertheless very expensive car. He owns two other properties, one in the south of France, where he spends part of every summer, and another in the Algarve, in one of those golfing complexes, where he regularly spends long weekends improving his command of the noble game. He does unco well for himself as a country GP in an overgrown Cotswold village, does he not?'

'Extremely well.'

'Too well, was my reaction. I'm quite an expert on lifestyles, and I wondered why yon man is living like a wee prince. Surely, I thought, the NHS does not pay so handsomely. It must be that he has a large private patient list. Not a bit of it. He has very few private patients. What he does have, though, is quite a reputation for being good with elderly people. There are plenty of retired ladies and gentlemen in the area. You know, the When-I-was-in-India type. Pedigree rich but cash poor, scrimping out a shabby genteel existence on a fixed income. The word on the street is that one of the reasons they go to him is that he has pull at, guess where, Willowdene. Yes, there are plenty of these old colonial boys and girls who would like nothing better than to see out their days in a comfy billet like Willowdene. But there's the mystery. What gives him this remarkable influence? Well, none other, of course, than his *petite amie*, the well-travelled Sister Monaghan SRN.

'I strongly suspect they formed a relationship that was more than merely professional when they were both in Hampshire. It's too much of a coincidence that they both ended up in the same area of the Cotswolds. There's no accounting for tastes, is all I can say. But I thought there was more to it than that. There must have been some reason for a brand-new residential home to have recruited the ugly sister, despite her extremely lucky escape from a hefty dose of porridge. OK, she wasn't convicted, but the case would have been widely discussed among the people involved in that world at the time. So. I have come to the conclusion that Anderson has some financial interest in Willowdene, though I can't prove it. As I said, the ownership of the Willowdene company is extremely opaque. Now the situation might be unethical in medical terms, given that Anderson recommends his patients to a place in which he has a financial interest. But it's hardly something he'd go to such elaborate and expensive lengths to conceal. But even if he does get some kind of pay-off from Willowdene, that doesn't in itself explain his expensive lifestyle. The company's accounts show that it doesn't make much of a profit. But I'm convinced that there's a link.'

Catriona turned away from the greasy river sliding by, and shivered. The air was damp and her black hair was beaded with moisture like hedgerow gossamer, but the chill feeling at her heart did not proceed from the weather. 'Let's walk shall we?' she suggested, and the Scotsman fell into step with her.

For a minute or two, they strolled together in silence along the Embankment towards Cleopatra's needle. Then she stopped, grabbing his coat-sleeve with a fierceness which startled him. 'It doesn't make sense, this business with Willowdene, does it? What you've uncovered about its odd financial structure might have some interest to someone on the look-out for illicit deposits of cash, but where does Flora come into it? But there has to be some kind of connection. Why would she have been taken there otherwise? Surely they're not in the business of kidnapping people to order? As you said, if Flora is under some kind of threat, the threat must also come from Willowdene. In other words, from Monaghan and possibly from this man Anderson. But that takes us back to the question. Why Flora? How could she have discovered something illegal going on at Willowdene? Something so incriminating that they were prepared to go to such extreme lengths to prevent her from revealing it.'

Urquhart shrugged. 'We won't know until she comes out of hiding, and the chances of her coming out of hiding are remote until the Willowdene scam and its perpetrators are dealt with. What you call a circular argument.'

Catriona almost stamped her foot in her impatience. 'If there's a reason, and there has to be a reason, then we can think it through.'

She lapsed into frustrated silence once more.

When they reached the monument, Catriona gazed up at the bizarrely incongruous obelisk, its hieroglyphs blurred and almost obliterated by millennia of desert storms and a century of urban pollution, the polished granite of the base pitted by shrapnel from the Second World War. Suddenly she experienced the kind of feeling she had when a textual crux resolved itself into clarity, or when the multiple knotted meanings of a difficult line of verse unravelled. How simple it all was!

Occam's Razor instructed that explanations were not to be multiplied. It was like doing a jigsaw puzzle as a child. That missing piece you couldn't find was one you had already, staring you in the face. The characters in the drama had been assembled. All that was necessary was to see the connections between them.

'Of course! The link must be Hazel Marchant. I just hadn't seen it until now.'

'Hazel Marchant? And who's she?'

'She and Flora were having a gay affair. When I found out about it by accident I was shocked. I know everyone takes that sort of thing in their stride these days, and in the abstract perhaps one can. But when it's your own sister . . . And Flora had never shared that part of her life with me. That reaction prevented me from seeing there might be another aspect to the relationship. Flora met Hazel in the course of her job at the estate agent's. The reason Hazel had gone to the estate agency was to arrange the sale of her mother's house. I assumed that the old lady had died. But this is the point. What if she hadn't died? What if she had gone into a home? And what if the home was . . .'

'Willowdene!'

'Exactly! What if she discovered something happening there, and shared the discovery with Flora?'

'Then shouldn't we go and ask her?'

'We can't. Hazel Marchant is dead. She was killed in an accident while out walking at a local beauty spot, only a week before Flora disappeared. A fall, apparently. But if she really had made a discovery about Willowdene . . .'

'Then she might have been pushed.'

'More tea, my dear?'

Mrs Richardson's slender hand, still beautiful despite the transparency imparted by age to its whiteness, grasped the china teapot and refilled her cup without a tremor.

'I'm frightfully sorry to barge in on you again.'

'Don't apologise. Our days are no longer so occupied that we mind spending time with an unexpected caller,' responded the elderly woman with a somewhat wistful smile.

'Always have time for a pretty woman,' added her husband with a flash of gallantry.

'Johnnie, really! That is not a politically correct thing to say in these days!'

'Never was one for being mealy-mouthed, was I?' retorted the old man. 'Dash it, I say what I mean, and I mean what I say. A woman's a looker, I say so! Never noticed anyone object, certainly not you, my dear!'

A ghost of a blush glimmered on Mrs Richardson's pale features. 'No, I never did,' she admitted.

'There you are then!' pronounced her husband triumphantly. 'You're as handsome now as you were as a girl, when I first saw you at the Astons' Christmas ball at the Hollies in '41.'

'Really, Johnnie, do stop your nonsense. You're embarrassing our visitor.' She turned to Catriona. 'I must apologise for my husband. He hasn't changed in sixty years either. Despite my best efforts.' She smiled at the reminiscence. Then she said, 'So, you've come to ask us whether we know of anyone to whom Hazel might have confided information about your sister?'

Catriona nodded. 'I've drawn a blank everywhere else. I think that she and Hazel were particularly close friends.' She stared at Mrs Richardson. She was old, but she was neither stupid nor naïve. She hoped that the broad hint might encourage more reminiscences.

'We knew Hazel better than one usually knows a neighbour, but even so there were aspects of her private life she did not share with us. Her . . . friendships, for example, such as that with your sister, were never mentioned.' She lowered her voice, glancing quickly over to the armchair in the corner. There her husband, his contribution to the entertainment of the visitor

205

concluded, and with the *Daily Telegraph* lying on his lap open at the crossword page, had subsided into a peaceful snooze.

'When first we came to know her, I asked Hazel if she had been married. It was not an unreasonable question to ask of a handsome woman presently unattached. I thought possibly she had been divorced, as so many young people are these days. She said that she had not, and that she had no intention of ever marrying. Then she looked at me and said quite plainly and without embarrassment that she was homosexual. In fact she used the word gay, but at my advanced age I find myself unable to accommodate myself to that usage of a word which is still, for better or worse, part of my everyday vocabulary. She added that she was very discreet and she would not intentionally cause us or our neighbours any embarrassment. When you first enquired about Hazel's relationship with your sister, I did not know whether you were aware of the implications which such a friendship might have for Hazel, and therefore I did not mention it.' She glanced once more at the gently snoring figure in the armchair opposite. 'Johnnie, of course, dear man, knows nothing of such things.'

'I appreciate your discretion. But if Hazel and Flora had more than just a friendship . . . If she did not discuss such matters with you, was there anyone else? Her mother, for instance?'

Leona Richardson laughed in a way which Catriona was surprised to hear had a bitter ring to it. 'Would you discuss such matters with your mother, my dear? In my day, personal problems of that nature remained exactly that, for oneself to cope with. There may be women now who are more fortunate in their parents, but poor Hazel was not one of them. She did not tell me much, but I know it was a great deal more than she ever shared with her own mother.'

'I gathered from the estate agency where Flora worked that Hazel had originally visited the office to discuss the sale of her mother's house. Apparently she had gone into a residential home?'

The elderly woman shuddered. 'I'd rather be dead than live in one of those places. If you're not a vegetable when you go in, it's only a matter of time before you become one. Nothing to do except eat, sleep and watch the television. It's the daily round that keeps Johnnie and me fit and alert. Take that away and we'd go rotten, like stored apples left too long in the drawer.'

'Is that what happened to Mrs Marchant?'

'I think her case was rather different. Poor Hazel. She had returned to the West Country from London, with the sole purpose of reconciling herself with her widowed mother, who lived in Owlbury. They had quarrelled many years before on, I believe, the subject of marriage, although as I have said, Hazel was not as frank about her reluctance to go in for it as she later was with me. Her mother was suffering from arthritis and unable to cope with the daily routine. A dreadful disease, from which Johnnie and I have mercifully so far been spared. It was Hazel's intention to support her mother emotionally and financially in her home. However, just before she took up residence here, Mrs Marchant decided, without consulting her daughter, or even mentioning her existence, to take up a place at a residential home. Apparently it was at the suggestion of her doctor, Dr Anderson of Stroud, whom we know well from our fundraising work with the Red Cross. Hazel felt she had been duped. Nevertheless, she arranged to visit her mother. Imagine her shock when she made the visit and found that the old lady refused to acknowledge her, denying that she had ever had a daughter, apparently unaware that she had ever been married.'

'Was her mother . . . ?' She hesitated, reluctant to use the word senile in such company.

'No, that is the curious thing. According to what Hazel was told by the home, her mother was mentally entirely well, displaying no symptoms of Alzheimer's or other forms of senility. The only explanation that her doctor could suggest was that the problem was psychological. The dispute with her daughter had caused her to deny her existence. In fact, I recall now what Hazel told me after her visit. Contrary to what I have suggested about such places, Mrs Marchant seems to have found the exception which proves the rule. This particular home did have an extensive programme of activities for their residents. There were opportunities for them to learn everything from foreign languages to contract bridge. There were classes and lectures in history and science. Hazel could not help but be impressed. Her own mother was becoming a fluent speaker of Spanish, never having learned a foreign language in her life! Yet she apparently could not or would not acknowledge that she had a daughter – or indeed remember anything about her life before she entered the home. Hazel was very distressed by this, so much so that she expressed her intention of, in her words, "getting to the bottom of the matter".'

'What did she mean by that?'

'It seemed to me that she was convinced that something was going on at the nursing home. She claimed it was unnatural that the elderly residents had such command of their faculties that they were playing poker and learning higher mathematics. I had to point out to her that not all senior citizens are vegetables. Johnnie and I were still dab hands at bridge, and in that we were not particularly exceptional, many players at the Cheltenham Bridge Club being even older. Hazel remained unconvinced. She had made up her mind that the level of activities in the home was, to use her words, unnatural. As was some of the behaviour she witnessed. She told me that she had observed a high level of aggression between some of the residents, which sometimes broke out in violent quarrels, even fights. Nothing I said would alter her opinion that the residents were being, in her words, brain-washed. If that's brain-washing, I said, I'd willingly undergo it myself! Poor Hazel. I'm sorry now I was not more sympathetic.'

Even as she asked the question, casually and with a smile, Catriona had the sick feeling that she knew what the answer would be. 'And what was the name of this splendid establishment?'

'Good Lord, I can't quite remember. It was quite local, though. Do you remember Johnnie, darling?'

It appeared that Johnnie had trained himself, even in sleep, to recognise enquiries from his wife. Opening his eyes, he asked mildly, 'Remember what, my love?'

'The name of the home that Hazel's mother went to?'

The elderly man shook his head. 'Tip of my tongue.'

Leona Richardson sighed irritably, then her face cleared. One more defeat for the advancing armies of time. 'It was Willowdene,' she announced, triumphantly.

It was as Catriona was passing the open kitchen door on the way to the bathroom that the opportunity presented itself. She could see straight into the small room. Beneath a wall-telephone was a board on which bunches of keys hung from cup hooks.

Before she had time for second thoughts, she darted inside, grabbed the set of keys with a plastic fob neatly labelled *Hazel*, and hurried into the bathroom.

There were three keys on the split steel ring: a bronze Yale, a bronze Chubb mortise, and another smaller Yale-type key in chrome. She guessed that the two bronze keys were for the flat door, the other for the outer door on the ground floor. She slipped the bunch of keys into her pocket, hoping that the Richardsons would not immediately notice the loss.

'Goodbye, my dear. We do hope your sister comes home soon.'

'No, please, I can find my own way down,' she said hastily

as Mr Richardson appeared to be about to escort her all the way to the street door.

She ran quickly down the stairs. Out of sight of the landing of the Richardsons' floor, she paused, waiting to hear the sound of the door closing. She waited a further few moments for them to return to the sitting room on the other side of the building, then, holding her shoes in her hand, crept back up the stairs in stockinged feet.

The Chubb key turned easily and soundlessly in the mortise lock. She removed it and slipped the Yale key into the slot in the circular bronze face of the lock. Holding the protruding metal finger pull, she gently revolved the key, holding back the bolt to avoid the tell-tale click of the return spring.

She had assumed from the absence of any other keys that there was no alarm, but she paused once inside the hallway, ready to flee if some nerve-jangling klaxon started up. There was silence. She shut the door carefully.

Hazel Marchant's flat appeared similar in layout to the Richardsons'. At the end of the hallway was the door to the sitting room. On the left before that was the kitchen, then the bathroom. On the right the two doors would lead to the bedrooms. She had no clear idea what exactly she was looking for, or where it would be kept, only that there might be some further sign of the relationship with Flora, more photographs, a diary, letters even. She decided to take the rooms in order, starting with the bedroom nearest to her.

She pushed open the veneered panel door.

Her first thought on seeing what was within was that Hazel Marchant had to be the most untidy person in the whole world. The room was in chaos, sheets had been pulled from the bed, the mattress was crooked on the base, every drawer was open, the contents spilled. Then, as her astonished eyes focused properly on the scene, it became clear that the disorder was not the random product of an habitual slut – and in any case that was hardly the impression of the occupant she had received from her starry-eyed and grieving neighbours.

To her horror, the room was in a mess because someone had conducted a thorough and ruthless search of it. The mattress was not only crooked, the ticking had been slit from end to end. Ditto, the fabric of the divan base. Ditto the duvet and the pillows. The fitted carpet had been wrenched up in several places, and the underlay rolled back to reveal the concrete floor. Books from the bedside bookcase had been torn apart, their pages scattered. The contents of the wardrobe had been dragged out and lay in heaps.

Stunned, she wandered through the flat to find that every room had received the same treatment. Everywhere there were open drawers, ripped cushions and upholstery, over-turned tables and cabinets, pictures and mirrors dragged from the walls. Even packets and jars in the kitchen had been opened and their contents lay on the vinyl tiles in sticky or gritty heaps.

What had been sought in this savage, pitiless fashion? What in God's name had Hazel Marchant possessed that someone had wanted so badly?

Urquhart's Volvo estate was parked out of sight round the corner. He was busy on his mobile as she opened the passenger door and climbed in.

He finished his conversation and turned to her.

'Any joy?'

'Joy. An odd expression in the circumstances. But I was right. Mrs Marchant was and probably still is a resident of Willowdene. And she's almost fluent in Spanish.'

'What?'

'Spanish. There's a regular adult education set-up there. A rival to Warbeck. There are classes in everything under the sun. No wonder it's popular.'

Urquhart furrowed his brow. 'That doesn't sound right to

me. That's the kind of facility you'd find offered to elderly people who are fit and active, not the residents of a nursing home.'

'That's what Hazel Marchant thought. She was upset because her mother did not recognise her or have any memory of her past life. Anderson – yes, he was the old lady's GP – insisted to her that there was nothing wrong with her mother except arthritis. Her memory lapse was psychological. Hazel wasn't convinced. She told Mrs Richardson that she thought her mother had been, in her words, brain-washed.'

'Brain-washed? That's a strange thing to say.'

'Mrs Richardson, who has many excellent qualities and is no kind of fool, isn't very imaginative. She thought this was a ridiculous idea. But what if it isn't so ridiculous? What if something is being administered at Willowdene that affects the memory? What if Hazel Marchant stumbled upon something of that kind and told Flora? Hazel is dead, in a bizarre accident, which we've already decided might have been engineered deliberately. Flora was abducted to Willowdene and has subsequently disappeared. And the most disturbing of all . . .' She hesitated. 'I did something very stupid just now.' She felt in her coat pocket and produced the set of keys. 'I stole these. The Richardsons had them. They're for Hazel Marchant's flat. I wanted to look inside. In case there was anything there about Flora. Someone had got there before me and trashed the place, very deliberately, as if they were looking for something.'

Urquhart brought his hand down with a thump on the padded top of the dashboard. 'Drugs! I knew there was something peculiar about what wee Mrs Arrowsmith told us about Sister Monaghan's routine at Willowdene. She said that she went round at regular times with a drugs trolley to all the residents! Now that might be usual practice in a hospital, but not in a residential home. There may be some residents on various kinds of prescribed medicines, but not all. But at

212

Willowdene, everyone gets a dose! Maybe this Hazel took a sample of what they were dishing out. Maybe that was why they decided to silence her. Then they went looking for what she had taken.'

'But why? Why take these extreme steps? Why commit crime after crime if all that's happening is that a few old people are being fed something to make them quietly go to sleep in the afternoon?'

'It isn't that, is it? You said just now that the old folks were the reverse of comatose. Look, a pharmaceutical company developing a new drug ultimately needs to conduct clinical trials. They use volunteers. But what if they're not absolutely sure about the safety of what they're testing? What if there's a risk, but they want to go ahead and test on human subjects anyway? Volunteers have friends, families, a whole circle of people who would be concerned for their welfare if anything went wrong. Much better to use a group that doesn't have close connections of that kind. And that also has another built-in advantage. The great advantage of using elderly people as guinea-pigs is that no one will be particularly surprised if they happen to die.'

A nasty little house in a nasty little street, Catriona thought, as she stood outside 27 Sebastopol Street, Stroud, the address that Urquhart had supplied for Mrs Arrowsmith. From inside the front window, in front of the closed curtains, three large, glossy cats – black, white and tortoiseshell – so immobile they might have been stuffed, were it not for the occasional blink of a green eye, watched her balefully.

She rang the doorbell again, then stood back, stepping off the vestigial pavement into the narrow road to see if there was any sign of life in the top storey of the red-brick, flat-fronted terraced house.

She pushed the plastic button of the doorbell once more. She had tried calling on the telephone, but the line seemed to have been disconnected.

She was about to walk away, still regarded with an air of disdain by the three cats, when there was the sound of footsteps and the door creaked open.

On the threshold stood a short elderly woman with wispy white hair, and a round pudding face on an equally round body. She was out of breath.

'I was in the garden,' she panted. 'You been there long?'

'I'm looking for Mrs Arrowsmith.'

The woman sniffed. 'I'm sorry, but whatever you're collecting for she won't be giving. She's gone to a better place.'

'You mean she's moved?'

'No, dear, I don't mean that,' she corrected, but without any show of irritation. 'I mean she's been taken to our Lord's bosom, God rest her soul.'

'She's dead?' Catriona's astonished rejoinder must have seemed like half-wittedness, but the woman remained stolidly patient.

'Yes, she died last Thursday. Sudden it was. Heart. I always told her that home job'd be the death of her, all that heavy lifting at her age. But she wouldn't listen. I'm her sister, Mrs Carter, by the way. I live round the corner. You're lucky you caught me. I was just here to air the place out and feed the cats. I don't know what to do about them now she's gone. Loved those cats she did, even more since George passed on. Maybe you like cats, do you? No, not everybody does. I can't say I'm really all that keen myself. There's something about the way they look at you as if they know what you're thinking. But there's me going on and you look quite pale, dear. Are you all right? What about a cup of tea?'

Catriona sat on a pvc-upholstered wooden chair at the formica table in the back kitchen, which smelled nauseously of cat and stale cat food. As she glanced around, she realised that the fitted units had an eerie resemblance to the ones she had thrown out of her house in Palace View Road.

Mrs Carter, an older, pumped-up version of the late Mrs

Arrowsmith, poured boiling water from a plastic kettle into a brown teapot. The loquaciousness of the deceased was clearly another family characteristic.

'There we are, dear. Not too strong? I can't bear a weak cup myself. I'm sorry, I didn't take you for one of Pam's friends. I thought I knew them, you see, and you didn't look like someone she'd . . .'

'I wasn't a friend, though the news of her death did shock me.'

'Well, you drink some tea and you'll soon feel better. You can't beat a good cup of tea.'

While she rattled on, Catriona was aware that Mrs Carter was eyeing her with curiosity.

'I met your sister at Willowdene. My mother was a patient and . . . Pam was very kind to her in her last illness. I came to see her to thank her.'

'She loved that job, she did. Cared for those old folks like they were her own flesh and blood. But like I said, it were too much for her.'

'Had she had heart trouble previously?'

'I don't believe she had, but that's what the doctor said it was she died of. He was there, you see, when it happened. They tried everything, him and that nurse who runs the place, but there was nothing they could do. She was dead before the ambulance arrived.'

'So she died at Willowdene?'

'Yes, took altogether sudden. In the midst of life, we are in death, as it tells us in the good book. But Dr Anderson told me she probably felt no pain. And she was doing what she loved to do. Wasn't a bad way to go, was it?'

Her voice broke and she started to sob. 'She were ten years younger than me, and I always thought she'd see me out. But it wasn't to be. The Lord giveth and the Lord taketh away.'

*　　*　　*

They were practically back in London before they spoke to each other again. Urquhart had taken a succession of calls on his mobile, and, driving nonchalantly with one hand, was in animated form on yet another.

'He was picked up drunk in St James's? And he gave his name to the desk sergeant as the Duke of Scarborough, and the desk sergeant said . . . Aye, I can well imagine what the desk sergeant said. So then the Royal Protection Squad turns up? . . . So where is he now? Back at the ranch? OK, that's great, Darren. Usual time, usual place? Great! So long!'

Catriona had stared listlessly through the windscreen as the countryside, drained of colour under a cloudy sky, flashed past.

Urquhart was right, of course. There was nothing they had discovered that would be of any significance to a policeman. There was no proof that any law had been broken. The death or disappearance of the actors had stopped the play. He was convinced that eventually a link between Anderson and Monaghan and Willowdene would be discovered, that he would be able to persuade his editor to back him, and that eventually, piece by piece, the story would emerge. As for Flora, the trail was cold.

Before she realised the time had passed, they were in the dismal suburbs of West London. At Gunnersbury, the rain which had been threatening all afternoon began to fall heavily.

She said, 'Drop me at Hammersmith tube, please.'

Urquhart seemed disappointed. 'No need. I'll take you home, of course.'

'No thank you. I don't want to take you out of your way.'

'It's no bother. I'm away back to Canary Wharf. I can go by Muswell Hill, no problem.'

'How do you know I live in Muswell Hill?'

He seemed taken aback by her tone. 'Och, I suppose you must have mentioned it.'

'No, I never have.'

He was staring straight ahead at the road, so she couldn't

read the expression on his face. The conversation reminded her unpleasantly of the scene with Michael Harwood.

He said, without disguising the irritation in his tone, 'I'm not trying to intrude on your privacy. You don't want me to know where you live, that's fine with me. I'll forget it right now.'

She didn't reply. Why was it that men, even apparently the kindest and most helpful men, couldn't simply accept a woman as she was? Why did the predatory streak emerge? They didn't want to know you, they wanted to possess you. Alan was no different. It was, he seemed to think, his God-given right to fix her place in his universe.

'You're sure you don't want me to run you home?'

'Quite sure, thanks.'

He stopped the car on a double yellow line in front of one of the entrances to the underground at Hammersmith Broadway. Around the vast one-way system the traffic roared in a ceaseless flood.

She reached over to the back seat to get the mac she had thrown there. In doing so, she knocked over his battered leather briefcase. It was full of files which slid out in a heap onto the floor.

'I'm so sorry. What a mess!' She scrambled out of the car, ran round, opened the nearside rear door, crouched down and started to pick up the scattered papers.

'Don't worry! I'll get them later,' he said, rather sharply, turning in the driving seat to look down on her. 'I can see yon traffic warden heading this way.'

'It's OK. They're not too jumbled. Oh my God! No! No!' She stared up at him, holding a slim manila folder. Scribbled at the top in Urquhart's sprawling capitals was the name MORRISON.

Before he could reach out to stop her, she had opened it. Inside were a number of photocopied newspaper cuttings. She stared at them and then at him.

'You treacherous fucking bastard!' She spat the words at

him, her eyes wild and staring in the white mask of her face, then hurled the file into his face. The stiff cardboard hit him on the forehead and its contents blown by the breeze through the open door flew around the interior like white leaves.

She ran towards the entrance of the shopping mall. She knew he was not built for running and had no chance of catching up with her. But, glancing over her shoulder, she could see he was somehow managing doggedly to keep her in sight. When she reached the top of the flight of steps that descended to the station level, she heard him yell, 'Catriona!' in a voice of thunder. This had the effect of stopping the crowds of homeward-bound commuters in their tracks; they turned as one towards the source of the disturbance and stared at the bulky, red-faced, gesticulating figure in the grimy trenchcoat with looks of contempt and distaste usually reserved for winos and beggars.

'Catriona!' he bellowed once more. But, despite the desperate note of appeal in his anguished cry, she did not falter as she ran headlong down the staircase.

TEN

Home. Her home. The word was like good Cognac, to be sipped and savoured. Here she was safe. In the dull suburban street, behind the solid front door, surrounded by the things which spoke to her of order and comfort. Her books. Her music. Her few but carefully chosen paintings and sculptures. Her furniture, rescued from car-boot sales and junk shops, lovingly refinished and restored.

She was sitting in her kitchen, at the big table that had been one of her earliest purchases, a beginner's bargain, coated in ten or so layers of thick paint, ranging from a hideous pale pink to a loathsome brown, spotted in a bric-à-brac dealer's in Minchinhampton in the Cotswolds, one day in the remote past, before normal life had come to an end. It had taken days of labour with stripper, scraper, white spirit, wire wool and beeswax polish before its true nature was revealed: it was genuinely old, made of yellow Baltic pine, a type and quality of timber that was no longer available, with a richness and density of texture and colour that the modern so-called pine reproductions, churned out by computer-controlled lathes and varnished with hideous polyurethane, could not remotely emulate.

On the table were two of her most precious possessions,

a Clarice Cliffe teapot and a matching tea-cup, from which she drank the nectar of the gods, the cup that cheers but not inebriates, the delicate straw-coloured China tea she bought loose from a tiny stall in Leadenhall Market.

She hardly ever used the expensive tableware. But this evening she had got it down from the glass-fronted cupboard in which it lived as a conscious gesture of defiance.

Urquhart's betrayal – there was no other way to express what he had done – was at that moment far more excruciating than the pain of Flora's loss, which throbbed continuously. Over the past weeks she had grown to trust and even to feel affection – the affection of a friend – for the huge Scot. Now it seemed that all his sympathy, assistance and courteous attention had been directed towards one goal.

Had he imagined that, eventually, in gratitude for his apparently selfless devotion to her cause, she would fall into his arms and into his bed? Did he think that in the tearful darkness of the night, after that banal interchange of bodily fluids which had been lately elevated by men and women, who ought to have known and who in many cases did know better into a mystical union, surpassing every other capacity of the human psyche, she would spill out the story of what had happened on the night of 12 February 1978?

That was the modern mantra. Love was fucking. Man and woman lived to fuck and be fucked. It was a truth universally acknowledged that a single woman was not complete in her happiness until she was regularly and definitively fucked. And once fucked she would divulge her most intimate secrets. Forget everything else that 5,000 years of human civilisation had taught: forget self-sacrifice, forget unselfishness, forget honour, forget loyalty, forget justice, forget beauty, forget truth. Fucking was the only god left alive in the pantheon.

The truly unforgivable thing was that Urquhart still believed that, after all he had learned about her from rooting with his fat pig-snout in the midden of the past, she could be purchased by him with a fuck. Well, fuck him! Fuck him! He would never be close to her, he would never know her. He might as well have stopped the car in a lay-by, pounded her into unconsciousness and raped her for all the good it would do him. She would never tell that swine what he wanted to know, never in a million years of fucking.

She finished her tea, carefully washed up and dried the beautiful earthenware and replaced it in the cupboard. How had he found out? What had made the connection between Catriona Mary Turville and Catriona Mary Morrison? There were those who knew, of course, but surely they would never have spoken, and how would he have found them? Perhaps it was enough that he was a reporter, and perhaps reporters had a nose for such things.

But somehow, he had found the old name, and that, like the key to Pandora's box, had opened up a whole world of woe. She had that key herself. She was drawn to the small mahogany portable writing desk which stood innocently on a bookshelf in her study. It had been some months since she had opened it. That had been when the phantoms had been stronger than usual; when, for several nights, sleep had been a distant memory. As with a ghastly wound she had been ordered not to uncover, the urge to rip off the white protective bandages to reveal and revel in the suppurating, gangrenous flesh beneath had been irresistible.

That compulsion had returned. The only antidote to torment was a surfeit of torment. She took the small brass key from the laquered tray on the desk and opened the chest.

Until Alan Urquhart, no one, other than her own self, had disturbed the black surface of the lake of memory beneath which lurked the horrors of that night. The newspapers at the time, with that sense of delicacy which all too rarely affects the British press, had never attempted to interview herself or Flora, or to seek them out subsequently.

The file of cuttings was in chronological order. Scholar that she was, she had compiled it with painstaking thoroughness.

DOUBLE TRAGEDY IN CORSTOPHINE

Police summoned last night to a house in Corstophine found the bodies of a woman and a young child. Urgent investigations are being carried out into the cause of the tragedy.

BRUTAL MURDERS IN CORSTOPHINE

The deaths of a middle-aged woman and an eight-year-old child, whose bodies were discovered last night at a house in the Edinburgh suburb of Corstophine, as reported in today's earlier editions, are being treated as murder. Police sources state that the child, a girl, had been asphyxiated, and the woman, the child's mother, had been beaten to death with a blunt instrument.

A forty-five-year-old man is being sought in connection with the deaths.

SUSPECT NAMED IN EDINBURGH MURDER HUNT

Edinburgh police have taken the unusual step of releasing the name of the man they wish to interview in connection with the murders of Claire Frances Morrison (42) and her daughter Morag (8) at their house in the Edinburgh suburb of Corstophine. He is James Allardyce MacGregor Morrison (45), the husband of the murdered woman and the father of Morag.

Morrison, Professor of Scottish History at Edinburgh University, well-known as an author and broadcaster and a prominent member of the Edinburgh intellectual and literary establishment, has not been seen since the night of the murders.

Colleagues today expressed astonishment at this turn of events, saying that the missing man was devoted to his wife and family.

EDINBURGH PROFESSOR HUNTED FOR MURDERS OF WIFE AND CHILD

A nationwide police search is under way to track down Professor James Morrison, the Edinburgh University don wanted for questioning in connection with the horrific murders of his wife Claire (42) and his youngest daughter Morag, aged eight, after their bodies were found on Wednesday night by police called to the family's home in the Edinburgh suburb of Corstophine.

It is alleged that Morrison (45) fled the house after Morag was smothered in her bed and her mother beaten to death with what is believed to have been a golf club.

Morrison was last seen by a neighbour, apparently in a distracted state, as he drove out of the gate of the substantial detached suburban house at the wheel of his dark green Range Rover.

Despite a massive police operation in the area, no trace has been found of either the missing man or his car.

THE HOUSE OF HORRORS
by our Crime Correspondent

There is nothing particularly unusual or distinctive about the pleasant grey-stone detached Victorian house, set back behind the shelter of its mature garden in the quiet tree-lined street. Larger and more opulent than some, it is nevertheless typical of many others in this up-market Edinburgh suburb. You might drive or walk past it without giving it a second glance.

The family who lived there were also typical of the inhabitants of this affluent, middle-class district. He was forty-five years old, a highly regarded professor of Scottish history at Edinburgh University, the author of several books on the Jacobite period and well-known as a broadcaster on Scottish radio and television. She was forty-two, a handsome woman in the prime of her life, a respected lecturer in modern languages at a local college, and the proud mother of three fine daughters aged 14, 12 and 8. To their friends, neighbours and colleagues, they were a model family.

Everyone this reporter spoke to has found it almost impossible to come to terms with what seems to have happened at the house of James and Claire Morrison on the night of 12 February, the events which turned it from a comfortable welcoming family home into a house of horrors.

Little Morag Morrison, who had celebrated her eighth birthday only a few weeks before, went to sleep as usual around eight o'clock in her bedroom overlooking the house's large rear garden. It was a sleep from which she never awoke. Some time around midnight, a pillow was placed over her face and she was smothered to death.

Then, minutes afterwards, a violent struggle broke out in the vestibule between James Morrison and his wife, as she attempted to telephone the police, and he tried to prevent her. It ended when she lay dead on the floor, her skull smashed by a blow of a heavy nine iron from the bag of golf clubs that Morrison had left in the hall when he had returned from the links that afternoon.

Professor Morrison left the house, leapt into his dark green Range Rover, which had been left parked on the entrance drive, and drove off. As it sped out of the gateway and roared off down the road, the car narrowly avoided colliding with Arthur Calder (74), his retired accountant neighbour, who was walking home with his dog from a midnight ramble.

'That was very unusual,' Mr Calder told me, 'because

Professor Morrison was the most careful and considerate of drivers, and also never failed to give me a cheery greeting when we met. It seemed to me that he was not himself at the time. I wondered why he was driving so fast and where he was going at that time of night. Perhaps there had been a family row which had upset him. But there were no lights showing and I believed all was well, never for one moment imagining what had actually happened.'

It was not until at least an hour later that the eldest Morrison daughter, Catriona, aged 14, came out of her bedroom to see her mother dead on the floor of the hall in a pool of blood. She had been awakened earlier by the shouting of her parents, and the sound of a car driving away, but had then gone back to sleep.

It was only after she, shocked, horrified, wracked with grief, had called the police that she discovered the fate of her youngest sister. Words cannot describe the horror that this young girl must have experienced as she waited in the house for the officers, alone except for her other sister who, in the deep and innocent sleep of the child, did not wake up until the morning.

James Morrison is now a fugitive from justice. Only when he is apprehended or returns of his own volition to face up to the consequences of what has happened will we have any chance of understanding what dark forces turned this perfectly happy ideal family into a shattered hell.

NO TRACE OF MISSING EDINBURGH MURDERS SUSPECT

Three months on, Edinburgh police admit that they are baffled by their failure to discover any trace of forty-five-year-old Professor James Morrison, sought in connection with the murders of his wife Claire (42) and their youngest daughter, Morag (8). Despite an extensive search, the alerting of ports and airports, and the involvement of Interpol, there has been no reliable sighting of the missing man or his green Range Rover since he fled from the family home in the Edinburgh suburb of Corstophine on the night of 12 February.

Morrison's bank account and credit card accounts have been monitored, but no withdrawals or purchases have been made since the date of his disappearance. 'It's as if he'd vanished into thin air,' said Detective Chief Superintendent Eddie Bell, the officer in charge of the enquiry.

BODY OF FUGITIVE FOUND IN QUARRY

The partially decomposed body of a man found yesterday in a disused flooded quarry a few hundred yards from the main Edinburgh to Queensferry Road is according to the Edinburgh office of the Procurator Fiscal almost certainly that of Professor James Morrison. The former Edinburgh University don was being sought by police in Scotland and the South since the murders last February of his wife Claire (42) and his youngest daughter Morag aged 8 at the family home in the Edinburgh suburb of Corstophine.

The body was discovered after the recovery of a vehicle seen submerged in deep water by children swimming during the recent spell of unusually hot weather. The car, a Range Rover bearing number plates identical to that of the similar vehicle owned by the fugitive, appeared to have been driven deliberately over the edge of the thirty-feet-deep excavation.

MORRISON MURDERS INVESTIGATION CLOSED

Reporters invited to a press conference held yesterday at Edinburgh Police Station were told that, following the positive identification of the body found in a disused quarry as that of Professor James Morrison, no further lines of enquiry were being pursued in connection with the brutal murders of his forty-two-year-old wife Claire and their daughter Morag, who was eight.

Detective Chief Superintendent Eddie Bell, the officer in charge of the investigation, said that he was satisfied that the evidence found at the scene, and the statements made by one of the Morrisons' two surviving daughters, indicated that the most likely explanation of the tragedy was that Professor Morrison had smothered Morag in her bedroom, and, after being confronted by his wife, had struggled with her, striking her on the head several times with a golf club, causing her death.

Morrison had then fled the scene in the family car. His flight was witnessed by an elderly neighbour, returning home from walking his dog. From the post mortem carried out on the body and the forensic examination of the vehicle, it was clear that the car had been driven into the quarry on the night of the murders, or very soon thereafter. Whether Morrison had driven into the quarry by accident, or in a deliberate act of suicide could not be determined from the evidence, and would probably never be known.

There is still no explanation as to why Professor Morrison, a renowned expert on Scottish history, and author of many books, committed these terrible crimes. He was known as a devoted family man, with no history of violence or mental illness, and had been married for more than sixteen years.

Asked about the surviving daughters of the family, Chief Superintendent Bell said that they had left Scotland to begin a new life in which they could try eventually to forget the tragic events of 12 February 1978. He hoped that no one would attempt to discover their whereabouts and to disturb them in their attempt to put behind them this horrific chapter in their lives.

But for the unspeakably horrific events of last February, which have forever stained his name with guilt for the most savage and heinous of crimes, the death of James Morrison, which has recently been confirmed, would have been an occasion on which to mourn and to celebrate the life, cut short in its prime, of a man who had been in so many ways an example of the best of Scotland's intellectual and literary endeavour.

Morrison, born and bred in Edinburgh, but of Highland stock, the scion of a long line of Scottish lawyers, numbering among his forebears writers to the signet, advocates, and judges of the Court of Session, commenced his studies in the discipline of his fathers at the University of Edinburgh. Quickly, however, he found that the taste for the law which had been so strong in previous generations, had by his time lost its savour. He turned to history, and in particular, the history of Scotland, for the young man was an enthusiastic patriot and had joined as a schoolboy the then virtually moribund Scottish National Party.

Although he would have been the first to admit that he had no future as a politician, being far too fond of speaking his own mind ever to do other than chafe impatiently under the discipline of a party, he was fascinated by the idea of politics. There are many who believe that the subsequent success of the Nationalist movement in Scotland – yet, alas, to see its final and richly deserved consummation – owes much to the intellectual rigour which Morrison contributed to the debates within the reviving body of the SNP.

More than that, however, it was his own championing of Scottish history, itself then regarded as of little more than parochial interest, which assisted in bringing forth the flowering of a new pride in the idea of Scottish nationhood, of a distinctively Scottish nation, valid not only for the years before the Act of Union, which Morrison called, with due regard for the resonances of the phrase, 'an Act which shall live in infamy', but for the future.

Morrison's publications were voluminous, but of an extraordinarily and consistently high quality, from the early works on the fifteenth and sixteenth centuries, of which *James IV Stewart and the Scottish Renaissance* is the most impressive, to the works on the Jacobite period for which he became most known, most particularly *The Lost Leader*, the definitive biography of Charles Edward Stuart, the Young Pretender. The two volumes of this, *Roses, Roses All The Way* and *Just for a Handful of Silver*, combined a scrupulous, almost painful adherence to the facts of the life of this most misfortunate of Scottish leaders, with an elegiac sense of what could, what should have been. Morrison was sometimes criticised for being a romantic in a realistic world, a cavalier in a roundhead society, but no one could ever fault him for the immense scholarship which informed his every utterance. Comment may have been free, but facts were sacred, and Morrison never confused the two.

Morrison's private life had always been regarded as exemplary. He had been married to Claire, daughter of the late Archibald Turville of London, for sixteen years and she had borne him three beautiful daughters. It is not for this obituary writer to speculate on what moment of madness could drive him to squander this legacy of love and fortune. That is for the psychologist. The historian must only record the facts, painful though they are. Morrison took the lives of his wife and youngest daughter, and afterwards his own. Those evil crimes will, rightly, live after him. In his case, however, the squalor of his end, like that of his hero, Bonnie Prince Charlie, had been preceded by years of triumph. Those years, too, should be included in his memorial.

There was one other item in the file. A bulky manila envelope, the flap of which had been firmly gummed down and in addition sealed there and at its seams with transparent adhesive tape. In the manner of a package entrusted to a bank to prevent tampering, the seams had, before sealing with the tape, been signed over at intervals with her initials CMT. In her precise cursive handwriting she had written:

'I, Catriona Mary Turville, previously known as Catriona Mary Morrison, have sealed within this packet various papers relating to the events surrounding the deaths of my mother Claire Frances Morrison, my sister Morag Kirstie Morrison and my father James Allardyce MacGregor Morrison.

'I leave it to be opened by my executors after my death, whereupon they may take such action as they see fit.

'IN WITNESS whereof I have set my hand the 25th March 1991.'

As she closed the file and locked the writing desk she reflected how much Alan Urquhart would have given to have got his filthy hands on the contents of that envelope. But he never would. Never.

She yawned, put the book aside, clicked up the button on the alarm clock by her bed and switched out the light. Despite her fatigue, she found it hard to go to sleep. The ceaseless whirl of activity in her mind would not be stilled. There were too many images crowding for attention in her mind.

Gradually, though, the images blurred and darkened, and she hovered on the threshold of sleep, dimly aware of the usual night sounds in her beloved house, lulling her with their normality.

That faint ticking was the clock, the intermittent creak was the sound of the house settling after the heat of the day. The nearby hum was the refrigerator in the kitchen, the more distant hum was the traffic on Muswell Hill. All was well. She turned in the bed, burying her face in the pillow.

Suddenly, from the sash window facing her, there was an explosive crash of breaking glass. In the same split second, blown by the cold incoming gust, the curtains billowed into the room. Then, with a kind of whooshing roar, most like, she was astonished to recall later, the sound of a Guy Fawkes Night rocket taking off, they burst into flames.

The Scotsman, accustomed to do everything commensurate with his own vast scale, appeared at her hospital bedside with a huge bouquet of flowers, an enormous basket of fruit and a massive box of chocolates.

He looked down on her, his craggy face softening with concern. 'So how are you?'

She coughed into a tissue. 'They're keeping me in for observation. I inhaled an awful lot of smoke. Plus I've some burns and cuts. Apparently, they should heal up OK.'

'You were very lucky. My God, when I saw the agency newsflash, I thought . . . I thought I'd lost you.' He reached out one of his great red paws and laid it on her slender hand. 'I think you know I care very much for you, Catriona.'

'Do you? You certainly went to a great deal of trouble to investigate me. Is that how you show your affection?'

'You're right to be angry. It must seem a betrayal.'

'There's a certain irony in it. I was worried that in involving you in Flora's disappearance, I was exploiting your crush on me.'

'Crush? I'm no fucking schoolboy!'

'No, but I thought you were. All your blushes and your cow eyes at me in the seminars! Your charming diffidence in asking me to go for a drink! Ha! Do you know, I went to the pub with you that time only because I'd had a dreadful scene with Michael Harwood? I wanted to get away from the bastard. He's been sniffing at my skirt like a mangy hound ever since he was appointed to the Disneyland Chair of Fun. But my self-reproach that I was leading you on was misplaced, wasn't it? Because all the time you were pretending to be interested in me only to fatten me up for your scoop. Murderer's daughter in new tragedy. Was that the headline you were planning?'

He shook his huge shaggy head, his eyes downcast. 'No, no. I swear that that was never my intention.'

'Really? So what was your intention when you began compiling a dossier on my life history?' Her face was deathly white, and her eyes were wide and bright, but no trace of tears shone there.

'It's true that I admired you from the beginning. If you want to call it a crush, then call it that. You are beautiful, sensitive, intelligent. All I'd ever looked for in a woman and never been fortunate enough to find. It was an honourable feeling. I never expected you to return it. Why should you? I had nothing to offer you. But then you shared with me what had happened to your sister. I thought that by helping you, I would be doing you some service.'

'Alan Urquhart, the courtly lover, the verray parfit gentil knicht? You must think I'm very naïve.'

'Sneer if you like. And yes, in some ways, you are very naïve. For a woman of almost forty, you're still a girl where feelings are concerned. I repeat, I wanted to help you. That was my sole intention. I didn't know or even suspect your history. I swear it. How could I have? How could I connect you with a twenty-odd-year-old murder case?'

'So how did you find out?'

'How?' He stared down at the polished vinyl of the floor, his mouth twisted in a wry, thin-lipped smile. 'You told me that you had been born and brought up in London, by English parents. Because I was fascinated by you, I wanted to know more about you. Your name Catriona! That wonderful name, so redolent of romance! So full of the smell of the heather and the broom! I fell in love with that name years before I ever met you! I hinted as much that time in the pub. I told you as a boy I wanted to be Alan Breck, but, unlike David Balfour, I never met my Highland princess. And then I walk into a seminar room thirty-five years later and there she is!'

He raised his head and stared into her eyes. 'How could I not fall in love with you? And then you told me of your sister, Flora. The name of a goddess. But also the name of a true Scottish heroine. Flora MacDonald, who helped Bonnie Prince Charlie to escape over the sea to Skye. Who were these Sassenachs who had given such iconic Scottish names to their daughters? It was a challenge to me to find out something about them, as I didn't flatter myself that we would ever be on such terms that you would tell me yourself. And I fear that that challenge became a passion to know.'

'So, this passion drove you to genealogy. You looked me up at Somerset House?'

'The great palace on the Thames has not housed such records for many years. The Office of Population Censuses and Surveys for England and Wales occupies a much less romantic building. Yes, I searched for the birth certificate of Catriona Mary Turville and it was not there. I searched for the birth certificate of Flora Turville and she wasn't there either. Had you been married? You hadn't. But Flora had. Now Flora's husband Bill is professionally eminent enough to appear on several databases. After a bit of digging I found the record of his marriage, at the British Consulate in New York, to one Flora Alice Turville. So your maiden name was Turville. Fortunately an uncommon name. So on I went to search the Turvilles. On the assumption that your father had been between twenty-five and thirty-five when you were born,

I searched the Births from 1939 to 1949. I found three male births in those years. I used computer records of registers of electors to find two of them. I telephoned them both. Neither of them had daughters called Catriona or Flora. The missing Turville I discovered in the Register of Deaths. He had died in 1955, long before you were born. So not only was there no record of your own or your sister's birth, there was no record of your father's. Then I had an inspiration. Perhaps your parents had not been married. In which case you might have taken your mother's surname. So back to the Turvilles. I found two Turvilles, who were born in Dulwich in what I had assumed were the relevant years. Claire Frances, and Charlotte Grace, and who were clearly sisters. Possibly your mother and your aunt. I was still puzzled by the lack of a birth certificate. I had a feeling about the two names, and neither of them seemed the type who would have a child out of wedlock. And then it hit me! You might have been born in Scotland! In which case there would be no record of your birth in the English system.

'Now, I have to admit that I've been so long in this country that my knowledge of Scottish administrative procedures is pretty non-existent. So, before mugging up on that, I took one more dive at OPCS. Your very bourgeois English-sounding mother would probably have married at home in London. That's when the whole thing unravelled. In 1962, Claire Frances Turville had married one James Allardyce MacGregor Morrison. And then I remembered. Morrison. I'd been a reporter in Manchester in 1978, but the case's notoriety spread far beyond Edinburgh. Morrison, the Edinburgh professor who had murdered his wife and his youngest daughter. I checked with an old acquaintance in Edinburgh and he remembered that the names of the surviving Morrison daughters were Catriona and Flora.'

'It was so easy, wasn't it? I always said we should have changed our names completely. But my aunt refused, saying there was no reason to reject our entire heritage. If we'd been called Smith, you'd never have found us. So now you know who I am. But that's as far as it goes. I'm never going to talk to you about that night. Never. There's going to be no scoop, Alan. No exclusive "as told to". If you want to break the story that it is James Morrison's daughter who has disappeared, go ahead. Reawaken the memories that have slept for twenty-four years. Destroy the lives of Flora's husband and her own daughter, neither of whom know who she really is. I hope there isn't an editor in the country who would have the inhumanity to let you do that, but, if there is, then publish and be damned.'

He seized her cold hands in his. 'Do you know me so little that you think I would do that? That I intended to do that? That file was purely for my own use. God, I wept when I read those stories. I tried to imagine you trapped in that house of blood, how those images must have seared your mind. But I never, never thought of breaking the confidence. Can you not forgive me my foolishness? Haven't I wished over and over that I'd never produced that file.'

'I understand now why you did it. I accept the purity of your motives. If that is forgiveness, then you are forgiven. And, now I'm recovered from the shock of your knowing, the fact that you know makes it easier for you to understand why I am as I am. And why I can never be your Highland princess, nor anyone else's.'

'You mean that because of what happened twenty-four years ago you live as you do, letting no one close to you? Why, for God's sake, why? Why punish yourself for what your father did?'

She held out her long slim hands, perfectly white and unadorned by rings or nail-varnish. 'His blood in my veins, Alan! Half my genes are his! Why should I want to pass on that heritage?'

'You're an intelligent woman, a brilliant woman! That

sort of talk, of tainted blood, is superstitious hogwash! And dragging in genetics doesn't make it any more sensible.'

'I don't wish to discuss this any further, Alan. Please.'

'But you have to discuss it. If none of that baggage from the past existed, could you feel something for me? Could you love me?'

She turned her head away, so that he wouldn't see the tears that were beginning to spring at the corners of her eyes. 'It's of no use to speak in hypotheses. No use at all.'

'It's of use to me,' he persisted, his blue eyes wet.

'Leave me alone! I'm no good for you, I'm no good for anyone. I should have been burned to death in the fire. I've exploited you, can't you see that, Alan? When you told me you were a journalist, I saw it as an opportunity to get help for a problem I couldn't solve myself. I used you. And the result of that has been to find mysteries where there are none and conspiracies in the everyday coincidences of life. There's no mystery in Flora's disappearance. There never was! Flora killed herself. She wrote to me and told me that was her intention!'

He stared at her in astonishment. 'She wrote to you?'

'Yes, a detailed, sane, reasoned declaration of her intent to commit suicide. She asked me to go to Owlbury, where I would find her body. I was to break the news to Bill and Charlotte.'

'So you went there?'

'Yes. Immediately. But she wasn't there, dead or alive. Nor was there any indication that anything was amiss. Or any other clue as to what she had done or what had happened.'

'So what did you do then?'

'I went home and waited. I thought, I hoped she might have had second thoughts and would simply turn up again. That she might have been ashamed and sorry for misleading me. But the longer her absence grew, the more confused the situation became. When I told you about it, I was still

236

hoping that she had simply gone into hiding and would come back.'

'Why didn't you tell the police?'

'Isn't it obvious? If I'd done that I would have had to disclose the letter. I would have had to explain what Flora meant when she wrote of the memories which had driven her to suicide. Our real identities would have been in the papers in no time. Charlotte's life, my life would be ruined. Besides, Flora forbade me to tell anyone else – to protect Charlotte.'

'So do you now believe she did commit suicide?'

'Yes. I do. I never knew how much she had taken in about that night. We never discussed it. But underneath that carefree exterior, she must have been as haunted as I was. She cracked under the strain of it. I think she's dead. I think she walked out of the house that day, and found a quiet place to die. The Cotswolds are not the Highlands, but there are plenty of unfrequented places where a body could lie for months or years without being discovered.'

'But what about Hazel Marchant?'

'Hazel's death was an accident which will have served to increase Flora's depression.'

'But what about Willowdene? Malcolm Thornton? And Mrs Arrowsmith?'

'Malcolm Thornton is a liar and a murderer. He attacked Charlotte and tried to kill her. I was responsible for encouraging him. I betrayed Charlotte's trust. Mrs Arrowsmith was a crazy frustrated old woman who imagined the excitement she never had in reality. There might be something going on at Willowdene. There might not be. Whatever it is, it isn't relevant to what happened to Flora.'

She lay back on the pillow.

'But why do you think your house was firebombed? Don't you think it was an attempt to silence you? Or was that another coincidence?'

'I don't know. London's full of gangsters who shoot and

kill one another. They got the wrong house, the wrong person.'

'I don't believe that! I don't believe your sister committed suicide. I don't think we can simply ignore the things we found out.'

'I can, because we haven't found them out. We've imagined them. Seen connections where there were none. Like reading more into a text than the author intended. You carry on if you want to. But it would be better for you and better for me if you didn't. Forget me, Alan. You think you love me, but you don't know who I am. You don't know what I might be capable of. I might, for instance, have killed Flora myself. I could have murdered her when I went there that morning. That's what the police are halfway towards thinking. That's something else I haven't told you. A few days before the attack on the Beacon, just after I had reported Malcolm Thornton's tale of the ambulance and the slipper to Stroud police, two detectives from Stroud came to beard the lioness in her den. They had found some old codger who saw my car in the lane that morning and gave me a very inept form of the third degree to find out what I was doing there.'

'And what did you tell them?'

'I denied being there. I lied. I found it remarkably easy. I've always been a good actor, hence a good liar, particularly to myself. You'd never know whether I was telling the truth. And I am the daughter of a murderer.'

He was looking at her with concern, but in his eyes was something else. It was uncertainty. She could sense it.

He said uneasily, 'You'd never have killed Flora. You loved her.'

'Perhaps I did, perhaps I didn't. Love can turn to hate. Perhaps I hated the things that she had and I didn't. A husband, a daughter. Love. You know one of the best pieces of literary criticism ever written? G. Wilson Knight's *The Embassy of Death*. It's a study of *Hamlet*. It's terribly unfashionable in these days to discuss Shakespearean characters as if they were real. But anyone who sees the plays, as opposed to French Marxist intellectuals who can't write their own language, never mind read anyone else's, knows that the two-hour traffic of the stage is real enough. Wilson Knight has no truck with the tortured intellectual justified-revenger view of Hamlet. He makes a good case for the sweet Prince being a nihilistic murderer: not the hero, but the villain. Does that remind you of anyone?'

She sank back on the pillow and closed her eyes. When she opened them again, Urquhart had gone.

There were two of them, WPC Edwards, a young woman with short blonde hair and a strong chin, and DS Collins in casual plain-clothes, also young and tough looking, with crew-cut dark hair.

WPC Edwards kicked off. 'How are you feeling, Catriona?' she asked brightly.

Catriona grimaced, wordlessly.

'I've seen your house. The investigator from the fire-brigade says he can't believe how you survived.'

'I thought I wasn't going to.'

The DS who had been gazing around the small room, as if searching for inspiration on the plain cream walls, joined the conversation. 'Perhaps you'd take us through what happened?'

'I went to bed that night as usual about twelve-thirty a.m. Then I read for about an hour before turning out the light.'

'Do you usually go to bed so late?'

'Yes. I work most evenings until about midnight. Then I have a snack, listen to the late news on Radio 4. Then I read until I feel tired enough to sleep.'

'What were you reading that night?'

'*The Bone Collector* by Jeffrey Deaver. An American detective novelist I've just discovered. Do you know the book?'

'I think I've seen the film. It's about a serial killer isn't it? Does that sort of thing make you sleep?'

'Usually. But on this occasion it didn't. Fortunately.'

'So anyone who'd been watching your house would have been able to observe a pattern of activity that they could be pretty sure would apply to any given night?'

'Yes, I suppose so.'

'Does anyone apart from yourself regularly stay in your house?'

'If you mean, a lover, the answer's no. If you mean anyone else, the answer's the same. Are you suggesting a man would have been of some assistance on that night, Detective Sergeant? Are men fireproof?'

He shrugged. 'You seem to have coped quite well on your own. So at about one-thirty, you put out your light. But you didn't go to sleep immediately.'

'No, I lay awake for several minutes. I was just turning over to try to sleep when there was a crash at the window. I didn't know what had happened for a moment. I had just realised that something had been thrown through the window, when there was a roar like a firework going off and the curtains burst into flames. In seconds the whole of that end of the room was in flames. I rolled off the bed and on to the carpet. I read somewhere that the air is clearest and coolest the lower down you can get. I pulled the duvet round me, as it was already scorchingly hot. I crawled towards the door, pulled it open and got out on to the landing, pulling it closed behind me.'

'You acted with remarkable calm in the circumstances.'

'Yes, I did. I thought afterwards that not panicking was what saved me. Particularly when they threw the second one through the front door.'

'There was a second device?'

'Yes. It came crashing through the glass panel just as I got out onto the landing. Almost as if it had been timed to catch me. It exploded as it hit the tiles. That was when I thought I'd had it.

The flames roared up the staircase towards me. I looked round and smoke was pouring through the gaps in the bedroom door. Then it broke apart and there was nothing but fire. I could smell that the duvet was burning. I was trapped.'

'So how did you get out?'

'I was almost fainting from the heat and smoke, but I was determined not to die like that. I kicked down the banisters and the handrail at the top of the stairs, and let myself drop down through the stairwell into the hallway. I thought I'd broken something, but I'd only sprained my ankle. I limped into the dining room, smashed the French windows open with a chair, and staggered out into the garden. I was only just in time. The fire took hold in moments. The roof fell in. I must have passed out. The next thing I remember is seeing a fireman bending over me.'

'So, someone waited for you to turn out your light, then threw two incendiary devices into your house. Someone must have been very keen to make sure you were caught by one or other of them.'

'Yes, if I'd been asleep I don't think I would have got out. It happened so quickly.'

'Who is this someone, Professor Turville? And why did they do it?'

There was something almost insolent in his tone, something which implied she was part of what had happened.

She responded tartly, 'What the hell is this about? I'm the victim here. How should I know why some hooligans firebombed my house? Why don't you catch them and ask them why they picked me?'

He gave a saturnine grin, sucking in his already hollow cheeks, so that the bones of his face stood proud and sharp. 'If we did catch them, they wouldn't tell us, and might not know anyway. They're only the soldiers. The people we'd like to catch are the ones who sent them. You see the perpetrators weren't just hooligans as you call them. Not kids making

Molotov cocktails out of empty milk bottles and petrol. The gear they used was state of the art. That's why your place went up like a Roman candle. A common-or-garden petrol bomb wouldn't have spread so quickly and destroyed the place so thoroughly. Could have damn near burnt down the street, too, if the brigade hadn't got there double-quick. No, these weren't yobboes out for a thrill. These were professionals. You were the victim of an attempted hit. Do you have any idea who might employ such people and why?'

WPC Edwards shot a not-entirely-friendly glance at her colleague.

She said in a soft, emollient tone, 'Catriona, we know you're upset. Who wouldn't be after what you've gone through? But we're on your side. We're not accusing you of anything. But is there anyone in your private life who might want to, well, punish you?'

'You mean one of my string of jilted lovers? Can I say for the record that I do not lead the kind of private life that would cause me to be the victim of attempted murder. My own theory, for what it's worth, is that these so-efficient professional assassins simply bombed the wrong house. I wouldn't want to cast aspersions on my neighbours, but there might be someone in the street who's a more suitable candidate for death by incineration.'

Collins said, stony-faced, 'That had occurred to us, surprisingly enough. Other lines of enquiry are being pursued.'

Waiting in her pigeon-hole at Warbeck, among a mass of business post, were two personal letters.

Dearest Cat,

I'm really worried about you. Daddy says you've been in hospital, just like I was. I wanted to come and see you straight away, but that wasn't on. He says there was a fire at your house, that's why I'm writing to you at the

242

college. Are you all right? Was your house burned very much? I know how much you loved it.

We're living in Chelt, as above, in this poxy little flat in a sad block near Pittville Park. Daddy would go ballistic if he knew my opinion. He thinks he's done the best for me by taking me away from Owlbury but he's dead wrong. I loved it at the Old Mill and I want to go back, but I don't suppose I ever will. He likes it because he's near his precious laboratory and really I don't think he ever liked the country. He's a townie at heart. It was Mum who loved the woods and fields and nature.

I'm not being allowed to go back to school yet, in fact I can't even go out at all yet. Daddy's promised to take me shopping at the weekend but he's hopeless at anything like that. Besides, I still have a bandage round my head and my hair hasn't grown back and I look a complete freak! Miss Big Bum – remember her? – came to see me yesterday and brought me some books. She went all sort of motherly and tearful, and said how much everyone was missing me, which was so amazing. I've had loads of letters and cards too, from people I've never even heard of. And flowers and chocolates and all kinds of stuff. I keep hoping there'll be something from Mum, but there isn't.

You thought I was loopy, didn't you, when I said it was Mum in the hospital, but I wasn't. You'll see. I'm worried though that she won't know where I've gone. You'll tell her won't you? Why won't she come back properly? I know she cares for me. Why won't she come back?

I miss my friends here as well. Dad said I can't see any of them yet. Most of all I miss Alice. We were really close. We knew each other's secrets. Dad told me what happened on the Beacon, when the doctors said it was OK for me to leave the hospital. I still don't remember anything of that day. Dad says that Malcolm is in prison.

I'd like to see him to ask him whether he was the one who did that to Alice and me and then I'd know. I don't want to believe it was Malcolm. I don't want to believe any of it happened. I wish it was all a bad dream I was going to wake up from.

I don't feel like writing any more now. Come and see me soon, or write if you can't make it.

Love,
Charlotte xxxxxxx

Dear Catriona,

Charlotte has written to you, as you are or soon will be aware. She will have said that she would like to see you or hear from you. For my part, I should be grateful if you would make no attempt to contact my daughter, either in person or in writing. Charlotte's state of health, emotionally and physically is still very delicate. Contact with you is not desirable at this stage, and may not be for some considerable future time. I do not, I am sure, have to rehearse to you the reasons why I consider this to be the case.

Yours sincerely,
Bill

How often had she seen on television or read in newspapers descriptions of those who had survived shipwreck or earthquake or some other natural disaster? How often she had seen victims of terrorism or bombing standing by the ruins of their homes? Now, sharing the fate of those unfortunates, she knew what was conveyed by the blank looks that their faces wore like masks.

Whether created by shock or grief, or both, indifference lay on her like a blanket of lead. Nothing mattered any longer. Nothing gave her joy or sadness, nothing moved her or excited her. Did she even exist? Everything that defined her existence had been lost. Things over which she had laboured, things to which she had given time and energy. Things on which she had lavished – it was not too strong a word – love. Precious and irreplaceable items had become ash.

Her house, her protective carapace, had been snatched away. A naked forked creature, growing in darkness and seclusion, she had been thrust suddenly into the daylight of the world. She was a blank figure in a child's colouring book. She was the ectoplasm of a ghost that had yet to rematerialise.

Through the grapevine, she had obtained a flat in Islington, in leafy Gibson Square, on the top floor of a large early Victorian house. The tenant, a lecturer in the languages department at King's, was going off on a visiting fellowship for six months.

Installed here, in borrowed surroundings, in new clothes which didn't seem to fit as well as the old ones, she found comfort, as she always had, in work. Her own books and papers, her computer and all its back-up disks had been destroyed, of course, but the files containing the Grasmere Edition papers had, mercifully, been kept in her room at the college.

Early every morning she ran across and around Highbury Fields, a tatty municipal park compared to the airy vastness of the fields around the Alexandra Palace, but better than nothing.

It was when returning from one of these runs a week after she had left hospital that she saw, parked outside the house, behind her own Fiesta, a police patrol car. On the pavement, pacing impatiently, was the recognisable figure of DS Collins.

'Have you some news?'

He didn't reply, but thrust a piece of official-looking paper at her.

'Catriona Turville. This is a warrant to search your flat and also your office in Warbeck College.'

'Is this some kind of joke?'

245

'I never joke about such things, madam.'

'To search for what?'

'Please, Dr Turville. May we proceed?'

'You understand, Dr Turville, that in order to act as your solicitor, I must be completely clear as to your position in this matter. Do you know anything about the alleged illegal substances that the police claim to have found in your office?' Jeffrey Goldman regarded her steadily and unsmilingly, his dark eyes disturbingly large through the pebble-lensed horn-rimmed spectacles.

She shook her head. 'Nothing whatsoever.'

'Have you any previous convictions involving the possession of or dealing in illegal drugs?'

'Certainly not.'

'Are you now a regular or occasional drug user?'

'No, absolutely not.'

'Have you ever taken any form of illegal drug?'

'No, never.'

He paused, tapping his pen on the counsel's notebook in front of him. Then he spoke sharply, a tinge of irritation creeping into his bland tones. 'Professor Turville, you do appreciate that whatever you say to me is entirely confidential? I do need to know if there is anything that the police may know or might subsequently find out about any involvement with drugs, however slight or long ago.' He glanced down at his notes. 'From what you've told me, you've spent your entire adult life in universities.'

She grimaced. 'And therefore you don't believe me? You consider it axiomatic that I'm a coke-sniffer, pot-smoker and pill-popper. Everyone knows that every don is a hopeless drug addict.'

'I didn't imply anything of the kind. But it's undeniably true that university is a place where many young people experiment with drugs.'

'Many, but not all. I won't embarrass you by asking you whether you did. But I didn't. I don't. I never have. There are people in the university who use recreational drugs, just as there are outside. But I'm not one of them.'

'Very well, those are your instructions. Now, I've spoken to DS Collins, the arresting officer. He says that the lab tests will show that the packet found in the box-file in your office at Warbeck College contained cocaine. Given the amount it contained, they intend to charge you, not just with possession, but with dealing. He also alleges in support that the recent fire-bombing of your house was the work of a professional hit man employed by your drug-dealing associates. Certainly, in my experience, such an attack would be consistent with the way scores are settled amongst the criminal fraternity. However I don't believe he will be able to substantiate this as the villains concerned are hardly likely to come to court to give evidence. Even so, on the basis of the charges already laid, I have to advise you that even for a first offence, conviction will result in a custodial sentence.'

'Drug-dealing? Me? But this is ridiculous, mad, absurd! I'm a university teacher, not a drug-dealer! I told the police that the fire was an obvious case of mistaken identity. Whoever it was attacked the wrong house. As for cocaine, I wouldn't know what it was if someone thrust it in my face. I don't know how that packet got into my room. But I do know that I did not put it there. Which means that someone else did.'

'Does anyone else have a key?'

'The porter, the cleaning staff, I suppose.'

'The fact that it is an office and not a dwelling does assist, as we can show that other people would have had access. But that is not the same thing as showing how the packet got there. Which raises the question as to why anyone would plant drugs in your office. Do you know of anyone who feels such animosity towards you that they might have done such a thing?'

'You mean a colleague who was jealous that I had had an article published and they didn't? Or whom I'd worsted in debate at the academic board? Or who didn't agree with my interpretation of the boating passage in *The Prelude*? Academia is full of feuds, but they're played out with words, not deeds. It would have to be someone who wanted me in very serious trouble; someone who hated me enough to have me sent to prison. I don't believe I know anyone like that. I certainly hope I don't.'

'There are other motives, besides professional jealousy.' He paused. 'If you sat in my chair every day, Dr Turville, you might be amazed at the savagery with which apparently ordinary men and women treat one another as a result of the tensions of an intimate relationship. It's a cliché, but true nevertheless. Hatred and love are sides of the same coin. The newspapers like to confine violent criminality to psychopaths, it's more comforting that way. But the truth is that most of us have the capacity for violence and destructiveness, even, or especially, towards someone whom they love.'

The letter – headed Warbeck College, University of London, From the Office of the Provost Jane Pelling MA Ph.D. DBE, OBE – was brief.

Dear Professor Turville, *[she read]*
 Having regard to the allegations contained in the criminal charges that I am informed are pending against you, I have, regrettably, no alternative but to suspend you from the post of Bloomsbury Professor of English Literature with immediate effect. A further condition of the suspension is that you do not enter college premises or discuss the matter with the staff or students of the college, except with my specific knowledge and approval.
 The suspension is, of course, imposed without prejudice to the outcome of any criminal proceedings, and will be

reviewed by the governing body at the conclusion of the same, at which time further disciplinary measures may be considered. The salary and other benefits to which you are contractually entitled will not be affected by the period of suspension.

Yours sincerely, etc.

She was packing books and papers into cardboard cartons when there was a knock at the half-open door.

Michael Harwood said, 'Hello, Catriona.'

She hadn't encountered him face to face since the scene several weeks before. 'Have you come to see how this frigid bitch copes with her own humiliation?'

'Actually I came to tell you I think this accusation is completely absurd and that our precious provost is a weak-kneed ninny even to entertain it.' He shut the door. 'It's political, you know. Jane is scared stiff of upsetting her friends in the Government if she appears soft on drugs. And she has four children, you know!'

Jane Pelham wore her quadruple motherhood as a badge of honour, and never ceased to remind everyone of the multiple burdens it placed on her overloaded back, only slightly alleviated by her multi-millionaire merchant-banker husband, a housekeeper, and a nanny.

'So you've come to support me in my hour of need, Michael?'

'Yes, I wanted you to know I spoke up for you in the SCR. There was a lot of stupid talk about how everyone knew there was something going on with you.'

'And you were able to put them straight about how normal I was? Is that right?'

'No one who knows you would ever imagine that you were doing drugs.'

'But you don't know me, do you, Michael? Not at all. It wasn't for want of trying, though, was it? Perhaps you thought I'd be easier meat once I'd been softened up a bit. Once I'd

249

been scorned by my colleagues and deprived of the only thing that makes my life worth living. Is that why you've come to see me? To ask me whether I'd like a spot of lunch to cheer me up? Whether I'd like to come back to your flat for some tender loving care?'

As she spoke she had moved closer to him, and he had unconsciously moved away, until he was standing with his back to the small metal-framed non-opening window, which enjoyed a view of a number of giant dustbins in the service yard below.

He gave her a look in which indignation was mixed with a touch of fear. 'Why are you behaving like this, Catriona? I thought you'd be grateful?'

'Grateful? For your attentions? Surely, even your cast-iron ego must appreciate the inherent improbability of my falling into bed with you after what you said to me in this very room only a matter of weeks ago? Or did you think I would be so desperate I would snatch any piece of comfort available? Or maybe it didn't matter. Was it enough to see me in the dirt? Was it the fire that gave you the idea, Michael? Did you think it was the sort of thing which might have happened to someone who'd fallen foul of a drugs baron?'

'If you're suggesting what I think you're suggesting, you're quite mad.'

'Am I? Am I really?'

'Raving. Now if you'd kindly excuse me, I'll leave you to your packing.'

He tried to push past her, but she made a sudden move. Without knowing how it had happened, he found himself face down on the floor, his right arm bent painfully up behind his back.

'What the hell do you think you're doing?' he managed to utter, his lips crushed painfully against his teeth by the concrete beneath the dusty cord carpet.

'Do you know I can quite easily break your arm, or merely

dislocate it in this position? A chap who'd been in the SAS showed my self-defence class this trick. Of course, the best form of defence is attack, so it's equally useful if you wish to do what my instructor called "serious damage".'

Harwood struggled in her iron grip but the pain simply grew more intense. 'You're fucking mad. Wait until the provost hears of this!'

'You'll go running to Jane, will you? After what you've just been saying about her? I don't think so. Someone might tell her who really is the coke-head around here. Tell me Michael, did you plant that cocaine in my office? Think carefully.'

'No of course I didn't!'

'Do you know who did plant it?'

'No! Let me go! Please! For God's sake, let me go!'

She went back to the house. There was a stench of burnt wood in the street. The emergency builders had put in scaffolding against the front to stop the facade from collapsing, and the lower storey had been hidden behind a screen of plywood. A notice affixed to it read DANGER. KEEP OUT.

She picked her way along the muddy, rutted cinder track, only just wide enough for a car, at the rear of the terrace. Her back gate had never been painted or had any other attention since she had been at the house. She had to barge the peeling panel hard with her shoulder to get it open. Once open it sagged on its hinges. On the other side, a curtain of ivy flopped down. She brushed it aside. She felt like Mary Lennox in *The Secret Garden*.

The brick path that led to the boarded-up kitchen door was slippery with wet ash. The flags of the sun-terrace still glinted with broken glass. The hole where the French windows had been was covered with a sheet of corrugated iron. She gazed up at the roofless shell, amidst the stench of soot and damp, then around her at the ruined garden.

The lawn was trampled to a quagmire by the feet of firemen,

workmen, surveyors, insurance assessors. Over the place where the pond and fountain had been was piled charred and broken furniture, dragged out of the house to improve access to the interior. In the process, the lead figure of the boy with a flute had been broken in half. Everywhere there were lengths of burnt timber and fragments of roof tiles. The shrubs and ornamental maples nearest the house had been shrivelled to a crisp by the heat of the fire. The flower beds and herbaceous border had a covering of grey ash, like a fall of dirty snow.

The debris would be cleared and the house would eventually be rebuilt with the insurance money. But it would be a recreation, a fake, not the original she had laboured for years to restore. She would never come back to live in it. She would sell it, pay off the mortgage. And what then? The idea of starting again, with somewhere else seemed pointless and bizarre. But not only that, disloyal. It was as if she had lost part of herself, or even a child. Such could never be replaced. What was dead had to be mourned, not replaced, as if the replacement could ever stand for what had been lost.

The key to the crumbling brick garage lived on a hook in the old outdoor lavatory. There was no electricity, as the supply had been cut off. In the gloom, amongst the old tins of paint and varnish, the gardening and do-it-yourself tools, were piles of old decor magazines – had she really read such things in that other life? – and stacks of paperback thrillers and detective novels, which she devoured at a sitting and covertly adored, but was vaguely ashamed to keep on her bookshelves. There was the cardboard box that she had brought from Frank Churchill's studio containing the clay models from Flora's hands, possibly the last things she would ever have to remind her of her sister.

She stepped into the back-alley, the box clutched in her arms. She set it down and, more out of habit than with any conviction that the security was necessary, dragged the collapsing door closed.

As she picked up her burden again, she saw she was not alone. Two small figures were kicking a black and white football from side to side, the thud as it cannoned against the wooden fences on either side echoing slightly in the enclosed space. As they took in her presence, they stopped their game, one of them heeling the ball out of the rank grass and flipping it up into his arms with the tip of his white trainer, where he clasped it to him possessively.

They were about ten, stocky and pale, with the aggressive watchfulness of street kids well-used to the unpredictable violence of the adult world. She vaguely identified one of them as belonging to a house about five doors down from hers, a family that went in for noisy parties and frequent visits from the police.

When they saw that she was a woman, they started to act in a swaggering manner. The local boy nudged the other, and asked his companion, no doubt copying his elders, without troubling to whisper, 'Shag that piece of cunt, wouldn't you?'

The path was narrow, and either she or they would have to step aside from the trodden mud and cinders of the tracks into the grass and litter of the verges to allow passage.

But, as she approached, ready for confrontation, she saw that over the face of the leader of the two, the boy from the terrace, spread a look of recognition, and, not only of that, of fear. He shuffled to one side and grabbed his companion's arm to pull him out of the way also.

As she drew level, he spoke. 'You're the woman who got bombed, aren't you?'

'Yes.'

'My dad was on about you. He's been inside, so he knows. He said you must be into something big for them to do that to you.'

ELEVEN

Catriona set the dusty, cobwebbed cardboard box on the floor and knelt down by it. Inside, shrouded in newspaper, were the clay figures that Flora had made. These crude creations were all that was left of the old life. Disregarded, they had survived the flames when other more precious things had been consumed. Their chance survival gave them iconic significance. One by one she removed each figure from the box and carefully unwrapped it.

There, impressed into the hard, grey surface of the clay, were the marks of Flora's long, dextrous fingers. Flora had made these. As she set them on the floor, these full-bellied, long-limbed figures, with their upraised arms, their bent knees and contorted torsos, their elongated heads, their pinprick eyes and tiny open mouths, she could see why when she had first seen them they had disturbed her. That was why she had concealed them.

Forcing herself to look at them with full attention, her initial reaction was confirmed. They were studies in terror and torment. They reminded her of those naked forked creatures suffering the torments of the damned in medieval doom frescoes, or in the paintings of Hieronymus Bosch. Whatever influence there might or might not be from such predecessors, the vision of human agony they represented was shared with those masters. It was a vision entirely at odds with the Flora she had thought she had known. These were part of that hidden Flora, the Flora who had indulged in a shamelessly sensual love affair with another woman, the Flora who had threatened to take her own life, the Flora who had deserted her husband and her child, the Flora who hovered still on the fringes of existence like a zombie creature, neither alive nor dead.

The figures were ranked on the polished boards of the floor by the open box, like a ghastly chess set made by an inmate of Auschwitz. Their pinprick eyes watched fearfully, their open mouths screamed at her.

One last figure lay in the box, larger under its newsprint winding sheet than the others. As she unwrapped it, she saw that it was the black cloth-bound figure that Frank Churchill had told her that Flora had refused to show him.

With trembling fingers, she unfastened the bindings, unrolling them like the bandages of a mummy. Finally, what lay beneath was revealed. Where the other representations had been emaciated, this was gross, with a huge belly, ringed with rolls of fat like the Michelin man. Where the features of the others had been vestigial, these were bloated, with bulging lips, protruding eyes and blubber cheeks. And, most shockingly of all, from the loins of this monster sprouted an obscenely large erect penis, swollen-headed and priapic.

The insight flashed like a mirror in sunlight. Flora knew. Flora had known everything. How? Had she watched? Had she spied? However she had found out, the knowledge she had buried in her heart smoked from this hideous figure, like foul incense rising from the idol of a Satanic religion.

The sour bile of it drove her to the lavatory, where she vomited long and copiously. Resting with her chin on the cold china of the bowl, her throat sore with retching, she recalled other occasions she had thought long buried in the darkest recesses of her memory, when she had knelt like this, when she had been sick like this, when she had wept like this.

In the small, neat modern kitchen, with its shiny laminate and stainless steel, she drank a glass of water, just as she had been instructed to on these occasions as a child by the grey haired, rosy-cheeked nanny they had called Mistress Collins. The kindly old woman had quarrelled with Daddy and he had called her an interfering old bitch and sent her away. After that, it had started.

It had seemed at the time that Flora had been unaffected by the tragedy. She had been asleep. She had slept through the horror, awakening in the dewy morning when the stench of blood had been replaced by the pine reek of strong disinfectant, to be petted and stroked like a fawn by the policewomen and social workers who had moved into the house, talking in hushed voices and brewing themselves endless cups of tea. Flora, the child of tragedy, had, phoenix-like, risen from the flames unburned.

In contrast, everyone had shied away from the tall, dark, slim girl with the pale face and the shadowed eyes. Those few who knew the truth about the saturnine private face behind the handsome public facade of James Morrison, those intimates who were cognisant of the black depressions, the drinking, the outbursts of furious self-loathing, whispered that it was she who was her father's daughter.

So the model set by their childhood had continued through their adolescence. They had continued to be opposites: the dark and the light; the friendly and the friendless; the heart and the head.

But now, as she stared at the obscene figure, she knew that the hidden truth had lurked below the surface, beneath the shining beauty, in the dark freezing water of her sister's soul.

She was roused by the sound of furious knocking at the door.

'Catriona!'

Calmly, mechanically, she rose to her feet and went out into the small lobby of the flat. She leaned her back against the panel.

'Go away, Alan. I've nothing to say to you.'

'Are you all right? You sound strange.'

'I'm quite all right.'

'I've been looking for you for days! I need to be sure. Please let me in. Please.'

It was as if she did not have the energy to keep him out. Her hand like that of an automaton turned the key in the mortise, then reached for the knurled knob of the Yale latch.

He stared with eyes full of horror and pity at her white face and her lethargic, defeated posture, and then around at the disordered room. 'My God! You're ill, woman! Have you been eating?'

'My whole life collapses and you ask if I've been eating!'

'This accusation, it can't stand up. Someone planted those drugs. I can help you, if only you'd let me. You shouldna' keep shutting me out.'

'I don't care any more. Not now I've opened Pandora's box.'

'What are you talking about?'

'The loathsome, crawling creatures I've spent my whole life keeping under lock and key are out. Here they are, look at them!'

She gestured at the ranks of figures on the floor.

He stared down at them, and then back at her face.

'My terracotta army, all set to accompany me to the grave.'

'What is this shite? This talk of death? You're a young woman, a brilliant woman. I won't let you destroy yourself.'

'I told you before. I was destroyed before I ever met you. I've kept going all these years because I believed that what I was was secret. Now I know it wasn't. I know that she knew, God knows how, but she knew. For all those years, she knew.'

'Flora, what did Flora know?'

'She knew this!' She grasped the squat clay figure and almost thrust it in his face. 'Take a good look! Do you recognise him? You should, you have the file!'

His face became ashen as he grasped the significance of the priapic figure. 'Oh my God, this is your father!'

'Yes, this is Professor James Morrison! Scotland's greatest historian! The toast of the liberal, Nationalist academic elite! As portrayed by his daughter. Flora made this figure years later, but she kept the vision of the twelve-year-old she was then. I didn't know she knew. But she must have seen my father . . . my father and me together.'

'Oh, Jesus Christ, you poor wee bairn!'

'You must wonder why I never told. Why I suffered in silence. That's the worst thing. When he came to my room that first time – oh yes, he'd seen to it that I, as the eldest, had the good, big room away from the rooms where Flora and little Morag slept, out on its own in what we used to call the west wing – he said that it was our secret. That it made us very special. Oh, he gave me chapter and verse, practically a monograph on father-daughter incest through the ages. The subject fascinated him, naturally enough. Then he . . . then he . . .'

Weeping uncontrollably, she fell into Alan's arms.

He stroked her hair, and tried to comfort her, but there was no comfort to be had from him, from any man.

Finally, she raised her head, the tears streaking her face, her eyes huge and bright. 'I believed him, you see. I thought I was special. I was clever, like him. I was beautiful, like my mother. I had the best of them both and that was why he loved me. The tortured love their tormentors, don't you know? They collude with them, protect them. That's what I can't forget. At some level, I wanted what he did to me. I lived only for his love, I longed for his abuse. If he was wicked, so was I.'

'Don't talk like that. He was a monster. You were a child. You were innocent.'

'No, Alan. There is no innocence. I was corrupted. That was why I acted as I did that night. Shall I tell you about it? Shall I?'

She drew away from him and stood up, her slender form drawn up to her maximum height. 'Shall I tell you what I really am?'

My mother would go to bed quite early, at ten or eleven o'clock. She slept heavily and my father would come to me around midnight, if we hadn't had any opportunity to be alone together earlier in the day. But that night when I awoke, it was not to the little shake he would give my shoulder when he leant over me as I slept. It was because I heard shouting coming from downstairs. Loud, angry shouting. The voices of my mother and father. I got out of bed, pulled on my dressing gown, and ran down the corridor to the main landing. There, there was a gallery which overlooked the huge square vestibule. To each side there were double doors, one set leading to the drawing room, one to the dining room. My mother was in her dressing gown, holding the telephone in one hand, and with the other was fending off my father. He had clamped one hand over the top of the main part of the phone, holding down the rest so that she couldn't get a line, the other hand was grabbing at her arm, the one holding the receiver. My mother was screaming at him, in a wild demented wail I had never heard before. Over and over again, she was saying, bastard, bloody bastard, bloody fucking bastard. This seemed to me particularly unusual and shocking. I had never before heard my mother use what she called gutter speech. But here she was swearing like a trooper, clutching the phone. My father had managed to grab her wrist, and was twisting it, trying to shake free her grip. He was yelling, 'No, Claire, please listen. You don't understand, wait.'

Then, instead of just pushing him away with her free arm, she began to hit at him, her fingers open like claws, gouging at his face, his eyes. He had to jerk his head away to avoid being scratched. All the time, she was screaming at him, fucking bloody bastard, fucking bloody bastard!

They had had rows before, in fact they were always having rows, but never anything as vicious and intense as this one. I shouted out, 'Stop it! What are you doing!'

Mum looked up at me and yelled, 'Get out, go for the police! It's Morag. He's killed her! He's killed Morag!'

For a moment, I thought I would faint. I just stood there, at the head of the stairs, holding on to the thick mahogany hand-rail of the banisters.

My father turned his face to me, and there was such a look on his face, of desperation and horror, and something else too, a beseeching, imploring look. I couldn't move. I was frozen while they both seemed to fight for my soul.

My mother screamed at me, 'Go, what are you waiting for? Get out! Go to the MacNaughtons!'

I ran down the stairs. My father still had one hand pressed down on the telephone. My mother's attack had made him let go of her wrist. He held the other arm over his face to protect his eyes. Still holding the receiver, my mother was alternately using it as a club to lunge at him, and with her other hand, tried to unclamp his grip from the body of the telephone.

As I reached the bottom step, my father moved to block my progress towards the front door.

He spoke quite softly. 'No, Cat. You mustn't. You mustn't. We must talk about this thing. Please, listen to me.'

My mother dropped the receiver with a clatter, rushed forward and took my arm, pulling me away from him. I could feel the tension in her arm, making it shake as if she were having a fit. Her eyes were wide and she was completely hysterical. 'Can't you hear what I'm saying? He's murdered her! She's dead! Poor little scrap, he's killed her!'

I couldn't take any of it in. My brain was buzzing, and I could sense the beginning of the sick feeling which meant a migraine. I struggled away from both of them.

I said, looking at my father, 'You've killed Morag?'

He started to move towards me and I backed away. Again there was the imploring look. 'Please, listen to me, my darling! It's a terrible mistake!'

My mother suddenly grew calm and stared at me and from the look of contempt in her eyes, I could see she knew everything. It was the gaze that a scorned woman turns upon her hated rival. 'I know you'd prefer to believe him, Catriona, darling, but there's no mistake. I saw him bending over her body, holding the pillow he used to suffocate her.'

Then she bent down and took something from near the hall-stand. When she stood up, I saw she was holding one of my father's golf clubs. I saw, disbelievingly, the flash from the steel shaft as she swept it at his head.

Still stunned by what she had revealed, I yelled, instinctively, 'Look out!'

He turned and saw the club scything down at him. Instead of smashing into his head, it glanced off the point of his shoulder. I saw the pain it caused him made his face crumple like paper; then the pain was replaced by the black rage that I had rarely seen, but which everyone in the house dreaded. It would come upon him when he had been drinking alone in his study, brooding on some slight, real or imagined, from a colleague, or from some criticism in an article, or it would flare suddenly when one of us had displeased or disobeyed him. Then nothing and no one was safe until the volcanic fury had blown itself out.

My mother was thrown off balance by the swing of the heavy club. With a roar like a wounded animal, my father charged at her with his full strength. He was a tall, burly man, the muscle and fitness of his rugby-playing youth had turned through years of high living to sheer bulk. One hand wrenched the golf club out of her grasp, the other thumped my mother full in the chest, and the weight of that blow knocked her flying. As she fell, her head hit the corner of the marble mantelpiece with a sound I shall never forget. Twisted by the impact, her body tumbled awkwardly into the tiled hearth and I could see from the way it fell and from the way she didn't move and from the trickle of blood at the corner of her mouth that she was probably dead.

Neither of us moved for what seemed an age. Both of us stared down at the body. Then I dropped to my knees and put my face to hers, and my hand to her neck as they had taught us to do in first aid. There was neither the faintest breath nor the least flutter of a pulse. For several minutes, as my father stood as massive and as immobile as an oak-tree, I massaged my mother's chest, as I had been instructed, with hands that seemed to belong to someone else. But it was quite useless, as I had sensed all along it would be. She was dead.

Finally, I looked up at him, but I couldn't see his face. It was a blur, something seemed to be wrong with my eyes. Then I realised that they were clouded with tears.

'Oh God!' he said.

He stood there, huge, but inert, staring abjectly down at my mother's body. A dreadful consuming fury rose in me. Where I had seen strength, there was only weakness. All my love and admiration turned to contempt and hatred.

I seized the golf club, which lay where my father had let it fall, stood up and swung it at his head.

I was already a champion golfer, unlike my mother who'd never held a club in her life until a few moments before her death. I did not miss my target. The blow hit him squarely on the temple. For a couple of seconds, everything seemed to stop. My father, as if in slow motion, put up his hands to the side of his head. Then he folded at the knees and fell towards the stone-paved floor.

As he fell, I very calmly raised the club in the air once more and brought it down with all my strength on the crown of his bowed head. I heard the noise of it as it hit him and it was the sound you get when you give a croquet ball a good thwack with the mallet, or when you hear someone chopping logs in the distance. He hit the floor in a heap and didn't move.

I stood there listening and the house was completely quiet.

I ran back up the stairs, two at a time, and into Morag's room. Her door was ajar and her night-light was on. She was lying there sleeping peacefully. My pounding heart began to slow down. Everything was all right after all. My father and mother had had a row, like they always did, but this one had gone a bit further than usual. My mother had had a bang on the head, but she would be all right. As for my father, he was indestructible. Only last year, he'd been on his pushbike in Princes Street, his great black hat on his head, his cloak flapping around him, and he'd been hit by a lorry, knocked clean off his bike and onto the pavement so hard he'd practically bounced. But he'd got to his feet and dusted himself off, and ridden off on his bike, no problem. So perhaps this time he might have to go to Casualty and say he slipped on the stairs. Or perhaps I'd dreamed the whole thing. I was always having bad dreams. This was just a bad dream. I'd wake up soon in my own bed and nothing would have happened, and I'd have forgotten all about it.

Then I saw that Morag wasn't moving at all. Normally she tossed and turned and mumbled in her sleep. I ran over to the bed, and put my hand on her neck and bent down to her mouth, and it was just as it had been with my mother. I couldn't feel anything, not the waft of a breath on my cheek, or the flutter of her pulse.

I ran to the landing and looked down into the hall again. It was as if I were watching a play from the dress circle. On the lit stage lay the two bodies, just as I had left them.

I knew that, however you approached it, what I had done was homicide of one sort or another. We'd had a talk about the law from the fiscal who'd visited the school, and, besides,

I knew a lot about it already from the detective stories I used to read. There would be a trial and I would go to some secure detention centre, and then, when I was old enough, to prison. I knew I couldn't ever explain or justify the surge of anger that had made me hit him. And not only that, they might say I had killed my mother as well, and Morag. No one else knew what had happened, except me. And what if they didn't believe me? There were plenty of people who didn't like me, who thought me hard and cold. Maybe that was how a jury would feel. When I'd hit my father, I hadn't been protecting myself, I wanted to hurt him. And that was revenge, which wasn't allowed. No matter what my father had done to my mother or to Morag, no matter what he had done to me. More than that, I didn't care that he was dead. It was his fault. He'd made me that way when he destroyed my love and my trust.

I thought, why the hell should I suffer any more for him? And that was when I came up with my plan. It might not work but it was the only way. It was the kind of plan I'd read about in detective stories. If I'd learnt one thing from reading those and from reading the accounts of murders in the newspapers, it was that the police tended to look at the most obvious solution presented by a given set of facts.

A wife dead after a struggle, a daughter murdered upstairs. The first person they would look for would be the husband. That was why it had to appear that my father had fled the house after committing his crime. If he was missing, the police would never even consider that his teenage daughter might have killed him. I knew enough by then about how most men regarded the thinking capacity of women. To the thick-headed plods of Edinburgh CID, I'd be only a wee bit o' a lassie.

I turned off the lights in the vestibule, opened the front door and stepped out into the night. It was crisp and cold, the frost glinting on the lawn and on the leaves of the densely planted laurels that screened the house from the road. My father's car, a Range Rover, was parked in the detached garage. I had dressed in what even in those days was my habitual black – black jeans, black T shirt and a black jersey. It seemed appropriate to the job in hand.

In my pocket, I had the keys to the car, which were always kept on a hook on the board in the kitchen. I could drive perfectly well. My father had given me lessons on a private airfield owned by a friend of his in the SNP. The garage door had been left open. I started the engine – how loud it sounded in the silence of the suburban night! – and drove the car round to the front of the house, backing it up close to the gabled porch.

In the utility room, in common with many middle-class families who practised petty economies amid the general lavishness of their lifestyles, there was a cupboard containing all manner of cardboard boxes and old packaging, kept for re-use. My mother had recently bought a new mattress, and the plastic cover had been thrown in there. I found it, and spread it out on the hall floor alongside my father's body. I rolled it over on to the polythene, then secured the bundle with sticky tape. Then I rolled the body over and over to the front door and out into the porch. With enormous effort, I heaved the body into the back of the car and covered it with a travelling rug.

It was then that I added what even now I think was a little stroke of genius. I ran back to the garage, took the little fold-up bicycle that my father used around the city, and put it into the boot.

I did not think I would be seen, but in case I was, I took down from the hall-stand the thick Harris tweed cloak that my father, who loved to cultivate the image of the eccentric Scottish genius, wore in his perambulations of the streets of Edinburgh. I put that on, and his tartan scarf, which I wrapped around the lower part of my face, and also his floppy-brimmed black fedora, which we used to make fun of, saying he looked like the Don in the Sandeman sherry advert – he would say that was all right because he was a don. I was as tall as he was and, wearing this outfit, I could pass as an adult male to a superficial observer glimpsing me at the wheel. That was all I needed.

I went out, locked the door and got into the car. As I started the engine, I tried to think myself into his shoes, the mind of a man who was escaping from a dreadful crime. Would he tear out of the gate in a great hurry, or would he proceed slowly, not wishing to draw attention to himself? As I pondered this problem, letting the car roll slowly towards the gate as I did so, it solved itself, as problems sometimes do. A small brown and white dog, yelping as it ran in through the entrance from the street, appeared in the headlights, followed moments later by the figure of a man.

I almost vomited with tension. The owner of the dog was Mr Calder, an elderly neighbour from several doors away, an insomniac who frequently exercised the animal in the small hours. He wasn't a friend, but his shrewd eyes knew all of us by sight. He would be sure to see immediately that I wasn't who I was dressed up to be. In no time at all, the old busy-body would be asking me what I, a slip of a lassie, was doing at that hour of the night, and did my mother and father know what I was about, and me not of an age to be at the wheel of a car as well I knew?

It was all up with me. I sat frozen, my hands clamped on the steering wheel as he came alongside the driver's door.

Then to my amazement, without the least hesitation or puzzlement, he addressed me as my father. 'Good e'en to you Morrison,' he called out. 'My apologies for this invasion of your home turf! The damned bitch slipped her lead again! Is all well in your house? It's nae often I see ye stirring in the sma' hours.'

It was then that I realised with a fierce elation that I had got away with the impersonation. Even from feet away, the old fool had seen only what he expected to see. And that meant that what I had thought would be the end of my desperate plan almost before it had begun was actually its crowning masterstroke! Not only could James Morrison be presumed to have driven off into the night, there was an unimpeachable witness who would swear that he had! Calder was exactly the kind of stubborn individual who would continue to aver that black was white once he had decided it was so.

Without a word, I revved the engine, let up the clutch and accelerated fiercely out of the gate and down the empty road. The nosy old devil wouldn't forget the night's encounter, and nor did he. He even said, irony of ironies, that he thought to himself at the time that Morrison could not have been himself to have behaved as discourteously as he did in driving off without even a word!

I must have hit eighty before I slowed for the junction with the Queensferry Road. Then I drove more circumspectly. I didn't want to be stopped by the police. After a mile or so, I slowed down, looking for the clump of trees that marked the lane. I turned down it and stopped after a hundred yards. Flora and I had played there when we were small. The quarry bottom seemed a million miles down to us, as we dared each other to stand right on the edge. That night, I couldn't see the lake, as there was no moon, but I knew it was there and more than deep enough for my purpose. I took the folding bike out first, then somehow I got him out of the back, too, removed his polythene shroud, dressed him in the coat, scarf and hat, and dragged him into the driver's seat. I pushed his feet on the pedals, restarted the engine and released the handbrake. The car bounced down the slope and then plunged straight over the edge. For a long moment there was nothing, then a massive bang, and then a rending, tearing and squealing of tortured metal, and then a splash, and then silence.

I wondered if it might have burst into flames, as they do in the films, but it didn't, which was just as well, because it might have been found too quickly. I stuffed the polythene sheet under my jersey, mounted the bike and rode back on the pavement. I saw no one and no one saw me. On the way I shoved the wadded-up plastic into a skip full of builder's waste. I came back to the house by the lane at the rear, returning the bike to the garage. I checked my watch. I had been out for almost an hour.

A great weariness was falling over me as I opened the front door. My mother's body lay where she had fallen. With a cloth from the kitchen I wiped the blood and hair from the corner of the mantelpiece where her head had struck. The golf club, smeared with my father's blood, lay where it had fallen. On it would be the fingerprints of my mother, my father and myself. I could not remove my own without obliterating theirs, and a completely clean murder weapon would be suspicious. I decided that, if I were asked, I would say that I had instinctively picked up the club when I saw my mother's body. I did say this and no one ever questioned me further about it.

Although the evidence of old Mr Calder was a bonus, I could never have committed what turned out to be the perfect murder without the assistance of the Edinburgh police and their forensic scientists. It should have been obvious to them that my mother had died not from a blow from the golf club, but from hitting her head on the corner of the mantelpiece. Similarly, it should also have been clear that my mother had got in at least one good blow, from the presence of her fingerprints on the golf club and the smears of my father's blood on it and on the hall carpet.

It was my good fortune that the wrecked car and my father's body was found only several months after the crime. Instead of observing, they, as Mr Calder did, preferred to assume. Thus the head injuries sustained by a woman lying beside a golf club were assumed to have been caused by a blow from that club, and the head injuries sustained by a man in a crashed car were assumed to have been caused by the crash.

You know the rest. Flora and I were brought up in London

by our aunt Charlotte, my mother's sister. The night we arrived in Kentish Town, I took a vow never to fall in love, never to marry, never to bear a child. I could not undo the past but I could prevent it from being repeated.

So, that was how it felt, to divulge the secret she had kept close these twenty-four years. She felt no sense of release, no feeling of exculpation. So much for the bletherings of psychotherapy. It confirmed what she had always known. The talking cure might be grand for the imaginary ills of the psyche. It was no help at all for reality. What she had done could not be undone. If she were damned before, she was still damned now.

She stopped pacing the room and turned to face him. 'There you are, Mr Journalist. The story of a lifetime. Go ahead. Publish it. I don't care. I shan't deny it. I have nothing left to lose now. I might as well spend the rest of my life in gaol.'

Urquhart raised his head from his knees where he had let it slump during her confession. 'You must know I'll never do that. Wild horses wouldna' drag from me what you've told me this day.'

The softness in her seemed to have been burned away by the heat of her remembrance. Her voice was harsh as she said, mockingly, 'The secrets of the confessional? Och, so you're the priest to give me absolution, is that it?'

'No, I canna do that. But I can say to you that however the law might regard what you did that night, I don't consider you a murderer. You were but a child, a child who had been abused and betrayed. You acted out of a child's anger and a child's sense of what was right. And who in truth could raise his hand against you now and swear solemnly that your father did not deserve his death? What good would it serve to punish you when you've already punished yourself?'

'So, I am Hamlet then? The justified avenger? I might have tried to believe that once, but I can't any longer. I can't forget how I felt that night, the sheer joy of it as I smashed his skull.

269

The sense of freedom as I knew that he was dead. The ruthless efficiency I used to escape from the consequences. Pity never ran in my heart that night. That came later. But even in my darkest times, I thought that my evil act might have done some good. I had avenged poor Morag's death. I had saved us from the misery of a trial and a condemnation. My father, a murderer and dead was one thing, but alive and in prison was quite another. And I took heart that Flora seemed to have survived unscathed. She was everything that I was not – carefree, loving, unhaunted by demons. I often envied and sometimes even despised that in her. Her freedom to roam the world, to have affairs, to subside into a dull marriage, to live a blameless life, to have a child. To have a child. My God, I did envy her that! I envied the fact that she had been spared. I envied her ability to have slept through that night. I envied her innocence of everything that had led up to it. I should have known, I should have suspected. There is no innocence, Alan! Look at these! These are what Flora knew! These are the things that writhed and squirmed within her. Yeats wrote, "I must lie down where all the ladders start, In the foul rag-and-bone shop of the heart." Flora dared to do what I never had. She went down the ladders, and she gave form to the foulness she found there. Look at them!'

Tears bursting from her eyes, Catriona lashed out with her foot at the ranks of clay figures standing with their tormented shapes and screaming mouths before her on the floor. Several fell over, their brittle limbs breaking off. Again and again, she kicked at those that remained standing, smashing them, scattering them. Then, as if possessed, she began stamping on them, crushing their friable material to powder under her heels.

When nothing was left but grey dust, she snatched up the obscene representation of James Morrison. With a fiercely skilful flick of the wrist, as if returning a ball hard across a cricket field, the throw of a boy, not a woman, she flung it at the wall, where with a thud it exploded into several pieces.

They both stared wonderingly down at the floor by the skirting board. A squat plastic cylinder, still partly cocooned in the clay in which it had been concealed, lay there among the fragments.

Catriona bent and picked it up and peeled away the remaining layer of clay from the object. It was a container of the type that pharmacists use for medicines. Within it were the jellybean shapes of capsules.

The self-adhesive paper label, though smeared with grey residue, could be clearly read:

AL74/06/02

RESTRICTED

The product code had been added by a word processor, and the words of the prohibition, leaving no doubt about their importance, had been printed in block capitals, in red.

Urquhart took a long pull at his tea, real workman's tea, mahogany brown with three sugars. Catriona sat opposite him on the sofa. She was still pale and hollow-eyed, but calmer. He had insisted that she ate the meal, consisting of tinned tomato soup and cheese on toast, which he had put together from the meagre supplies in the kitchen. He set down the Charles and Di mug – the flat was full of this sort of kitsch – and once more scrutinised the plastic drum of capsules.

'So, what the hell is this?'

'Isn't it obvious? Flora must have obtained this from Hazel Marchant, and she in turn must have stolen it from Willowdene when she visited her mother. It's some form of experimental drug that Monaghan and Anderson have been testing on the residents.'

'It's one thing to assume that. It's quite another to prove it.'

'She clearly didn't buy it over the counter at a chemist's!'

'Maybe not. We still can't prove it came from Willowdene. Hazel Marchant is dead. Only Flora can say where she did get it from. And even she couldn't prove it wasn't a run-of-the-mill prescription product. The truth is we don't know what this drug is or what it does. Sure we could get someone to analyse it, but what would that show about its actual effects on a human subject?'

'My God, I understand now. I understand what she was doing when she wrote me the letter.'

'You mean the letter you told me about in the hospital? The suicide note?'

'Yes. She thought I would find her and that the whole thing would make sense. She relied on my being clever, but instead I've been stupid. If only I'd understood! If she hadn't been abducted, I would have done!'

'Understood what?'

'What she was saying in the letter. She told me exactly what she was going to do. She did know what the drug was, or rather what its effects are. But she had to prove it in the most direct way possible, in the way scientists used to do. Don't you see, she took the drug herself!'

'What? She told you this in the letter?'

'Yes.'

'But how? Let me read it.'

'I burned it.'

'So we don't have the exact words she used?'

'Yes, we do. The exact words.'

'But you said the letter was burnt.'

'Alan, there are more ways to preserve things than committing them to paper. The old skills are still valid. The letter has been burnt, but the text survives.'

'You mean you have a copy?'

'The hardest copy possible. It's contained on an instrument a million times further advanced than any computer. An instrument whose potential we've hardly begun to understand. Here.' She tapped her forehead. 'I can remember the text of Flora's letter, word for word. I can remember it backwards. It's a trick, a knack, a gift. I've always had it in some measure, but I've also developed it. So, you see, it's no problem for me to reproduce the exact text of Flora's letter.'

She pulled a sheet of paper from the ream on the desk, opened her fountain pen. Without any hesitation, she wrote swiftly in her meticulous copperplate.

'There.' She pushed the pad back towards him.

He read it slowly and carefully, like a child or a medieval monk, running a finger under each word, his lips moving slightly as he whispered them to himself.

When he had finished, she said, 'Well?'

He hesitated, then plunged. 'I'm sorry, Catriona. But I don't see it. It seems to me a perfectly plain statement of her intention. She even refers to the dreadful events of your childhood as the reason why she is taking this step.'

'There's no such thing as a plain text, is there? Ambiguity, in the Empsonian sense, is inherent in any form of discourse. Even the apparently plainest of texts will be fraught with a host of other meanings. The legendary sign on the escalators in the Underground. 'Dogs must be carried.' Does it mean that no one is allowed on the escalator without a dog? Or is it a universal statement that dogs cannot walk? Or could I allow my cat, or my pet iguana to walk down the escalator? And what happens if the dog in question is a Great Dane? Why then speak as if this text was capable of bearing only the one meaning that you extracted from it? The more complex the motives behind the utterance, the more complex will be the codes, the words used to express that utterance. When I recalled that letter just now, after our discussion about the drug, I saw at once that Flora omitted to say directly that she was going to commit suicide. Did it seem strange to you that she does not actually in so many words say that she is going to kill herself?'

'What on earth do you mean? "By the time you receive this letter, the sister you know and love will be dead." What could be clearer than that?'

'It isn't clear,' she contradicted sharply. 'She doesn't simply say, "I am going to commit suicide" or "I am going to die", does she? She says the sister you know and love will be dead. Why? Could it be that a being who has the reference "Flora", and the sister I know and love may not always be synonymous?'

He gazed at her in astonishment. 'I see what you're about! She's using death as a metaphor. She's saying she might be a completely different kind of person. As a character in a Victorian melodrama might say, "Henceforth, my feelings shall be dead to you . . ."'

'Precisely. She is going, as we will see, to take this probably very dangerous experimental drug. She knew that it would alter her mind in some way, even if it didn't kill her. She warns me that she will have suffered "a sea-change into something rich and strange".'

Alan jabbed at the paper with his forefinger, caught up in the intellectual excitement of the quest. 'She goes on to say that she has "found the drug to put an end to my suffering." A drug, not a poison. A drug that may not kill, but may lead to an altered state of mind – or to a coma or loss of faculties. That's why she's clear she is being strong to "seize the remedy for my agony".'

Catriona nodded. 'Yes. Like Hamlet's soliloquy: the ambiguity between life which is action, and death by suicide, which may be an escape but may also be a leap into something worse: "What dreams may come when we have shuffled off this mortal coil must give us pause." If this drug did cause changes in her mind, she might be dead to herself, dead to me, dead to the other people she loved and who loved her, but still alive. But she had no way of knowing what her new being would be like. It would be akin to Hamlet's "undiscovered country from whose bourn no traveller returns."' Her voice fell to a whisper.

'She carried a burden I'd never even suspected until a matter of hours ago. She wanted to forget. But she also ensured that the change wrought by the drug would not go unnoticed.'

'But all this is complete speculation,' Alan put in. 'Unless or until Flora returns, there's no proof of what the drug is capable of.'

'No, we do know what this drug is. Mrs Arrowsmith told us. I remember what she said, but at the time, it seemed so much verbal diarrhoea. Leona Richardson said the same thing, except that she made light of it, given that she is one of the sharpest elderly persons I have ever come across. They both said that the elderly residents of Willowdene were mentally very lively, but they couldn't remember their own histories. They had none of the usual tendency of elderly persons to dwell on the past. Hazel Marchant's mother had forgotten she ever had a daughter. Forgetting. That's what this drug is all about. You function normally, perhaps even better than you did before you took it, but you don't remember your past. And nor is it true that we can't prove it. There is one other person who knows what this drug is, what it can do, and the whole story about Willowdene.'

'Who's that?'

'Isn't it obvious? This drug was not produced at Willowdene. Anderson and Monaghan are not scientists. They're simply part of the front office. It's the backroom boys who call the shots. Look at the code. AL. I'm convinced that stands for Avalon Laboratories. In which case, Bill Jesmond is the man who knows. I should have realised it from the start. Flora certainly must have suspected her husband's involvement the moment she saw that label. It would have confirmed her distrust of Avalon and multinationals in general. She believed they would be more than capable of fudging research and selling what may turn out to be lethal substances to consumers, in the interests of profit. I remember her saying as much to me. But she must have been in a dilemma. Perhaps she delayed going to the authorities not only because of Bill but the effect it would have on Charlotte. Bill, whatever his other faults, does love his daughter.'

'But she resolved it, didn't she? By taking the drug and writing to you, she opted for disclosure.'

'Yes. She must have, whatever the consequences. That's why she wrote to me in the way she did. She knew I would rush to her bedside without thinking, that I would find her. If she were alive but changed or incapacitated, then I would be there as a witness and to challenge the authorities.

'Anderson and Monaghan, though, had already discovered that the drug was missing. They must have been desperate to recover the missing pills – once in the hands of the authorities, those pills would have been the smoking gun that revealed what Avalon had been doing at Willowdene. They went after Hazel Marchant. They killed her, making it look like an accident. They searched Hazel's flat, looking for the missing drug. They found photographs of Flora, and probably letters as well, revealing her relationship with Hazel. They suspected Flora's involvement. When they couldn't find the capsules, they tracked her down and abducted her. They took her to Willowdene, to silence her and eventually perhaps to force her to reveal where she had hidden the drug. But Flora escaped. She knew that the Willowdene pair would search for her. And if they caught her again, they might kill her. So she went into hiding.

'After Flora disappeared, I started trying to find out why. I blundered into part of the truth. They killed Mrs Arrowsmith merely to close off my investigations. Then they tried to silence me as well. If only I'd listened to you in the hospital, instead of pretending to myself that the arson attack was some sort of mistake. Now they're continuing to target me, someone close to Flora, in the hope that she will be flushed out into the open. Oh my God.' She paused as the implications of what she had said became clear. 'Someone close to Flora? Who's closer than her own daughter? What would have happened if, God forbid, Charlotte had been killed on the Beacon, as well as Alice? Flora wouldn't have been able to keep away then, would she?'

'You're saying that Alice Peters was murdered and Charlotte attacked simply in order to make Flora reappear? But that's hideous, monstrous, unspeakable!'

'Yes, it is. But it's an explanation linking the two events. And it succeeded. Flora did reappear, to protect her daughter. After that attempt failed, they turned their attention to me.'

He was shaking his head. 'These people, if your theory is correct, had no scruples about killing an entirely innocent child and attempting to kill another merely to find Flora. Why would they go to those appallingly ruthless lengths? What stakes would, even in the most corrupt mind, justify that?'

She pointed at the capsules in the plastic container. 'You said it yourself once. Follow the money. We have followed it. It's led to Avalon.'

'Hold on a moment! Would Bill Jesmond have conspired to murder his own daughter? I know you dislike him, Catriona, but would he do that?'

She shook her head. 'No, I might accuse him of many things, but not that. Besides, he didn't know that Flora had the drug. How could he have? Flora never told him. I don't believe he knew about any of this. Maybe Anderson and Monaghan were so scared at losing the drug sample that they embarked on a scheme of their own to get it back. Surely if I can convince him what's been going on, he'll change sides?'

'Perhaps. I think I should go with you.'

'No, it's best if I go alone. He might talk to me. He won't want a third party present.'

'Aye, I suppose, particularly not a journalist. The question still remains, though, doesn't it? Where on earth is Flora? And why doesn't she come forward?'

*　　*　　*

277

They stood together on the stone flags before the door of the elegant house, the sun glinting on the rain-wet stock-bricks of the facade, and on the moisture-beaded black paint of the elaborate curlicues of the iron balconets.

'You're sure you want to do it this way?'

'Quite sure.'

'For God's sake, be careful! This whole business stinks.'

'Don't worry.'

'Of course I'm worried! How could I not be, I mean I . . .' he blushed and began to stammer. 'I love you.'

She hoisted the bag on her shoulder. 'Do you, Alan?'

'Yes.'

She shook her head, sadly, and her eyes were bright. 'You poor wee man,' she said softly in the accent of her childhood.

Then he was grasping her in his arms, kissing her cheeks, her lips, her forehead. And she stood there, her face turned towards him, while he kissed her. And though she did not return his kisses, she did not pull away. He held her gently, while, face buried in his bosom, she wept as she had not wept for countless years. Finally, for the moment, all her tears were over. She raised her head.

'Alan, please, I have to go.'

'Will you call me?'

'Yes, I will call you. Please, go now.'

He drew away from her and planted one last gentle kiss on her pale forehead.

Catriona watched him for a moment as his tall, broad shouldered figure strode away down the side of the square. Then her attention was distracted by a clattering sound from the roadway. A man dressed in the white coveralls of a painter and decorator was unloading his impedimenta from the back of a van. Collecting an old, paint-dribbled five-litre tin, from which brush handles protruded, the workman closed the doors of his vehicle. Then with a quick glance at a crumpled sheet of white paper he was holding, he crossed the street, whistling tunelessly through his teeth as he did so.

'Professor Catriona Turville?' he enquired as he reached the the bridge over the front area.

'Yes, but I'm not expecting . . .'

With a rueful grin, he casually set down the paint-tin on the paving and waved the order form in front of her face. 'Look, it says here . . .'

Then, as she came forward and bent her head to look at the document, he grabbed her shoulder hard and painfully, pulling her down to the pavement level beside him, at the same time reaching down towards the tin.

But for his powerful grip she would have overbalanced.

Struggling, she said angrily, 'What the hell do you think you're . . . ?' when his hand appeared in front of her face holding not a paint-brush but a pistol, its barrel grotesquely elongated by the sausage shape of a silencer.

She felt the cold pressure of metal boring into her forehead. In the dreamy milliseconds of the moment, she seemed to have time to notice that the man's face was quite expressionless, his blue eyes cold and dead; then her knee jerked upwards hard and straight, crashing into his groin. At the same time, her hand chopped at his wrist, knocking his gun hand away just as he squeezed the trigger.

The blast scorched the side of her face and she felt a pain sharp and acute as a wasp sting as the searing hot bullet grazed her temple before she heard the cough of the silencer. Her nose filled with the firework stink of the explosion and the acrid odour of her burnt hair. She staggered, and, trying to regain her balance, her questing hand sought the stanchion of the area railings behind her. The assassin did not release his grip on her shoulder as he stumbled back, but dragged her with him. She fell and sprawled full length, striking her head on the cold damp stone.

Bent double, the gunman held his bruised privates with one hand for only a moment, the other still gripping the weapon. As he stood up, his right arm swivelled smoothly downwards.

Dazed by the impact of the fall, she raised her head. The pistol, only a foot away, pointed straight at her face. Only then did she scream.

Then there was the sound of heavy feet pounding the pavement, and Urquhart's huge voice bellowing, 'No!' Then, 'Run Catriona! Run!'

She dragged herself upright, reeling and confused from the throbbing pain in her head, and half blinded by the blood that poured from the bullet graze on her temple. The hitman ignored her as he calmly turned in one single movement to face the direction of the new threat, his gun arm tracking round unwaveringly like a tank turret, his finger squeezing the trigger.

Alan was only a matter of feet away when the gun was fired. He gave a strange choking sound, dropped to his knees, then collapsed face down. The man had stepped back as he would have to avoid a falling tree he had cut down. From beneath Alan's trenchcoat, rivulets of dark red blood spread out over the paving and trickled in the gutter.

Catriona was on her feet now, staring down at Urquhart's body, shocked into immobility. The man was in front of her, raising the pistol yet again. He was close enough for her to smell the sweat of him and the sour reek of his breath. Close enough for her to . . .

Her hand shot out, fore- and index fingers extended, and she felt the jelly of his eye splatter under the impact.

Then he had dropped the gun and was scrabbling with both hands at his face, and though he did not scream, she heard the great sucking intakes of his breath as he fought the agony. She ran for her car, wiping her fingers on her jeans as she ran.

Her hands shook as she forced the key into the lock and yanked open the door. Twisting desperately at the ignition, the engine fired, then roared. Slamming the wildly swinging door closed, she wrenched at the wheel, the bumper smashing the tail-light of the car in front as she pulled heedlessly out into the road. In the rear-view mirror, she could see that the gunman, blood streaming down his face from his ruined eye, was on his feet yet again, pointing the gun, aiming, firing. She heard the clang of a bullet hitting the tailgate as she crushed the accelerator to the floor.

TWELVE

JOURNALIST KILLED IN DRUGS FEUD SHOOTING

A gunman described by the police as a professional hit-man is being hunted following yesterday's shooting in Gibson Square, Islington, in which freelance journalist Alan Urquhart was fatally injured.

Mr Urquhart (50) was killed by a single shot to the heart fired at point-blank range from a high-powered automatic pistol. A resident of the square, who did not wish to be identified, witnessed the incident from the sitting room of her flat. She told our reporter that, alerted by a sound like a car backfiring, she saw a man dressed as a workman in white overalls pointing a handgun at a woman lying on the pavement. A second man, Mr Urquhart, ran towards them from the far end of the square. As he approached, the gunman fired the fatal shot, then made his escape in a white Ford Transit. A vehicle stolen that morning, which may have been the one involved in the shooting, was later found burnt out in the yard of an abandoned warehouse in Southwark, and is undergoing forensic tests.

The shooting happened outside a flat occupied by London University Professor Catriona Turville (38). There is reason to believe that Ms Turville, who had been suspended from her post at Warbeck College following her arrest on a charge of possession of cocaine, was the target of the attack. Possibly injured, she fled the scene at the wheel of her white Ford Fiesta. Neither she nor the vehicle have been traced.

Detective Inspector Collins of the Metropolitan Police Drugs Squad appealed for Professor Turville to contact the police. It is understood that the investigation is working on the theory that the incident was drugs related. Earlier this month, Professor Turville narrowly escaped death following a fire, believed to be arson, which completely destroyed her Muswell Hill home. Mr Urquhart appears to have been a bystander who bravely intervened, with tragic consequences.

Mr Urquhart had worked as a journalist first in his native Scotland, then in the North of England and in London for many years. Most recently he had specialised in news items concerning the Royal Family. Well-liked by colleagues, his scrupulous integrity and avoidance of sensationalism were respected by Buckingham Palace. A spokesman said today that the Queen was distressed to hear of his death, and a letter of condolence would be sent to his family.

The tall redhead in the lime-green tracksuit and trainers took the copy of the *Daily Telegraph* from the rack in the supermarket and paid for it at the counter, searching a little clumsily in her purse for the change, apparently encumbered by her excessively long fingernails which were painted a vivid scarlet, matching her lipgloss.

In the car-park, she climbed into the driving seat of the shiny red Volkswagen Golf. For half an hour she could do no more than sit, holding the wheel with hands clenched, her whole body shaking with sobs as she wept.

He should never have done what he had done. She wasn't worthy of such a sacrifice. She wasn't worthy of such love. All her adult life, she had abhorred intimacy, spurned human contact, rejected love. Despite those endeavours, love had sought her out. Then, just as it was beginning to enfold her in its warm embrace, bringing her back from the chilly death in life she had chosen, it was snatched away. It was as if she were being reminded that such things were not for her. The priests of her childhood had averred that evil deeds resulted in damnation. But they were wrong in one respect. To be sure, Hell existed, but not after death. Before.

'You all right, dear?' The concerned face of an elderly woman peered down on her through the car window.

She nodded, 'Yes, a migraine. Thanks for asking.'

She glanced at the alien face in the vanity mirror of the sun visor. Tears black with dissolved mascara had carved rivulets through the heavy pancake make-up.

What had happened had happened. She could not go back to what she had been. For Alan's sake, for the love he had so selflessly borne her, she had to go on.

When Catriona had driven hell for leather out of Gibson Square on the afternoon of the previous day, she had had no plan other than to put as much distance as she could between her and the man with the gun and anyone else who might be after her.

She abandoned the Fiesta in a run-down street at the back of Kings Cross station. She left it unlocked and the keys in the ignition. She had no doubt it would have disappeared in no time at all.

In the station she scanned the departure board for a train leaving immediately, hurriedly bought a ticket to Stevenage from a machine and scrambled aboard at the last moment.

In the shopping centre of the town she bought the gear for her new personality: a bright auburn wig, the loud tracksuit, and the accompanying accessories. Then she locked herself in the loo of a pub, donned the wig and the new outfit, and emerged as the woman she had dubbed Maggie Baxter, a wee whoor, who'd got hersel' respectably wed, and was now off to conquer the bourgeoisie.

From Stevenage, secure in Maggie's identity, she bought a ticket back to Kings Cross, and from there travelled on the underground to Paddington. She then took a train full of commuters to Kemble. In the gathering dusk, she set off to jog by footpaths and bridleways across country to Owlbury.

It was a risk to return to the Old Mill, but there was no choice. The police had probably checked it out in the course of the day, but it was unlikely they would have set a twenty-four hour watch on it, and so it proved. Just in case, however, she had entered the property from the wood that bordered its western edge, climbing stealthily over the dry-stone wall.

In the darkness, the noise of the mill-stream falling over its spillway seemed like the roar of an express train. Her footsteps crunched the gravel of the yard as she crossed to the front door. For a moment, her ears seemed to be playing tricks as, mingled with the rushing water, she heard what might have been musical notes, but when she strained to hear more clearly, there was only the sound of the weir.

The spare front door key was still in its usual place. She took the key of the garage and the spare key to Flora's Golf. She opened the up-and-over door slowly, so as to minimise its oil-drum rumble, which sounded dreadfully loud in the cold, clear night air.

The car engine turned over sluggishly but then coughed and fired. She drove it out on the shingle, then closed the garage door, hiding the key under a stone. A few cautious minutes later, the Golf was driving down the dark deserted High Street of Owlbury in the direction of Cheltenham.

*   *   *

'Good morning, Dr Jesmond.'

Bill looked around to discover who had accosted him at this hour of the morning in the parking lot at the rear of the small apartment block. A woman, in a luridly coloured tracksuit and dark glasses, what was visible of her face absolutely caked with make-up, was standing on the passenger side of his car. It was obvious from his look of puzzlement that he didn't recognise her.

'Good morning.'

The woman was now draping herself rather provocatively on the bonnet of the car. He disengaged the central locking, and even the slithering click of the mechanism did not make her move.

'You'll have to excuse me, Ms ... er ... I'm in rather a hurry.'

'Maggie Baxter's the name. My wee car won't start and I was wondering if you'd care to give me a lift?'

'I don't go into town, I'm afraid. I work over towards Gloucester.'

'No matter. Wherever you're heading will be fine.' The strange woman with the excruciatingly thick Scots accent descended gracefully from her perch, opened the door and climbed in. Despite the bizarre outfit, she had a slim figure, and under the make-up could be discerned the fine bone structure of an attractive woman. Although, it seemed an odd time of day to be propositioned ...

He lowered himself into the driving seat and glanced at his watch. 'Look, it'll only take five minutes to run you down to the Promenade at this time of the morning ...'

'That would be extremely kind of you.'

He started the engine and drove out of the car-park.

'Have you just moved into one of the flats?'

'Aye, very recently indeed.'

'Do you work in the centre of town?'

He heard the sound of laughter. His passenger was laughing.

'Is that the latest pick-up technique, William?' Catriona said in her own voice.

Astonished, he took his eyes off the road to glance to his left. He had not been mistaken.

'Christ!'

She whipped off the sunglasses and leant close to him. 'The masquerade's over, Bill. You and I have to have a serious talk.'

'I told you to stay away from Charlotte and me. That decision has been amply justified by subsequent events. If only half of what they printed in the newspapers was true, then you're a danger to yourself and to others. You should give yourself up. You and I have nothing to talk about.'

'Oh yes we do. This.'

She held up before his face a shiny gelatine-encased capsule, white with a black central ring. 'Recognise this? You should.'

'Where the hell did you get that from?'

'Careful! Keep your eyes on the road! Now I've settled the topic for the morning, I want you to pull off the main road at the next left turn.'

Without a word, he complied.

'OK. Stop here.'

He drew up beside one of the stretches of tree-dotted parkland which stretch green fingers towards the commercial centre of Cheltenham.

'I asked you a question. Where did you obtain that capsule?'

'It's a long story, Bill. And I'm not in the mood to mess around. I'll answer your questions, but first, you're going to answer mine. If you refuse, I shall go to the authorities with what I already know. If I do that there'll be enough mud to smear you with for the rest of your life. Even if you escape gaol, I doubt that anyone will think you a fit person to have sole custody of a child. Your only hope is to co-operate with me. Do I make myself clear?'

He said nothing, but made no move to drive off or get out of the car.

'Good. Now, to business. This,' she held up the capsule again. 'This, as you and I both know, is a drug code-named AL74/06/02, made by you and your colleagues at Avalon Laboratories.'

'I can't discuss anything to do with the company's activities. All product information is strictly confidential. There has obviously been a breach of security. I demand that you tell me where you got that from. I shall have to make a report.' He spoke defiantly, but his normally ruddy outdoor complexion had paled and there was a tremor in his deep voice.

'Bill, I don't think you heard me. You are in serious trouble. You're not in a position to demand anything. You'll lose Charlotte. Is that what you want?'

He stared ahead through the windscreen.

'You know as well as I do the source of this capsule,' Catriona continued. 'It was part of a batch delivered to a clinical trial centre for administering to human subjects. Those subjects did not know they were taking part in a clinical trial. They were not told of any risks they might be open to. They were not volunteers. They were not even appropriate persons to be volunteers, as they were in all cases vulnerable elderly persons. Not only was that unethical, and a negligent breach of the duty of care to which those in charge were bound, but criminal. You and your colleagues and your company, and the directors of your trial facility, are therefore guilty of a criminal conspiracy, for which I don't doubt that the penalties are severe and the professional and commercial consequences devastating. I don't need to tell you that this clinical trial centre, set up covertly with Avalon funds, employing staff either ignorant or unscrupulous enough to do the company's bidding, purports to be a residential home for elderly persons under the name Willowdene.'

The scientist made no reply.

'You don't deny any of that?'

Again there was silence from her brother-in-law.

'Bill, I've told you what I shall do if you don't co-operate. Is that what you want?'

He raised his hand and ran it through the thick mop of grizzled curly hair. He shook his head ruefully, an over-grown schoolboy, up in front of the beak for blowing up the stinks lab.

'Put like that, it does sound bad. But there were strict guidelines. There was no harm suffered by any of the old folk. Quite the reverse.'

Struggling to conceal her elation that her threatening bluff had worked, and that the closed door into the world of Avalon had begun to open, she replied, scornfully, 'Come off it! We're not talking about test-marketing a new flavour of toothpaste! This was a drug designed to affect the mind. You can't be sure with a substance of that nature, can you, what kinds of side-effects are going to appear?'

'I repeat, there were no harmful side-effects.'

'But the anticipated effects were dramatic enough, weren't they? To destroy someone's memory. Is that a trivial thing to do? Why did you do it, Bill? Why is this thing so important? What is it for?'

He shook his head impatiently. 'Listen, and I'll explain. First of all, although it was not my idea to set up Willowdene – that decision was taken before I returned to England to take over the laboratory – I fully concurred with the logic of the arrangement, given the research path the company wished me to follow. The subject group were chosen because they were isolated from other influences. They were passive recipients. They had no commitments to fulfil. No responsibilities. Nothing to think about. Nothing to live for.'

'They were human beings! They ought to have been given a choice!'

'No, in order to progress, it is sometimes necessary to

289

eliminate superfluous and usually harmful choices. Fluoride is added to our water supply, calcium to our bread and so on. It is not necessary to be able to choose to have bad teeth or brittle bones. In consequence we are healthier and, I daresay, happier.'

'An experimental drug is not a food additive! You were recklessly endangering their lives.'

'Catriona, you have blackmailed me into explaining. You could at least listen to the explanation. The drug was entirely beneficial, designed not to destroy, but to enhance the power of the mind – in pursuit of a greater goal, which I'll tell you about in due course. You're right that the drug was intended to have certain affects on the human memory. The memory is one of the brain's most mysterious functions, in that we know very little about where it is located or how it works. To put it into layman's language, the brain is composed of a system of tiny triggers which react to the presence of chemicals. Once the chemical reaches the trigger, it fires a burst of electricity; that passes the message through the nervous system to whatever part of the body requires direction. For example, a message is passed from the stomach in a chemical form to signify hunger or thirst. In the brain, the message is evaluated. Possibly a simple action is called for. The body is required to act in whatever way the need may be most quickly satisfied. It gets up out of its armchair and fixes itself a sandwich. Or, depending on the circumstances, a more complex reaction is required. The body's location may be in a desert where neither food nor drink are available. So the brain has to use other resources to suppress the demand for hunger. Now, even in a less sophisticated brain than that of a human, the capacity of the brain to react to such triggers and stimuli is massively enhanced if the reaction does not have to arise from new every time a similar message is received. The storage in the brain of the association between needs and the means to fulfil those needs is what we can assume to be the primary function of memory. That function is seen in animals. Animals remember food sources. They remember the good places to sleep, to hide, to build nests. More developed animals, particularly those which live closely with human beings, such as cats and dogs, can learn, through repetition and through remembering, a variety of more or less complex tasks. How to open a fridge door to steal food, for example. So learning and memory are obviously intimately linked. In the days before we could record data, on paper, or electronically, there is evidence that human beings were capable of enormous feats of memory.'

As he spoke, it was evident that the scientist in him had taken over. No longer was he speaking under compulsion. He was expounding a subject dear to him. She had never heard him so animated. It was infectious. For the first time, irony upon ironies, they had something to share.

'Yes. That's something I do know something about. To become learned in philosophy or literature or theology in the ages before printing, and before paper was cheap and available, it was vital to have a highly developed memory. A scholar could not afford to have a copy of every book he read. He had to remember vast amounts of material. And not only that, but discourse; examinations were oral, not written. Consequently, there were all kinds of artificial memory systems – Frances Yates describes them in *The Art of Memory*. Mostly they involved imaginary rooms or places in which the items you wanted to remember could be arranged. You searched the relevant location in your memory room and there was everything you needed, logically arranged, much as it would be in a modern paper or electronic filing system.'

'Yes, that's right. And those things do work. I've tried them. But we know a great deal more about memory now than that. We've learned from studying people whose brains are defective. There are different kinds of memory. The everyday short-term needs of the brain to recall where we left our shoes or our spectacles, what we were doing an hour ago, what we need to be doing in an hour's time: we hold those memories only for as long as we need them. I don't remember in a year's time the colour of the socks I'm wearing today, for example, unless of course there's a particular reason why I should – say the socks become associated with a particular event which we readily call to mind. It's those things, along with fundamental aspects of our identities, our names, our dates of birth, our likes and dislikes, which are more deeply embedded. We don't forget those, even if we don't necessarily call them to mind every few minutes. I know my name is Bill Jesmond. I'll remember that without having to remind my conscious mind of that. Similarly there are certain classes of physical skills that we remember as if they were part of us, through repetition as children, so that there never seems to be a time at which we never knew them. Walking, for instance. We learn to walk, we remember the technique, and, unless something serious happens to our brains, we don't forget how to do it. We don't wake up every morning trying to remember the technique for walking. Similarly, swimming, cycling, driving, riding a horse, catching a ball, going to the lavatory, dozens of other physical actions are perfectly embedded.

'There are other things that seem not to adhere so perfectly. I, for example, can never, no matter how hard I try, remember how to set the VCR. Charlotte, though, remembers perfectly. Most people can remember a few frequently used phone numbers, but not by any means all the numbers of all the people they might call in a year. Historians might remember many significant dates, but for most of us, that and other kinds of stuff we learned at school is lost. Maybe it was no use learning it in the first place, but then to learn it and then forget it seems even more of a waste of time.

'The modern world is, of all commodities, the most short of time. The computer is vaunted as the great saviour of modern society, but the kinds of skills it displays are, even now, totally elementary compared with the power of the human brain. I'm not one of these people who believe in machine intelligence. It's the ideal of technicians. To me, a machine, no matter how advanced, will always be a machine. The vital ingredient of human intelligence is consciousness. I do not believe that a machine can be programmed by a human being to be self-conscious. There's a paradox there, a logical impossibility which can never be overcome. Artificial intelligence will progress enormously, but it will reach a very advanced dead-end. I'm far more interested in harnessing and enhancing those latent powers in the brain which we know are there and can at the moment reach only imperfectly.

'What if every schoolchild could read a text once, then remember it word-perfectly thereafter? Think of the savings one could make in education and training. Think of the advances in human communication! At present the Western world is locked out of any real understanding of a major part of the world's societies because of the problem of language. How many businessmen, politicians, academics properly understand Chinese, for example? To learn even the basics of Mandarin can take a well-motivated student working full-time a year or more. To improve the memory would make every language on earth theoretically available in a matter of weeks. And I'm convinced that the more languages the brain can absorb, the easier it is to learn others. The human brain can invent short-cuts, see parallels where no computer could. I do believe in intuition, you see. Because without it there would be no science. All great scientific discoveries have demanded inductive reasoning, which is only the name that logic gives to intuition.'

'Bill, isn't this loading too much on memory? I don't forget things I read. It gives me an advantage over most people. But I'm not, in consequence, a super-brain. I don't know Chinese! I shan't win a Nobel Prize! Most of the time I can't remember where I put my handbag.'

'I'm not saying that exceptional memory will turn everyone

into a genius. But even if a person has only average intelligence, an enhanced memory is going to massively increase his potential. As it has yours. And if your memory is as good as you claim, then there's no question that it could be further exploited.'

'Exploited? The human brain is not a resource to be ruthlessly mined like a mineral deposit. Nor do I believe that I have an infinite capacity to learn and remember. That means that there must be some limit on memory. Computer storage memory systems become full. Doesn't something similar happen to the brain's?'

'I think the computer is a false analogy. The computer is a machine. The brain is an organism. The phenomenon that we call memory has one enormous advantage over any machine. It has a body attached. The body is also a memory system. That is why I believe that those physical skills I spoke of, once learnt, become embedded. The body itself remembers. The memory extends to every cell of the body, and has infinite capacity, for all practical purposes. The problem is the access to that storage, to embed knowledge as effectively as the knowledge of how to walk or to hold a knife and fork. For that, you need a trigger.'

'Like Proust. The madeleine dipped in tea? That signified to him the taste of childhood and brought the memories flooding back.'

'Yes, on this occasion, a literary analogy is appropriate. But not everyone functions like Proust. For the rest of humanity, a scientific solution is required. And that was where the drug came in. It was intended to be that trigger, to open up the organic memory, to facilitate learning. To revolutionise human life.'

'You say was intended to. Did it not work?'

'It worked extremely well. The sample at Willowdene consisted of a group of elderly persons, most of whom had not received much in the way of higher education. They were unaccustomed to undertake sustained intellectual endeavour. The majority did not read anything more demanding than a tabloid newspaper or a light novel. Within weeks of taking the drug, we were able to start advanced learning programmes. Their memories for facts, figures, ideas, techniques, enormously improved. But there was another effect which we had not, it must be admitted, built into our calculations.'

'A side-effect.'

'If you like. It was observed that although, as I've said, their procedural memories were massively enhanced, and their other short- and medium-term memory functions functioned as well or better, what one might call their historic memories – of their infancy, youth, and indeed the whole of adulthood prior to their taking the drug – were curtailed to the point of being completely blocked. This would happen quite suddenly and quickly, usually after the drug had been taken for several weeks, but occasionally much sooner. A profound sleep was followed by a state akin to a very specific kind of amnesia. Yet without the distress and trauma associated with that condition, as of course it was not that they forgot their own identities, but merely the historical background of those identities.'

'Merely? Wasn't that a serious thing to do, unasked, to destroy the memories of elderly people? Weren't you destroying much of the beauty and the worth of the lives they had lived?'

'Destroy is an extremely emotive word. I should prefer a more scientific description such as blocked or inhibited or suppressed. And as for their memories being a source of beauty and worth, that's exactly the kind of romantic view I'd expect you to take. In the real world, it isn't Wordsworth and daffodils and the glory of childhood. These people were old. Their memories constantly reminded them of the tragedies and the disappointments of their lives. No, there was no regret for a lost golden age when their memories vanished. It was the loss of such memories which gave them the ability to live in the present with renewed vitality.

'The amazing thing was that those who had been so locked into negative states that they could not move from the chairs in which they were placed, not even to exercise bodily functions, began to flourish again. They awoke every day clear and refreshed. Every day was new! New every morning! A spiritual rebirth every day! Their minds were relieved of the dross that cluttered them. It was a revelation to me. The burden of depression had lifted like morning mist, and the bright sunlight flooded in!

'When I read the reports of what was happening, I knew I had made the most extraordinary breakthrough in the treatment of one of the most common and insidious illnesses afflicting modern man. If depression were an epidemic plague like cholera or typhoid, governments would devote massive resources to its eradication. But because its effects are more subtle and more secret, the deaths and disabilities it causes less visible and less conducive to publicity, its presence amongst us is accepted. Of course the word depression covers a variety of mental states, from what the psychiatrists call clinical depression, because that's the one they've cornered the market on claiming to treat, to stress, grief, and plain unhappiness. And there are dozens, hundreds of drug treatments. Occasionally, a brand comes along which gains a brief notoriety: once it was Vallium, now it's Prozac. The most modern drugs are supposed to work – and whether they do actually work is a matter of dispute – by inhibiting the reabsorption by the nerve cell of the chemical neurotransmitter serotonin. Enhancing the quantity of the chemical in the brain has been found by some researchers to alleviate the symptoms of depression. Eventually, of course, the effect of the pill wears off and you have to pop another, and another and so on. It's a controversial area, but there are claims that these drugs may have unpleasant side-effects, both physical and mental.

'What the Willowdene effect made me consider was whether my colleagues who developed these drugs were not falling for the old medical trap of treating not the disease but the symptoms of the disease. There's no evidence that people who are depressed have lower serotonin levels than those of people who are not depressed – unlike, say, the inadequate production of the neurotransmitter dopamine that causes Parkinson's disease. It's simply that increasing those levels may alleviate the depression. The depression has its roots elsewhere. And where else should one look than at what causes normal, non-clinical unhappiness in healthy people? For most of us, it's life itself that is the source of our unhappiness. We have bad things happen to us. If we have more good things than bad things happen to us, or if we are able to shrug off the bad things, then maybe we're not depressed. But for many people, the bad things predominate and persist, and that makes them unhappy. The way in which the bad things persist is through the memory. It seemed to me obvious that without memory of the act, there can be no guilt, because to all intents and purposes the act has ceased to exist. There can be no pain felt for the consequences, because in fact, without memory, there are no consequences. The old cliché is that time is the great healer. But that isn't true. Over time, one's stock of memories grows, it doesn't diminish. An old memory is no less painful than a new one. I shall remember the day they told me Charlotte might die in all its fresh agony until the day they cart me away. I expect there are things that have happened to you about which you feel the same. Nothing is ever truly forgotten. Even if all memories aren't present all the time, they still exist in the deep recesses of the brain. Freud and Jung called that place the unconscious, but I believe that term is simply another word for the deepest historical memories. Such memories are embedded in the way that the memory of how to tie shoelaces is embedded.

'No one had ever before thought of targeting those memories, but the Willowdene drug has proved to my satisfaction that it is possible to eradicate them, in the way that one would eradicate any other noxious life-threatening organism, without damage to the host. I have proved that, by suppressing that compartment of the memory in which the horrors and the errors of one's past are preserved, one can improve the happiness level of any individual, not only an elderly person in a retirement home. The mental cess-pit will be replaced by a well of crystal water.'

'And this justified what you were doing? You were playing God, weren't you?'

'Playing God is what makes us human. How would mankind progress, if outstanding men had not taken decisions to benefit the majority. How would, for that matter, any child be raised and educated if its parents and teachers did not play God? I observed what was happening to these old persons. They were mentally more alert, psychologically more healthy. But that was not the whole effect it had. The subjects were also observably – which was then proved by medical examination – physically fitter! Yes, their bodily ailments were responding to the cure occurring in their minds. Healing has always been suspected amongst so-called alternative practitioners to be at least partly a psychological process. Here was living proof. I realised what I had done. I realised that what had been created was, in embryo, not merely a drug to enhance the learning capacity of the brain, but to improve an individual's whole quality of life. *And, as a corollary, not only to improve, but to extend it.*'

As he spoke those last words, his face glowed with a kind of fervour, and his eyes brightened. He was no longer a scientist expounding an experiment, he was a preacher extolling a new creed.

He was almost laughing as he continued. 'I had a glimpse of the Holy Grail. Yes, I did feel a little bit divine that day. I knew then that we could make men immortal.'

'Immortal? You're crazy.'

'No, it was entirely within the bounds of possibility. Further research was needed, of course. But the unlocking of the latent power of the brain was the key. Everything else was a technicality.'

'And the bosses of Avalon knew what was at stake?'

'Of course.'

'The profits from this discovery would have been astronomical.'

He shrugged. 'Possibly. But to me that was as nothing compared to the benefits for mankind.'

'For you, maybe. I don't think the men who run the company are quite so high-minded. You wouldn't be allowed to publish, would you?'

'There is a company policy: the publication of any research that has commercial implications has to be postponed until the necessary intellectual property rights have been secured.'

'I'm sure there is. If the company knew that this discovery had leaked out, would there be some concern? If the authorities had discovered the setup at Willowdene, the experiment would have been terminated, and the scandal would have resulted – at the least – in massively bad publicity for the company.'

He shifted uneasily in his seat. 'Look, I'm not concerned with security. The company operates a need-to-know principle among its managers. It's more efficient that way. There are others within the company who have that role. I was never involved with the management of the Willowdene establishment, only with the clinical research.'

'You wanted to separate yourself from the dirty work?'

'There was nothing dirty about it.'

'Oh no? It's convenient for you, isn't it, that need-to-know principle? But do you realise just how much there was that your precious company decided you didn't need to know? You didn't need to know that the manager of Willowdene narrowly avoided a conviction for grievous bodily harm? That a care assistant at Willowdene died, allegedly of a sudden heart attack, shortly after she gave me certain information about what was happening there? That agents working for Avalon fire-bombed my house in an attempt to kill me, planted cocaine in my office to destroy my credibility as a witness, and yesterday, while trying to murder me, instead shot and killed my . . . my friend?'

'That's preposterous. You're completely paranoid.'

'No, I'm the victim of an unscrupulous, dangerous opponent. All because of this.' She held up the capsule. 'I have the original container, with its label. There would be no difficulty in proving it came from Avalon. You asked where I obtained it. Now I shall tell you yet more things you didn't need to know.

'The container was stolen from Willowdene by a woman called Hazel Marchant. Her mother was and probably still is a resident of the home. Hazel became suspicious of what was happening there. She died in what appeared to be an accident, but which I'm convinced was murder: by the Willowdene managers, trying to cover up the loss of the drug by a desperate attempt to retrieve it. After killing her, they ransacked her flat, but she had already passed the container on to her lover. So they kidnapped the lover, in the hope that they could discover where it had been hidden. The attempt was complicated by the fact that the lover had already, as a way of calling public attention to what was going on, taken the drug. Before the hiding place could be discovered, the lover escaped. Don't you want to know how I became involved? Wouldn't you like to hear why Avalon was scrupulously careful not to relax the need-to-know principle in your particular case? They were undoubtedly nervous that your loyalties would be strained to breaking point if you had known that the person against whom the whole weight of their security apparatus was directed was none other than your own wife.'

'Flora? No, you're wrong. Not Flora.'

The sick pallor which spread over Bill's rugged features

could not have been faked. There was no doubt that the scientist knew nothing of what she had told him.

'Yes, Flora was Hazel Marchant's lover, the lover I told you I had discovered. But I was wrong that Hazel's death drove Flora to suicide. It made her determined to stop the experiment at Willowdene. She took not poison but the Avalon drug. I was to find her, and help her. Instead of which, Anderson and Monaghan from Willowdene arrived first on the scene and abducted her. After being locked up, she escaped. She went into hiding.'

'Where is Flora now? Why can't she return and tell me these things herself?'

'I don't know where she is. Nor does Avalon. I suspect that after her escape, Anderson and Monaghan had no alternative but to inform their Avalon controllers. The methods they adopted to deal with Flora were even more unspeakably ruthless. I think you now have a need-to-know the kind of people you have been working for. To find Flora, they adopted the methods of hunters staking a cub to trap the lioness. They attacked Charlotte and her friend on the Beacon.'

The Stroud surgery of David Anderson MA (Oxon) MB BCh. D.Phil. was an eighteenth-century town-house in Lowcroft. She pushed open the heavy wooden door. At the end of the hallway, from which rose a steep cantilevered stone staircase, a panelled door was marked: *Reception. Please enter.*

At the counter within was a sharp-featured woman in her fifties.

'Yes?'

'Hello, dear. I've an appointment with Dr Anderson. My name's Maggie Baxter.'

'Baxter.' The woman clicked the mouse of her computer to scroll through a data-base. 'Margaret Rose Baxter, Lilac Cottage, Arnolds Lane, Rodborough? New patient?'

'That's right, dear. Just moved in.'

'And you wish to become a private patient?'

'That's right.'

The receptionist's manner became marginally more polite. 'The waiting room is the next door on the left. Dr Anderson will be with you shortly.'

Despite the handsome exterior, inside the surgery was shabby. In the waiting room, there was a pleasantly carved grey marble mantelpiece, but it had been crudely boarded up with hardboard. Over it hung a discoloured oil painting of cows drinking at a stream. There were a few grubby red leather-effect vinyl-covered armchairs, a sagging brown sofa and a low, varnished deal coffee-table laden with dog-eared glossy magazines. On the rear wall was a pinboard to which were attached posters exhorting her to avoid unprotected sexual intercourse, dangerous drugs, cholesterol-rich foods, smoking and alcohol.

Catriona stood by the window staring unseeing at the busy street. Then she heard the door behind her open. She turned to see a tall figure advancing towards her, hand out-stretched.

'Ms Baxter? I'm David Anderson. My consulting room is this way.'

He ushered her up the stairs to the first floor and through an open door into a large room at the front of the build-ing. The voices of passers-by and the hum of traffic drifted through the half-open lower sash of one of the pair of tall windows.

A table cluttered with files and papers stood at one end of the room. On the window side of the white marble fireplace, boarded up like the one downstairs, was a desk on which were more piles of files and correspondence, the receiver of a cordless telephone and an open lap-top computer.

The recesses on either side of the chimney breast were shelved in white-painted wood from floor to ceiling, and filled with bulky medical volumes in various subfusc hues.

David Anderson pointed to an upholstered chair considerably smarter than those in the waiting room. 'Do sit down, Ms Baxter.'

She sat on the edge of the cushion, the tension humming in her limbs.

He sat down in the swivel armchair behind his desk. There was a faint creak as he tilted back, his hands clasped together over his chest. For a moment they regarded one another. David Anderson was in his mid-forties, with thinning dark hair greying at the temples, over six feet tall and a heavily built, even burly man into the bargain, an ex-rugby player gone slightly to seed.

'Now, Ms Baxter. As this is your first visit, I wonder if you'd first of all mind completing our registration form? There are questions about your medical history, but your answers will of course remain entirely confidential. Let me know if there's anything you don't understand. Unless there is anything specific you'd like to consult me about now?'

His voice was measured, deliberate and monotonous, the tones of a man in the habit of regarding the people he was addressing as having limited intellectual powers.

'Och no, I'm as fit as a flea. Despite having my wee house in London completely destroyed by a fire-bomb, and me barely escaping with my life.'

The habitual blandness of his professional manner all but hid the faint flicker of alarm that spread across his face and vanished almost as soon as it appeared.

She carried on as if what she had said was the most normal thing in the world. 'Aye, I could have been burnt to death. And then, after that, to cap it all, my guid friend is shot to death in the street by a gunman. I thought, I'd better move to the country where it's more peaceful. I'll go and see that doctor who was so helpful to my friend Hazel. Poor Hazel, she had a terrible accident and is no longer with us.'

He stood up. 'I'm sorry, Ms Baxter, but it appears to me

303

that you require the services of a psychiatrist rather than a general practitioner. To help you deal with what are clearly distressing fantasies.'

'Sit down, Dr Anderson,' said Catriona in her normal voice. 'I'll dispense with the play-acting. I'm Catriona Turville. Flora's sister.'

He wrinkled his brows. 'Flora? Flora who?'

'Flora Jesmond.'

'I know no one by the name of Flora Jesmond.'

'You certainly do. You and your colleague Monaghan abducted her from her house and took her to Willowdene.'

'Ms Turville or Baxter or whoever you are, you are clearly a very disturbed woman to make such groundless, indeed utterly fantastic allegations, which I totally and contemptuously refute. I don't know what Willowdene represents in your fantasy, but to anyone in this part of Gloucestershire, it is a residential home for senior citizens.'

'You don't deny that you have a connection with Willowdene?'

He shrugged. 'Several of my elderly patients have taken up residence there over the years. It is an excellent establishment. A model of its kind.'

'You admit you know Sister Monaghan, the manager?'

'Naturally.'

'You've known her for many years, haven't you? Since your time as a doctor in Southampton. When she was also employed in an old persons' home.'

'You've clearly been doing some homework, Ms Baxter, though why you have taken such pains is beyond me. Yes, it's perfectly true that I met Sister Monaghan at that time. We were both surprised to encounter each other again in this part of the country.'

'Quite a coincidence, wasn't it?'

'I suppose it was.'

'It was far more than that. It was at your behest that Sister Monaghan became manager of Willowdene.'

He shook his head, smiling. 'Good Lord, Ms Baxter. You credit me with an influence over the institution that I as a mere physician simply don't have. Those matters are firmly in the hands of the trustees.'

'So you had nothing to do with Sister Monaghan's appointment.'

'Nothing whatever.'

'But nor did you see fit to warn those who did appoint her?'

'Warn them about what?'

'About the case heard at Winchester Crown Court in 1989. Sister Monaghan was accused of GBH against an elderly patient.'

'She was acquitted. She left the Court without a stain on her character.'

'You gave evidence in her favour. Such evidence would have weighed heavily with a jury.'

'I was asked by the defence team to appear as a witness, as I had had dealings with the home concerned. I described what I had seen on my many visits there. That was all.'

'So you had no qualms about her employment at Willowdene?'

'None whatsoever.' He shot the cuff of his silk shirt and looked at the broad face of the gold Rolex on his wrist. 'Now, look here, I have another appointment in five minutes' time, Ms Baxter. I've had quite enough of you and your crazy fantasies. I've listened to you out of courtesy and out of compassion for your condition. But I now think I've humoured you for long enough. I have suggested you need more specialist treatment than I can offer you. You must seek that elsewhere. Would you please leave immediately. Otherwise I shall be forced to call the police.'

He was very convincing, there was no doubt about that. She could see him as he must have appeared in the witness box at the trial of Sister Monaghan: the calm, rational professional man, giving his objective opinion of a fellow professional. It would have taken more determination than a provincial jury would possess to go against the weight of such a testimony.

Now he was smiling down on her, the mad woman. Despite everything she knew and believed, such massive self-assurance was daunting. He almost convinced her. This man would never break under even the roughest police questioning. And what policeman would dare to subject a man like Anderson to such treatment?

She said, 'Bill Jesmond. He's going to reveal everything he knows about the Avalon Project. He's going to break with Avalon. Blow the whistle on the whole scheme. He's compiling a dossier for the prosecuting authorities.'

'You can't stop, can you? It's a compulsion. I know nothing of any of this. Avalon Project? Bill Jesmond? I've heard of Avalon – they're a household name – but not this man Jesmond.'

'You thought he would never put his career on the line. That he was in too deeply. That he'd never risk going to prison. But you went too far when you attacked Charlotte. Bill understands now that it wasn't Malcolm Thornton who was responsible. He'll make the police listen to Malcolm's account of what happened on the Beacon.'

He wasn't smiling now, he was laughing. 'My dear Ms Baxter, how you do manage to weave everything into your tissue of fantasy! It's the Beacon murder now, is it? Well, you obviously haven't caught up with the latest developments in that distressing case. That blighter Thornton isn't going to be giving any story to anyone. It was on the news earlier. He was found hanged in his cell in Gloucester Prison this morning.'

A huge midden of horse muck, on which a luxuriant thatch of turf and weeds flourished, rose up at the end of the muddy shingle of the car-park. A girl of about Charlotte's age, dressed in jodhpurs and sweater, appeared round the corner of the prefabricated steel and asbestos building alongside.

She was pushing a wheelbarrow bearing another aromatic yellow-brown load to add to this mound. She stopped when she saw Catriona beckoning to her.

'I'm looking for Sam Thornton.'

'She's giving a lesson in the manège there.' She indicated the building. 'She'll be finished soon.'

In the muddy, straw-littered concrete yard on the other side, there were half a dozen timber loose-boxes, all empty at that moment. Hand-painted plates over the doors bore names such as Chestnut and Sooty. She stood in the shadow of an open door, wrinkling her nose at the zoo smell of hay and urine.

There was a squeaking groan as the double steel doors of the covered exercise arena were slid back and a string of ponies and young riders emerged, followed on foot by Sam, in jeans and wellingtons. Her usually high-coloured cheeks were pale.

Catriona waited until she went alone into the tack room-cum-office, then followed her in, closed the plank door and leaned against it.

The young woman looked up at the sound, then stared at her in obvious surprise. Catriona had abandoned the wig, and washed off the make-up, but she still wore the outlandish clothes.

'Sam. I'm so glad I've found you. I tried your house, and a neighbour said you were here.'

'I might as well be here as anywhere. There isn't anything I can do to help Malcolm now.'

'I'm probably not someone you want to see right now. I just wanted to say I was desperately sorry.'

'I don't blame you for what happened. I pestered the lawyer like you told me. But all he kept saying was that we had to wait for the trial. I knew Malcolm wouldn't last being in there. I should have done more. I don't know what, but I should have done something.'

'You shouldn't criticise yourself. We did what we could. If

only he could have held on for the trial, there might have been a chance.'

'There never was a chance. They'd made up their minds there wasn't going to be no chance. You don't believe he done it himself, do you? No way would our Malcolm hang himself. He wouldn't know how. He wouldn't even think of it. No, someone decided to help him. Just like I knew they would.'

The tears coursed down the girl's glowing cheeks. For a moment Catriona hesitated, then she enveloped her in a hug.

They stood in silence together, then Catriona pulled away.

Sam said, 'Are you staying at the Old Mill?'

Catriona shook her head. 'No. I've been back in London since Charlotte came out of hospital. You obviously haven't heard the news lately?'

'No, I never bother with that. But why?'

'It doesn't matter.'

'I wondered whether you might be staying over at the Old Mill again. Only, when I was coming down the lane the other evening after seeing to some ponies I look after, I could have sworn I saw a light on in the little flat over the garage. An au pair used to stay in it a few years back. A Swiss girl who liked riding. We got quite friendly. So it wasn't you?' she added in a disappointed tone.

'No.'

'It must have been my imagination, then. Hey, what's up?'

Catriona had pulled open the door. 'Sorry. I have to go.'

Sam stood shading her eyes against the sun, watching as the tall dark-haired woman raced away across the muddy yard to the stares of the novice riders.

As she ran back to her car, Catriona heard in her head the same sounds she had heard at the Old Mill, only this time she recognised them. The chimes at Westminster, preliminary to the striking of Big Ben. Sam might not listen to the news, but someone else she knew certainly did.

THIRTEEN

A clothes-horse hung with drying underwear stood in the kitchenette. On the windowsill was a pot of scarlet geraniums, the bright flowers like a declaration of intent.

Flora boiled water for tea. Catriona stood looking out of the small grimy window. In the spinney beyond, a grey squirrel negotiated with dainty precision the spider's web of branches between two silver birches.

'How did you work out I was here?'

'I should have realised much sooner. The principle from the Edgar Allan Poe story of the purloined letter, where the compromising letter is secreted in the letter-rack. If you want to hide something, conceal it in the most conspicuous place. I even mentioned it to Frank Churchill in his studio. So here you are, hiding out in your own house.'

'And so, in the end, you've found me.'

'Yes, I've found you. I thought I would be so elated. But instead, I can feel only . . .' She hesitated, but the thing had to be said. 'I feel so angry with you, Flora. Deeply angry and wounded. I don't understand why you've behaved as you have. So much has happened, and yet you have remained in hiding. From the very start of this business, it seems to me that you've been so detached and cold. Why did you write that horrid letter to me, in such a deliberately ambiguous way? You wanted me to believe you were literally, not just metaphorically, dead. Why didn't you simply tell me about the drug and what you were doing?'

'I wanted you to react with pure emotion. To come immediately, without stopping to wonder what was going on. If I'd said I was taking an experimental drug, it would immediately have made you think of Bill, and I didn't want him involved. I wrote another letter explaining what I had done. You would have found that. Besides, if the drug had worked, it would have been as if I were dead. I wouldn't have known you. I would have known nothing about my life or my family. It would have been as if my mind had been wiped clean. I would have been a new person. If that isn't a kind of death, I don't know what is.'

'A sleep and a forgetting. A death and a birth. Instead of which Anderson and Monaghan came for you.'

'Yes, when I woke up, I was in Willowdene. They stomach-pumped me to flush out the drug, and, in the course of time, my memory gradually returned. The drug doesn't work permanently straightaway. You have to have a series of doses spread out over several months. I managed to convince Monaghan and Anderson that I hadn't recovered my faculties. Their security became slack, particularly on the nights when Monaghan went to have it off with her lover-boy Anderson. A grisly sight that must have been. So I smashed the window with a chair and lit out for the territory.'

'But why then didn't you return? Why didn't you contact us? Why did you go into hiding? Why did you let us spend this time looking for you? I don't understand how you could do that. You've been skulking here like a spider at the centre of her web. Don't you realise the consequences? The effect on my life has been catastrophic, but far, far worse, your refusal to reappear has devastated the life of your own daughter, and caused the death of another woman's child.'

Flora shook her head sadly. 'Yes, there's a great deal that must seem puzzling to you. Yes, my behaviour must have appeared strange. But there was a reason for it, which I shall explain. It has had consequences for you, for which I'm desperately sorry, but I never thought you'd get involved to the extent you have, nor did I imagine how low Avalon would stoop. As for my darling Charlotte . . .' Her voice faltered and tears shone in her clear blue eyes. 'Don't you know how often I've blamed myself for what happened? Surely you know I'd have given anything to prevent that? If only I hadn't been so trusting and so naïve. That's why I came back here – to make sure that my darling was all right. I watched over her. Do you know what it cost me not to burst from my hiding place and hug her? I wanted to so much. If I'd done that that day when I watched them going up the Beacon, I could have . . . But I've gone over what happened so often. If only I'd stopped him following them that day. But, stupidly, I never believed that Malcolm presented any danger . . .'

Catriona stared at her, her head beginning to throb with the onset of a migraine. 'Malcolm? But it wasn't Malcolm! It was Monaghan who followed them up the Beacon! She'd dressed herself in clothing similar to Malcolm's.'

Flora's lovely face was twisted in an expression of astonishment. 'Monaghan? I don't know what you're talking about. The person I saw was most definitely Malcolm Thornton. There's no question that it was Malcolm Thornton who killed poor Alice and attacked Charlotte. To think I used to entertain that dreadful pervert in my own kitchen! I nurtured that viper in my bosom! I despise myself for it. And, may I be forgiven, I'm glad the bastard is dead. I'm glad he acted as his own hangman.' She began to sob. 'I did my best to make amends, Cat. I sneaked into the hospital, disguised as a nurse. I wanted to make sure they were looking after my darling. And oh, the joy in my heart when I saw that she would recover so completely.'

'So you're absolutely sure it wasn't Monaghan who followed the two girls up the Beacon that day?'

'No, I've told you. I'm certain she was nowhere near the Beacon. Why should she be? Sister Monaghan is a heartless bitch, but I'm quite sure she's no Myra Hindley. What happened on the Beacon has nothing to do with what happened at Willowdene. What connection could it conceivably have? Even the Avalon Corporation, ruthless and acquisitive as it is, has no reason to murder innocent children.'

'Not even as a way of forcing you to come forward?'

'Is that what you conjectured? Sometimes, my dear sister, you are what is known as too clever by half. You miss the obvious. I suppose it's a result of your spending your life poring over texts looking for obscure meanings that even the author would never have intended.'

As Catriona listened to her sister, the pain in her head grew. Now it was as if a cold blade was slicing through her brain. Could she have been so stupidly, so utterly wrong-headed?

'But you don't deny that Avalon's agents were behind the fire-bombing of my house? That they planted cocaine in my office? That they sent a hired assassin to kill me, that a friend of mine was murdered as a result?'

'The journalist? He was your friend? They said in the newspaper he was an innocent bystander. I didn't know you had friends, Cat. But yes, those seem far more likely. Much more their style. I never thought you would become so involved.'

'I was looking for you, Flora! I followed the way the clues pointed. I didn't ask to be involved in any of this. As a result, I've lost everything I ever lived for. My whole life is ruined.'

'So you said. And I've said I was sorry for it. Sorry, but not responsible. You have to take responsibility for your own life, just as I have had to. And when you come to think of it, what have you really lost? Yours wasn't much of a life, was it? You were hardly alive, were you, Cat? You existed in the crevices of life, like a mouse. Hardly anyone noticed you were alive, and no one would care if you were dead.'

Catriona stared at her sister in horror. Flora's blue eyes were wide, her ivory face was flushed, her mouth twisted in contempt. It was as if a switch had suddenly been thrown. Her whole being seemed suddenly to have changed. Never had Flora spoken to her like that. And those few words seemed to encapsulate the way in which this new Flora regarded her, perhaps had always, deep-down, regarded her. Was that so? Behind the veil of love, had there been lurking this shadowy loathing?

'A mouse? Is that how you really think of me? Is that all I amount to in your opinion? So you really wouldn't care if Avalon had succeeded in having me killed? You wouldn't, I can see it from the way you're looking at me.' As she spoke, she felt the hot pricking of tears at the corner of her eyes.

Flora shrugged, apparently unmoved. 'I need a drink.' She got up from the formica table and took a bottle of whisky and two tumblers from one of the wall cabinets. She set them on the table and carelessly slopped a generous slug of the spirit into each glass. She shoved one over to Catriona, picked up the other and knocked back about half of it in one gulp. Catriona took a mouthful of the burning liquid and choked as she swallowed it.

Flora laughed harshly. She had already refilled her glass. 'You were never much of a drinker, were you? That was one respect in which you did not take after our father.'

Catriona shuddered. 'Why, on top of everything, do you have to mention him?'

'The great unmentionable? Why not? Why not now? Why do we have to spend the whole of our lives never communicating about the one and only thing we have in common? Why did we always pretend that our lives began with our arrival at Aunt Charlotte's house in Kentish Town? That before then, we had no history? As if our memory of what had happened to us could be as easily expunged as the administrative records. But we colluded with the officials who wanted to bury us as completely as they had buried our mother and our sister and our father. Better that way. No one wanted to be reminded that the nuclear family is a bomb waiting to happen and, in our case, as in many others, it had exploded. Oh Cat, there are so many things we have never discussed! Did you never feel that? Or were you as content as you always seemed to be with your compulsive scratching amongst other men's archives, other men's lives? Of building your immaculate fortress house, so full of things and so lacking in emotion!'

Catriona gulped what was left of her whisky, and with a shaking hand poured more from the uncapped bottle.

'Emotion! You're a fine one to talk of emotion! You've left everyone who loved you in a state of anguish since your disappearance. You could have returned. Why didn't you? You haven't answered the crucial question. Why didn't you return after you escaped from Willowdene? And even before that, why didn't you speak out when Hazel Marchant was murdered?'

Flora drank up her whisky and turned to stare out of the window at the gathering dusk.

'You know Hazel was murdered, do you?'

'Once I realised that she must have been the means by which you obtained the drug from Willowdene, it was clear that she would have become a target for Anderson and Monaghan or the Avalon security service. I found out that her flat had been searched. It seemed far too coincidental that she had met with an accident.'

'You don't understand, do you? You don't understand what happened between Hazel and me, do you? If you did, you'd understand why I couldn't return.'

'Tell me then! I do want to understand! I'm involved as much as you are now! I have a right to know more! All I know about you and Hazel is that you were lovers. I found the photographs in your bag at Frank Churchill's studio.'

'I suppose you were shocked?'

'Yes, I was. Were you really in love with her?'

'You'll find that difficult to comprehend, but I was. Not at first, though. I was like you. Embarrassed by the very idea of women making love. But also perhaps, although I never would have admitted it, a little intrigued. But that came later. A day or so after she'd been in the office, I met her in Cheltenham, in Cav, as a matter of fact, by chance. We chatted for a moment politely – she was a client! – then she suggested we had tea together in the café of the department store. I was naïve, of course. I never even suspected that she was gay. I didn't think that that invitation betokened an intention on her part. She didn't fit the lesbian stereotype – cropped hair, boot-face and boiler suit! – that heterosexual men use to put down women who don't regard them as the lords of creation. You've seen the photographs. She was entirely feminine. Good-looking, beautifully dressed, sophisticated in her tastes. A successful career woman. Independent, free. Everything I had once set my heart on being. Everything I wasn't any longer. We exchanged life stories, as one does. Listening to her, her travels, the things she'd done, made me realise, yet again and even more forcefully, what I had given up when I married Bill.'

'You didn't have to marry him.'

Flora set down her mug with a bang on the table-top. She turned a look of fierce scorn on her sister. Catriona almost flinched at the expression in the blue eyes.

'You don't understand, do you? For all your so-called cleverness. All those exams, Cat. What were they for? All those dead white male poets? All that paper? And you can still come out with a statement so crass! I didn't have to marry him! Of course I had to fucking well marry him!'

'Had to? You mean?'

'Yes, I mean! Bill Jesmond was the first non-moronic, non-shitty man who hove into view just after the blue line gave me the news.'

'After? You were already pregnant?'

'Brilliant, Cat! Go to the top of the class! Bill told me he was a biochemist, but he didn't seem to know anything about biology! Nor about psychology either. I had to practically frog-march him into bed. When I told him the good news, he did the decent thing, as I knew he would. In fact he was delighted. He was totally besotted by me then. What was that verse you used to quote? Something about a whirligig?'

'The whirligig of time brings in his revenges.'

'That's it! Well it certainly does.'

'So if Bill isn't Charlotte's father, who was?'

'I'm not sure. One of a dozen or so hunks who were around at the time.'

'Oh, Flora.'

'Oh Flora? Don't you oh Flora me, you bloody prude!'

'Why didn't you tell me?'

'Isn't it obvious? I didn't tell you because I didn't want you to know. I didn't want any suggestion of it showing in your attitude or your demeanour. You may think you're good at concealing your emotions, but you're not. You're not even a beginner.'

'I never knew you were like this. I never knew you at all.'

'No, you didn't. To you I was the air-head, the dozy blonde. The one who didn't do well at school. What never crossed your mind was that I had my own ideas about what my life was going to be. I was going to be rich and successful. And I nearly was. When I got pregnant, I was a senior flight-attendant. But I didn't want to stay as cabin crew. I was determined to get into management. The glass ceiling was dissolving. The sky, as they say, would have been the limit. Instead of which, I blew it. Being pregnant was like taking a drug. It switched off all that hunger, all that ambition. My metabolism fucked me up. I could think of nothing except finding a secure nest for my child. In that I succeeded. But,' she smiled wryly, 'it was at some cost to myself. That afternoon in the restaurant at Cav, I found myself spilling this out to a complete stranger. Who in return told me that she was gay and madly attracted to me. That did it. I was turned on by her. I suddenly felt what it was in myself that was crying out to be recognised. It wasn't simply sex. If I'd wanted that I could have had any number of affairs. Frank Churchill was desperate to get into bed with me. But Hazel reached something deeper in me. It was as if I had been buried alive, and then around the edges of the coffin lid appeared the wonderful daylight as strong hands lifted it.'

'You used to meet in the studio?'

'Yes. What the newspapers would have called our love-nest. We were discreet. I for obvious reasons. Hazel because she wasn't in the scene, or "out" as far as her colleagues and clients were concerned, and she had elderly neighbours she was fond of whom she didn't want to embarrass. But in that studio amongst Frank's macho constructions – erections, Hazel called them – we played out our fantasies. Hazel liked pornography. She told me she spent hours on her computer, manipulating the images she'd loaded from her digital camera. But it wasn't all sex. We made plans. We were going to run away together. To somewhere warm. Greece or Italy. Hazel had some money of her own, from her father, and the expectation of more from her mother. Her flat was worth quite a bit. I would have had to fight Bill for custody of Charlotte, but I was sure she would want to be with me. Hazel and I were going to start a property business. Hazel knew all about finance – she'd trained as an accountant, and I had picked up most of what there is to know about estate agency – which isn't much, after all – from working at Marshalls. Anne Marshall was always on at me to become a fee earner, but I couldn't be bothered. Why the hell should I help pay for her Porsche and her designer clothes?

'But all that was in the future. So, to tide me over, I started my own escape fund. Although Bill was mean, he wasn't actually very clever with money. When I got a raise from the agency, I carried on paying the old salary into the joint account and the increase into a new cash-card account that I opened at a building society in Cheltenham. I also paid in money that I kept back from the household expenses. I soon had quite a tidy sum. It came in handy, later. When the dreams had evaporated. I really thought I was going to be happy, do you know? Then Hazel told me about a visit she had paid to her mother at the home she was in. Willowdene. Hazel and the old bat had never got on. Hazel's father had been killed in a car-crash when she was thirteen. After that, Mrs Marchant put all her energy into her daughter's future. But it was her version of that future, not Hazel's. She didn't care that Hazel was doing well at school. That she wanted to go to university. All she wanted was that Hazel should settle down with a man with money and have a family. Barmy, wasn't it? Like something out of Jane Austen. It ought to have been bloody obvious to her that her precious daughter had no liking for men. She had never had a boyfriend. As for being a mother! Eventually, Hazel got sick of being nagged morning noon and night. She told her mother there was no chance that she was ever going to settle down and raise a family, and if she was hoping for grandchildren, then she had better forget it. She stormed out of the house. She went to London, got a job as a dogsbody in a financial services company, just as I had in the travel agency before I joined BA. God, how you sneered at me for that! She worked hard and got herself qualified. She went abroad, to Sydney, Hong Kong and New York. She moved back to London and started her own business. She started to communicate with her mother again, and she found out that the old woman had become infirm and moved into a home for the elderly. She moved her business to Cheltenham to try to mend the relationship before her mother died. It was at that point that I wandered into her life. I tried to warn her that she would be disappointed, but she took no notice. As she continued to visit her mother in the home, she began to be obsessed with the idea that her mother's lack of response was due to some physical ailment, and not merely the effect of the psychological estrangement between them. It wasn't that Mrs Marchant refused to acknowledge her daughter, as she had in the old days. She had been unable even to recognise her or to remember anything about her own life before she had entered the home. This was a genuine inability to recall. Hazel said that sometimes there seemed to be something flickering on the edge of her mother's mind, reflected in the strange looks she gave her, as if she knew that she ought to know who this person was. But even when Hazel prompted her, there was nothing. She simply could not remember who Hazel was. Yet in other respects, she was completely well. She was playing a full part in the activities of the home. Willowdene insisted that there was nothing wrong with the old lady. Whatever problems there were between the two of them, they implied, were down to Hazel's failure to care for her mother. But Hazel wasn't convinced.

'As I said, it became an obsession. She took it upon herself to observe the behaviour of the other residents. They seemed, for elderly people, very active. They played bridge and chess and one or two of the men played computer games. They had classes in learning languages and lectures on history and art. It was, she said, more like a cruise ship than an old people's home. Yet when she tried to strike up a conversation with any of them, they were, in her words, quite opaque. They never talked of their old lives, of their families, of their previous occupations. In short, they didn't behave like normal old people. Their brains were unnaturally alert in some ways and unnaturally dead in others. It was as if, she said, that they were being brain-washed.'

'So that was when she started to think that it was something that was being done to them at Willowdene?'

'Yes. I told her she was exaggerating. I felt it was driving us apart. She could hardly think or talk of anything else. Were they being drugged? And why? She speculated on the nature of the imagined drug. A substance that would boost the short-term memory and suppress the long-term. It was as if it were designed to force someone to live constantly in the present. It made me speculate too. I fantasised how it would be to have no memory of the past. And the more I fantasised, the more attractive the idea became. I didn't tell Hazel. I'd never told her anything of my early life, and she knew very little of my marriage. She never knew that Bill was a research biochemist with Avalon. But the Willowdene situation began to intrigue me as much as it did her. If these old people were being drugged, then the drug had to come from somewhere. I knew a fair bit about pharmaceuticals, from what I had picked up from Bill and contacts in the Green movement. I had never heard of a drug that targeted the memory. It certainly was not an ordinary tranquilliser or even an SSRI such as Prozac. It must be new. So it must be being administered at Willowdene as part of an experiment. And that of course was illegal. There was no way that all these elderly and infirm people could be legitimate volunteers. They were unsuspecting guinea-pigs. I had more than an inkling that Avalon might be involved. They were very much a member of the military-industrial complex with a reputation for way-out research. In the sixties, there had been some suggestion that they had evolved a drug for the CIA to assist in interrogating Vietcong prisoners. I wouldn't have put anything past them.'

'But you didn't share any of this with Hazel?'

'No.'

'But why not?'

'She might have decided to go after Avalon, caused a stink and ended up achieving precisely nothing. I knew how these multinationals operated. They denied, denied, denied, denied. They threatened with writs from their expensive teams of lawyers anyone who persisted. They got one of their paid mouthpieces in Parliament to stand up and say what a wonderful contribution they were to the economy of the country, and how they should be regarded as a national treasure. In the meantime they buried the bodies. They destroyed records, wiped computers, sacked employees or bribed or threatened them into silence. There was no proof that Avalon was involved. It would come out that Bill was my husband. It would probably be the end of our relationship. So I said nothing. It would fizzle out. The old lady would die, and Hazel would get her life back, her life with me.

'Then came the day when we had arranged to meet for a ramble on Cleeve Hill. Hazel was late. She had been to Willowdene. She was elated. Her first words were, "I've caught them! I've nailed the bastards!" And she showed me the little plastic canister of capsules she had stolen from Willowdene.

'I knew the moment I saw that container that my suspicions had been right. I knew that the capsules must have come from Avalon. I had seen enough of that kind of thing over the years from items that Bill had brought home to recognise the style. And that meant that, whatever was going on, Bill must be in on it. Nothing could happen in that laboratory without his directing it. Knowing him, I can't say it surprised me. I knew he valued intellectual discovery over any other consideration. Morality was irrelevant. If you could do something, you did it. To be that kind of scientist, some part of your humanity must be missing. Otherwise, you could never attain the necessary level of objectivity.'

'Isn't that a definition of evil? To do something without caring about the consequences?'

'Perhaps. But in Bill's case I think it was more an almost child-like naïvety, a kind of innocence. I'm sure he was the kind of boy who pulled the wings off flies merely to see what happened, without thinking whether it was cruel.'

'"As flies to wanton boys are we to the gods. They kill us

for their sport." So when you saw the container, you felt you had to tell Hazel the truth?'

Flora shook her head.

'Was that because, in the end, you wanted to protect Bill? You wanted to have time to warn him?'

Again the blonde head moved from side to side, as irritatingly coy as she had been as a child. 'No, I felt no such protective instinct. Bill was a piece of flesh who provided a home for my child and occasionally shared my bed. I cared nothing for him. He was on his own.'

'Then why not give her the information she needed?'

'I've already said. It would do no good. I told her that if she went public with those capsules, they would prove nothing. An analysis would not reveal their effects on human beings. The company concerned, whoever it was, would deny and conceal. I said there was only one way she could prove that those capsules contained what she claimed that they contained. Only one way that their effects on a human being could be determined.'

'And that was to take them and to see what happened?'

'Of course. I volunteered myself as the guinea-pig.'

'And what was Hazel's reaction?'

'Can't you guess? She absolutely refused to entertain the idea. She said she was going that very afternoon to tell the police what she had found. I argued with her, I pleaded. But she was adamant.'

'But why Flora? Why were you so determined to take the risk? Why take that upon yourself?'

'When I saw Hazel standing there with the drug whose effects we had discussed so intently, when I saw it in her grasp, I wanted it. I wanted it as I had never wanted anything. I wanted it not as an experiment, not in some quixotic attempt to bring down a company richer than most nations – I was not so stupid as to imagine I could do that. No, I wanted it for myself. For however short a time, I wanted to experience oblivion. To

322

get the peace of mind that can only come from freeing oneself of the past. From being able to forget. It was what I had always dreamed of. And I thought that, if it worked, I could persuade or blackmail Bill into guaranteeing a supply of it.'

'But why, Flora?'

'How can you ask me that question? How can you?'

'I can. It's something I haven't been able to understand. You never went through what I went through that night. You never saw what happened. You were asleep in your bed! If you had nothing to remember you had nothing to forget. We've never talked of it. You've never shown the least sign of wanting to talk about it.'

'You've never understood anything, have you? For all your brilliance, your cleverness. You never reached out to me and I could never reach out to you.' Suddenly, the calm, steady manner which had been Flora's trademark for all those years seemed to dissolve. The tears poured down the perfect skin of her peaches-and-cream cheeks. Her lovely mouth twisted in pain and anger.

'You know nothing about me. But how could you? You were so determined to see me as unlike yourself. You had suffered as a child. Your sufferings blinded you to what was happening elsewhere. You cried out in the darkness of the night, and I heard you. But did you hear me, when it was my turn to scream? Did you think you were the only one? Did you really believe that you suffered alone?'

The words jolted her like a physical blow.

'Oh, my God. You as well?'

'Yes, me as well. Didn't you know our father was a lapsed Catholic in everything but his tastes, which had been well nurtured by sadistic priests? Perhaps he was paying back God for his own misery by degrading and abusing his own daughters.'

'But you never told me!'

'Just as you never told me!'

323

The pain in Catriona's head screeched as if an electric drill was grinding the bone at her temples. 'I couldn't tell you, Flora, because, because I wanted to protect you.'

She shook her head. 'No, Cat. You didn't even think of me at all. You thought only of yourself. And why not? You didn't know whether you could trust me. But the irony was that I already knew everything. Not only everything that happened between you and Daddy. Everything that happened that night.'

The nausea caused by the unaccustomed alcohol was spreading from Catriona's stomach to her head in the familiar way, the thudding hammer blows of the migraine battering the inside of her forehead, making her skull feel as if it would crack.

'No, you're lying! You know nothing of that night, except what you were told. You were asleep.'

'I tell you I know what really happened. I saw it.'

'No, that isn't possible.'

'Yes. It is. You see, I woke up a little after you did. I saw what was going on. I watched you from the gallery of the landing, crouching down in the shadows. I saw the struggle between the two of them, I saw you intervene – you were so tall and strong, even then. Even though Daddy was over six feet, you seemed to tower over him, like a dark angel. Do you not want to remember? Does the revulsion at the act come between you and your synapses? I heard you shout that craven warning to our father. I saw him lash out at our mother. I saw her fall and lie still. I saw you pick up the fallen golf club, I saw you . . .'

'No! No! It isn't true!'

'Yes. I saw you whirl it round double-handed as if you were throwing the hammer at the Highland Games. I heard the kerchunk! as it connected with the side of his head. I saw the blood spurt. I was simultaneously sickened and elated. I didn't know whether to vomit or cheer. Then as he went down, you hit him again. Kerchunk! And he was flat on his face on the floor. That great big unholy terror of a man was felled like a tree. I loved you then, I really loved you. I wanted to rush down the stairs and hug you. You were heroic. In your long white broderie-anglaise night-dress, as tall and as chaste as Sir Gawain himself when he chopped off the head of the Green Knight. Kerchunk! You remember how father used to read that poem to us in the nursery, explaining the difficult bits. You could see how much he relished the part of the Green Knight. And now, here he was, playing it for real! Kerchunk! What a childhood we had! No television! Only books, books and more bloody books. We were so cultured you could wring it out of us. If you'd squeezed us, out would have come Shakespearean blank verse and Jane Austen and Walter Scott and Robert Louis Stevenson. What a preparation for your life, eh, Professor! Like father, like daughter. If only they knew, those weedy academics who promoted you and hungered after you – as I'm sure they did – that they were nurturing in their midst someone who had committed the worst of all crimes: cold-blooded, deliberate parricide. Kerchunk!'

'Stop it! Stop it! Have you gone mad!'

'You don't like to remember what happened, do you? You'd prefer to forget. I don't blame you. I longed to as well. But that was your part in the play. You've never even suspected my own leading role, have you?'

'What do you mean your role?'

'Have you never wondered what drove our father to murder little Morag? Killing wasn't really his style was it? He was fattening her up, but not for the kill. When he'd tired of us, she would have been ripe enough for those Catholic tastes of his. Why would he spoil all that by killing her?'

The calm, matter-of-fact manner in which she spoke chilled Catriona to her very soul. A nameless, formless shape, whose horror she could but dimly grasp was materialising inside her skull.

'Of course he killed her. Mother saw him. Almost her last words to me were that she had seen him bending over her.'

'When he found her, she was already dead.'

'No! You can't know that! No, don't speak to me! I don't want to hear!'

'Oh yes, but you must hear! All these years, you thought you were alone in your guilt and in your innocence! But you weren't. I know that Morag was already dead when our father found her, because I had taken it upon myself to save her from the shades of the prison house that would close on her, as they did on us, when her body told her that the lease of childhood was expiring. Remember your beloved Wordsworth? "A simple child, That lightly draws its breath, And feels its life in every limb, What should it know of death?" Or of sex. Or of brutality. Or of corruption. Well, she never did, thanks to me. I did her a big favour when I crept on tiptoe into her room that evening. She was already asleep, the night-light shining on her beautiful little face, her lips apart, murmuring slightly as she wriggled under the covers. She was so innocent, and the only thing that ensures innocence in this world is death. So very very gently I put the pillow over her face, and she struggled only a little. I don't believe she ever truly woke before she died. I saved her, Cat. I saved her. I saved her from pain, and betrayal. I saved her from the flames of Hell. I did it because I loved her. But she's so little she doesn't understand. And often in the night she comes to me, and stands by my bed and asks me why. And whatever I say to her, she always asks me again and again. Why? Why? Why? Over and over. And I can never make her understand. Is it any wonder that I wanted to get away from her? That I might sleep and when I awoke, I would remember nothing of that night. Is it any wonder I wanted oblivion?

'So when Hazel appeared that windy day on Cleeve Hill, waving that little plastic drum in triumph, I was desperate to get hold of the drug it contained. But she wouldn't hand it over. She was stubborn. She refused, no matter how much I begged.

When I snatched the canister, she struggled to retrieve it. We struggled and she fell. I watched her body as it crashed onto one rock then another, before it finally came to rest, broken and bloody at the bottom of the cliff. I killed her, God help me, I killed her too.'

Flora turned away, hiding her face, and sobbing with great convulsive shudders. Catriona felt her entire body become cold and heavy and rigid, as if her skin were made of lead. She longed to be able to reach out to her sister, but the weight of the metallic carapace enveloping her prevented all movement. With a voice that issued with difficulty through the frozen mask of her face, she said, desperately seeking rationality from the overwhelming, titanic flood of chaos, not only for Flora but for herself, 'With Morag, you were only a child. You weren't responsible for your own actions, after what you had suffered. With Hazel, it must have been an accident. You could never have intended . . .'

Flora whirled round, her face blanched, her eyes glittering. 'Even I can't excuse myself so easily. I wanted that canister and at that moment I would have done anything, including murder, to get it. That's what I've been hiding from! Hazel was followed that day. By Anderson. When the theft of the drug was noticed, he immediately suspected her. She had been a troublemaker from the start. She was virtually the only visitor to Willowdene. They admitted only those elderly men and women who had no close relatives likely to cause a fuss about any personality changes that might occur. They made a mistake with Mrs Marchant. Anderson would never have admitted her if he had known she had a daughter like Hazel. So he followed her, looking for an opportunity to tackle her. Instead of which he witnessed what happened between the two of us – the struggle, the fall, everything. He was dressed up like a tourist. He had a camera! He used the photographs to try to blackmail me into handing over the drug. They had already decided to kidnap me, using a fake ambulance, but they hadn't realised that I would already have taken some of the drug and be unable to reveal the place where I had hidden the rest. I escaped, but I knew I could never return until Avalon was satisfied that there was no longer a threat that their activities at Willowdene might be revealed. So I was trapped, trapped as I had been throughout my entire life. Trapped, trapped, trapped!'

Catriona dragged off her outer clothes. Her fingers seemed thick and clumsy. She supposed she might be drunk. She had never been drunk before. She had always been horrified by the loss of control it must involve, of what she might blab in an unguarded moment. In the small bathroom, she cleaned her teeth with the toothbrush she always kept in her handbag to use after every meal, and dragged a comb through her hair, this night-time ritual so ingrained that it persisted even in a state of total collapse.

Over the basin was fixed a medicine cabinet, with a mirrored front. Catriona had striven to turn her eyes from the glittering glass, as she did whenever she was presented with any reflective surface. Her aversion was such that there had been no mirrors in her house. But her languor lulled her instinctive avoidance as she automatically pulled the comb through the remaining snags of her thick black locks, and she did not avert her gaze from the other woman in the looking glass.

It was not only the pale face, the dark-blue eyes with their deep shadows, the aquiline nose and the generous, sensual mouth that captured her attention, but also the sight of the smooth skin of her neck and shoulders, and her breasts swelling under the white sports bra. She hardly ever looked at her body. She closed her eyes when she undressed. She worked her body, drove its muscles and sinews to sweat and strain in the gym or out on a run, but she did not look at it or take pleasure in its hard perfection or allow others to do so. She strove with it blindly, struggling against its reminder of other places and

328

other sensations, feelings, emotions that must be crushed and destroyed, if she were not to fall back into the fiery hell of the pit from which she had emerged.

For a dazzling moment, she stared at her white flesh, flawless, pearlescent in the harsh light of the bathroom. Slowly, as her eyes blurred with tears, she inclined her forehead to the cold surface of the glass. Its chill kiss roused her. She snatched at the cord of the light switch and stumbled out of the bathroom.

She was running through the cool night. Above her the sky was bathed with the radiance of an infinity of stars. The road ran white and clear over the heath, like a parting in dark hair. She was running through a forest. Black tree trunks sprouted on either side. Overhead, branches black as charcoal arched against the sky, blotting out its illumination. Something was running behind her. She could hear its feet pounding on the hard ground, a pounding louder than the pounding of her own heart. She ran faster, widening her stride. The black tree trunks flashed past, as quickly as telegraph poles seen from a speeding train. Faster and faster she ran, and still behind her she could hear the thing behind her, pounding like the beating of her own heart. It was nearer now. She could hear its breathing. Ever faster, but still the creature gained. And now it was as if she was running on the spot, and that only the dark forest was moving. The creature was no longer behind her, it was in front of her, its hot weight was upon her, crushing her. Its hot face was against hers. Kiss me, it whispered with a sibilant tongue of fire, kiss me my darling, my only darling. She tried to scream, to cry out, but her mouth was full of the creature. It was inside her mouth. Its loathsomeness was forcing itself between her teeth and onto her tongue. Its hot pulsing loathsomeness. She was growing fainter the more she struggled. The creature pressed against her face. There was a scent, a sweet flowery scent, of cupboards and drawers, of crisp sheets in sunlit sickrooms – Why can't I go out to play, Mummy? Not now, darling; you must stay in bed a while longer till your temperature goes down. Stay in bed. She was in bed, and something, something that smelt of lavender – yes, that was it, lavender! – was against her face and in her mouth. *Dreams don't smell.* She had said that once. *Dreams don't smell.* The weight against her was heavier now. It was pushing her down into the bed, into the mattress. Lavender! *If dreams don't smell, this was no dream!* A pillow, yes, a pillow was over her face and she couldn't breathe. She was awake, but she couldn't breathe. The weight was on top of her and the pillow was on her face and she couldn't breathe. She must push the weight away from her and then she could breathe. There was a humming in her head, and there were lights flashing, beautiful lights, pink and green and yellow, flashing on the blackness inside her skull. Don't look at the lights. Push, push, push. PUSH! The weight moved. It moved! She had an arm free from under the duvet where it had been trapped. She clawed at the pillow, twisting her head to one side, sucking in one glorious breath of oxygen, until the sickly lavender scent clamped down on her again. But now, with her free arm, she was hitting out at the weight on top of her, lashing wildly in her frenzy to breathe. The weight was soft, the weight cried out, in pain or anger, and the pillow on her face lifted a little and there was another glorious breath. She fought and struggled and heaved and kicked. Then the weight screamed – it screamed! – and there was a thud as it slid from the bed to the floor. The pillow was gone from her face and she drew in great sucking lungfuls of wonderful, wonderful air, retching and coughing as she did so. Then into the blackness was a flash of light, the door of the room had opened, and a dark figure stood for a moment against a lighted rectangle and then vanished.

'Flora, Flora!' Catriona screamed as she staggered out of the bedroom. No answer. Oh God! Had the intruder attacked her first, had he succeeded?

The door to Flora's room was open, the light was on, but the bed was empty. Empty!

'Flora!' She screamed again in an agony of fear.

From outside there was the roar of an engine revving, the crunch and crackle of tyres on shingle; then the sound of the motor was in the lane, whining up the hill and fading into the silence of the night.

She hurtled down the bare wooden stairs and ran out through the open door into the yard. The Golf which had been parked in front of the garage had gone.

'Flora!' But there was no answer from the surrounding darkness.

FOURTEEN

The sky was pale at the horizon with the approach of morning. Under the fading starlight, the black metalled surface of the carriageway gleamed dull silver like the polished cast iron of a fire-grate. In the dew-soaked hedgerows and in the copses, birds were singing.

Catriona ran as she had never run before, not as in her dreams, pursued by the demons of her past, but in pursuit of a new devil from the present.

At the moment she had stood in the courtyard of the Old Mill staring wildly around into the night, everything had fallen into place with sickening clarity. It had been no abductor sent by Avalon, she realised with a certainty that was burned into her like a brand, who had placed that pillow over her face in an attempt to suffocate her.

She heard again in her mind the scream that had filled the room as she had lashed out at the weight that lay upon her, a scream she recognised, as a bird recognises the call of its own species. Once more she saw the dreadful change obscure her sister's features, like an eclipse. Once more she heard the scornful, wounding note in Flora's voice as she had told her hideous story. Once more, Catriona felt the terrible pain at her heart as she realised that she had been destined for the same fate that poor helpless Morag had suffered two decades before.

But that was not the farthest extent of the pain she felt. The violence had awakened doubt. She recalled the tremor of uncertainty she had experienced when she had heard Flora claim that she had watched Malcolm Thornton follow Alice and Charlotte up the Beacon. Malcolm had told his sister that he had preceded the girls. It was verging on the impossible that he would have had the presence of mind to lie about the sequence of events. Yet if Flora were correct, that had to be the case. But if Malcolm had told the truth, then Flora had lied. But why? Why had she lied? The only reason was that she wished to conceal the truth. The truth about her own part on that cruel day.

The unimaginable had forced its way into Catriona's mind. Its loathsomeness could not be ignored. The appalling suspicion had to be confronted. To fail to act might be to allow the tragedy to be repeated. If evil there was, it had to be stopped.

But she could not do that here, alone. She who had always spurned help, needed it now. And then, as if by chance, she recalled the white card she had been handed outside the old wool mill in Stroud, and at which she had casually glanced before thrusting it into her handbag. The handbag, the card and everything else had been consumed by fire, but the words remained. She summoned them and, like familiar spirits, they answered her summons.

Woodcombe is a straggle of houses, a pub and a petrol station on the Cheltenham road five miles from Owlbury. She paused for a moment, lungs on fire, under the glow of the amber street lamps outside the darkened bulk of the Cross Keys. Then she was away again, driving her aching legs like pistons. She could recall from the many times she had driven this way the metal sign reading Mulberry Lane, at the far end of the village. And there, just down from the corner, was a small stone-tiled cottage, by the front gate of which was a carved wooden post like an Indian totem pole. That had to be his house.

She vaulted the picket gate, sprinted up the flagstone path, and without hesitation hammered on the boards of the front door. The sound echoed in the brightening air. For a long minute, there was silence.

She was about to knock again, when there was a grating sound from above her head. She looked up to see that a light had come on in a first-floor window, and the casement was being pushed open.

A dark head appeared against the lighted panel.

'Who the bloody hell is that at this time of night?' Frank Churchill's deep voice called out.

'It's Catriona. Catriona Turville. I need your help.'

He was yawning and rubbing the sleep out of his eyes when he opened the door. He was dressed only in a pair of blue-and-white striped boxer shorts, and his grey-brown hair was tousled.

'I haven't time to explain but I need to borrow your car. I need to get to Cheltenham. It's very urgent. Life or death, literally. You did say you'd help me if ever I needed it. At any time.'

He shook his head, wonderingly. 'I didn't expect to be taken quite so literally. You're something else, aren't you? Hang on a sec. I'll get some clothes.'

'Just give me the keys. You don't need to . . .'

'You don't look in any fit state to drive. Not my car, anyway.'

She stood by the open door, leaning against the jamb as pain surged and eddied in her skull like a wave threatening to burst apart its fragile bones.

In a moment, Frank was back, dressed in jeans and sweater.

His car, a Volvo estate almost as ancient as her Fiesta, was parked in a layby further down the narrow lane. She slumped into the passenger seat.

'Cheltenham, you said?'

'Yes, please.'

He tipped an imaginary cap. 'Right you are, guv!'

He drove expertly and swiftly. Soon they were on the ascent to Cranham Woods and Coopers Hill. To the left, in the broad valley below, was the amber-lit sprawl of Gloucester.

'Are you going to tell me what this is about?'

She passed a hand over her aching head. 'I can't. Not now. But later, I will.'

Flora had at least a half an hour's start.

They drove through the shopping centre: Cheltenham could have been a city of the dead, its population obliterated by a neutron bomb.

'Turn left here, then next right, then left again. It's over there. Oh God.'

Flora's red Golf was drawn up on the forecourt of the small apartment block. On the third floor, lights were on at an uncurtained French window giving on to a balcony.

Desperately Catriona jabbed the bell push for Jesmond on the security panel.

To her inexpressible relief, Charlotte's voice crackled through the speaker.

'It's me.'

'Cat? Cat! You'll never believe what's happened! Mum's come back and she's all right.'

Followed by Frank, Catriona pounded up the vinyl-covered treads of the concrete and steel staircase.

Charlotte, in her Mickey Mouse pyjamas, was standing by the open door of the flat.

Without a word, Catriona grabbed the astonished child and shoved her through the open door of what seemed at a glance to be her bedroom and slammed the door. She turned to her companion. 'Frank, hang onto that door handle and don't under any circumstances let her out.'

Frank raised his eyebrows in ironical enquiry at this peremptory command, but, seeing Catriona's wild and stricken face, took the metal lever in one large brown hand. He leant close to the door panel and said calmly, 'Charlotte, I don't know what this is about any more than you do. But you do as your aunt says and stay put for a bit.'

Bill, a brown shapeless dressing gown over his pale blue striped pyjamas, stood at the sitting-room door.

'What the hell are you doing here?' Becoming aware of the tall figure of the sculptor behind her, he said sharply, 'And who the devil are you?'

Flora appeared at his shoulder. 'Hello, Cat. And Frank, too! What an unexpected pleasure. I didn't know that you two were acquainted.'

Catriona ignored her sister. 'Bill. Please listen to me. Charlotte is in great danger.'

'What the hell are you talking about?'

'Flora. She isn't the person you think she is. She's been affected by the drug. When you told me it had no serious side-effects, you either lied to me, or others had lied to you. There are very serious side-effects. In enhancing the cognitive power of the brain, and suppressing the long-term memory, the reservoir of experience, bad or good, on which we can draw and which, ultimately, enables us to distinguish good from evil is destroyed. That is the function of the memory. To keep alive the means by which we learn to be human. Make people forget, and you make them less than people. By remembering a bad deed, we remember the remorse and the unhappiness associated with it. Through that we are conditioned not to repeat it and not to do something even worse. Psychopaths can forget what they've done, or remember it selectively in a manner that reassures them. By switching on the power to forget, your drug can turn a disturbed mind psychopathic, unleashing violence and aggression. It had that effect on some patients at Willowdene. It has had that effect on Flora. She was already deeply disturbed. She had killed her lover. And taking the drug made her far more ill. After she escaped from the hospital, she hid out in the flat over the garage at the Old Mill. It was she who, dressed as Malcolm Thornton, followed the girls onto the Beacon that day. She killed Alice and tried to murder Charlotte. When she pretended to be a nurse in the Royal Gloucestershire Hospital, she wasn't there to look after Charlotte. She was trying to kill her! But she won't remember any of that! A matter of an hour or so ago, she tried to kill me. To suffocate me as I slept. She's forgotten that as well. That's what your playing God has led to! That's where your scientific fascism will always lead.'

He was shaking his head. 'I don't believe it. You're the madwoman. There are no side-effects. I would have heard of them if there had been. Besides, Flora has not taken the drug. She has reassured me of that. You were completely mistaken. Her disappearance had nothing whatever to do with Avalon or Willowdene. She has explained everything. She was depressed and wanted to get away for a while, that's all. She was travelling abroad. When she heard what happened to Charlotte, she hurried back.'

'Flora! Try to remember the truth! Only that will save you! We can help you! But only if you admit that you need help.'

The calm blue eyes stared guilelessly into hers. 'I think you've been under terrible stress, Cat. Bill told me that your lovely house had burned down. And there's some problem with drugs. You're the one who needs help, darling.'

Catriona looked wildly from one face to another. Bill's pugnacious, contemptuous. Flora's full of winsome compassion.

There was a crash from behind her as Charlotte's bedroom door was torn open, the handle wrenched out of the astonished Frank Churchill's less-than-concentrated grip.

'Let me fucking well go!'

Charlotte cannoned into Catriona, attempting to push past her in the narrow corridor.

'I want my Mum!'

Catriona had her arms around the child, who was kicking and screaming, and yelling obscenities.

'Listen to me, Charlotte! If you never listen to me again, listen to me now! I swore to protect you. I failed once. I shan't fail again. Your mother is very sick. Very very sick. She needs urgent medical treatment. Please go back to your room. This is the truth. I would never lie to you. You know that.'

Flora came forward, holding out her arms. 'Charlotte. I told you how sorry I was for leaving you for so long! When I heard you'd been hurt, I thought I should die of anxiety. Come and hug me.'

Catriona tightened her grip on the child's thin shoulders. Charlotte wasn't struggling so much now, as if a dreadful doubt was casting its shadow over her mind.

'You wanted to kill her, didn't you, Flora, when you caught her in your uniform? That uniform you'd worked so hard for, that uniform which represented the bright future you'd lost through your own carelessness. Charlotte knows how much you hated her then. She saw it in your eyes.'

'Nonsense. Nonsense! I love my daughter more than my own life. But you wouldn't know about that, Cat. You've never loved anybody. Only your work. Your stupid sterile, pointless work.'

Catriona felt her strength ebbing. In this contest of wills, she was going to lose. And Charlotte would die. Sometime soon, her mother would kill her. As she had killed the others. Morag. Hazel. Alice. As she had tried to kill her own sister. Out of love, out of jealousy, out of madness. And she, Catriona, would go mad with grief.

She bent her mouth to Charlotte's ear, whispering into it with a desperate urgency. 'You're in the hospital, Charlotte. You're lying in bed still feeling woozy from the drugs. A nurse comes in. A beautiful nurse. She bends over you. You can smell her. It's the scent you recognise. Your mother's. You're feeling light-headed, as if it's a dream, but it isn't a dream. It really is your mother. You smile at her. She whispers that she loves you. Then what happens, Charlotte? Try to remember what happened next. Your mind blanked it out. You don't want to remember it, because you can't believe it. But you know it happened. Deep inside you, you know that the worst thing in the world actually happened. I know that feeling, my love. I know it so well. Please remember. Please remember.'

It was as if the child were in a hypnotic trance as she grew still and listened to these words. Then she spoke. 'She's bending over me. I can smell her lovely smell. She's bending down to me. She says I love you. She's going to kiss me. Then . . . then . . . I feel . . . I feel something soft over my face. I can't breathe. I can't breathe. I try to speak to her but I can't breathe. I can't breathe. The soft thing is pressing on my face. I can't breathe. I'm beginning to float away and everything's getting dark. Then I hear a voice in the room, a doctor's, and he's like, How's our little patient today? And the thing over my face has gone, and Mum's gone.' She stopped speaking and raised her head, her wide blue eyes meeting her mother's. 'Mum! Why did you do that, Mum? Why? Why did you try to suffocate me? Why? Why? Why?'

With a scream of rage, Flora hurled herself forward, her hands hooked into claws. Catriona lifted Charlotte clean off her feet, swung the girl into the arms of Frank behind, then jabbed forward with her clenched fist.

The blow hit Flora in the solar plexus and she collapsed, curled up on the carpet in the foetus position like a child, gasping for breath, weeping and sobbing. Raising her tear-streaked swollen face, she howled in agony like a wounded animal. 'Help me,' she cried. 'Yes, yes, it's true. It's all true. Please, help me. Please help me. I do remember! I remember everything! I'll do whatever you want. Please, I do need help! Please help me!'

DRUGS COMPANY TO AXE RESEARCH LAB

Avalon, the US-based multinational pharmaceutical corporation, is to close its laboratory near Cheltenham with the loss of over a hundred and fifty jobs. Only a few key research personnel are likely to be offered relocation to other Avalon facilities in the US, Europe and the Far East.

The decision has been taken, according to a company spokesman at its headquarters in Cincinnati, following a strategic review of its global operations. It is a blow to hopes of further development of high-tech industry in the south-west region.

STROUD DOCTOR VICTIM OF M5 CRASH

Dr David Anderson, 45, the well known Stroud GP, was killed yesterday in a collision between his luxury Bristol saloon and a foreign container lorry near the Almondsbury motorway interchange. Dr Anderson was pronounced dead on arrival at the Royal Gloucestershire Hospital. The driver of the Romanian-registered vehicle was reported to be shocked but otherwise unhurt.

MANAGER DIES AS OAP HOME DESTROYED BY FIRE

Police are treating as suspicious the blaze in which Sister Oonagh Monaghan SRN, the manager of Willowdene, the residential home for the elderly near Stroud, was killed on Monday. Elderly residents were shepherded to safety after staff were woken by an alarm at about 2 a.m. Despite the prompt attendance of applicances from Gloucester and Cheltenham, the building was almost totally destroyed in the inferno. It is believed that Sister Monaghan may have been attempting to save computer records from her office, where her body was found later by firefighters.

Ms Samantha Thornton (25) last week opened the doors of Jodhpurs, her new riding school in her home village of Owlbury.

'Cat, look! There's old smoothy-chops Churchill. He's seen us!'

Catriona was discovering that one of the benefits, or disadvantages, depending on one's mood, of provincial life is the inability to indulge in one's everyday activities without encountering one's acquaintances similarly engaged. In the crowded High Street of Stroud, there was at that moment no polite way in which she could avoid the encounter with the sculptor, particularly as Charlotte, taller, more willowy, riper of figure, and more glowing with youth and health than ever, her blonde hair bleached and her clear skin deliciously tanned by exposure to the sun of the Greek island where they had recently holidayed together, stood out on that drably damp English autumn day like an exotic bloom on a compost heap.

'Well, hello, Professor. Long time no see! And hello, Charly, you look absolutely gorgeous!'

They shook hands. 'Hello, Frank.'

Charlotte was not yet so used to compliments as not to blush. 'What about Cat? Doesn't she look gorgeous as well?'

'Charly!'

'She's right,' he responded, his eyes twinkling. 'You do look very well, Professor. Very well indeed.'

He glanced at Charlotte, who had wandered away to chat to some wildly over-dressed teenagers, presumably her schoolfriends, and lowered his voice. 'And how is Flora?'

'She came out of hospital last month. She's hoping she can go back to work soon. Anne Marshall has kept her job open for her.'

'So what about you? Are you here for the weekend?'

'Oh, no, since the beginning of term I've been a resident. Flora and Charlotte and I are living at the Old Mill. Bill's in Bristol, doing research at the university. Into the long-term side effects of prescription drugs. I've resigned from Warbeck. Ten years at any institution is long enough. I've been lucky enough to get a grant from an American foundation in Cincinnati to pay for a research assistant to help me with my edition of Wordsworth. And next January, I'm starting my new post as Dean of continuing Education at the University of Gloucestershire. I'll be teaching in the Literature faculty, but also administering the extra-mural work in the community. Quite a challenge!'

'"And thus the whirligig of time brings in his revenges."'

She looked at him sharply, but the handsome face under the greying thatch of hair smiled back blandly. She turned to her niece. 'Come on, Charly. We've still got Waitrose to endure. Goodbye, Frank.'

'*Au revoir*, surely? We'll see each other around. You can't avoid it in a place like this. Not that I'd want to avoid you. In fact, I'd enjoy another midnight drive.'

'You didn't have to hustle me away like that! I was having a good chat. And so you were you. Why fight it, Cat? He fancies you, you can see it written all over him. He's not bad for quite an old guy.'

'Have you got the shopping list or have I?'

'You don't need the list, Cat. Not with your memory. You're trying to change the subject. But I can see you're blushing. Yes, you are!'

342

Blood on the Tongue

Stephen Booth

It wasn't the easiest way to commit suicide. Marie Tennent seemed to have just curled up in the snow on Irontongue Hill until her body slowly and agonizingly froze. But hers wasn't the only corpse lying hidden beneath the Peak District snow that January . . .

DS Diane Fry is trying to build a murder enquiry, but she's not finding it easy. The snow and ice have depleted half the 'E' division and her partner, DC Ben Cooper, is otherwise engaged trying to solve a 50-year-old wartime mystery.

To DS Fry, Ben's interest in the case seems a waste of police time - until a vicious attack in the dark Edendale backstreets suggests that the past could provide a motive for the present violence.

'Best traditional crime novel of the year'   *Independent*

ISBN: 0-00-713066-X

Arms and the Women

Reginald Hill

When Ellie Pascoe finds herself under threat, the men in her life assume it's because she's married to a cop. But while they trawl after shoals of red herrings, Ellie is blasted off course with a motley crew of women on a voyage of discovery whose perils make Scylla and Charybdis look like a pair of Barbie dolls.

Irish arms, Colombian drugs, and men who will stop at nothing, create a tidal wave which threatens to sweep her away. She heads out of town in search of haven, but instead finds herself at the very edge of the storm in a remote clifftop house undermined by the sea where she must reach deep down into her reserves to find the strength to survive.

'Luminously written, thrilling in the best old-fashioned sense of the word'   *Daily Mail*

ISBN: 0 00 651287 9